NEW TESTAMENT LITERATURE

BY THE SAME AUTHOR

THE FOUNDATION OF THE
CHRISTIAN CHURCH

NEW TESTAMENT
LITERATURE

IN THE LIGHT
OF MODERN SCHOLARSHIP

BY

T. HENSHAW
M.A.

LONDON
GEORGE ALLEN AND UNWIN LTD
RUSKIN HOUSE   MUSEUM STREET

FIRST PUBLISHED IN 1952

Meth. Pub. H.
4.00
8-22-56 slm
9-25-56 cdm

PRINTED IN GREAT BRITAIN
11 point Baskerville type by Jarrold & Sons Ltd. Norwich

PREFACE

My aim in writing this book has been to acquaint the reader with the light which modern scholarship throws on the literature of the New Testament. In the wide field of New Testament study there is such a mass of available material and so much that is controversial, that it is extremely difficult to give, in a small compass, a true picture of present-day opinion. Anyone undertaking the task must of necessity resort to a process of selection and condensation. In this volume, therefore, will be found what I consider to be the relevant historical facts and the main theories of the different theological schools. On disputed points the view of the majority of experts has not always been taken: in some cases the matter has been left open, and in a few a minority view has been accepted.

The opening chapters of the book are concerned with the background of Christianity, the Canon of the New Testament, the Pre-Literary Period, the Earliest Written Sources, and the Synoptic Problem. These are followed by chapters dealing whenever possible with the authorship, recipients, date and place of composition, sources, purpose, contents, characteristics, and historical value of each of the twenty-seven books of the New Testament. There is also an introductory chapter on Paul's Epistles. In the Appendices will be found much useful information, including short biographies of persons mentioned in the text, summaries of the "Didache" and the "Muratorian Fragment", a list of the Principal Manuscripts and Versions of the Greek New Testament, and a note on Writing Materials. Those readers who wish to pursue the study of the subject further will find a Bibliography at the end.

In writing the various chapters many authorities have been consulted—far too many to permit of my expressing the debt which I owe to each one. My obligations to some of them are acknowledged in the footnotes.

In conclusion I wish to express my deep indebtedness to

5

Professor R. L. Archer, M.A., D.Litt., Professor Emeritus of Education in the University College of North Wales, without whose generous assistance the book could not have been written. My sincere thanks are due to my friend, Mr. J. C. W. Ludlow, M.A., for his kindness in correcting the proofs.

T. HENSHAW

CONTENTS

7

CONTENTS

PART IX

Appendices

9

PART I

THE WORLD OF THE NEW TESTAMENT
AND THE CANON

CHAPTER I

THE WORLD OF THE NEW TESTAMENT

UNIFICATION AND HELLENIZATION OF THE EAST

Alexander's Conquests and Policy

The world of the New Testament was built on the foundations laid by Alexander the Great who, in the fourth century B.C., conquered the East and threw it open to the influences of the West. In ten years (333–323 B.C.) he succeeded in forming an Empire which stretched from Athens in Greece to the Punjab in India. People, made conscious of the fact that the world was much larger than they had imagined, became cosmopolitan; hitherto they had been content to remain in their native city but now many preferred to wander forth to other lands. Alexander believed implicitly in the superiority and power of Greek culture. His policy was to break down all racial barriers and to bring about the unification of East and West by encouraging inter-marriage, by fostering trade and commerce, and by furthering the spread of Greek culture. He himself married an Oriental and compelled or persuaded his soldiers to follow his example. This has been called the Marriage of Europe and Asia. According to Plutarch the two continents were to be joined "in lawful wedlock and by community of offspring". He not only enlisted Orientals in his army and trained them in Greek discipline, but also organized regiments in which Greek and Persian soldiers were combined. Persians were appointed to high offices and set over provinces as satraps. At important points on his lines of communication he built many towns, bearing his own name, such as Alexandria in Egypt, and transferred Greek colonists to them. These towns embodied the chief features of Greek life, such as theatres, amphitheatres, baths, and gymnasia, and were not only centres of trade but also of Greek culture. The population of Greece declined as people emigrated to these new towns and as commercial prosperity and leadership passed eastward. Wherever the Greeks settled they became missionaries of Greek culture. Men everywhere learnt Greek, which became a universal language, at least over the western half of the conquered territories. The people of the country districts and the lower stratum of society doubtless retained their native tongue and followed the old ways of life, but among the educated classes and those who were not entirely illiterate Greek culture was predominant.

On Alexander's death his Empire collapsed. After a period of confused fighting three kingdoms gradually emerged, namely, those of Antipater in Macedonia, of Ptolemy in Egypt, and of Seleucus in Syria, which included Babylonia and parts of Asia Minor. These rulers and their successors were also missionaries of Greek culture. Ptolemy I built a kind of university in Alexandria and attracted the foremost Greek scholars of the day to his court. His example was followed by the Seleucids in Syria and by the Attalids in Pergamum. It was the Hellenizing policy of Antiochus IV (175–163 B.C.) that led to the revolt of the Jews under Judas Maccabaeus (165–160 B.C.). Thus, the world opened up by Alexander became in the course of time increasingly unified and Hellenized.

Roman Conquests and Policy

The process of unification and Hellenization was continued by the Romans. Rome, originally a small city-state on the Tiber, gradually extended her power over Italy, Sicily, Southern Gaul, parts of Spain, Northern Africa, Greece, and Macedonia. The year 133 B.C. is a landmark in the history of the world, for in that year Attalus III, king of Pergamum, dying without heirs, bequeathed his dominions to the Roman people, who thus became a territorial power in Asia. Later, there followed the conquest and annexation of the rest of Asia Minor, Syria, Palestine, and Egypt, the Euphrates becoming the eastern frontier of their Empire. In the West Gaul and Spain were conquered before the beginning of the Christian era, Britain was subdued in the principate of Claudius (A.D. 41–54), and the northern frontiers were extended to the Rhine and Danube. By the beginning of the Christian era Rome had brought all the civilized world under her dominion: all opposition had been crushed and the conquered countries united into one vast Empire, within which the people enjoyed peace, order, security, and prosperity. Her newly conquered territories were secured by a network of military roads and piracy was suppressed, so that people were able to travel in safety both by land and sea. The world became more cosmopolitan than ever. "Under the advancing power of the Roman Republic, separate nations had ceased to exist, so that all were either citizens or subjects of Rome; the growing autocracy of the Empire was destined to diminish the distinctions between citizens, provincials and slaves, and to lead toward a cosmopolitan equality among all men."[1]

The Romans were in one sense a Hellenistic power. They conquered the Greeks, it is true, but the latter "took captive their conquerors". In their laws and principles of government they were original, but in their literature, science, and philosophy they were debtors to the Greeks. In the eastern half of the Empire they were the champions of Hellenism against Oriental encroachment. They made no attempt to substitute the Latin language for the Greek which had become the dominant language. Under their rule Hellenism not only held its own but also advanced: in Asia Minor, which had only been partially Hellenized, the remains of Greek cities belong mostly to Roman times. In the course of time the civilizations of two great peoples—Greeks and Romans—were fused and unified. It should be remembered, however, that while the West had been influencing the East, the East had been exercising a powerful influence on the West, especially in the realm of religion. To this composite culture which resulted from the interaction of East and West, we apply the term Hellenistic to distinguish it from the pure Greek or Hellenic culture.

[1] Jackson and Lake (Eds.), *The Beginnings of Christianity*, vol. I, 1939, p. 231.

RELIGION AND PHILOSOPHY IN THE
GRAECO-ROMAN WORLD

Loss of Faith

Long before the beginning of the Christian era, Romans and Greeks, especially the educated classes, had begun to lose faith in their ancestral gods. The old Roman religion had become little more than a prescribed ritual. Traditional Greek religion was less moral, although it probably had a stronger hold on the affections of the people as it was enshrined in a magnificent literature, and the festive worship associated with the deities of the city-states provided them with what they needed in the way of holidays, festivals, and processions, and drew many visitors who were excellent for business. The new conception of the physical world, consequent on the conquests of Alexander the Great, the fall of city-states, and the practice of deifying great leaders, resulted in a decline of interest in local gods. Caesar worship, which came to be firmly established in the Empire in the course of the first century A.D., cannot strictly be called a religion at all, being merely a bond of union, binding the people of the province to the throne and serving as a test of loyalty: as such it was absolutely devoid of spiritual content.

Study of Philosophy

Among the cultured classes the study of philosophy tended to kill superstitious beliefs. It brought out the defective morality of the traditional religion: men longed for a righteous God who would set before them the ideal of moral perfection. They longed, too, for a "Saviour" who would release them from the grip of Fate and Fortune, the terrors of the magician, the sense of guilt and moral failure, and the fear of death. In educated circles these feelings had long been felt among the Greeks: as early as the fifth century B.C., Euripides had cast doubts on the reality of the existence of the gods, while the same feelings had spread to Rome after the conquest of Greece in the second century B.C. In their craving for spiritual satisfaction, some turned to philosophy, especially to Epicureanism and Stoicism, which professed, not only to deal with the problems of the universe, but also to provide for men a way of life; others, less coldly intellectual, turned to the Mystery Religions.

Epicureanism

Epicurus (342–270 B.C.) taught that the universe is a chance conglomeration of atoms. The gods—if they exist at all—live in a region far removed from the earth and are not in the least concerned with the affairs of mankind. He ridiculed ancient mythology, explained such phenomena as eclipses and thunder on purely natural grounds, and denounced the belief in Fate. The chief end of life is the pursuit of happiness: the ideal life is the simple life devoid of all excess. All the conventions of the world to which men conform, and all its glittering prizes, such as power, wealth, and rank, are worthless: a picnic by a river is to be preferred to all the crowns of the Greeks. The soul of man, like his body, is material, and at death is resolved into its primordial atoms. Since the gods are indifferent to mankind, and there is no survival after death, men should banish the degrading fears of death and of future punishment beyond the grave. Men later distorted his teaching into a justification for a life of sensual pleasure.

Stoicism

The Stoics, who were followers of Zeno (336–264 B.C.) believed in a universal reason (also called breath, spirit, Nature, providence, or destiny) which is diffused through all things, including man. In the cosmic process there is evidence of the rational working out of a divine purpose which is essentially good; but there is no movement towards a final consummation—nothing in fact but a succession of cycles of long but finite duration, each ending in conflagration and in a meaningless renewal. It must be man's endeavour to live in accordance with Nature, that is, in harmony with the principle and purpose of the universe. The chief end of life is the cultivation of virtue, which should be cultivated, not to win the approval of gods or of men, but for its own sake. The wise man will exercise strict self-control and rise superior to all the circumstances of life. Since nothing can happen to him which is

2   17

not part of the system of the universe, he will be able to be calm and self-sufficient, even in extreme adversity. Since men partake of the divine nature, being "fragments of God" or "Sons of God", all are members of a great commonwealth that knows no barriers of race or class, and all have obligations of service to it. Such service, however, is not to be animated by feelings of good-will, pity, or compassion, but only by a sense of duty, for a wise man will allow neither suffering nor adversity to disturb his equanimity. Some believed that at death the soul is reabsorbed into the universal reason, and others that it enjoys a continued existence among the stars in contemplation of the heavenly bodies until the final conflagration, when it will be reabsorbed into its Source and the world process will begin again.

Mystery Religions

In the course of several centuries the so-called Mystery Religions had spread throughouth the Graeco-Roman world. Among the most important of them were those of Demeter and Kore from Greece, Isis and Osiris from Egypt, Cybele and Attis from Asia Minor, and Mithras from Persia. Candidates for admission became members after a solemn ceremony of initiation, which included baptism and participation in a sacred meal. These Mystery Religions were cosmopolitan, transcending all barriers of race and class. Greeks, Romans, barbarians, bond, and free—all were admitted to the brotherhood. At the same time they were individualistic, for they were concerned with the relation of the soul to its God. Here men found what they longed for, namely, the promise of deliverance from the dangers of this life, union with God, and the hope of a blessed life in the world beyond. In these cults there was a good deal of pageantry and of solemn ritual, performed under the direction of an official and consecrated priesthood. The daily services, held at definite times of day, helped to establish them as a solemn and necessary part of the recurring daily round. There is no doubt that their worship made a powerful appeal, and often lifted the worshipper into a state of exaltation in which he seemed to enjoy fellowship with the deity.

HISTORY OF PALESTINE

Introductory

On their return from exile in 537 B.C. the Jews were successively under the rule of Persia, Macedonia, Egypt, and Syria; but in 129 B.C. they finally succeeded in throwing off the Syrian yoke, and for sixty-six years they enjoyed complete independence under the Hasmonaean dynasty. On the death of the Priest-King, Alexander Jannaeus, (102–76 B.C.), his widow, Alexandra, became Queen with her elder son Hyrcanus as High-priest. Her death (*c.* 67 B.C.) was followed by a period of civil strife. Her younger son, Aristobulus, seized the throne and compelled his elder brother, the rightful heir, to retire into private life. The latter, acting on the advice of Antipater, governor of Idumaea, appealed to Rome to arbitrate in the quarrel and was given a decision in his favour, but Aristobulus and his followers rejected alien domination.

Pompey, who was campaigning in Asia, thereupon invaded Palestine and captured Jerusalem in A.D. 63. Judaea, greatly reduced in size, was incorporated in the province of Syria, while Hyrcanus was confirmed in the High-priesthood and appointed civil governor with the title no longer of King but of Ethnarch. Hyrcanus proved to be a weak, indolent ruler, and the power virtually passed into the hands of Antipater. On the death of the latter, his son, Herod, afterwards known as Herod the Great, received the title of King from Rome, and with the help of a Roman army captured Jerusalem in 37 B.C.

The Herods

Herod the Great (37–4 B.C.) was hated by the bulk of the Jews because of his Idumaean birth, his tolerance of idolatry, his ruthlessness, and his friendship with Rome. He was, nevertheless, a capable administrator who succeeded in maintaining peace and order in his dominions. He was distinguished by a love for building: he founded practically new cities at Samaria and Stratonis Turris, calling the former Sebaste and the latter Caesarea in honour of Augustus; built or strengthened fortresses at Herodeion, Alexandreion, Hyrcania, Machaerus, and Masada; and completed many public works, such as theatres, amphitheatres, gymnasia, baths, and market-places. His greatest undertaking, however, was the rebuilding of the temple at Jerusalem.

On his death his kingdom was divided among his three sons. Archelaus was given Judaea, Samaria, and Idumaea, with the title of Ethnarch. Herod Philip became Tetrarch of Ituraea, Batanaea, and Trachonitis, and Herod Antipas Tetrarch of Galilee and Peraea. Archelaus was quite out of sympathy with Jewish aspirations and was deposed in A.D. 6, his territories being placed under a Roman procurator. Herod Philip was a conscientious and just ruler, who maintained good relations with Rome and held office till his death in A.D. 34. His rule, however, had little or no bearing on Jewish history. Herod Antipas, like his father, was a capable administrator and a great builder, maintaining peace and order in his territories, and founding cities like Sepphoris, Bethsaida Julias, and Tiberias. On the other hand, he roused public feeling against himself by his marriage with the daughter of the Gentile King, Aretas, and still more when he divorced her to marry Herodias, the wife of his brother Philip. Seeking to obtain the title of King, he roused the suspicions of the Emperor Caligula and was deprived of his tetrarchy and banished to Gaul (A.D. 39). Caligula bestowed the vacant tetrarchies of Philip and Lysanias, and later that of Antipas, on Herod Agrippa I, a grandson of Herod the Great. On the death of the Emperor in A.D. 41 he supported the new Emperor Claudius and was rewarded with the territories of Judaea, Samaria, and Idumaea, with the title of King. During his reign of three years (A.D. 41–44) he endeavoured to conciliate the Jews by his punctilious observance of the Law, and the Gentiles by the erection of theatres, amphitheatres, and baths, and by the organization of games and gladiatorial shows. On his death this kingdom was brought under direct Roman rule. His son, Herod Agrippa II (A.D. 44–100), was given the tetrarchy of Philip and certain districts of Galilee and Peraea. He was also granted the power to appoint the High-priest and the guardship of the Temple and its treasure. In the Jewish war of independence he sided with the Romans, and after the Fall of Jerusalem retired to

Rome where he died (A.D. 100). His kindgom was then merged in the province of Syria.

Political Divisions

1. *Galilee.* In the north lay the fertile province of Galilee with its fields, gardens, oliveyards, and vineyards. According to Josephus it contained 204 cities and villages, the smallest of which numbered at least 15,000 inhabitants, but this is probably an exaggeration. It had a mixed population of Jews, Phoenicians, Arabs and Greeks, and well deserved the name of "Galilee of the nations" (Is. ix. 1), or "Galilee of the Gentiles" (1 Macc. v. 15). Many of the inhabitants were probably bilingual, speaking Aramaic and Greek, but the former was their native tongue which they spoke with a special accent, so that at Jerusalem Peter was easily recognized as a Galilean (Mt. xxvi. 73; Mk. xiv. 70). They were an industrious people, their chief occupations being the cultivation of the land, fishing, weaving, dyeing, and the making of pottery. The prosperity of the province was enhanced by the close proximity of the Phoenician seaports and by the network of roads which traversed it in all directions. The inhabitants were not only industrious, but also warm-hearted, impulsive, and enthusiastic, as is shown by the Gospel portrait of Peter who was a typical Galilean. Josephus pays a tribute to their courage. "The Galileans are inured to war from their infancy and have been always very numerous; nor has the country ever been destitute of men of courage." It was Galilee that supplied most of the rebels against Roman rule.

In their religion they held the same fundamental beliefs as the Judaeans; like the latter they used the same sacred book in their worship and were devoted to the Law, observing the Sabbath and making pilgrimages to Jerusalem for the great religious festivals. From the Gospels we infer that they were a pious people, and that they lived in expectation of the advent of the Messiah. Their acquaintance with Hellenistic ways of life and thought had given them a wider outlook and made them more tolerant than the Judaeans, and this probably accounts for the contempt in which they were held by the latter

21

(Jn. VII. 52). The contempt shown by the Judaeans naturally roused resentment on the part of the Galileans and prevented the establishment of harmonious relations between the two provinces.

2. *Samaria*. The origin of the Samaritans dates back to 722 B.C., when the King of Assyria conquered the northern kingdom, transferred some 27,000 Israelites to various centres of his empire, and resettled the land with conquered foreigners from the region of the rivers Euphrates and Tigris. These settlers intermarried with those of the Israelities who had been allowed to remain, and ultimately took the name of Samaritans. They naturally brought with them their religious beliefs, but in time they abandoned idolatry and adopted the Hebrew religion, accepting only the Pentateuch as authoritative Scripture.

It is probable that Jewish-Samaritan hostility had its origin in the rivalry between the tribes of Judah and Joseph. There is evidence for believing that the tribe of Judah was settled in Palestine before the Conquest and was only merged in the Hebrew nation after the main settlement. It may well be, therefore, that there was some resentment on its part against the new-comers, especially as for centuries the latter definitely took the lead, the tribe of Judah not becoming prominent till the time of David. After the death of Solomon violent hostility broke out between the Kingdom of Israel, consisting of the ten northern tribes, and the Kingdom of Judah, consisting of the two tribes of Judah and Benjamin. The immediate cause of the revolt of the ten northern tribes was Solomon's oppression and the refusal of his son, Rehoboam, to grant reforms; but it is clear that the North was glad of an opportunity to break away from the South. Political separation naturally increased the bitterness, and in spite of occasional alliance and co-operation this continued till the conquest of the Northern Kingdom in 722 B.C. The opposition up to this time had been purely political. There was no mutual hatred of Samaritans and Jews after the fall of the Northern Kingdom, nor was there any idea of the northern Israelites being a mixed race; on the contrary there is evidence of co-operation and friendliness. The antagonism between Samaritans and Jews is usually held to have originated with the building of the Temple, but the whole idea of Samaritan interference is probably a mere fiction of the chronicler of the books of Ezra and Nehemiah. The first overt act of hostility took place when the Samaritans tried to prevent Nehemiah from rebuilding the walls of Jerusalem. This, however, was probably due to political and personal reasons, for the Samaritans feared the revival of a rival province so near them; and Sanballat, the governor of Samaria, did not welcome a rival governor in Judaea, especially one who was a favourite of the Persian king. From this time onward religious and racial differences came to be emphasized. The final breach between the two communities came when the Samaritans built a rival Temple on Mount Gerizim (*c.* 332 B.C.) and disparaged the central sanctuary at Jerusalem. The destruction of the Samaritan Temple by John Hyrcanus in 128 B.C. would increase the bitterness on the part of the Samaritans.

Herod, a half-Jew, knowing that he would find more support from the Samaritans than from the Jews, practically rebuilt Samaria and called it Sebaste in honour of the Emperor Augustus, and showed them favour in other ways. The Samaritan support of Herod was never forgotten nor forgiven by the Jews: the spirit of antagonism was at its height in Jesus' day. To call a man a Samaritan was a term of the vilest reproach (Jn. VIII. 48); no Jew would pass through Samaria if he could possibly avoid it or have any dealings with its inhabitants (Jn. IV. 9). This hatred was returned by the Samaritans with interest. We read in the Gospels, for example, that the inhabitants of a Samaritan village refused hospitality to Jesus because he was apparently on His way to Jerusalem (cf. Lk. IX. 52–53).

3. *Judaea.* In the south lay Judaea, a poor province compared with Galilee. Many of its cities were in decay and some in ruins while much of its land was unsuitable for cultivation, but within its borders was the great city of Jerusalem, with its Temple, the central shrine of all Jewry and a place of pilgrimage. The inhabitants of the province, who probably numbered about 240,000, were reserved and haughty, claiming

to be the only true representatives of their race and religion. Proud of their traditions and blood, they looked down with contempt upon both the Samaritans and the Galileans.

Parties

1. *Pharisees.* The Pharisees were the spiritual successors of the Hasidim or Saints, who, in the days immediately preceding the Maccabaean rebellion against Antiochus IV of Syria (175–163 B.C.), opposed the Hellenization of their country. The word "Pharisee" is derived from the Hebrew word "Perushim" which means "the separated ones", and was applied to those who separated themselves, not only from the heathen, but also from the mass of their own people, who had neither the desire nor the ability to keep the Law. They were essentially a religious party whose chief object was the strict observance of the Law, since in their view it was the only way by which a man could become righteous before God. By the Law they meant the Unwritten as well as the Written Law, both being regarded by them as equally authoritative and binding. One of their distinctive beliefs was that of the resurrection of the dead: according to Josephus they held that after death the souls of good men returned to life but in other bodies, while those of the wicked were condemned to eternal punishment under the earth. They did much to keep alive the expectation of the advent of the Messiah among the people. Politically they were intense nationalists, opposed to all foreign influence, whether it was that of an alien culture like Hellenism or of a foreign power like Rome. Unlike the Zealots they would not appeal to force to overthrow the Roman domination, but were content to submit to it until it should please God to remove it. There were probably not more than six thousand of them altogether, but their influence was out of all proportion to their numbers. Their devotion to the Law, their ardent patriotism, and their championship of the cause of the people, made them the most influential factor in the Jewish life of Palestine. After the Fall of Jerusalem in A.D. 70 they devoted more time than ever before to the development of the Law and became the founders of what was to be orthodox Judaism.

24

2. *Sadducees*. The Sadducees were the spiritual descendants of those Jews who had welcomed the spread of Hellenistic culture in the days of Antiochus IV. It is thought that the name is derived from Zadok, the High-priest in the time of Solomon. They were men of wealth and position, the majority of them being members of the high-priestly and distinguished priestly families. They accepted the Written Law as authoritative Scripture but repudiated "the tradition of the elders"; hence no doctrine that was not clearly taught in the Written Law possessed for them any validity. For this reason they refused to believe in the doctrine of the resurrection, and in angels and spirits. Though they were not strong numerically they wielded great power. As members of the priestly aristocracy they had charge of the Temple and its services: the High-priest was generally a Sadducee, as was also his chief executive officer, the superintendent of the Temple guard of Levites. The revenue of the Temple was also under their control. They formed the majority of the members of the Sanhedrin, although they had to bow to the wishes of the Pharisees in order to conciliate the people with whom the latter were popular. They were not averse to the spread of Hellenistic culture and acquiesced in Roman domination in order to retain their power and privileges. As political control was largely in their hands, they were opposed to all projects of revolution. They did not share in the Messianic hope, believing that a Messianic movement might lead to a revolution and the overthrow of the established order. They were detested because of their political power, their arrogance, and their acquiescence in foreign domination. As a party they produced no great men, nor did they have any permanent influence on the life of the nation. On the Fall of Jerusalem in A.D. 70 they disappeared from History.

3. *The Zealots*. The Zealots were extremists of the national party who stood for everything Jewish and were opposed to all foreign domination or heathen influence. Their rallying cry was, "No Lord but Jehovah; no tax but the Temple tax; no friend but the Zealot". Extreme nationalists of this kind had existed since the time of the Maccabees, and it was one of the achievements of Herod the Great that he was able to hold them

in check. After his death they took advantage of the unrest in the land and revolted under Judas the Gaulonite, capturing the town of Sepphoris and overrunning the whole of Galilee. The revolt was eventually crushed but the nationalists succeeded in maintaining themselves in spite of the Roman might. In the time of the census of Quirinius (c. A.D. 6) Judas again revolted with the help of a priest, named Zadok, but the revolt was stamped out with exemplary ferocity. To this national party Josephus gives the name of "The Fourth Philosophy", the members of which held views identical with those of the Pharisees, except that they allowed only God to be acknowledged as King and advocated deeds rather than words. Actually the term "Zealot" does not appear in literature till A.D. 66 when it was applied to the followers of John of Gischala, who escaped to Jerusalem when the Roman army subdued Galilee.[1] These extreme nationalists, by their turbulence, kept the country in a state of constant unrest and finally precipitated the fatal rebellion of A.D. 66 which culminated in the Fall of Jerusalem four years later.

4. *The Herodians.* The Herodians were members of a political party who accepted the rule of the Herods and favoured friendship with Rome. Their existence proves that the Herod dynasty had secured a certain measure of support among the people. Their religious and political views approximated to those of the Sadducees; hence they were bitterly opposed to the Pharisees, but combined with the latter in their opposition to Jesus. In Mark's Gospel they appear twice (Mk. III. 6, XI. 13)—once in Galilee, and once in Jerusalem when, according to Luke, Herod Antipas, Tetrarch of Galilee and Peraea, was in that city. The question which they, in conjunction with the Pharisees, put to Jesus during His last week in Jerusalem gives us a clue to their political faith. "Is it lawful to give tribute unto Caesar or not?" Had Jesus said that it was not

---

[1] This absence of mention proves nothing, since there was no systematic writer on the Jewish history of the period before Josephus. The word "Zealot" is used as a translation of an Aramaic word, "Quanan", and the Aramaic word may have been used long before a Greek translation was found for it. One of the Apostles is called by Mark (followed by Matthew) "Simon the Canaanite", which Luke gives as "Simon the Zealot". This suggests that Mark knew the Aramaic name but not the Greek name.

lawful to pay tribute they would have denounced Him to the authorities. They were, however, apparently satisfied with the answer that Caesar, and therefore Herod, had his rights in the political affairs of the country.

5. *The Essenes.* The Essenes were ascetics who withdrew from the turmoil of the age and sought by strict discipline to live a life of absolute purity. They numbered some 4,000 people, the majority of whom lived in settlements on the western shores of the Dead Sea: they were also found in the smaller towns but not in the large cities, which they considered to be too immoral for habitation. They formed an order to which candidates were admitted by passing through various degrees, after probationary tests. With the exception of a solemn oath of initiation, they abstained from all oaths on the ground that their word was as good as their bond. Marriage was allowed if used solely for the continuance of the community. They earned their livelihood by agriculture and handcraft, and dwelt together on a communistic basis. Pious and hospitable, they were prepared to help those in need; to this end they studied the medical property of herbs in order to heal the sick who might seek their aid. They disdained riches, and abhorred war and slavery.

Their ideas of worship differed from those of their fellow men. They observed the Sabbath scrupulously and visited the Temple, but took no part in its sacrificial rites. They were dualists in so far as they recognized the existence of Good and Evil as opposing principles in the universe: it has been supposed that they worshipped the sun, but the probability is that they worshipped towards the sun, as it represented light in its mystical sense. They believed in the immortality of the soul but not in the resurrection of the body. It is thought by some scholars that their beliefs and practices were a combination of Jewish, Greek, and Oriental ideas.

Apocalyptic

Apocalyptic exercised a deep influence upon Jewish thought. This was found in a type of literature which belonged approximately to the last two centuries B.C. and to the first century A.D., and comprised a large number of books. It was the product of an age of pessimism and despair. The great prophets of Israel had prophesied a glorious future for the nation but the hopes had never been realized; instead they had been conquered in turn by Babylon, Persia, Egypt, and Syria. During the Syrian conquest certain pious, patriotic Jews sought to encourage their faith in God by the prediction of their deliverance through the dramatic interposition of God. These writers varied considerably in their ideas, but they all had certain common assumptions. All believed that God would intervene catastrophically and establish His kingdom on earth; all believed in a life after death and a final Judgment when due rewards and punishments would be meted out to both men and nations; and all believed in the advent of a great deliverer—the Messiah.

Among these apocalyptic books are the "Book of Daniel" in the Canon of the Old Testament; the Books of 2 "Esdras", and "Baruch", in the Apocrypha; and the "Testaments of the Twelve Patriarchs", the "Book of Enoch", the "Sibylline Oracles", and the "Assumption of Moses", in the Pseudepigrapha (i.e. books regarded as heretical and rejected by the Jews). In all such writings a symbolical language was employed, the meaning of which was generally understood. It was against this apocalyptic background that John the Baptist proclaimed the immediate advent of the Kingdom of God, and it was in an atmosphere charged with these expectations that Jesus proclaimed His message. Whether Jesus was familiar with these books may be doubted, but some of the ideas contained in them are plainly reflected in His teaching on the Kingdom of God. In the New Testament, the apocalyptic element in the Gospels is all taken from the thirteenth chapter of "Mark", which probably consists of a Jewish apocalypse blended with some authentic sayings of Jesus, and in the Epistles is practically confined to 1 and 2 "Thessalonians". "The Revelation" is wholly apocalyptic except for the charges to the seven churches at the beginning. Apocalyptic literature was early abandoned by the Jews, partly on account of its popularity among Christians, and partly because they became wholly absorbed in the study of the Law. The Christian Church also abandoned it, since it had served to encourage fanatical movements, such as the millenarian outbreak of Montanism in the second century A.D. though it continued to be written right down to the Middle Ages.

THE INFLUENCE OF HELLENISM ON JUDAISM

The great significance of Greece in the history of the world has lain, not in the realm of conquest, but in that of ideas. After the conquests of Alexander, Palestine became part of the Hellenistic world, and settlers, following in his wake, built cities in many districts, especially on the western seaboard in Galilee, and in the region east of Jordan, afterwards known as Decapolis. These cities became centres from which Greek culture was disseminated. The Jews could no more escape its charm and subtle appeal than any other thinking people, though their peculiar genius and charm were such as to reduce that influence to a minimum. Tradition played a great part in their lives. In spite of the universalistic trend which developed in such writers as Deutero-Isaiah and the author of the "Book of Job", Jewish hatred of Babylonians, Persians, Syrians, Samaritans, and Idumaeans, and the teaching of such men as Ezra and Nehemiah, led them to emphasize exclusiveness and separation. They divided mankind into two classes—Jews and Gentiles. The Jews were God's chosen people. He was their God in a sense in which He was not the God of other people. Hence there was fierce opposition to the penetration of Greek culture; but in spite of all their efforts the appeal was so powerful and pervasive that they could not wholly escape it.

So far as Greek influence appealed to the Jews, it was not so much through Greek penetration of Palestine as through the dispersion of the Jews throughout the Graeco-Roman Empire. Jews in such cities as Alexandria, Antioch-in-Syria, Tarsus, Ephesus, and Corinth, would naturally come into closer contact with Greek culture than their fellow countrymen in Palestine, while in Palestine the Galileans would be more susceptible to foreign influence than the Judaeans, since the former were in closer touch with the Hellenistic world.

The Greeks do not seem to have imposed their system of government on Palestine. The Greek system was that of the city-state, the city being the civic centre of the surrounding district and the government being an annually elected representative council. While the Jews did not adopt this system, they were undoubtedly influenced by the conciliar idea. From days of old the large towns of Palestine had formed centres of political life. "The influence of Hellenism marks, however, a turning-point in this respect, as in others; for, on the one hand, it transformed the existing communities fundamentally, while on the other, it founded numerous new ones, and made the municipal communities in general the basis of the political organization of the country in a far more thorough manner than before. Wherever Hellenism penetrated, and especially on the Philistine coast and the eastern boundaries of Palestine beyond Jordan, the country districts were grouped around single large cities as their political centres."[1]

The influence of the Greek gymnasium had a profound effect upon the young Jewish manhood. This was the modern equivalent of sport and was a new idea to them. The "First Book of Maccabees" gives us a picture of the true state of affairs. "In those days came there forth out of Israel transgressors of the Law, and persuaded many saying, Let us go and make a covenant with the Gentiles that are round about us: for since we were parted from them many evils have befallen us. And the saying was good in their eyes. And certain of the people were forward herein and went to the king, and he gave them licence to do after the ordinances of the Gentiles. And they built a place of exercise in Jerusalem according to the laws of the Gentiles, and they made themselves uncircumcised, and forsook the holy covenant, and joined themselves to the Gentiles, and sold themselves to do evil."[2]

Greek influence is more definitely seen in the sphere of literature. This influence is apparent in both form and content. The Greek language, in its colloquial form, had spread throughout the Mediterranean world, and was superior

[1] Oesterley and Robinson, *History of Israel*, 1932, p. 180.
[2] "The Apocrypha", p. 312 (*The World's Classics*, Oxford University Press, 1931).

30

to the Hebrew as a medium of expression. We do not know to what extent Greek was understood in Palestine in the first century A.D. Aramaic was the language of the common people, but in view of the large number of Greek cities scattered throughout the land, it would have been easy for an intelligent Jew to acquire sufficient Greek for purposes of conversation. It is probable that many, especially those belonging to the educated classes, were bilingual. All the Jews of the Dispersion spoke Greek and used in their synagogues the Greek translation of the Old Testament made in Alexandria.

From the middle of the third century B.C. until about the end of the first century A.D. a mass of Jewish Hellenistic literature was produced. Long before Josephus the Jews were writing their history in Greek: they composed tragedies on Greek models, taking as their subjects stories from the Scriptures, like that of the Exodus from Egypt. They had no philosophical works till after the time of Alexander the Great, when they began to study philosophy in earnest. The "Book of Job" is a philosophical discussion on the problem of evil and still retains its place as a contribution to the subject. The "Fourth Book of Maccabees" has for its purpose the attempt to show that Greek philosophy is really implied in the Mosaic Law, while the "Third Book of the Sibylline Oracles" seeks to express Judaism in terms of Greek thought. Philo (c. 20 B.C.–A.D. 50), a Jewish philosopher of Alexandria, endeavoured to bring about a synthesis of Greek philosophy and Hebrew religion.

The influence of Greek thought on Hebrew religion is not great, for Jewish traditionalism and exclusiveness would naturally show itself in this sphere. The spectacular element in Greek religion—its ritual, shows, and processions—made its appeal, and tended to loosen the ties which bound the Jewish people to their ancestral faith. Even in the realm of thought some influence can be traced. It is seen especially in the belief in the immortality of the soul, as distinct from the hitherto Jewish belief in the resurrection of the body. It was the attempt to harmonize these two tenets which led to the belief in an intermediate state in which the soul underwent a process of purification.

31

THE INFLUENCE OF HELLENISM ON CHRISTIANITY

Greek rapidly became the language of the early Christian movement. It was probably the increasing number of Greek-speaking Christians in the Roman Empire that led to the writing of the books of the New Testament in colloquial Greek, which had become a universal language. It is significant that when Paul sent a letter to the Christians in Rome it was written, not in Latin but in Greek. When New Testament writers quote from the Old Testament they generally used the Septuagint, that is, the Greek version of the Jewish Scriptures. The Greek language gave many words to the Church, such as Christ, baptism, eucharist, apostle, evangelist, bishop, priest and deacon.

The question of the language in which our Lord taught has often been discussed. It has been suggested that since He was reared in and confined His ministry largely to Galilee, where Greek influence was strong, He must have addressed the people in Greek, and that since His message was meant for the whole world, it was fitting that He should speak in an international language. For reasons given later this view cannot be accepted.

After the Exile, Aramaic began to supplant Hebrew as the language of everyday life. By the beginning of the first century A.D. Hebrew had become unintelligible to most of the people, so that when the Scriptures were read in Palestinian synagogues, an interpreter had to be employed to translate into Aramaic in order that the people, who had no knowledge of the "holy tongue", might readily understand. Hebrew, however, continued to be used in the Rabbinical schools down to the nineteenth century when it again became a spoken language.

Aramaic, then, was the language of the ordinary people, but it is probable that many were bilingual. Peter, for example, must have been bilingual otherwise he could not have addressed a Gentile audience. Jesus, also, must have spoken Greek in addition to His native tongue, Aramaic, for His conversation with the Syro-Phoenician woman and with the Roman procurator, Pilate, must have been in Greek, the only language all three could have understood. We know, too, that He could read Hebrew, since He read from the "Book of Isaiah" in the synagogue at Nazareth; but it is practically certain that He taught in Aramaic. Though the Gospels were written in Greek, some of the material was probably derived from Aramaic originals. The document Q, for example, is apparently a Greek translation of an Aramaic original. It follows that if there is a case for a translation from Aramaic into Greek, Jesus must have spoken Aramaic, for the idea of a double translation (Greek-Aramaic-Greek) is inconceivable. The presence of certain Aramaic sayings in the Gospels (e.g. Mk. v. 41, xv. 34) and their translation into Greek suggests that Aramaic was His habitual language. The presence of Semitic constructions alone, however, does not necessarily imply Aramaic originals, since they may be due to the underlying thought of people normally speaking Aramaic and writing Greek as a second language. If Jesus had carried on His disputations with the scribes and Pharisees in Greek, he would surely have been attacked as a Hellenist. Professor Manson suggests that in His formal disputations with them He used, not Greek or Aramaic, but Mishnaic Hebrew as they did. Finally Jesus confined His ministry, for the most part, to His own people and made no effort to exercise a world mission. The work of evangelizing the Gentiles was left to His disciples after His death, when the question of international contacts would become important.

Though the early Christians used the Greek language, they were not influenced to any great extent by Greek culture. Luke reveals the Greek spirit in his works, namely, the Third Gospel and "Acts", but especially in the former. John's Gospel and Paul's Epistles show that their authors were familiar with Greek philosophical ideas, while Paul also shows some acquaintance with Greek literature. It was not till the second century that Greek culture began appreciably to influence Christianity. The Apologists, who undertook the literary defence of Christianity, appealed for toleration on the ground that Greek philosophy taught very much the same as what Christians believed. Harnack, in fact, goes so far as to say, "In the earliest Christian writings, apart from Paul, Luke, and John,

I cannot find any considerable trace of Greek influence. The real influence of Greek thought and life began about 130."

CHRISTIANITY AT THE END OF THE FIRST CENTURY

The destruction of Jerusalem by the Romans in A.D. 70 marked the extinction of the Jewish state. The only party which survived was that of the Pharisees, who retired to Jamnia on the Palestinian coast, where· they devoted more time than ever to the study and inculcation of the Law. The Jews as a nation continued to be the enemies of Christianity, expelling its adherents from the synagogue and even appointing a prayer to be read against them on the Sabbath. "For the apostates let there be no hope; may the proud kingdom be speedily uprooted in our day; may the Nazarenes and the heretics perish in a moment." The controversies between Jesus and the Jews, which are recorded in the Fourth Gospel, written within the period A.D. 90–110, reflect the bitter opposition which Christian missionaries had to face from the Jews of the Dispersion.

Before the commencement of the siege of Jerusalem the Jewish Christian leaders fled to the country east of Jordan, especially to Pella some twenty miles south of the Sea of Galilee. After the destruction of the city, a few scattered communities lingered on in Palestine, but by the end of the first century A.D. Christianity had become a western religion and had severed its connection with the land of its birth. It was now firmly established in Syria, Asia Minor, Greece, and Rome, and had probably reached Gaul, Spain, and northern Africa. Now that the mother-city of Jerusalem was destroyed, the chief centres of Christianity were Antioch-in-Syria, Ephesus, Rome, and perhaps Alexandria.

The Christian Church had always regarded the Old Testament as a sacred book and had used it in their worship, in their private devotions, and in their controversies with Jewish opponents to prove that Jesus was the Messiah. By the close of the century they possessed, in addition to the Old Testament, nearly all the books of the New Testament as we know it

34

to-day, though they were not all in free circulation till some years later.

The Jewish Christians or Judaizers, whose chief stronghold had been Jerusalem, had declined in numbers and in influence, and were now a negligible quantity, though a few traces of them survived in the second century A.D. There was no longer any danger that Christianity might become an insignificant sect of Judaism: it was now recognized by the whole Church that Christianity was a universal religion, transcending all barriers of race or class.

Christianity now had to face not only the opposition of the Jews, but also that of the Roman government. The persecution under the Emperor Nero (A.D. 64–68) marked the end of the period of its more or less peaceful development, for from that time onward, it was regarded, not as a branch of Judaism, but as a distinct religion with certain peculiar features which rendered it dangerous to the state. The Church was now looked upon as an illegal society, and to belong to it was a punishable offence. Christians were called "atheists" because they refused to worship the heathen gods; and "traitors" and "enemies of the human race" because they refused to worship Caesar as Lord. In the reign of Domitian (A.D. 81–96) certain persons of high rank were put to death as Christians, but the persecution does not seem to have been of wide range. The correspondence of the younger Pliny, governor of Bithynia (c. A.D. 112), with the Emperor Trajan (A.D. 98–117) reveals the attitude of the imperial government towards Christianity. Christians were not to be hunted down, and no anonymous accusations against them were to be received. Any person, who was proved to be a Christian, after information had been laid against him, was to be punished if he did not recant. Thus, though it was illegal to practise Christianity, a chance of escape was to be given its followers.

By the close of the century the heresy, known as Gnosticism, had arisen and threatened to undermine the historic foundations of the Church. It was an amalgam of Oriental religious ideas, Greek philosophical ideas, and ascetic practices. Among other things it denied the reality of the Incarnation, and was fundamentally opposed to the Christian doctrine of salvation for all men. Moreover, it was especially dangerous at this time, since it attacked Christianity in its infancy before its theology had received rigid definition.

Finally, the Church was in the process of organization. In the lifetime of Paul each local church founded by him had been in charge of a board of elders or presbyters (sometimes called bishops), assisted by a number of deacons. By the end of the century we begin to hear of the monarchical episcopate in Syria and Asia Minor. Under this system the administration of a local congregation was in the hands of a single bishop, with the presbyters as his advisers and the deacons as his personal assistants. The monarchical episcopate, however, was at present merely the headship of the single congregation of a city: Christians were not sufficiently numerous to have more than one congregation in a city, and there were few Christians in rural districts. Clement of Rome, in his "Epistle to the Corinthians" (c. A.D. 96), traces the existence of church officers to apostolic succession. Ignatius (c. A.D. 115), though he urges the value of the monarchical episcopate as a bond of unity, makes no mention of apostolic succession. In the second century A.D. the union of these two principles—a monarchical episcopate in apostolic succession—greatly increased the power and prestige of the bishopric.

CHAPTER II

THE CANON OF THE NEW TESTAMENT

Definition of "Canon"

By the Canon of the New Testament we mean the list of books recognized as authoritative by the Christian Church. The word "canon" is derived from the Greek "canna" (a reed); it came to denote first a bar or straight rod, then a carpenter's rule or level, and then a standard of accuracy. Finally it was used metaphorically for a collection of books which attained such a standard.

Three Stages of Development

The intention, therefore, of this chapter is to trace the steps by which the twenty-seven books included in our New Testament were selected, and certain others, which were at some time and in some place included, were finally excluded. It is not intended to treat matters which will be discussed in other chapters when we come to deal with individual books, such as the reasons why the books were written, the conditions of the Church at the time they appeared, or their date and authorship, though reference will have to be made to those chapters whenever the arguments for inclusion or exclusion turn on such considerations.

Three periods can be traced in the development of the Canon: (1) that in which these books were read in Church services, treated with great respect and quoted, but were not regarded as "Holy Scripture" like the Old Testament; (2) that in which the Gospels, "Acts", and Pauline Epistles came to be treated everywhere as Holy Scripture, on a level with the Old Testament, but the remaining books were accepted, some in one locality and some in another; and (3) that in which agreement took place on which of these books should be accepted and which excluded, which in the full sense is the formation of the Canon.

(1) The first period covers roughly the lifetime of the oldest eyewitnesses of Our Lord's ministry and the generation which followed. During this period, at first all the converts and later the older ones (whose influence would be greatest) had obtained their knowledge of Christ's life and teaching from eyewitnesses, and the written records of what some of these eye-witnesses had said were of secondary authority to what they had themselves heard from them. Perhaps the last expression of this view is Papias's assertion that things out of books were less useful to him than what could be learnt from "a living and abiding voice" (c. A.D. 140). But already by the close of the Neronian persecution, the leading eyewitnesses had passed away, and the Gospels met a demand—they did not create it. It is remarkable how quickly each of the four Gospels became generally known and recognized, though we are in almost complete ignorance how it was effected. In particular, as we should expect, "Mark", as the Gospel of Rome, from and to which all roads led, was known to the writers of the other three Gospels. There is slight evidence of some opposition to "John" in Rome, and possibly to "Matthew" in Ephesus; but it must soon have been overcome. In Egypt a tiny fragment of "John" has come to light, which experts say must have been transcribed before the middle of the second century A.D. The earliest quotation of Our Lord's sayings in post-apostolic writers are identical in substance with those in the Gospels, but are not exactly in the language of any of them; but Ignatius of Antioch definitely draws his quotations from "Matthew", and it soon becomes apparent that all four Gospels were in general use. "Acts" is not quoted much at first; but we should hardly expect it to be as popular as the Gospels. There is abundant evidence for the use of Paul's Epistles, which are quoted during the period c. A.D. 96–115, by Clement of Rome, Ignatius, and Polycarp, the three outstanding post-apostolic writers, who speak of them in language which implies familiarity on the parts of their readers.

(2) As the written records came to be the only source for the knowledge of the acts and teaching of Our Lord and His Apostles, and a generation grew up which had from childhood

been used to hearing them read in the Church services, the distinction between the infallibility of the sayings of Christ and that of the only record of them which the Church possessed, or between the authority of Paul's preaching (which was forgotten) and that of his writings (which remained) was bound to vanish. The authority of Christ and the Apostles devolved on the writings, which thus came to be regarded as Scripture. In the so-called "Epistle of Barnabas" (c. 110–130 A.D.) we have what is probably the first quotation from a New Testament book with the authoritative formula, "It is written". ("Let us beware lest we be found cast out, as it is written, 'many are called but few chosen' ", Mt. xxii. 14). It must be remembered the "Scripture" is merely a Latin translation of the Greek word for "Writings", so "it is written" means exactly the same as if he had said, "to quote Scripture". The heretic Basilides (c. A.D. 120–130) refers to "Matthew" ii. 1 and to some of Paul's Epistles with the same formula. But the process was hastened by the need of authoritative documents to refute heretics. In fact, the first known Canon was that of the heretic Marcion (c. A.D. 140), who rejected the Old Testament and based his version of Christianity on an expurgated version of "Luke" and the ten Pauline Epistles (excluding the Pastorals)—an extreme form of Paulinism. A little later another heretic, Montanus (c. 156), claimed that the original revelation had been superseded by the utterances of the Holy Spirit through certain members of his own sect. In opposition to this view the Church was driven to assert the finality of the revelation given by Jesus to His disciples and to indicate the books in which that revelation could be found.

We might have expected that a definite Canon would at once have been produced, and may be surprised that two hundred years were to elapse before this actually occurred. But we must remember that Christianity was an illegal, underground movement, and anything approaching a General Council was quite impossible. The British constitution, for example, is not unique in disregarding logic when it has something which will work. Without any formal acceptance the four Gospels, "Acts", and the Pauline Epistles were treated as authorities in every church, and, if we exclude all the books from "Hebrews" onwards, the exclusions are less than a sixth of the whole: and, however valuable some of these books are, it would be difficult to affirm that our view of what Christianity means would be materially altered by their absence. In point of fact no church excluded all, though none was included by every church.

The unanimity on the five-sixths was not entirely due to one cause. The Gospels were certainly passed on to other churches with the prestige of the church in which each originated. "Acts" was accepted because it was written by Luke, the author of the third Gospel. We are inclined to account for the acceptance of the Pauline block by the assumption that they were kept by the Apostle himself and published together after his death, rather than collected from the various churches to which they were sent. This position is worked out in Chapter XII.

(3) We have to wait until the end of the second century before we get any list of recognized books anywhere. The first list we possess is the Muratorian Fragment, a mutilated Latin manuscript, probably not earlier than A.D. 170, discovered by the Italian scholar Muratori in 1740. In addition to the Four Gospels and the thirteen Pauline epistles (including the Pastorals) he admits 1 and 2 "John", the "Apocalypse of John", and the "Apocalypse of Peter", which was ultimately not accepted and which he admits to be rejected by some; he rejects the "Shepherd" of Hermas. Other books may have been included in the missing portions of this manuscript. Unfortunately its statements about the writing of the Gospels are obviously incorrect, and, from the modern standpoint, the writer is quite lacking in the historical sense. It may be noted that Marcion's list of Pauline Epistles which excludes the Pastorals, though it is written later than the time of Ignatius who quotes from them, may well represent an earlier tradition of the Roman Church; but during the greater part of this period they must be counted among the books which were everywhere accepted.

Eusebius, writing in the time of Constantine, was a scholar

trained in the science of literary criticism at Alexandria, the birthplace of that science in the field of secular Greek literature. His treatment is on an entirely different plane from the author of the Muratorian Canon. He states that 1 "Peter" and 1 "John" are universally accepted, and he himself concurs. He does not regard "Hebrews" as Pauline, though he values it highly; he mentions several theories about its authorship but concludes: "Who wrote this epistle God alone knows." He states that opinion differed on "James", "Jude", 2 and 3 "John", and 2 "Peter", but he himself rejects the last of these without reservation. Apparently he regards the "Apocalypse of John" as being accepted by most, though it is doubtful if he concurs. He rejects the "Shepherd" of Hermas, the "Didache", the "Epistle of Barnabas", and the "Apocalypse of Peter".

After the acceptance of Christianity by the Empire, concerted action became possible. Athanasius, in his Paschal Letter (A.D. 387), gives a list identical with our own; in addition, he wishes the "Didache" and the "Shepherd" of Hermas also to be read by catechumens but not in the service of the Church. His views are entirely his own but his position made it very important; his list was adopted at Rome in A.D. 383 and by the Council of Carthage in A.D. 397. We may regard the Canon as practically fixed by the end of the fourth century, though no Oecumenical Council ever pronounced upon it.

Principle of Selection

It may be well to consider the factors which determined the choice, and to compare them with those which would weigh with a modern body of experts if they had to determine the question independently.

The choice was limited to books, which, in some localities at least, were read in the Church services. Orthodoxy was essential. The attitude to authorship strikes us as curious. Apostolic authorship was not required for a Gospel or for "Acts", but was considered essential for an Epistle; consequently discussion on authorship was prejudiced. "Hebrews" was ultimately accepted as Pauline in spite of the evidence, because its high spiritual quality was recognized; and the same is more

41

or less true in the case of many of these books. Thus a recognition of the spiritual level of a book, though it was rarely put forward as an argument because it is subjective, actually played an important part in determining the choice and accounts for the rejection of the "Didache", which was long regarded as a genuine pronouncement of the Apostles, and the "Shepherd" of Hermas, in spite of its early date and the claim of the author to be a prophet.

Comparison of Ancient and Modern Methods of Selection

We shall now try to compare the reasons which led to the ultimate decision in doubtful cases with those which would guide us to-day if these cases had been left open. In the first place evidence of date and authorship would to-day be much more scientifically considered: even Eusebius, though in recognizing resemblances or differences of style he was equal to the best modern critics (possibly, as Greek was his mother-tongue, superior to them), would not notice all the slight indications of date which a modern critic is able to notice. Theological prejudice would be much more largely kept out, but we should be less exacting in demanding apostolic authorship. Date would count for more and the name of the author for less. What we should be aiming to secure would be the body of literature which would show us the mind of the Early Church at its best. We have abandoned such theories of inspiration as require acceptance of any view or of the historicity of any event on the evidence of a statement by a single author, whether apostle or otherwise; but we accept the cumulative evidence of those who represent the Primitive Church. Hence we should unhesitatingly include "Hebrews", though we are as uncertain of the authorship as was Eusebius. If, indeed, it was the work of Apollos, who would probably secure a majority of votes, we should be unmoved by the fact that Apollos was not an Apostle and impressed by the evidence of "Acts" and "Corinthians" regarding his importance in the Gentile churches. 1 "Peter" clearly dates from the age of eyewitnesses; and Streeter, while attributing it to Aristion, would never have thought of excluding it from the Canon; his view would raise our estimate of Aristion, not lower our estimate of the Epistle. James, indeed, differs from Paul, or rather from what he supposed Paul to mean; but we feel it to be a benefit to realize how truly those who differed from specifically Pauline views were at one on the essentials of the faith. The identity of the author of the three Johannine Epistles with the author of the Fourth Gospel is accepted by most of those who regard that Gospel as the work of John the Presbyter, not of John the Apostle. Even the Pastorals, though largely not by Paul, are representative and of high quality. The three books which moderns would have most hesitation in accepting, though owing to their actual inclusion many who would reject them if the question were perfectly open try to marshal arguments in their favour, are "Jude", 2 "Peter", and the "Apocalypse of John". The first two would be rejected on the grounds of date, and the date is reflected in the contents; no reader can avoid feeling that we have descended from the trumpet-call of early Christianity to commonplace moral sermons. The "Apocalypse" passes muster as far as date is concerned, but it stands for a tendency which we deplore, a tendency which we regard as opposed to Our Lord's teaching. Our imaginary modern commission would probably not include any book which is not now included, though it might consider the claim of 1 "Clement" to be above those of "Jude" and 2 "Peter".

Rejected Books

The reader may be desirous of knowing the nature of the books which came very near inclusion.

1. The "Didache" or "Teaching of the Twelve Apostles" was probably written in Syria about A.D. 100. Except for the "Two Ways", a piece of moral exhortation which appears also in the "Shepherd" of Hermas and the "Epistle of Barnabas", it is concerned with Church order, and its aim seems to be to establish an orderly system in churches in which it was lacking. It was long accepted as a genuine pronouncement of the Twelve Apostles, even after monarchic episcopacy had everywhere taken the place of the system which it contains and after the Johannine view of the relation of the Son to the Father had

taken the place of its theology. The modern objection to it is that, whereas "the letter killeth, but the Spirit giveth life", its outlook is that of the letter. Its inferior quality must have had much to do with its rejection, though even Athanasius wishes it to be read by catechumens.

2. The "Shepherd" of Hermas was written in Rome, probably about A.D. 100, and consists of a number of quaint visions and prophecies. It has no literary and little spiritual value, and is useful only as showing the thoughts of the ordinary Christian of Rome at the time. It is quite harmless and was accepted by writers of such prestige as Irenaeus, Clement of Alexandria, and Origen, while Athanasius treats it as he treats the "Didache". Thus it came very near acceptance, which shows the weight attached by most early Christians to contemporary "prophets". The author was undoubtedly sincere; he had been a slave, and he was orthodox. It is, however, a very tedious set of repetitions.

3. The "Epistle of Barnabas" is an anonymous homily, written in the form of a letter like the Catholic Epistles— "James", 1 and 2 "Peter", 1 "John", and "Jude". It seems practically certain that it was written in Alexandria, but its date is very doubtful, but probably not later than A.D. 130. It contains the "Two Ways", but its marked feature is its use of the Old Testament allegorically, an exaggeration of the tendency of the author of "Hebrews", himself (if he were Apollos) an Alexandrian. It was accepted in the city of its origin, as for example by Clement of Alexandria and Origen, but nowhere else; Eusebius counts it among the spurious books. Had it not been for the immense importance attached to Alexandria as the home of scholarship, it would never have had a chance of inclusion; but it is noticeable as being included in the Sinaitic codex of the New Testament in the British Museum, which is recognized as the best manuscript after the Vatican codex.

4. The "Apocalypse of Peter" dates from as late as c. A.D. 150, but, unlike the apocryphal "Gospel of Peter" of about the same date, got as far towards recognition as inclusion in the Muratorian Canon. It seems to come from the province of Asia. It shows how strong the apocalyptic tendency was in some

quarters that it should ever have obtained recognition at all. Like the three preceding books it was decisively rejected by Eusebius.

5. The "Epistle of Clement" is a letter written about A.D. 96 from the church of Rome to the church of Corinth on the dismissal of certain presbyters, an action which to the church of Rome seemed an abuse of power. It does not contain the author's name, as he does not write on his own responsibility, but it has always been quoted as Clement's. At first there was a tendency to include it, but it did not survive as a competitor when the final list was made. On grounds of date and quality it has better claims to inclusion than most of the other excluded books, but neither seems quite to warrant it.

PART II

THE PRE-LITERARY PERIOD AND EARLIEST WRITTEN SOURCES

CHAPTER III

THE PRE-LITERARY PERIOD

Evidence of an Oral Period

None of the Gospels could have been compiled for many years after the Crucifixion which probably took place about A.D. 29 or 30. Since it is generally agreed that the "Gospel of Mark" is the earliest of the four and that it was written about A.D. 65, there is a period of some thirty-five years before the first record of the life of Christ, preserved in our New Testament. But we must not assume that nothing bearing on that life was written during these years, for Luke in his dedicatory preface says:

"Forasmuch as many have taken in hand to draw up a narrative concerning those matters which have been fulfilled among us, even as they delivered them unto us, which from the beginning were eyewitnesses and ministers of the word, it seemed good to me also, having traced the course of all things accurately from the first, to write unto thee in order, most excellent Theophilus; that thou mightest know the certainty concerning the things wherein thou wast instructed."

From these words we may conclude:

(1) that before Luke wrote his Gospel, previous attempts had been made to write an account of the life and teaching of Christ. With the exception of "Mark", none of these attempts is extant; for even if Matthew's Gospel was written before Luke's, which is uncertain, Luke was almost certainly unacquainted with it. (It is doubtful if certain papyri fragments discovered of recent years are from these "lost Gospels");

(2) that the words and deeds of Christ had been handed down, both in writing and by word of mouth, by the original "eyewitnesses and ministers of the word";

4

(3) that Theophilus had gained his knowledge of the Christian faith, not from written documents, but by oral teaching (the word translated "instructed" in the Revised Version is from a Greek word meaning "to teach orally");

(4) that Luke was not acquainted with Christ personally. We conclude, therefore, that a generation elapsed before a complete biography of Our Lord was written, that during all that period the instruction of converts was mainly oral, and that during the earlier part it must have been entirely oral.

Reasons for Non-appearance of Documentary Records

The lateness of the first Gospel puzzles us who live in the twentieth century. In our day some accredited person usually sets about writing a biography of every distinguished man shortly after his death. But there is nothing puzzling about it. The really astonishing fact is that in all the centuries before the birth of Christ no biography of anyone had ever been written in any language. The first century A.D. invented biography, and it at once became an important branch of Greek and Latin literature, as the names of Suetonius, Tacitus, and Plutarch show. Consequently, it was not till Christianity was well established in the Graeco-Roman world that the first thought of writing a biography of Christ arose; then the four, which we call Gospels, came within a shorter period than had elapsed before the appearance of the first.

At an earlier period the early Christian missionaries, being Jews, were more likely to follow contemporary Jewish custom than Graeco-Roman. Now "Rabbi" was a title given to our Lord, both by His own disciples and by the people at large. The teaching of Jesus was therefore likely to be preserved in the same manner as was that of Jewish Rabbis. Somewhat later than the Gospels the Jews began to write down the teaching, not only of contemporary Rabbis, but also of those who lived in Christ's time. At an earlier date, however, no records were committed to writing: their teaching was learned by heart by their pupils and committed to memory. We shall shortly see that a written record of Our Lord's teaching was probably completed somewhat earlier than the earliest Gospel, that is, before any written record was made of His deeds.

Indeed, people accustomed to the method of oral instruction gave precedence to the spoken word: it was thought that by this method a person with a retentive mind could acquire and pass on knowledge with a greater degree of accuracy than was possible to one who relied solely on documents, which were suspect. The teacher or preacher was present, and, if necessary, could be questioned as to the truth of his utterances, while the information supplied by a document could not be checked. A careless scribe might commit many errors in the process of transcription and no one would be any the wiser. An unscrupulous person, with ulterior motives, might deliberately tamper with the text: the writer of "The Revelation" had such a person in mind when he wrote at the close of his vision, "And if any man shall take away from the words of the book of this prophecy, God shall take away his part from the tree of life, and out of the holy city, which are written in this book" (Rev. xxii. 19). Moreover, there was the possibility that the document, purporting to be the work of a well-known person, might be a forgery. Paul was alive to this danger, and warned the Thessalonian Christians to be on their guard against the receipt of spurious letters. He usually dictated his letters to an amanuensis, but to prove their authenticity he sometimes added a postscript in his own handwriting. In his second letter to the Thessalonians he wrote, "The salutation of me Paul with mine own hand, which is the token in every epistle: so I write" (2 Thess. iii. 17).

We are familiar with this oral method in the Gospels. There was nothing unusual in the fact that the child Jesus was found in the Temple, "sitting in the midst of the doctors, both hearing them, and asking them questions" (Lk. ii. 46). The extraordinary retentiveness of the Oriental mind made possible a degree of literal accuracy which to the modern Westerner would seem incredible. The fact that many of the sayings of Jesus have a poetic form, following as they do the laws of Semitic parallelism, shows that He adopted the oral method in

His teaching.[1] Such examples as the following could easily be committed to memory by repetition:

> Judge not,
> that ye be not judged (Mt. VII. 1).

> With what measure ye mete,
> it shall be measured unto you (Mt. VII. 2).

> Every good tree bringeth forth good fruit;
> but the corrupt tree bringeth forth evil fruit
> (Mt. VII. 17).

> He that findeth his life shall lose it;
> and he that loseth his life for my sake shall find it
> (Mt. X. 39).

> He that receiveth you receiveth me,
> and he that receiveth me receiveth him that sent me
> (Mt. X. 40).

Needs which eventually led to Written Records

Written accounts of the deeds and words of Christ were not therefore expected by those to whom the early Christian missionaries preached. When they came, an explanation has rather to be sought why they came then than why they did not come before. Some need of them must have been felt.

For some time, however, no such need was felt. The early disciples lived in eager expectation of the speedy return of Christ on the clouds of heaven to judge mankind and to establish His kingdom on the earth. How firm was that belief may be gathered from "Acts" and the Epistles. Some of the Thessalonian Christians, for example, became concerned about the fate of their friends who had died before Christ appeared, while others abandoned their occupations in preparation for His advent and claimed the right to be supported by the Church (1 Thess. IV. 13-18; 2 Thess. III. 6-15). Under the

Burney, *The Poetry of Our Lord*, 1925, pp. 137-40.

circumstances, therefore, there would be no desire to record the life and teaching of One for whose appearance they were watching with such eager expectation.

For some years after the Ascension the main facts of the life of Christ were common knowledge among the people of Palestine, especially in the districts of Galilee and Judaea, which were the chief scenes of His ministry. On one occasion the Pharisees, in their jealousy and anger, declared, "Lo, the world is gone after him" (Jn. xii. 19). Cleopas, one of the two disciples whom Jesus joined on the way to Emmaus, described him as "a prophet mighty in deed and word before God and all the people" (Lk. xxiv. 19). Paul, speaking of His death and resurrection before King Agrippa, declared, "For the king knoweth of these things, unto whom also I speak freely: for I am persuaded that none of these things is hidden from him; for this hath not been done in a corner" (Acts xxvi. 26), implying that the facts of the death and resurrection were so well known as to be beyond dispute. Since there were so many eyewitnesses of His ministry and so many people who had heard it from the lips of others, the early disciples would feel no urgent need of written records.

Further, in the work of conversion the personal appeal was far more effective. Christ Himself left no record which His disciples might consider it necessary or advisable to follow. Unlike many other prophets and some of the great founders of religion, he wrote nothing; there is no evidence that He ever commissioned one of His intimate friends to perpetuate the memory of His life and teaching through the medium of the written word. We know that He could both read and write, for in the synagogue at Nazareth He read from the book of Isaiah, while on another occasion He wrote, not on parchment, or papyrus, or in clay, but in the dust.[1] That He, a great spiritual genius and religious teacher, wrote no book was certainly not due to His lack of ability, ignorance, or infirmity of purpose. According to Sir William Ramsay, the Jews of that time were the most highly educated people in the ancient world. The Jewish Scriptures, especially the works of the psalmists and

[1] Deissman, *The New Testament in the Light of Modern Research*, 1929, p. 25.

prophets, in which Jesus was deeply versed, would be a constant reminder of the power of the written word; but He chose to follow the example neither of psalmist nor of prophet. Instead of embodying His teaching in a book, He appointed a small band of twelve men, and having trained them, sent them forth to preach the Gospel, not with a book in their hands, but with a memory in their hearts. That is all the provision which He made for the continuance of His work. It was not by the promulgation of a creed, or the formulation of a code of ethics, or the compiling of theological treatises that Jews and Gentiles were drawn into the Church, but by men and women who were inspired by His spirit to proclaim what they had seen and heard, and who in their lives and conversation bore witness to the truth of the Gospel.

But the lapse of time produced changes, and with them a need was felt for written records. So long as memories were fresh and the deeds and words of Jesus were the possession of a small group, no need of authoritative documents would be felt; but as the Gospel spread and new communities were founded, often far removed from the mother-church at Jerusalem and from one another, as the vividness of recollection became dimmed by time and the original eyewitnesses began to pass away, and as the Lord's return was delayed, there would be an ever-increasing demand for permanent records, in order to preserve and safeguard the knowledge of the Faith and to supply missionaries and teachers with an authoritative account of the life and teaching of Christ. That there was such a demand may be gathered from the study of patristic writings. Clement of Alexandria (c. A.D. 150–215) states that Mark was urged to write down the reminiscences of Peter, and that "he, having made his Gospel, gave it to those who made the request of him". This testimony is supported by Eusebius (c. A.D. 265–350) who declares that Peter's hearers were not content with the unwritten teaching of the Gospel, and that "with all sorts of entreaties they besought Mark, a follower of Peter, that he would leave with them a written monument of the doctrine which had been orally communicated to them". From the same writer we learn that the four daughters of

Philip the Evangelist "transmitted stories of the old days", a statement which may indicate that they possessed written documents. Thus Mark and others endeavoured to satisfy the insistent demand for permanent records, producing the "attempts" of which Luke speaks and of which he availed himself when he came to compile his own Gospel.

The Moulding of the Oral Teaching

We must now consider what was the nature of the knowledge of the deeds and words of Christ which was possessed by the early Church, how it was created, and how maintained. In the earliest period of its history that knowledge was based entirely on personal testimony. When the Christian brotherhood met for social intercourse, common worship, and participation in the breaking of bread, its members would share with one another their memories of the deeds and words of their Master. With the decision to embark on the work of evangelization beyond Jerusalem there came great changes. As the Gospel spread, the new converts were formed into communities and loosely organized. Since there was no one fixed form of organization drawn up and imposed upon the local churches by a supreme head or central body, there was naturally a variety of local usage throughout the mission field. As regards officers, we hear of apostles whose function was to rule the united body of believers and to preach the Gospel as witnesses of the Resurrection; prophets, who predicted events, preached and perhaps taught; evangelists who were probably sent out as missionaries by the apostles or a particular church; elders or presbyters (sometimes called bishops) who were responsible for the government and discipline of a local group; deacons whose main duty was to administer relief; and teachers to whom was entrusted the task of instructing the new converts in the Christian faith as a preliminary to their baptism and admission to the fellowship of the Church. Since there was no clear distinction between the various orders, it was possible for an officer to perform more than one function. For example, it is recorded that five "prophets and teachers", namely Barnabas, Niger, Lucius, Manaen, and Saul, ministered to the Lord at

Antioch-in-Syria. Of these, two, Barnabas and Saul exercised the apostolic functions as well; it is evident, therefore, that apostles and prophets could be accounted among the teachers. Outside "Acts" the last named appear more definitely as a class. Paul, in his first letter to the Corinthians (xii. 28), ranks them next to prophets, while in his letter to the Ephesians he places them in the fourth rank together with pastors (iv. 11), from which it will be seen that they occupied an important position in the life of the Church. Of these officers, the preachers and teachers played a fundamental part in the selection and preservation of the content of the oral teaching.

It is probable that there would grow up in the important centres of Christianity like Jerusalem, Caesarea, and Antioch-in-Syria, cycles of narratives, and that some of these narratives would be transferred from one church to another as missionaries passed from one centre to another. Intermingling and constant repetition would thus lead to greater resemblance in the teaching of the various churches on Christ's deeds and words. Now it is evident that these cycles of narratives did not contain all the knowledge of the life and teaching of Jesus which must have been accessible at the time through the original eye-witnesses and their immediate successors, nor was their growth merely a matter of accident. There must have been a process of selection by which certain portions were preserved and the rest ignored and soon forgotten. The choice of this material was chiefly the work of the preachers and teachers, mentioned above, who were guided by the needs of the Church.

In the first place there would be need for practical guidance on the many problems which confronted members in their daily lives. For some time after Pentecost they neither contemplated forming a new Church nor did they grasp the world-wide implications of the teaching of Christ. They formed a sect within Judaism, differing from orthodox Jews only in their belief that Jesus of Nazareth was the long-expected Messiah. If they were members of the Jewish Church, they were also an integral part of the nation, and as such subject to the domination of a foreign power. When the Gospel spread, many converts, both Jews and Gentiles, were called upon to practise the new

Faith in the midst of a pagan society. Moreover, the person of Christ, who claimed the allegiance and worship of all the members of the scattered Christian communities, would be the dominating interest in their lives. Guidance would be sought from His teaching on such questions as the observance of the Sabbath, fasts, food-laws, marriage and divorce, payments of tribute to Caesar, and the eating of food offered to idols. If they could only obtain "a commandment of the Lord" on such vexed problems, they would feel that they had real assistance. "For if they had problems, they also had a solution; and their solution did not lie in a process of acute reasoning, but in the ready acceptance of the authoritative words of Jesus. It was only when His word seemed ambiguous, or was entirely wanting, that serious difficulties arose, as when questions concerning Gentiles were discussed at the Apostolic Council of 'Acts' xv. For the most part there was little room for uncertainty or friction; their Lord had spoken and His words were spirit and life."[1]

The choice of the material would also be conditioned by the opposition of enemies without the Church. As the Gospel spread rapidly, the early disciples had to face the growing hostility of the orthodox Jews, who formed the majority of the nation. To the latter the idea of a suffering Messiah was an absurdity; the Messiah would come with great pomp and power to inaugurate His kingdom on the earth. The fact that Jesus of Nazareth had been crucified, a form of death on which the Law pronounced a curse, was conclusive proof that He was not the Messiah but a blasphemer and impostor. Peter and the other Apostles evidently knew the arguments they would have to refute, and the strength of the opposition they would be called upon to face, in commending Jesus of Nazareth as the Messiah to the unbelieving Jews. To substantiate their claims the Church would need an account of the Passion and Resurrection, and also texts from the Jewish Scriptures to prove that Jesus had fulfilled the Messianic prophecies.

We can see how the apostolic preaching would meet this need for proof of the Messiahship of Jesus. In the early days of

[1] Vincent Taylor, *The Formation of the Gospel Tradition*, 1945, p. 173.

His ministry Jesus "appointed twelve, that they might be with him, and that he might send them forth to preach" (Mk. III. 14), and just before His Ascension He commissioned His disciples to preach repentance and remission of sins in His name, beginning from Jerusalem (Lk. XXIV. 47). "It was God's good pleasure," said Paul, "through the foolishness of the preaching to save them that believe" (1 Cor. 1. 21). Christianity thus began with the preaching or proclamation of a message which formed the Gospel of good news. From Peter's speeches in "Acts" and Paul's letters we can obtain a rough idea of the content of the apostolic preaching. It is as follows:

(1) Jesus is the fulfilment of Old Testament prophecy.
(2) With His coming the Messianic prophecies have been fulfilled and the New Age has dawned.
(3) He was born of the Davidic line, approved of God by mighty works and wonders, crucified, raised from the dead, and exalted to the right hand of God.
(4) He would return to judge mankind and to establish His kingdom on the earth.
(5) Salvation was to be obtained, not by obedience to the Law, but by faith in His name.[1]

It will be observed that the chief emphasis is laid upon the death, resurrection, exaltation, and return of Christ. The Passion narrative was probably the first part of the common oral teaching to attain a fairly fixed form. In support of their argument as witnesses of the Resurrection, the Apostles probably carried about with them a book of Messianic prophecies which they considered had been fulfilled in Jesus of Nazareth.

Although there are but few explicit references made to the ministry of Christ in the apostolic preaching, we must not conclude that the Apostles confined themselves to the subjects of the Passion and the Resurrection. Argument from silence is precarious. Peter's speeches and Paul's letters give the impression that the ministry of Christ formed an integral part of their message, although it was not stressed to the same extent.

[1] Dodd, *The Apostolic Preaching and its Development*, 1944, p. 17.

In Peter's speech before Cornelius the life of Jesus prior to His Crucifixion is summed up in the words:

"The word which he sent unto the children of Israel, preaching good tidings of peace by Jesus Christ (he is Lord of all)—that saying ye yourselves know, which was published throughout all Judaea, beginning from Galilee, after the baptism which John preached; even Jesus of Nazareth, how that God anointed him with the Holy Ghost and with power: who went about doing good, and healing all that were oppressed of the devil; for God was with him. And we are witnesses of all the things which he did both in the country of the Jews and in Jerusalem" (Acts x. 36–39).

Now the Apostles were highly successful missionaries, but bald statements, such as the one above, would have little power to rouse enthusiasm and create faith. The speech is evidently a mere outline; if we could read a verbatim report of it, we should probably find that Peter had dealt with the life of Christ in much greater detail than Luke's account would seem to suggest. As regards the speeches and letters of Paul, there is sufficient evidence to prove that he was well acquainted with the ministry of Christ, and that it exercised a profound influence upon his own life and character. Moreover, the Apostles see the Passion as the culmination of the ministry. We therefore conclude that the narrative of the Passion and Resurrection was not delivered in isolation, but in conjunction with stories and sayings of Jesus, of which there must have been no lack, for we read in the closing words of John's Gospel, "And there are also many other things which Jesus did, the which if they should be written every one, I suppose that even the world itself would not contain the books that should be written" (Jn. xxi. 25).

Finally the content of the oral teaching would be shaped by dissensions within the Christian community itself. The early Church formed a close fellowship, but brotherly intercourse and frequency of meeting do not necessarily imply perfect harmony. It was not long before controversy broke out on the question of the relation of Gentile converts to Judaism. Two parties

59

emerged, namely, that of the Judaizers and that of the upholders of Gentile liberty. The Judaizers consisted of those Jews who, while professing the Christian faith, remained within Judaism and retained their devotion to the Law which they sought to impose upon all Gentile converts. The upholders of Gentile liberty, recognizing that Christianity was not a national but a universal religion, demanded that Gentile converts should be admitted to the Church without the imposition of any legal restrictions upon them. The adherents of each party would wish to select and preserve those portions from the life and teaching of Christ which would best support their arguments.

This leads us to perceive an important truth concerning the Gospels which are based on the oral teaching. They were not written by men working independently and in isolation. Each Gospel, to a certain extent, expresses the point of view of a particular school or tendency of Christian thought. Matthew, with his Jewish leanings, is at pains to present Jesus as the Son of David and the fulfilment of Messianic prophecy; Mark's purpose is to portray Him as the Son of God with power and authority; Luke, a friend and travelling companion of Paul, has Gentile sympathies and stresses the universality of the Gospel, while John is concerned to prove that Jesus is the eternal Word who was in the beginning with God and was God. Tendentiousness was a common characteristic of ancient writers. As Professor McNeile says, "To the true historian the past is not the 'dead past' which can be left to bury its dead; it is alive, with a meaning for the present. And an ancient historian generally allowed his conceptions of its meaning to set their mark upon his narrative more strongly than is permitted by the modern feeling of the importance of accuracy. He always wrote with presuppositions and a purpose, political, moral, religious, and so on. And the writers of the Gospels show that they were not exceptions; each of them emphasizes particular aspects of the message which he felt to be important."[1]

[1] McNeile, *An Introduction to the Study of the New Testament*, 1927, p. 7 f.

Form-Criticism

Reference must be made to Form-Criticism, which seeks to investigate the oral tradition which has received literary form in the Gospels and to discover the "Sitz im Leben", or Life-situation, out of which it sprang. Form-Critics assume that during the oral period the Gospel narratives and sayings, with the exception of the Passion-narrative, circulated as separate and self-contained units according to their forms. The German theologian, Dibelius, the leading exponent of the theory, classifies the narratives and sayings as follows:

Paradigmen (Paradigms): short stories in which the main interest is concentrated on a saying of Jesus. They were used as illustrations or models in preaching; e.g. the Paralytic (Mk. ii. 3–12), the Man with the Withered Hand (Mk. iii. 1–6), the Tribute Money (Mk. xii. 13–17).

Novellen (Tales): miracle stories told to show the power of Jesus over disease and nature. They were valued for themselves alone, not for any saying in them, and served as examples to Christian healers and exorcists; e.g. the Leper (Mk. i. 40–45), the Daughter of Jairus (Mk. v. 21–24, 35–43), the Feeding of the Five Thousand (Mk. vi. 35–44).

Paränesen (Exhortations): sayings of Jesus which served the purpose of catechetical teaching. They differ from the sayings embodied in the "Paradigmen" by the fact that they have no narrative framework. Among them can be distinguished the maxim (e.g. Mt. x. 26–27), the parable (e.g. Lk. xviii. 9–14), the prophetic call (e.g. Mt. xi. 25–30) and the commandment (e.g. Mt. v. 21–24).

Legenden (Legends): religious narratives of saintly men and women. They were intended to satisfy a double need—to give some knowledge of the holy men and women who were associated with Jesus, their virtues and also their lot, and to know Jesus Himself in this way, e.g. the Birth and Infancy Stories (Lk. i. 5–ii. 52), the Repentance and Death of Judas (Mt. xxvii. 3–8), the Dream of Pilate's Wife (Mt. xxvii. 19).

Mythen (Myths): stories which deal with particular relations and actions of divine beings, e.g. the Baptism, the Temptation, the Transfiguration.[1]

It is further assumed that the Gospel narratives and sayings sprang out of the practical needs of the Church. Dibelius finds their origin in preaching and teaching, and Bultmann in "community debates" in which they grew up under the influence of apologetic, polemical, and dogmatic needs. The Evangelists, therefore, were collectors of tradition or editors rather than authors.

The Nature of the Content of the Oral Teaching

The growth of the content of the oral teaching was not an orderly, progressive development, beginning with the Nativity and passing through several phases to the Ascension. The early disciples were not primarily biographers or historians, seeking to preserve for posterity a full and reliable account of the life and teaching of Jesus. Their chief concern was not the mere accumulation of facts but the building up of His Church according to the pattern on the Mount. In the pursuit of that ideal many personal and circumstantial details, which to-day would be of absorbing interest, would be considered of little or no value for their purpose and would therefore be ignored and in time forgotten. It was the fundamental needs of the Church which were the deciding factor in the selection and preservation of the material which found its way into the oral teaching. The Gospels, therefore, which are based on the material preserved in that teaching, are not primarily biographies or histories, though they doubtless have a biographical and historical interest. They lack the chronological sequence and completeness of presentation which are generally associated with these forms of writing.

[1] The leading exponents of Form-Criticism do not adopt the same terminology in their classification of the Gospel material. Where, for example, Dibelius (*Die Formgeschichte des Evangeliums*, 2nd ed., 1933) speaks of "Paradigmen" (models) and "Novellen" ("tales", "stories"), Bultmann (*Die Geschichte der synoptischen Tradition*, 2nd ed., 1931) speaks of "Apophthegmata" ("apophthegms") and "Wundergeschichten" ("miracle stories") respectively. Vincent Taylor (*The Formation of the Gospel Tradition*, 1945) classifies the Gospel material as follows: (1) "Pronouncement-stories", (2) "Miracle-stories", (3) "Sayings and Parables", (4) "Stories about Jesus".

Elaboration

In spite of the efforts of the early disciples and the proverbial retentiveness of the Oriental mind, it would be found impossible to preserve the content of the oral teaching intact, with complete accuracy and without any accretions. Imagination would soon begin to weave legends round the figure of Christ. It was inevitable that as the narratives and sayings passed from mouth to mouth some transformation should take place in the process. Some disciples would seek to modify them in accordance with their own particular views. We must also remember the practice of ancient historians of condensing the opinions and policy of their characters into the form of speeches, which were meant, not to state what was said at a particular time, but to give the gist of numerous utterances. The Sermon on the Mount, for instance, gathers together many utterances which are quite separate in "Mark" and "Luke". Occasionally, therefore, things which the Church later on believed to be part of Christ's teaching may have slipped into these addresses wrongly, though the consistency of His teaching, as represented in the various sources, shows that this cannot have happened on any large scale.

In our search for the truth we should not treat the Gospel records as if they were sacrosanct and therefore beyond criticism. We should recognize that they were written by men liable to error like ourselves, and that they should be tested by the same rules of historical and literary criticism as the works of any other chroniclers.

CHAPTER IV

THE EARLIEST WRITTEN SOURCES

Introductory

We have described in the previous chapter how the knowledge of the life and teaching of Jesus was transmitted by the original eyewitnesses, how the selection of events and teaching which were to be remembered was moulded by the practical needs of the Church, and finally, how with the passage of time an urgent need was felt for written testimony. Whether the attempts mentioned in Luke's preface, other than the Gospel of Mark, were merely fragmentary records or something approaching the dimensions of a Gospel like Mark's we cannot be certain, but we shall see that those which have been used by the authors of our four Gospels probably dealt only with sections of the material, and it is unlikely that anything like a full Gospel should have disappeared without leaving some trace. We will therefore now examine the evidence of the existence and nature of several of these probable documents, which can be derived from a comparison of the structure of the Gospels themselves.

Evidence of the existence of Q

There is practically universal acceptance of the view that Matthew and Luke used other written sources in addition to the Gospel of Mark in the composition of their own works. Critical analysis of the three Gospels demonstrates:

(1) that some 200 verses of non-Marcan material are common to the Gospels of Matthew and Luke.
(2) that the language of many of the verses in the two Gospels is either identical or almost exactly similar.
(3) that there is general agreement in the order in which the longer sections of this common material occur, namely the

Work of John the Baptist, the Sermon on the Plain, the Healing of the Centurion's Servant, the Baptist's Question, Would-be Disciples, the Missionary Charge, and the Parable of the Pounds.

(4) that in "Matthew" or "Luke" the same saying sometimes occurs in two forms, of which one is evidently taken from "Mark" and the other, by inference, from another source. These are sometimes called "doublets" of which there are twenty examples in "Matthew" and eleven in "Luke".

The presence in the two Gospels of these 200 verses, with their marked similarities, can only be accounted for on the supposition:

(1) that Matthew copied from Luke or vice versa. It is, however, unlikely that one copied from the other, since the genealogies and the narratives of the Nativity, Passion, and Resurrection are so different in the two Gospels that we must assume that they are independent works, written in churches some distance apart. As they were not written for the whole Church, their use for some time after their composition would be confined to particular localities.

or (2) that they both made use of different cycles of oral narratives. The use of different cycles of oral narratives would explain the passages more or less dissimilar, but not the striking similarities. When different people report the same event, there will be a general similarity between the two accounts but each will select different details, and none will give the facts in the same words. The same holds good of memories of speeches. Sometimes we find these differences and in such cases we assume that the evangelists who give the two accounts are not using the same written source; they are either using oral accounts or different written accounts. But when in their Gospels they use words no more different than they use when copying that of Mark, we assume that they are using the same written source. The small changes which the two others make in

"Mark" are usually due to a wish to improve Mark's Greek, which is often that of a man to whom Greek was a foreign language, or to shorten a statement as Mark often repeats himself.

or (3) that they both used a common source. As this is the most obvious explanation, we therefore conclude that both Evangelists made use of a single document, which is now referred to as Q, the initial letter of a German word *Quelle* (source).

Authorship

The hypothetical document Q is no longer extant, at any rate in an independent form, so that we cannot speak of it with any degree of certainty. Such questions as authorship, date of composition, place of origin, the language in which it was written, and the nature of its contents, must therefore be largely a matter of conjecture; only its discovery by an archaeologist would answer the questions which have for so long engaged the attention of New Testament scholars.

A clue to the identity of the compiler may perhaps be found in the *Ecclesiastical History* of Eusebius, who quotes Papias, Bishop of Hierapolis (*c.* 140), as saying, "So then Matthew arranged in order (or composed) the 'Logia' in the Hebrew tongue and each one interpreted (or translated) them as he could." Unfortunately there is no general agreement as to the exact meaning of these words. Some scholars hold the view that they can hardly refer to our present Gospel since it is not a translation: a few scholars believe that they refer to a *Book of Testimonies*, or proof-texts, put together from the Old Testament to prove that Jesus was the fulfilment of Messianic prophecy. The chief objection to this theory is that there are not enough proof-texts to make up a book. There is, however, a wide acceptance of the view, that since "Logia" can be translated "oracular utterances", they are identical with those found in Q. If such be the case, the author is Matthew who, it is thought, gave his name to the first Gospel because it incorporates this older document.

Language and Purpose

It is generally assumed that it was originally written in Aramaic and afterwards translated into Greek. There are two chief reasons for this assumption:

(1) the form of much of the teaching is Aramaic poetry, and Burney's translation into Aramaic not only brings out the poetic form, but also the occurrence in places of rhyme, which, though not a feature of the most classical Semitic poetry, was sometimes used in popular Aramaic.

(2) in one instance (Lk. xi. 41) Aramaic scholars are convinced that there is a mistranslation from the Aramaic, due to the translator's misreading of one of two words, which are very much alike, for another, and that a better sense can be got by substituting the other; in fact that we have an instance of just what Papias alleges.

The Epistles constantly show a distinction between the proclamation of the Gospel, that is, the recounting of the Passion and the Resurrection, the proofs that Jesus was the Messiah and fulfilled Old Testament prophecy, and His approaching Second Coming as Judge (this was addressed to the heathen), and the teaching on Christian life and conduct, intended for the converted. We should never have thought of making the distinction from the Gospels. Q, however, is principally concerned with the "teaching" of the converted. It has been conjectured that it was a manual of instruction in the meaning of discipleship for newly converted members of the Christian Church.

Contents

The following list of passages which Canon Streeter assigned to Q at least serves as a statement of the passages which appear in almost identical form in the Gospels according to Matthew and Luke, and may serve as a starting-point for considering what Q contained.

	Luke	Matthew
1. The Baptist and the Baptism of Jesus.	III. 7–9 (10–14), 16–17, 21–22.	III. 7–12, 16–17.

	Luke	Matthew
2. The Temptation and Appearance in Galilee.	IV. 1–16a.	IV. 1–11.
3. The Sermon on the Plain and the Centurion's Servant.	VI. 20–VII. 10.	V. 3, 4, 6, 11, 12, 44, VII. (*passim*), VIII. 5–10, 13, and Sayings elsewhere reported.
4. The Baptist's Question and the Witness of Jesus to the Baptist.	VII. 18–35.	XI. 2–11, 16–19.
5. The Journey to Jerusalem, Would-be-Disciples.	IX. (51–56), 57–60 (61–62).	VIII. 19–22.
6. The Mission of the Seventy.	X. 2–16 (17–20), 21–24.	IX. 37–38, X. 16, 9–15, XI. 25–27, XIII. 16–17.
7. Various Sayings, Defence against the Beelzebub Charge.	XI. 9–52.	VII. 7–11, XII. 22–27, 43–45, 38–42, V. 15, VI. 22–23, XXIII. (*passim*).
8. Warnings against fears, cares, etc.	XII. 1b–12, 22–59.	X. 26–33, XII. 32, VI. 25–33, 19–21, XXIV. 43–51, X. 34–36, V. 25–26.
9. Parables of the Mustard Seed, etc.	XIII. 18–35.	XIII. 31–33, VII. 13–14, VIII. 11–12, XXIII. 37–39.
10. Warnings to the Disciples.	XIV. 11, 26–27, 34–35.	X. 37–38, V. 13.
11. The Law and Divorce.	XVI. 13, 16–18.	VI. 24, XI. 12–13, V. 18, 32.

	Luke	*Matthew*
12. Warnings against causing others to stumble, etc.	XVII. 1–6, 20–37.	XVIII. 6–7,15, 21–22, XVII. 20, XXIV. (*passim*).
13. The Parable of the Pounds.	XIX. 11–27.	XXV. 14–30.

Now it is probable that each of the two Evangelists would treat his sources, "Mark" and Q, in the same way. Each has quite a different method of combining into a coherent narrative the material derived from these two sources. "Luke" has large blocks taken from Q: but in "Matthew" we often find the two mixed, everything dealing with a particular subject-matter being grouped together. There are, of course, inevitable exceptions; for example, in cases where Mark and presumably Q describe the same incident, such as the work of John the Baptist or the "casting out of devils by Beelzebub, the prince of the devils", Luke confines himself entirely or almost entirely to Q, while in "Matthew" the two are carefully combined. Matthew does not hesitate to depart from the Marcan order, so that it is unlikely that he is any more careful in preserving that of Q. Luke seems to keep more closely to the Marcan order, and probably does the same in the case of his non-Marcan source. We have, therefore, a test which will probably be sound for the bulk of the matter of Q as regards its order. If we assume that Q contained everything which appears in almost identical language in "Matthew" and "Luke", and that it was set out in Luke's order, we shall probably be right in the majority of cases. Our chief difficulty is about matter in Q which is omitted in either "Luke" or "Matthew". But, apart from one long omission by Luke of a part of "Mark", which we shall see was probably due to the loss of a sheet in the manuscript which he used, both omit so little from "Mark" that it is probable that they omitted little of Q, and, though we can never be sure what small parts are preserved only in one of them, we can be reasonably certain it was not much.

Dr. T. W. Manson thinks that it was arranged in four divisions: (1) Jesus and John the Baptist; (2) Jesus and His

Disciples; (3) Jesus and His Opponents; (4) Sayings about the
Last Things. Certainly these sections stand out, but there is a
large number of sayings in the material common to the two
Gospels which hardly admit of classification.

This view of Q derives some support from an analogy with
the prophetic books of the Old Testament, which, to a Jew
living in the days before the teaching of contemporary Rabbis
was written down and unfamiliar with the Gentile biographies,
would be the most natural model. If we look at the books of
Isaiah, Jeremiah, and Ezekiel, we find that, though the
sayings of the prophet occupy the bulk of each book, their call
is described—and the baptism of Jesus, when He saw the vision
of the Holy Spirit descending and heard the voice from heaven,
and subsequently meditated in the desert on His mission,
corresponds to the prophetic call—and occasional historical
incidents are recorded to explain the circumstances of His
utterances. This is exactly what we have in Q, if its contents
were such as we have described.

A few other theories may be mentioned. Some hold that it
was a Gospel and that the Gospel of Mark was compiled as a
supplement to it; others that it contained nothing but sayings
of Jesus; and others that it contained, in addition, a certain
amount of historical narrative. According to Professor Buss-
mann, Q is a fusion of two documents, one written in Greek,
which contains narratives and sayings, and the other written
in Aramaic, containing sayings exclusively. Professor Vincent
Taylor thinks that it began merely as a sayings-source and that
it was afterwards expanded by the inclusion of a number of
stories.

Place and Date of Composition

As regards the place of its composition cases have been made
out for some centre of Christianity in Palestine and for Antioch-
in-Syria. An Aramaic original with a strong Jewish colouring
implies a connection with Palestine, not necessarily Jerusalem,
as there were many Christians in Galilee. It had, however,
been translated into Greek before Matthew and Luke used it.
A Greek translation implies a community of Hellenistic Jews,

70

or of Gentiles, or of both, living within easy reach of Palestine. Its contents also suggest the same conclusion. Now Antioch-in-Syria was within easy reach of Palestine: it had a flourishing church, composed of both Gentiles and Jews, and was an important centre of Christianity, being the headquarters of missionary enterprise. There are grounds for believing that Luke was a native of that city, and Matthew's Gospel appears to have been of Eastern origin, as it is quoted by writers of Syria and Palestine earlier than by Western writers. We therefore infer that the Greek translation was closely connected with Antioch-in-Syria.

The date of its composition cannot be fixed with any confidence, but an Aramaic original and a Greek translation connected with Palestine and Antioch-in-Syria respectively, suggest an early date. It is generally agreed that it is earlier than Mark's Gospel (c. A.D. 65): we are probably safe in dating it within the period A.D. 45–65.

Mark and Q

The question has been raised whether Mark was acquainted with Q and whether he used it. The two questions are not identical, as he might have been acquainted with it and not have used it, though it seems hardly likely: or he might have read it at some time but not have had a copy, or even merely have heard of its existence. But he does not seem to have used it. His account of John the Baptist selects quite different features from those given in Luke's Gospel, which is probably taken from Q; Matthew combines the two. His missionary address to the Twelve stands in a similar relation to Luke's missionary address to the Seventy, which is presumably Q. Matthew again combines them. The same is true of the Beelzebub controversy. Mark has a much longer account of the teaching about divorce and the washing of the "outside of the platter", both of which are condensed by Q into two verses. There are about twenty verses scattered up and down "Mark" which are in substance the same as Q, but they all differ substantially in wording and do not appear in the same context, so much so that both "Matthew" and "Luke" repeat some of them in both contexts. They were probably well-known sayings which could easily be remembered, and it would be quite easy for Mark to know them even if he knew nothing of Q, though he may have read Q at some time and remembered the substance of them. But if Mark wrote in Rome and Q was in existence in Antioch-in-Syria, it is not necessary that Mark should have seen it.

The Historical Value of Q

The document Q is of great historical value. Forgotten as an independent record when once it had been incorporated in the larger works of Matthew and Luke, and reconstructed in recent times, it is now a priceless heritage of the Christian Church. It has preserved for all time the teaching of Jesus which has changed the whole course of human history. Its early compilation, combined with the inherent nature of the material composing it, convinces us that in it we have the authentic words of Jesus. It was written a few years after the Crucifixion when the original eyewitnesses were yet alive and memories were still undimmed. The teaching which it enshrines is the noblest ever given to mankind, while the profundity of the thought, prophetic fervour, and deep under-standing of human nature which characterize the utterances, bear the unmistakable signs of being the work of a great religious genius.

The document sheds some additional light on the ministry of Jesus. From this source we gain a juster appreciation of the character of John the Baptist and a clearer understanding of the meaning of the Baptism and the Temptation. We infer, too, that the work of healing performed by Jesus was not merely incidental to that of preaching but formed an integral part of His ministry, and that in the fulfilment of His mission He visited places rarely if ever mentioned by the Evangelists. He bade the disciples of John the Baptist return to their master and tell him what they had seen and heard; "the blind receive their sight, the lame walk, the lepers are cleansed, and the deaf hear, the dead are raised up, the poor have good tidings preached to them" (Lk. vii. 22). His denunciation fell upon the inhabitants of Capernaum, Bethsaida, and Chorazin, because, in spite of the mighty works done in their midst, they had not repented. Apart from Q little is known of Bethsaida and nothing of Chorazin. From His lament over Jerusalem we gather that He must have visited the city on many occasions.

The sayings preserved in Q reveal something of the character of Jesus. He is seen to be a poet, with a deep love of Nature and the homely things of life, and with the ability to express His thoughts in language of rare beauty and simplicity. The countryside and the home provide Him with much of the imagery which He uses in His illustrations. The sparrows sold for two farthings, the ravens which have neither store-chamber nor barn, the hen gathering her chickens under her wings, the foxes in their dens, the lilies of the field arrayed in a glory greater than Solomon's, the grass cast into the oven, the reed shaken by the wind, and the grain of mustard seed growing into a tree—He had noted them and had gazed on them with the eyes of perfect understanding. He is seen, too, as a man resolute and courageous, patient and humble, stern and yet compassionate—that rare combination of strength and gentleness which is characteristic of the great soul.

Other Written Sources and Archaeological Discoveries

It is generally agreed that Q is only one of many such collections of sayings used by members of the Christian communities. Three of these will be discussed at some length in the chapters on the Gospels which make use of them. They are:

(1) a source of some length used in "Matthew", containing a collection of sayings analogous to Q, which probably represented the recollections of the church at Jerusalem.

(2) a collection of discourses on subjects of controversy between Jesus and the Jews or particular sects of the Jews, which continued to be vital issues between Christian missionaries and their Jewish opponents. This is incorporated in "Mark".

(3) Mark's chapter on the Second Coming.

Whether written collections of parables existed is uncertain. If we exclude comparisons extending only to a verse or two in length, it is remarkable that, apart from Mark's parables which are incorporated by the other two Synoptists practically as they stand, only two parables are common to "Matthew" and "Luke", and they differ enough to make it probable that they are not from the same source. Parables are easily remembered, so it is unnecessary to assume that they were written before the Synoptists included them; on the other hand, there is nothing to show that several collections of parables existed.

The only narrative source of which we have any clear evidence is the Passion narrative. Matthew follows Mark's version; Luke's version appears to be a slightly different version with some facts from "Mark" added; even the Fourth Gospel, which never copies a source verbally, follows the same general lines as the others with many omissions and additions, in such a way as to suggest that the author assumed the familiarity of his readers with the narrative. The slight divergences between "Mark" and "Luke" must have taken place while the narrative was still being taught orally; but either version or both versions may have been written before they were used by the two Evangelists.

It is thought that there existed a book of proof-texts, consisting of quotations, collected from the Old Testament, and used as evidence that Jesus of Nazareth had fulfilled the Messianic prophecies.

In connection with these early written sources mention should be made of recent archaeological discoveries. In 1897 Messrs. Grenfell and Hunt, exploring in the village of Oxyrhyncus in Egypt, found a leaf of a papyrus codex, containing what purported to be eight Logia (or Sayings) of Jesus. These sayings are not in an ordered series but are detached and independent of one another, while each is introduced by the formula, "Jesus saith". They date back to about A.D. 150 or perhaps earlier. Further exploration in the same locality led in 1903 to the discovery of five more sayings, written on a survey list of various pieces of land, and prefaced by the words:

"These are the (wonderful) words which Jesus the Lord spake to —— and Thomas, and he said unto (them), Everyone that hearkens to these words shall never taste of death."

Of these thirteen sayings the most memorable are perhaps the following:

(1) Jesus saith, Except ye fast to the world, ye shall in no wise find the kingdom of God; and except ye make the Sabbath a real Sabbath, ye shall not see the Father.

(2) Jesus saith, Wherever there are two, they are not without God; and wherever there is one alone, I say I am with him. Raise the stone and there shalt thou find me; cleave the wood and there am I.

(3) Jesus saith, Let not him who seeks . . . cease until he finds, and when he finds he shall be astonished: astonished he shall reach the kingdom, and having reached the kingdom he shall rest.

Whether the recently discovered sayings are authentic reminiscences of these early collections or forgeries of a later age is a matter of opinion. On the one hand Professor Milligan believes that "they contain a distinct residuum of the Lord's teaching rescued from the floating tradition", while on the other Sir F. Kenyon declares that "they can have little claim to authenticity and are akin to some sayings recorded in the early Christian writings".

The earliest fragments we possess of what may possibly be a non-canonical Gospel, were discovered in Egypt in 1934, and published the following year. They contain four episodes in the life of Christ, three of which have affinities with incidents related in the Four Gospels, while the fourth is something apparently quite new. It is thought that they date back to about A.D. 150, and that the author is "following a stream of tradition independent both of John's Gospel and of the Synoptists".[1]

[1] Bell and Skeat, *Fragments of an Unknown Gospel and other Early Christian Papyri*, 1935.

Whether in these fragments we have an authentic record of another written source is uncertain.

There are, of course, many Apocryphal Gospels which were condemned as untrustworthy by the Church and excluded from the canon. These are all later than the Apostolic Age.[1]

---

[1] James, *The Apocryphal New Testament*, 1950.

PART III

THE FOUR GOSPELS AND ACTS

CHAPTER V

THE SYNOPTIC PROBLEM

Comparison of the Synoptic Gospels and the Fourth Gospel

A comparison of the four Gospels reveals a substantial resemblance among the first three and a marked difference between them and the fourth. Naturally all four contain the essentials of the Gospel message as it is set out in "Acts" x. 38–41: "how that God anointed him with the Holy Ghost and with power: who went about doing good, and healing all that were oppressed of the devil; for God was with him. And we are witnesses of all things which he did both in the country of the Jews, and in Jerusalem; whom also they slew, hanging him on a tree. Him God raised up the third day, and gave him to be made manifest, not to all the people, but unto witnesses that were chosen before of God, even to us, who did eat and drink with him after he rose from the dead." Within these limits, however, there are differences as regards (*a*) the selection of events recorded, (*b*) the form and content of the teaching, (*c*) the attitude of the writers.

(*a*) The first three, commonly called the Synoptic Gospels, confine themselves to Galilee from the arrest of John the Baptist up to the last week, whereas the Fourth devotes far more space to incidents occurring in Jerusalem during visits to various feasts than to the Galilean mission. Some differences of fact can be found: for example, John the Baptist in the Synoptics occupies a prominent position as a preacher and religious reformer and is cast into prison before Jesus enters on His ministry, whereas in the Fourth Gospel he is reduced to being merely a witness of Jesus and is still preaching when the latter enters on His ministry; the Cleansing of the Temple occurs according to the Synoptists in the last week, in the Fourth Gospel at the beginning of the ministry; the Last Supper is in the Synoptics the Passover meal, while in the

Fourth Gospel it takes place the day before the Passover. Very few of the incidents recorded prior to the Triumphant Entry are the same; in fact, it looks as if the Fourth Evangelist was deliberately omitting all events except those of the greatest importance which were recorded by the Synoptists simply because he knew that his readers were already familiar with them; but some of the omissions may well be dictated by this difference of attitude which we shall shortly discuss.

(b) The differences in the record of teaching concern both form and substance. Parables, so numerous in the Synoptics, are entirely absent in the Fourth Gospel, their place being taken by allegories like those of the Good Shepherd (x. 1–18), and the Vine (xv. 1–8). Instead of the brief, incisive utterances of the Synoptic Gospels, expressed in simple, direct language which all can understand, we find in the Fourth Gospel long, mystical discourses, expressed in a style closely resembling that of the Evangelist himself. The differences of substance are equally marked. In the Synoptic Gospels the central theme of Jesus' teaching is "the Kingdom of God and His righteous-ness", whereas in the Fourth Gospel He is represented as being chiefly concerned with the nature of His own person and with His relation to the Father. In the Synoptic Gospels Jesus conceals the fact of His Messiahship till towards the close of His ministry; but in the Fourth Gospel He presents Himself as the Messiah from the beginning.

(c) Finally, the attitude of the writer seems to be different. It produces a marked difference in our impression of Jesus. The Synoptists are in no doubt as to His divinity, but it is something which discloses itself on supreme occasions and is then realized with astonishment, at the Calming of the Storm, at the Transfiguration, and on the Cross. Ordinarily the spectators only recognize the great religious teacher, the Rabbi who, unlike the scribes, "speaks with authority", the healer, and the Man with power over unclean spirits. In the Fourth Gospel divinity is apparent at every moment: emphasis is constantly laid on His omniscience and omnipotence; He is subject to no outward compulsion; His betrayal and crucifixion are in accordance with His own will, and are manifestations, not of His weakness but of His power. The Synoptic attitude may be summed up in Paul's well-known words: "Who, being in the form of God, counted it not a prize to be on an equality with God, but emptied himself, taking the form of a servant, being made in the likeness of men; and being found in fashion as a man, he humbled himself, becoming obedient even unto death, yea, the death of the cross" (Phil. II. 6–8). Great though His powers were on earth, they did not amount to omniscience (Mk. XIII. 32), or omnipotence (Mk. VI. 5). And so we find that the Fourth Gospel omits the Temptation, the Agony, and the cry of desertion from the Cross, which imply human limitations. From the beginning of this Gospel, in which Jesus is introduced as the incarnation of the pre-existent, eternal Logos, who came from God and would return to God, the emphasis is on His Divinity: and, though His human feelings are stressed, any human limitations are virtually denied, and the miracles, which in the Synoptic Gospels are deeds of mercy, become less the outcome of compassion than designed to reveal the divine nature of Jesus.

Comparison of Synoptic Gospels

When we compare the first three Gospels, however, we are struck not so much with the differences as with the many striking similarities among them. This is not true of the Birth and Infancy narratives, which do not appear in "Mark" and are completely independent in "Matthew" and "Luke". Afterwards, however, the three Gospels tell the story of the life and teaching of Jesus in much the same way. The ministry of Jesus is preceded by the preaching of John the Baptist, the Baptism, and the Temptation. Then follow the ministry in Galilee, with withdrawals east and north beyond its borders, the journey to Jerusalem, and the events of the last week. Within the limits covered by Mark, Matthew and Luke follow the same general outline. They also show a remarkable agreement in the selection of the incidents and discourses, and in the general order in which they are presented. The Gospels can frequently be arranged in three parallel columns, when it will

6

be observed that the triple and dual agreements are more numerous than the isolated material. "Mark" can be divided into 105 sections, and only four of these are absent from "Matthew" and "Luke": of the remaining 101 sections, 93 are found in "Matthew" and 81 in "Luke". There is also a considerable amount of material in "Matthew" and "Luke", which cannot be found in "Mark", but in this there is much that is common to the two Gospels. Again, when the same incident is recorded in all three Gospels we find that they are characterized by remarkable verbal agreements. These agreements are not confined to the language only, but are also seen in the structure of the sentences, as for example, the parenthetical insertion of a detail of fact in the middle of a speech (Mt. ix. 6=Mk. ii. 10=Lk. v. 24).

The first three Gospels are called the Synoptic Gospels because they largely present a synopsis or common view of the life and teaching of Jesus (Greek, "sunoptikos"="taking a general view"). The striking parallelisms existing between them constitute what is known as the "Synoptic Problem". It cannot be accidental that three authors, apparently writing independently, adopt the same general outline, make a similar selection of incidents and discourses and arrange them in a similar order, and often employ identical or almost identical language. The common outline, the common selection of material, the common order, and the common language, demand a common source or sources; for independent biographers, with so great a wealth of incident and teaching from which to choose, would, apart from the all-important events, be likely to make a vastly different selection, as the author of the Fourth Gospel does.

Augustine's Solution of the Problem

The first to attempt to solve the problem of the interdependence of the first three Gospels was Augustine (c. 354–430), who advanced the theory that "Matthew" was the first to be written and that "Mark" was an abridged version of it. He also held that Luke had the Gospels of both Matthew and Mark before him when he came to compose his own Gospel.

The substantial agreement of the three Gospels was judged to be a providential guarantee of the truth of the Gospel message, and an old Jewish proverb, "a threefold cord is not quickly broken" (Eccles. IV. 12), was often quoted. This theory prevailed until the rise of modern critical investigation in the eighteenth century, when it was proved to be false. Had Augustine taken the trouble to compare the Greek texts of the Gospels of Matthew and Mark, he would have discovered that it is Matthew and not Mark who generally does the abridging. Canon Streeter shows that the number of words employed by Mark to tell the stories of the Gadarene Demoniac, Jairus' Daughter, and the Feeding of the Five Thousand are respectively 325, 374, and 235, whereas Matthew tells them in 136, 135, and 157 words. Moreover, it is inconceivable that Mark should have omitted Matthew's accounts of the Birth and Infancy, the Sermon on the Mount, and practically all the parables, merely to write at greater length on the remainder of the material.[1]

Modern Solutions of the Problem

The many modern theories which have been advanced to solve the problem of the interdependence of the first three Gospels fall into two classes, namely (a) the oral, and (b) the documentary.

(a) Oral Hypothesis. According to this theory the first three Gospels were based upon a primitive Gospel, which, though unwritten, had become more or less fixed by constant repetition. This oral Gospel originated in Palestine and was Aramaic in language, forming the content of the apostolic preaching. Its fixity and accuracy were due, it was alleged, to the catechetical method adopted in the teaching of converts and to the extraordinary retentiveness of the Oriental memory. The first to reduce the oral Gospel to writing was Mark; and later on another version was produced by Matthew. Later still, Luke using this Aramaic Gospel in conjunction with that of Mark, which had by this time been translated into Greek, prepared the Gospel which now bears his name.

[1] Streeter, The Four Gospels, 1930, p. 158.

This theory, which was once popular, is now rejected by almost all scholars, mainly for the following reasons:

(i) It is difficult to explain the fixity of the oral Gospel in the matter of selection of the incidents, the order in which they are arranged, and the language in which they are expressed. If the oral Gospel arose to meet the practical needs of the Church, we should expect to find several different cycles of narratives, not one. Mark's order is generally followed by Matthew and Luke. There would be no difficulty in accounting for the fixed order of the narratives if they were chronological, but Mark's order is probably not so. We have, therefore, to account for the formation of an artificial order. Even if we make allowances for the extraordinary retentiveness of the Oriental memory, it is inconceivable that the incidents should have been repeated for over thirty years with such little variation in language.

(ii) It does not account for the material common only to the Gospels of Matthew and Luke. If we assume that it must have been included in the oral Gospel, the question arises why Mark should have excluded some of its most valuable matter from his Gospel.

(iii) If the oral Gospel was more or less fixed, we should naturally expect to find general agreement, at any rate in the main incidents, but it is otherwise. In addition to slight verbal differences, we find that accounts like those of the Last Supper, the Crucifixion, and the Resurrection, differ in all three Gospels.

(iv) An official oral Gospel would have been considered authoritative, and consequently it is unlikely that the Synoptists would have taken such liberties with it as they undoubtedly have done.

(v) The original instruction of converts must have been given in Aramaic, but the coincidences in the Greek texts of the Synoptic Gospels are such that they cannot be accounted for on the ground that the authors translated independently from an Aramaic original. It is hard to believe that the same fixity of verbal expression would persist throughout the whole process of translation.

(vi) The exponents of the theory assumed that the oral

84

Gospel took shape in Jerusalem. It is remarkable, however, that though it is evident from the Fourth Gospel as well as from indications in the Synoptics that there was a Judaean as well as a Galilean ministry, the oral Gospel should have omitted all account of the former ministry until the Triumphal Entry.

Though the oral hypothesis has been abandoned, it is generally agreed that the oral teaching has exercised a considerable influence on the Synoptic Gospels.

(b) *Two-Document Hypothesis.* There is now almost universal agreement that two basic documents underlie the Synoptic Gospels. These are "Mark" and a document, commonly called Q (from the German word *Quelle*=Source). The theory that "Mark" is the earliest account of Jesus' ministry and that it was utilized by the other two Evangelists is supported by the following arguments.

(i) *Common Contents.* There is very little in "Mark", apart from details, which is not found in "Matthew" or "Luke". Matthew reproduces about ninety per cent and Luke about fifty-five per cent of the subject-matter of "Mark".

(ii) *Common Language.* When three parallel accounts are given, we find that the language of "Matthew" and "Luke" is often identical or almost identical with that of "Mark". Matthew retains about fifty-one per cent and Luke about fifty-three per cent of the actual words of Mark.

(iii) *Common Order.* The order in which the events are recorded by Matthew and Luke agrees very closely with that of Mark. When Mark and Luke differ in order Matthew agrees with Mark, and when Mark and Matthew differ in order Luke agrees with Mark. There is no case where Matthew and Luke agree in order against Mark.

(iv) *Arrangement of Marcan and non-Marcan material.* The way in which Marcan and non-Marcan material is distributed in "Matthew" and "Luke" suggests that the authors had "Mark" before them, and that each devised his own method of combining the material derived from his various sources into a coherent whole. Matthew makes "Mark" the framework of his Gospel, combining Marcan and non-Marcan material in such a way as to make appropriate contexts, while Luke, except

85

in the Passion narrative, sets the Marcan and non-Marcan material in alternate blocks.

(v) *Improvements in Mark's Version.* Matthew and Luke show a constant tendency to improve upon Mark's version. Statements which might be misunderstood or raise difficulties are sometimes omitted or changed. Thus, in "Mark" Jesus is only once addressed as "Lord", whereas Matthew uses it nineteen times and Luke sixteen. In the account of the Rejection at Nazareth Mark declares: "And he could there do no mighty work, save that he laid his hands upon a few sick folk, and healed them. And he marvelled because of their unbelief" (VI. 5–6). Luke omits this statement altogether, while in "Matthew" it appears in the form: "And he did not many mighty works there because of their unbelief" (XIII. 58). Mark's words: "Why callest thou me good?" (X. 18), are changed in "Matthew" to: "Why askest thou me concerning that which is good?" (XIX. 17).

Sometimes changes are made in both style and grammar. For example, in "Mark" there are 151 cases of the Historic Present, that is, the verb is used in the Present Tense for the sake of vividness. Matthew has parallels to these in only twenty-one cases, and Luke in only one. They omit most of Mark's Aramaic words. Luke uses none of them, while Matthew preserves only one, namely, "Golgotha" (XXVII. 33), but substitutes for the words: "Eloi, Eloi, lama sabachthani?" (Mk. XV. 34), the Hebrew equivalent: "Eli, Eli, lama sabachthani?" (Mt. XXVII. 46).

Ur-Marcus Theory. The acceptance of the view that Matthew and Luke used "Mark" as their main source in the composition of their Gospels raises a problem which calls for a solution. A comparison of the three Gospels shows that:

(i) there is a number of minor verbal agreements of "Matthew" and "Luke" against "Mark";

(ii) certain sections of "Mark" are omitted by Matthew and Luke. Matthew omits fifty-five verses, while Luke, in addition to several short passages, omits one long passage of seventy-four verses, namely VI. 45–VIII. 26.

The problem is how to account for these phenomena. According to the Ur-Marcan Theory, none of the three Evangelists was dependent upon any one of the others, but the three used an earlier form of "Mark", or an "Ur-Marcus", which contained both incidents and discourses. "Mark", as we have it to-day, is an expanded version of this earlier Gospel and has a slightly different text. This theory, however, has been abandoned by almost all scholars. Some of the verbal agreements are due to the fact that Matthew and Luke, who sought consistently to improve Mark's style and grammar, occasionally made identically similar corrections, while others are due to the modifications of the text by copyists familiar with the parallel Gospel. In most cases the readings found in "Matthew" and "Luke" as regards style and grammar are improvements, and consequently, if the verbal agreements are not due to the causes above mentioned, the authors must have used a revised text of "Mark". In that case our present "Mark" is earlier and more primitive than that used by Matthew and Luke.

As regards omissions in "Matthew" and "Luke", they are, with one exception, few and unimportant. The case for an Ur-Marcus rests chiefly on the fact that Luke omits the long section, Mk. vi. 45–viii. 26. Several reasons have been advanced for this omission. He may have deliberately omitted it because he preferred his non-Marcan source which had similar incidents; or he may have omitted it by accident, or used a mutilated copy of "Mark" from which the section was missing. On the Proto-Luke theory (see pp. 89–91) the difficulty disappears since, on his theory, Luke takes from "Mark" only what he needs to supplement Proto-Luke. "To Luke 'Mark' was a supplementary source, from which, if pressed for space, he would refrain from extracting material, which seemed to him of subordinate interest."[1] We should remember, however, that the Evangelists were not mere transcribers, whose object was to produce exact copies of manuscripts, but historians who were free to select the material which best suited the purpose which they had in view.

[1] Streeter, *The Four Gospels*, 1930, p. 214.

The Document Q. A comparison of the three Gospels shows that "Matthew" and "Luke" have in common some two hundred verses which are not found in "Mark". This material was derived from the document Q which is no longer extant. (For an account of Q see Chapter IV.)

Marcan Sources. Although "Mark" is the "Foundation Gospel" of "Matthew" and "Luke", it is not itself an absolutely independent production but is to a certain extent derivative. It contains not only the reminiscences of Peter and Mark's own personal recollections, but also a certain amount of material derived from other sources. The Conflict Stories (II. I–III. 6), are characterized by an orderly development which suggests that they existed as a whole before they came into Mark's hands. There are probably at least three doublets in the Gospel, namely, the Feeding of the Five Thousand (VI. 35–44) and the Feeding of the Four Thousand (VIII. 1–9), the Healing of the Deaf and Dumb Man with Saliva (VII. 32–37) and the Healing of the Blind Man (VIII. 22–26), and the two instances in which Jesus rebukes the disciples for their personal ambition to occupy the highest places in the Kingdom (Mk. IX. 33–35, x. 41–45). To account for these doublets we must suppose that Mark had at his disposal two distinct sources which covered much the same ground. The Little Apocalypse (XIII. 3–37), which combines older apocalyptic material with genuine utterances of Jesus, is written in a different style from the rest of the Gospel and was presumably derived from another source. Mark also must have derived material from the Passion narrative, which was one of the earliest parts of the Gospel story to take shape, but whether he found it in an oral or written form we do not know.

The Four-Document Hypothesis. We have shown that Matthew and Luke compiled mainly from two main sources, namely "Mark" and Q. This Two-Document Hypothesis, however, does not take into account a large amount of material peculiar to the two Gospels. Canon Streeter claims that in addition to "Mark" and Q, Matthew used a collection of sayings and parables which he designates by the symbol M, and that Luke (besides "Mark" and Q) used a collection of sayings, parables, and narratives, to which he assigns the symbol L. The Judaistic character of much of the material in M suggests that it was closely associated with the Church in Jerusalem, which was the chief centre of the Jewish Christians. The material in L represents the information collected by Luke during his two years' stay in Caesarea. (For further accounts of M and L see Chapters VII and VIII.) Each of the four sources was probably connected with an important church. "Mark" was the Gospel of the Church in Rome; Q was an Antiochene translation of an Aramaic original, perhaps compiled for Galilean Christians; M was connected with Jerusalem and L with Caesarea. "The connection of these Gospels with the traditions of the great churches explains the authoritative position which, as against all rivals, they soon achieved, and thus their ultimate selection as the nucleus of the Canon. It was because the Synoptic Gospels included what each of the great churches most valued in its local traditions, and much more also, that the records of these local traditions were allowed to perish."[1]

We should remember that in addition to the above four sources Matthew and Luke must have employed material from other sources. In "Matthew", the Birth and Infancy narratives (I.–II.), together with a number of parables and incidents and some minor details connected with the Passion and Resurrection (see pp. 119–121), are not derived from "Mark", or Q, or M. They probably belonged to a cycle of tradition current in the church where the Gospel was composed. He may also have used a "Book of Testimonies"—a collection of Old Testament Messianic proof-texts. The Birth and Infancy narratives of Luke (I.–II.) are probably a Greek translation of an Aramaic or a Hebrew original, and must be assigned to another source than L, though some scholars include it in the latter.

Proto-Luke Theory. We have already shown that there is in Luke's Gospel a large amount of non-Marcan material, mainly derived from two sources, Q and L, and that in addition there are the Birth and Infancy narratives, derived from another source. The account of the Preaching of John the Baptist, the

[1] Streeter, *The Four Gospels*, 1930, p. 269.

89

Baptism, the Temptation, and the Rejection at Nazareth
(III. 1–IV. 30), would appear to be derived from Q and L, and
that of the Call of Simon (v. 1–11) from L. There are three
sections, namely, VI. 12–VIII. 3 (called the Lesser Interpolation),
ix. 51–xviii. 14 (called the Great Interpolation), and xix. 1–
28, which are also drawn from Q and L. The narrative of the
Passion is mainly, and of the Resurrection wholly, derived
from L, since Q had no Passion and Resurrection narratives.
Taken all together these non-Marcan sections are greater in
extent than those derived from "Mark" and form a more or
less continuous narrative, beginning with the preaching of
John the Baptist and ending with the post-Resurrection appearances. On the other hand the Marcan sections are self-
contained and supplementary. It is wrong, therefore, to call
any of the non-Marcan sections "Interpolations".

Further, critical analysis shows that:

(1) Marcan and non-Marcan material appear in alternate
    blocks;
(2) Marcan and Q material stand apart, while L and Q
    material are fused together;
(3) where "Mark" and Q overlap, Luke prefers Q as in the
    account of the Temptation, and when "Mark" and L
    overlap he prefers L as in the account of the Rejection at
    Nazareth.

In view of the above considerations Canon Streeter claims
that Luke first combined material from Q with material from
his special source L. To this first draft Canon Streeter gives
the name Proto-Luke. Later Luke came across Mark's Gospel
which contained a good deal of material with which he was
unacquainted. He therefore expanded his original draft by
inserting into its body at suitable places extracts from the second
Gospel. Finally he completed the work by pre-fixing the Birth
and Infancy narratives, and by adding a brief preface.

The Proto-Luke Theory has several advantages. It explains
the position of the elaborate date (Lk. III. 1), and the genealogy
(Lk. III. 23–38). The former reads as if it was originally written
as the opening words of the book, while we should have

expected to find the latter somewhere in Chapters I. and II., in connection with the Birth and Infancy narratives. If, however, the Gospel originally began at Chapter III. 1, the position of the genealogy is explained, for it occurs immediately after the first mention of the name "Jesus". The large non-Marcan section IX. 51–XVIII. 14 is more easily accounted for if it originally formed part of Proto-Luke than as a section inserted at a later date in the Marcan material. The theory also helps to show that Luke adopted the same method of composition in the Gospel as he did in "Acts". In both we have the same orderly progress; in the Gospel from Galilee, through Samaria to Jerusalem, and in "Acts" from Jerusalem, through Judaea, Samaria, Syria, Asia Minor, and Greece to Rome. In both the author uses material which he had himself collected—in the Gospel the source L, and in "Acts" the "We" sections.

CHAPTER VI

THE GOSPEL ACCORDING TO MARK

Authorship

Early tradition assigns the composition of the second Gospel to Mark who is said to have written down the reminiscences of the Apostle Peter. The first of the ancient writers to ascribe it to Mark was Papias, Bishop of Hierapolis, a town of Asia Minor, in a work which is unfortunately no longer extant. He is, however, quoted by the church historian Eusebius (*c.* 265–350) as saying:

> "This also the Presbyter used to say, 'Mark, having become the interpreter of Peter, wrote accurately, though not in order, all that he remembered of the Lord's sayings or doings. For he was neither a hearer of the Lord, nor a follower of Him, but afterwards, as I said, followed Peter, who adapted his instructions to the needs of his hearers, without any attempt to give an ordered account of the Lord's Sayings. So Mark was not wrong in writing down some things in this way from memory; for his one concern was not to omit or falsify any of the things he had heard.' "

This view was universally accepted in the early Church, but in all probability the subsequent writers, Irenaeus (*c.* A.D. 142–200), Origen (*c.* A.D. 185–253), Tertullian (*c.* A.D. 150–225), and Jerome (*c.* A.D. 340–420), all derived their original authority from the statement of Papias. It has, however, been disputed in modern times, the view having been put forward that the Gospel is not based on any first-hand authority but on the general tradition which was the common possession of a local church, probably that of Rome. This line is particularly taken by the form critics, but it is hard to see how a view of a suitable classification of material can throw light on its source. It may show for what kind of information there was a demand, but it cannot reveal the source of the supply. The truth of the theory can only be settled by its consistency or inconsistency with the internal evidence.

It is a striking fact that, from the call of Peter to the end of the Gospel, there is nothing of which Peter could not have been a witness or hearer, with two notable exceptions, and a vast amount of which he is definitely recounted as a witness (the execution of John the Baptist was a matter of well-known history and not part of Our Lord's life). These two exceptions are the Agony in the Garden, when Peter was present but asleep, and the Trial and Crucifixion, when he was in the court of the High Priest's palace and then a fugitive. A point on which sufficient stress has never been laid is that, though Mark never directly tells us his sources—ancient historians rarely did—in both these cases he practically does so indirectly. The close of the account of Gethsemane is as follows: "And a certain young man followed with him, having a linen cloth cast about him, over his naked body: and they laid hold on him; but he left the linen cloth, and fled naked" (xiv. 51–52). Now this young man was the only person who could have heard Jesus' prayer (xiv. 35–36), as the disciples were asleep. Whether, as has been often suggested, the young man was Mark himself, we can never say, but that he was the original source of the account is clear: and the detail of his escape is a presumption that it was Mark himself and that it had stamped itself on his mind. The second case is at the end of the Crucifixion narrative where it is stated: "And there were also women beholding from afar: among whom were both Mary Magdalene, and Mary the mother of James the less and of Joses, and Salome" (xv. 40). Mary Magdalene might well be mentioned as a prelude to the resurrection appearances, but the others are in themselves persons of whom nothing else is recorded; yet Mark is clearly interested in their identity, as well he might be if they had described to him what they saw.

We must be careful, however, in distinguishing between the narratives of acts and of teaching. It would be most difficult to prove satisfactorily that narratives of teaching, except where it consists of a verse, or as given in answer to a question, or arising out of an incident, were derived from any one person. Several long portions of teaching occur in the Gospel, as for example, the chapter of parables of the kingdom (IV. 1–34), the controversy on the traditions of the elders (VII. 1–23), the answers to various Jewish sects (XI. 27–XII. 40), and the Apocalyptic chapter (XIII. 3–37).

In the narrative sections, one long exception to the Petrine origin occurs. In Chapter VIII. 1–9 we have the account of the Feeding of the Four Thousand, which so closely resembles the Feeding of the Five Thousand (VI. 34–44) that most critics are convinced that it is an account of the same incident, derived from another source, while the Healing of the Deaf and Dumb Man with Saliva, which precedes it (VII. 32–37), is so closely analogous to the Healing of the Blind Man with Saliva, which follows it (VIII. 22–25), that another duplicate is possible.

But, with these, and probably other shorter omissions, we can interpret the bulk of the narrative as the career of Jesus as it appealed to Peter. Peter was a man so little self-centred that it never occurred to him that what he was giving was a record of his own religious experiences; it is because of this complete absence of self-consciousness that the record is so valuable from this point of view. In accordance with the invariable Christian "proclamation", Mark has to begin with Jesus' call at His baptism, that is, with John the Baptist and the baptism and temptation of Jesus, but it is all disposed of in thirteen verses. The full narrative begins with the call of Andrew and Peter, though it can be safely assumed that some time must have been occupied in preaching before any call of disciples began. Then comes a graphic description of that day's events (I. 21–34), for it marked one of the great days in Peter's life. When the multitude are said to have been "astonished at his teaching: for he taught them as having authority and not as the scribes", we may assume that the astonishment was equally Peter's; otherwise why record it? The amazement continues and increases. In Chapter II. 12, after the healing of the paralytic the comment is, "We never saw it on this fashion". After the calming of the tempest the disciples—no doubt Peter was one of them —say one to another, "Who then is this, that even the wind and the sea obey him?" (IV. 41). The crescendo continues till Peter admits that it was he personally who said, "Thou art the Christ" (VIII. 29), after which the Transfiguration follows. Peter is now so overwhelmed that he records what he said, though he sees its pointlessness, "For he wist not what to answer; for they became sore afraid" (IX. 6). This seems the clearest instance of the record being coloured by Peter's recollections of his own state of mind; it would be far too subtle a piece of character sketching for anyone to have invented. From this time on Peter is mainly concerned with his failure to grasp Jesus' foreshadowing of His coming fate, which had already begun immediately after his confession, when he "began to rebuke him" (VIII. 32) and was told that "thou mindest not the things of God, but the things of men" (VIII. 33).

This contrast between the disciples' expectation of a Messiah and Jesus' pronouncements was clearly the dominant element in Peter's mind for a short time; he recounts the dispute who should be the greatest and the reply that it is the man most like to a little child: as for the prophecy of His death and resurrection, "they understood not the saying, and were afraid to ask him" (IX. 32). They clearly expect worldly promotion in the Messianic kingdom, and are told that it is hard for a rich man even to enter that kingdom; they are "astonished exceedingly" (X. 26) and Peter again becomes spokesman. The climax is reached in the request of James and John, culminating in, "the Son of man came not to be ministered unto, but to minister" (X. 45). But, along with this surprise, the journey to Jerusalem now acquires an element of awe, a sense of utter weakness in the presence of the unintelligible Divine, which we can only call Aeschylean: "And they were in the way, going up to Jerusalem; and Jesus was going before them: and they were amazed; and they that followed were afraid" (X. 32). The conduct of the disciples generally, and of Peter in particular, during the final scenes would be unintelligible without this psychological clue—on the one hand sincere protests of loyalty, on the other hopeless confusion and flight at the crisis, and, in Peter's case, denial. Their minds had been in confusion from the beginning of the journey; the two elements were jarring and no reconciliation between their own view of the Messiah and Jesus' view had been reached; and circumstances could incline the balance either way.

Even in the Passion narrative, we still have Peter's standpoint. Almost as much space is given to Peter's denial as to the trial; we imagine that Peter's denial was not part of the ordinary Passion narrative, but was derived by Mark directly from Peter. But we may go further; the Gospel really ends at XVI. 8 (vv. 9–20 not appearing in the two best manuscripts or being recognized by Eusebius, and being obviously an attempt to sum up what happened afterwards, mainly out of "Luke"). Whether Mark never lived to finish the Gospel, or whether the last page was lost, he clearly never meant to finish at XVI. 8. In XVI. 7 the women receive the command to "tell his disciples and Peter"; and we learn from Luke and Paul that there was a special appearance to Peter. It is not a very rash assumption that Peter recorded what was of supreme importance to him in the Resurrection, as he did in the Trial; and that an appearance, in which he was forgiven for his denial, was the climax of the Gospel. How far this resembled the account given in the last chapter of the Fourth Gospel, we shall never know; but we can see that in the Fourth Gospel the main interest is in "the beloved disciple", and that the interest in Peter is secondary.

Arguments based on the characteristics of a whole book, on its psychology in short, are by their cumulative force so much more telling than arguments based on single passages, which can be multiplied indefinitely and inconclusively, so that, when they tell in favour of a view which was held from the earliest times, they seem to be overwhelming.

There is nothing in the internal evidence to prove that Mark was the author; but he was not a person of sufficient importance to make anyone attach his name to the Gospel unless he wrote it, or at least a substantial portion, so that this attribution can be safely accepted. But one reservation must be made. At first sight it may seem a grotesque anachronism to suggest that a Gospel could be edited by a committee. But in "John" XXI. 24, "and we know that his witness is true", we have a clear statement that the Fourth Gospel was accepted and accredited by some body of persons, probably the Ephesian Board of Presbyters. It is not therefore impossible to reconcile the view that the Gospel is mainly Mark's record of Peter's teaching with the view that it represents the work of a local church, presumably that of Rome, by assuming that the Church of Rome regarded a biography of Our Lord as necessary, and obtained it by combining materials otherwise at their disposal with an account which Mark wrote for them of Peter's memories. Such a view can only be an unproved hypothesis, but it may satisfy those who detect non-Petrine sources in the Gospel.

Place of Composition

Early tradition affirms that Mark composed his Gospel at Rome, primarily for Roman Christians. We know from the Epistles that Mark was with Paul during the latter's imprisonment at Rome. Paul claims him as a fellow worker and sends greetings from him in his letter to the Colossians (IV. 10), and to Philemon, 24: later, in his second letter to Timothy, he requests Timothy to bring Mark, who was probably at Ephesus, to Rome (IV. 11). So unanimous was the early Church that Peter ended his career at Rome that it must be accepted, but it could hardly be within the period covered by "Acts". Assuming the genuineness of I "Peter", and that Babylon, mentioned in the text, stands for Rome, we find Mark in close touch with Peter, who claims him by the affectionate title of "Son". Early association at Jerusalem and the fellowship of the church at Rome would naturally bring the two together in the capital of the Empire.

Most early writers, including Irenaeus, Clement of Alexandria, Origen, and Eusebius, assert or imply that the Gospel was written at Rome. Attempts to connect Mark with Alexandria are quite late, but Christianity at Alexandria for more than 150 years was cut off from the main current of church life. Internal evidence tends to confirm the tradition that the Gospel was written for Gentiles. It translates Aramaic words such as "Boanerges", "Talitha cumi", "Corban", and "Eloi, Eloi, lama sabachthani", explains Jewish customs, such as those connected with ceremonial ablutions and the Passover, and geographical allusions, such as Jordan and the Mount of Olives. No such translations would be necessary had it been written for Jewish readers. Mark makes less use of proof-texts and has fewer references to the Mosaic Law than the other Synoptists. The frequent use of Latinisms is generally cited in support of the Roman origin of the Gospel; it is true that they are more frequent than in the other Gospels, but they are such as would be easily learnt and used in various parts of the Empire. He mentions Rufus, a son of Simon the Cyrenian (xv. 21); and Paul sends greetings to a Rufus in Rome (Rom. xvi. 13). But the name was common and it does not necessarily follow that they were the same person. The survival of "Mark", even after it had been almost entirely incorporated in "Matthew" and "Luke", can best be explained by attributing it to a Roman origin.

Its Primitive Character

Its Palestinian Atmosphere. Its publication at Rome, however, must not blind us to the fact that Mark's Gospel does not represent the atmosphere of Rome at Peter's death but that of Galilee at the time of the Ministry; to such an extent is it flavoured by Peter's reminiscences. Had we no other Gospel but "Mark" we should believe that Jesus never visited even Jerusalem till the final journey, though we shall find evidence in later chapters which make it certain that He did so. What is not specifically Galilean is still Palestinian.

The Parables. The parable of the sower is an exact description of Palestinian agriculture; its whole point, that the farmer has to scatter seed over good and bad soil and must be content with a good yield from a small part—the analogy being that the Christian missionary cannot expect wholesale conversions— would be as untrue of Italian agriculture as of modern British or American. The mustard seed is Palestinian; Italy has not this tropical rapidity of growth. Even in the parable of the vineyard (xii. 1–9), the departure of the owner to a distant country would be normal in the case of a Gentile land-owner in Palestine, whose family would not be there, but in Italy things would go on as usual when only the head of a family went abroad on military or government service.

The Controversies. At one point undoubtedly we have an attempt to extract from Our Lord's teaching a pronouncement on the later controversy of the food laws (VII. 19), which should be translated, "This he said, cleansing all meats"; but this comment is obviously an insertion into a controversy with the Jews on the frequent topic of the "tradition of the elders", and Jewish legalism. The controversies on fasting (II. 18–22), on the sabbath (II. 23–38, III. 1–6), on the charges of being a sorcerer (III. 22–30), which we know from Jewish as well as Christian sources was the accepted Jewish explanation of the cures, on giving tributes to Caesar (XII. 14–17), and on the resurrection (XII. 18–27), all breathe the air of Palestine and of the earliest struggles with Jewish opposition. Some of these issues, it is true, had not died down at the time of Peter's death; but the setting, with Sadducees, Herodians, and scribes, is Palestinian: it has only to be compared with Paul's treatment of points of controversy with Judaizers to see that, though all his Epistles are earlier than Mark's Gospel, yet "Mark" is far more primitive.

The Passion Narrative. We cannot tell whether Mark or the compilers found this in a written form. Quite likely it was known by heart by the early missionaries. Peter from his personal recollections would be able to contribute the Last Supper and something of the events in the Garden, and was the only person who could recount his own denial, but much he was not in a position to recount from his own experiences. In an oral form the narrative must have been one of the earliest parts of the Gospel narrative to take shape.

The Apocalyptic Discourse. One other probable source, namely the Apocalyptic Discourse (XIII. 3–37), is of quite a different character. It looks as if vv. 1, 2 were part of the main narrative and seemed to provide a suitable point to introduce this source. That we are dealing with a written source seems to be indicated by the words, "let him that readeth, understand" (XIII. 14) which could not be part of a discourse. It seems to be made up of:

(*a*) Genuine sayings of Our Lord. Some are taken verbally from Q, which ended with an apocalyptic section, given in

99

Luke xvii. 20–37; from this are taken Mark's verses 6, 15, 16, 21: while Mark's verse 11 is taken from the Q missionary charge (Lk. xii. 11–12). Probably Mark's verses 34–37 are a condensation of the Parable of the Pounds (Lk. xix. 12–27), and v. 30 is from a saying which is given in "Mark" ix. 1 in the form, "There be some here of them that stand by, that shall in no wise taste of death, till they see the kingdom of God come with power". Verse 28 sounds like a genuine saying, being much akin to other "signs of the time".

(b) Statements having a basis in Our Lord's teaching, but made more concrete in the light of what had actually happened in their fulfilment. Thus v. 9 echoes warnings of persecutions, but has in mind particular events in the life of Paul; and vv. 12–13 are based on "Luke" xii. 51–53, but probably has in mind happenings of the Neronian persecution. There is nothing which suggests that Jerusalem has actually been destroyed.

(c) Prophecies of woe in the Old Testament, for the most part not reproduced verbally, even Joel's, "The sun shall be turned into darkness and the moon into blood" appearing as "The sun shall be darkened and the moon shall not give her light". The verses of "Mark" of this character are vv. 7–8 (wars, earthquakes, famines, etc.), vv. 17–20 (ending in the usual Old Testament hope of the preservation of a faithful remnant), vv. 22–23 (the existence of false prophets, to which Christians added false Christs, in the light of actual rebellions against the Empire led by such pretenders), and vv. 24–25 (signs in heaven).

(d) Jewish Apocalyptic. This took up much of the aforementioned material from the prophets, but it can be distinguished from it in one set of prophecies, based on "Daniel" vii. 9–14, in which, however, considerable changes have taken place. It has been closely connected with "Daniel" ix. 25–27, where we get the "abomination" and the "desolation", connected with a cutting off of the Messiah and the destruction of Jerusalem. The original meaning of these passages in connection with the Maccabean revolt has been forgotten; the abomination (originally the image of Zeus set up by Antiochus in the Temple) has become a personal Antichrist; the Son of Man has ceased to be a symbol of the Jewish people and become a heavenly being; and he has taken the place of the Ancient of Days as judge. Mark's verse 14 seems to be a specific apocalyptic prophecy which the larger discourses incorporated, and which may permeate vv. 17–23, though it is difficult to say to what extent. Some such prophecy must have been known to Christians long before the Gospel of Mark was written, as we can see from the Pauline Epistles, especially 2 "Thessalonians" II. 3–12. But even the Second Coming and the general Resurrection are post-Old Testament ideas derived from Jewish Apocalyptic (1 Cor. xv. 51–54, describing the Second Coming, begins by saying that a mystery is being revealed). They are developments of the Old Testament "day of the Lord", as Paul still calls it in 1 "Thessalonians" v. 1–3. It is noticeable that Luke, writing after the destruction of the Temple, omits the Abomination and substitutes another prophecy, much more like Our Lord's frequent predictions, dealing only with the Desolation of Jerusalem.[1] Mark's v. 26 is again from the first

---

[1] It used to be thought that Luke had, without any previous authority, so altered the text of "Mark" as to bring it into line with what had actually happened. Professor C. H. Dodd, however (*Journal of Roman Studies*, vol. XXXVI, pp. 47–54), has convincingly argued that what he has done is to substitute another pre-existing prophecy for Mark's prediction of the Antichrist. He takes the non-Marcan portions of Luke XXI. 20–24, and shows that they are in the form of Semitic poetry.

> When ye see Jerusalem surrounded by armies
> Then know that her desolation draweth nigh.
> Let those who are in the midst of her go forth
> And those in the country not enter into her.
> And they shall fall by the edge of the sword
> And be taken prisoners into all Gentile nations.
> And Jerusalem shall be trodden down by the Gentiles
> Till the times of the Gentiles shall be fulfilled.

The word "desolation" in the phrase the "abomination of desolation" doubtless suggested this other prophecy to Luke's mind; but Dodd shows that all the substance and language are taken from Old Testament prophecies of the destruction of Jerusalem by Nebuchadnezzar, whereas the "Abomination" prediction is drawn from "Daniel" and 1 "Maccabees". He shows that it contains nothing which implies a knowledge of what actually happened in Titus' siege as distinct from the predictions of what would be done by Nebuchadnezzar. "Luke" XIX. 42–44 shows that Luke was quite convinced that Jesus had prophesied the destruction of Jerusalem. It may be added that as the Apocalyptic discourse in "Mark" arises out of Christ's prediction of the destruction of the Temple, Luke was justified in thinking this prophecy more relevant than that used by Mark in v. 14, which, as Matthew sees, implies that the Temple is standing.

passage in "Daniel". Verse 27 recounts the part which the angels will play; this was part of all Christian eschatology, and appears in the Parable of the Tares (Mt. xiii. 41–42).

(e) Some editorial comments, e.g. v. 10 (that the Gospel must first be preached to all nations) and v. 32 (that the exact date is not known even to the Son), which are attempts to explain the long delay which troubled Christians from the early days when Paul wrote to the Thessalonians till the end of the New Testament period, when the so-called "Second Epistle of Peter" was written.

It is plain (1) that the document is a compilation from authorities already made before Mark took it over, as "Mark" shows no verbal acquaintance with Q, (2) that it is a document of Gentile, not Jewish Christianity (vv. 9–10), (3) that it represents the general views of Apostolic times, however much it differs from Our Lord's own teaching, if Q is a typical representation of that teaching, and (4) it is the earliest evidence of the existence of Q, as its quotations from two different parts of Q are too exact to be taken merely from oral tradition.

Date of Composition

The date of the composition of the Gospel has been variously fixed. Some scholars assign it to the period A.D. 42–49. The tradition that Peter came to Rome in A.D. 42,[1] becoming its first bishop and holding office until his martyrdom in A.D. 67,[2] is derived from one of the numerous "Acts" of particular Apostles which sprang up in the second century and is worthless.

Harnack puts the date about A.D. 50. Irenaeus says, "After their deaths Mark, the disciple and interpreter of Peter, himself also handed down to us in writing the things which Peter had proclaimed". According to Harnack the words, "after their deaths" do nothing to fix the date of the Gospel, but mean that the apostolic preaching was handed down after their deaths by means of written records. It was therefore compiled before the death of Peter which took place about A.D. 64. "Acts" was written at the close of Paul's imprisonment at Rome, from which

---

[1] Eusebius, *Historia Ecclesiastica*, ii. 25, vi. 14. [2] Jerome, *De Viris Illustribus*, i.

it follows that the third Gospel and the second (since it is one of the sources of the third) must be earlier still.

The majority of scholars date the Gospel within the period A.D. 65–70, as this is the only period when it is likely that Peter and Mark were together in Rome. Irenaeus states that it was written after Peter's death, while according to Clement of Alexandria it was written during Peter's lifetime. Of the two writers Irenaeus is the better authority. The Temple still seems to be standing in the Apocalyptic Discourse (XIII. 14); "standing where he ought not" must refer to the idea that the Antichrist would set himself up in the Temple, as Matthew states in XXIV. 15, where for "where he ought not" he writes "in the holy place", which fixes A.D. 70 as the latest date. The references to persecution in the same chapter are reminiscent of the Neronian persecution, thus making A.D. 65 the earliest date.

A few competent scholars date the Gospel later than A.D. 70 on the ground that the vagueness of the references to the Temple in the Apocalyptic Discourse (XIII.) is due to the fact that Jerusalem had been destroyed. But surely Mark would have been more explicit in his references had he been writing after the fulfilment of the prophecies, just as Luke is.

Original Language

It has been argued that from the Semitic idioms to be found in the text the Gospel was originally written in Aramaic and afterwards translated into Greek. It is unlikely, however, that a book written primarily for the Roman church would be written in a language which they did not understand. The translation of Aramaic words into Greek suggests that the Gospel is not a translation. It is certain that Matthew and Luke used the Gospel in Greek: it is inconceivable that they would go to the trouble of translating it from Aramaic into that language. The explanation for the use of Semitic idioms can probably be found in the fact that Mark was bilingual, speaking and writing both languages; he would think in his native tongue but write in Greek. We may safely assume, therefore, that the Gospel was composed in Greek.

Purpose

The purpose of Mark in compiling his book was to present Jesus as a man of such power as to prove that He was the Son of God. His Gospel stresses the fact that He was a great teacher who spoke with authority. In the synagogue at Capernaum the congregation were astonished at his teaching, "for he taught them as having authority, and not as the scribes" (i. 22). As they listened to His teaching in the synagogue at Nazareth the people, who had assembled to hear Him, exclaimed, "Whence hath this man these things?" (vi. 2). He had power over disease, nature, and death. He healed the leper (i. 40–45), and the paralytic (ii. 1–12), made the deaf hear and the dumb speak (vii. 37), walked upon the waves (vi. 45–52), stilled the storm (iv. 35–41), and raised the dead to life (v. 21–24, 35–43): evil spirits obeyed His voice, recognizing Him as the "Holy One of God" (i. 24). He faced His captors in Jerusalem with such self-possession that even Pilate marvelled (xv. 1–5).

His great power, combined with His "new teaching", served to attract crowds from every quarter. All the city was gathered together at the door of Simon's house (i. 33); so great was His popularity that He "could no more openly enter into a city, but was without in desert places" (i. 45). On one occasion, as He withdrew to the sea, "a great multitude from Galilee followed: and from Judaea, and from Jerusalem, and from Idumaea, and beyond Jordan, and about Tyre and Sidon" (iii. 7–8); on another occasion He withdrew to a desert place, "for there were many coming and going, and they had no leisure so much as to eat" (vi. 31). Those who flocked to hear Him preach and to see His mighty works were moved to wonder. After the healing of the paralytic "they were all amazed, and glorified God" (ii. 12); those who saw the damsel restored to life "were amazed straightway with a great amazement" (v. 42); when He walked on the sea to His disciples "they were sore amazed in themselves" (vi. 51). Sometimes astonishment was mingled with fear; in the presence of His glory on the Mount of Transfiguration the three disciples, Peter, James, and John, "became sore afraid" (ix. 6); when He stilled the storm, "they feared exceedingly, and said one to another, Who then is this, that even the wind and the sea obey him?" (IV. 41). To Mark Jesus could only be explained on the assumption that He was divine: the words of the centurion at the foot of the cross expressed his own thoughts, "Truly this man was the Son of God" (xv. 39).

Characteristics

The Messiahship of Jesus. The Gospel stresses the Messiahship of Jesus. At His Baptism (I. 11) and Transfiguration (IX. 7) a voice from heaven declared Him to be God's beloved Son. He took for granted Peter's confession of His Messiahship and commanded His disciples to keep their knowledge secret (VIII. 27–30). He was not the Messiah, born of the Davidic line, but the Son of God. To the High Priest's question, "Art thou the Christ, the Son of the Blessed?" (XIV. 61), He made answer, "I am: and ye shall see the Son of man sitting at the right hand of power, and coming with the clouds of heaven" (XIV. 62). The centurion, who stood near the cross, expressed the conviction that he had witnessed the death of the Son of God.

Not only does the Gospel stress the Messiahship of Jesus, but also the fact that He is a suffering Messiah. The shadow of impending doom seems to be over the story from beginning to end. In the early days of His ministry He warned His disciples that one day they would mourn His loss (II. 20), while His enemies, roused to anger by His teaching and popularity, conspired with the Herodians to destroy Him (III. 6). Opposition gradually increased until the inevitable clash came which resulted in His death. No sooner had Peter grasped the truth and acknowledged Him as the Messiah, than He at once warned the disciples that He must suffer many things and be rejected by the nation: as He passed through Galilee and on the journey to Jerusalem He foretold His death and resurrection. In teaching His disciples the meaning of true greatness, He described His own mission in the words, "For verily the Son of man came not to be ministered unto, but to minister, and to give his life a ransom for many" (x. 45). In the hour of His death the Scribes and Pharisees mocked Him with the words, "He saved others; himself he cannot save" (xv. 31).

The Atmosphere of Awe and Secrecy. Another notable feature of the Gospel is the atmosphere of awe and secrecy in which Jesus moves. In a time of great expectancy, when John the Baptist is proclaiming to crowds from "all the country of Judaea" and from Jerusalem the near approach of the Messiah, Jesus appears abruptly out of the unknown and preaches the "Gospel of God" (I. 14). The people are at once conscious that a powerful personality has come among them, and are filled with astonishment and even with fear: similar feelings are roused in the hearts of the twelve disciples, who become more and more impressed by the greatness of their Master, until the day comes when at Caesarea Philippi Peter declares Him to be the Messiah. Later, as they journey towards Jerusalem, the headquarters of His enemies, He appears even greater still, and the disciples, especially Peter, awed by the splendour of His personality, are bewildered by His refusal to proclaim His Messiahship. The crowds fall away from Him, Peter denies Him, and the other disciples forsake Him, but He remains to the end a great, lonely, awe-inspiring figure.

His greatness is beyond Mark's comprehension: apparently he cannot understand His reasons for desiring to conceal His Messiahship, but he keeps to the historical facts as he sees them. Demoniacs, who recognize Him as the Son of God, are silenced, "And the unclean spirits, whensoever they beheld him, fell down before him, and cried, saying, Thou art the Son of God. And he charged them much that they should not make him known" (III. 11–12). He commands those whom He has healed "to say nothing to any man" (I. 44, V. 43), and the disciples to keep secret the knowledge that He is the Messiah (VIII. 30). He teaches the people by means of parables in order to conceal the true significance of His teaching (IV. 11–12), but He "expounds all things" privately to His disciples not, however, that they may possess some mysterious knowledge denied to the people at large, but that they may instruct others after His departure, "for there is nothing hid, save that it should be manifested; neither was anything made secret, but that it should come to light" (IV. 22). Finally, shortly after His triumphal entry into Jerusalem, He makes secret preparations for the Last Supper, at which He gives His disciples the bread and wine (XIV. 12–25). Owing to the stress laid on the attempts of Jesus to conceal His Messiahship, His teaching, and at times, His presence from the people, and on His method of instructing His disciples privately, the Gospel of Mark has been called "a book of secret manifestations".

Structure. As regards the structure of the Gospel there is a conflict of opinion. Some critics see in it nothing but a number of disconnected incidents strung together like beads on a string. In support of their view they quote the words of the Presbyter (mentioned by Papias) that Mark wrote accurately but not in order; others hold the view that there is in the story a definite dramatic structure, beginning with the baptism of Jesus and culminating in the Cross and the Resurrection. Something may be said for both these views, but the truth seems to lie somewhere between the two. It is evident that there are many omissions in the story. For example, no mention is made of the birth, parentage, childhood, education, and character of Jesus. He appears out of the silence in mature life. "And it came to pass in those days, that Jesus came from Nazareth of Galilee, and was baptized of John in the Jordan" (I. 9). No hint is given as to the duration of His ministry. There is an apparent lack of proportion in the amount of space given to the various incidents narrated. The story of the Passion and the Resurrection occupied one week of His ministry but its narration takes up about one-third of the book. Long periods are passed over in silence while the events of one day are recorded in detail. There is no reason to doubt that the account of the Passion and the Resurrection is written in chronological order, but the same cannot be said of the rest of the story. Some incidents are evidently arranged according to subject-matter with little or no regard to historical sequence. In spite of the omissions, vagueness, looseness, and lack of proportion, there is, on closer examination, a consistent development of the story. After His baptism Jesus commences His ministry and is immediately hailed as a great teacher and prophet. His teaching rouses the opposition of the Scribes and Pharisees and their increasing hostility leads Him to withdraw to the neighbourhood of Tyre and Sidon. Returning to Galilee He resumes His work, but again retires to the region of Caesarea Philippi, where Peter recognizes Him as the Messiah. Finally He makes His way to Jerusalem, the headquarters of His implacable foes, who compass His death, but He is raised from the dead. In its broad outline the story has an element of dramatic unity, which, however, has not been artificially created by the conscious selection and manipulation of the material; it is rather the result of the nature of the story itself which is of the essence of tragedy.

Power of Vivid and Realistic Description. The Gospel is written in a simple, clear, but vigorous style, devoid of all ornamentation: it is, in fact, the homely language of conversation rather than that of literature. There are no apt figures of speech, felicitous expressions, choice words, or literary devices, which reveal the master-hand of the great artist. This lack of polish is apparent even in the English version. We shall look in vain for command over language or skill in the arrangement of ideas. Sentences are often joined together by the conjunction "and", while the adverb "straightway" is employed to mark the transition from one incident to another; the latter word is used no less than eleven times in Chapter i. and forty-two times in the whole book. Sometimes pronouns are used ambiguously so that the reader has to guess the reference, the same idea is repeated in the same sentence but in a different form, and clauses and phrases are loosely strung together. Still, whatever faults of style may be found in the Gospel, they are insignificant compared with the writer's power of vivid and realistic description. He was evidently a keen observer with the ability to describe faithfully what he had seen. This gift is seen in such pen-pictures as those depicting the call of the four disciples, the stilling of the storm, and the feeding of the five thousand. Others might have given him the main outline of the stories, but his was the power of imaginative reconstruction.

He shows a fondness for minute details which bring the scenes before the mind's eye. Jesus put forth His hand and touched the leper (i. 41); at the height of the storm He was in the stern, asleep on a cushion (iv. 38); the Gadarene demoniac was found "sitting, clothed and in his right mind" (v. 15); the mourners in the house of Jairus "laughed him to scorn" (v. 40); He commanded His disciples to make the multitude "sit down by companies upon the green grass" before feeding them (vi. 39); on the Mount of Transfiguration "his garments became glistering, exceeding white, so as no fuller on earth can whiten them" (ix. 3); before leaving the upper room for the Garden of Gethsemane, they sang a hymn (xiv. 26); as He hung on the cross His enemies "railed on him, wagging their heads" (xv. 29).

The writer's honesty and love of realism prevented him from giving an idealized picture of Jesus. He was not afraid to record facts which some might imagine would detract from His greatness. Jesus, the man of power, was driven by the spirit into the wilderness (i. 12); a leper (i. 45) and a deaf stammerer (vii. 36) disobeyed His command to tell no one of their cure; as His enemies watched to see if He would heal on the Sabbath, He "looked round about on them with anger" (iii. 5); on His visit to Nazareth "he could there do no mighty work, save that he laid his hands upon a few sick folk, and healed them" (vi. 5); to the man who addressed Him as Good Master, He disclaimed any pretensions to goodness with the words, "Why callest thou me good? none is good save one, even God" (x. 18).

The Lost Ending

We have already mentioned that the Gospel really ends at Chapter xvi. 8 and have also suggested the probable contents of the missing ending. The concluding verses probably formed no part of the original manuscript. The distinct style and vocabulary, so different from the rest of the book, the description of Mary Magdalene as if it is her first appearance in the story, and the brief summary of the events, lead us to doubt their authenticity. The internal evidence serves only to increase that doubt. Two of the oldest manuscripts—the Codex Vaticanus and the Codex Sinaiticus—and some other authorities omit them. In the Codex Vaticanus a blank is left after the words, "for they were afraid", evidently indicating that the chapter is incomplete. Eusebius states that these verses are wanting in "the accurate copies", and again in "nearly all the copies".

Some good manuscripts give an alternative and shorter ending, which reads thus: "And all that had been commanded them, they briefly reported to Peter and his company; and after these things Jesus appeared, and from the east to the west sent through them the sacred and incorruptible proclamation of eternal salvation." This is merely an attempt to provide a suitable ending and sheds no light on the problem of how the gap came to exist.

In a tenth-century Armenian manuscript the longer ending is attributed to Ariston the Presbyter, but it is too late to be of any value.

CHAPTER VII

THE GOSPEL ACCORDING TO MATTHEW

Authorship and Original Language

The author of the first Gospel is anonymous, but an early tradition of the Christian Church attributes it to Matthew, one of the twelve Apostles. Eusebius quotes Papias as saying, "So then Matthew arranged in order (or composed) the Logia in the Hebrew tongue, and each one interpreted (or translated) them as he could". Similar statements are made by other patristic writers, notably Irenaeus, Clement of Alexandria, Origen, and Jerome, all of whom take it for granted that by "Logia" was meant the Gospel of Matthew, which was originally written in Aramaic and afterwards translated into Greek. Jerome goes much further: he not only accepts the common view that Matthew wrote his Gospel in Aramaic, but also states that a copy of it was preserved in the library of Pamphilus at Caesarea, and that he himself had translated it into both Greek and Latin with the permission of the Nazarenes who used it. This statement was not denied and the translated Gospel was quoted by some writers as the work of Matthew.

Most competent critics, however, have abandoned their belief in the accuracy of this tradition for the following reasons:

(1) it is incredible that one of the twelve Apostles should have used as his main source the Gospel of Mark who was not an eyewitness of the ministry of Jesus.

(2) the material peculiar to "Matthew" does not suggest that they are the personal recollections of an eyewitness.

(3) Matthew, the converted publican, could not have had the rabbinic training necessary for the codification of the teaching of Jesus into a complete system of Law.

(4) it is unlikely that Matthew translated the "Mark" portions into Aramaic and that the retranslator of the book should

have used in so many cases the exact phraseology of the original "Mark".

(5) the term "Logia", mentioned by Papias, was probably used, not of a Gospel, but either of a "Book of Testimonies", or a collection of the sayings of Jesus, preserved by Matthew and identical with that of Q. If it was used of the latter, as many critics believe, then the fact that the anonymous author of the first Gospel used a source supplied by Matthew would naturally suggest the title.

(6) the book which Jerome translated was probably a copy of what has come down to us only in fragments—the apocryphal "Gospel according to the Hebrews". The fragments that have survived show a wide divergence from the narratives of the first Gospel and have no connection with the latter. Moreover, there was no need to translate the first Gospel into Greek, since it already existed in that language. Jerome gives no hint that he wished to improve on the original.

The Title of the Gospel

The title "the Gospel according to St. Matthew" is obviously intended to distinguish it from "the Gospel according to St. Mark", and both titles must have been given at the same time. It was "Mark" which was first called "The Gospel", taking its name, in accordance with Jewish usage, from the first significant word: "Mark" begins: "The beginning of the Gospel (i.e. good news) of Jesus Christ;" the word "beginning" is not very significant and was already appropriated to "Genesis", and so the word Gospel became the name of the book. As soon as "Matthew" was compiled, the natural thing was to distinguish the two by calling "Mark" after its main author, and probably therefore "Matthew" after the author of the main sections other than "Mark", probably Q but possibly M.

Place and Date of Composition

The place and date of composition of the first Gospel are both matters of conjecture. As regards its place of composition, the fact that it sets forth Christianity as both a national and a universal religion, points to some place where there was a church consisting of both Jews and Gentiles, and in which the question of the relation of the new religion to Judaism and the Gentile world was a pressing problem. Antioch-in-Syria seems to suit the conditions best. It was a cosmopolitan city with a large colony of Jews, an important centre of Christianity, and the headquarters of missionary activity. If Antioch-in-Syria was the place of its composition then the reference to the Gospel by Ignatius, who was for some years Bishop of the city, can be explained.

Some idea of the date of its composition may be derived from the following considerations:

(1) since it incorporates "Mark", it cannot be earlier than about A.D. 65.

(2) if the words, "But the king was wroth; and he sent his armies, and destroyed those murderers, and burned their city" (XXII. 7), and "Behold, your house is left unto you desolate" (XXIII. 38), refer to the destruction of Jerusalem and its consequent misery, then it must have been written after A.D. 70.

(3) such sentences as, "And from the days of John the Baptist until now the kingdom of heaven suffereth violence" (XI. 12); and, "Wherefore that field was called, The field of blood, unto this day" (XXVII. 8); and, "This saying was spread abroad among the Jews, and continueth until this day" (XXVIII. 15), suggest that a long time had elapsed between the occurrence of the events described and the composition of the book.

(4) the allusions to Peter as the rock on which the Church was to be built (XVI. 18), the tendency to exalt the Apostles by minimizing their short-comings, and the appearances of false prophets (VII. 15, 22), suggest the latter part of the century, by which time the theory of Petrine supremacy was being proclaimed, the veneration of the Apostles had increased, and heresy had arisen.

(5) if Clement of Rome knew of the Gospel, as his letter to the Corinthians seems to suggest, then it must have been written before A.D. 96.

(6) Ignatius, writing about A.D. 115, apparently refers to the Gospel when he declares that Jesus was baptized by John, "that all righteousness might be fulfilled by Him". It would seem, therefore, that the Gospel was already in existence about that time.

From the evidence at our disposal, it is reasonable to suppose that the Gospel was composed within the period A.D. 80–90.

Use of his Materials

Before discussing other sources besides "Mark" and Q, it may be well to consider the use made by the compiler of this Gospel of those two sources.

(1) He reproduces almost the whole of "Mark", and no special significance has been discovered in the few omissions: but by pruning Mark's repetitions and somewhat cumbrous phraseology, he considerably reduces the length of what he has taken from "Mark".

(2) On the whole he follows Mark's order, the exceptions being at the beginning. The material from Q is not arranged in Luke's order but is introduced into the Marcan narrative at points where something in "Mark" suggests its suitability. In other words, he follows what he conceives to be chronological order as regards events, and logical order as regards teaching.

(3) Wherever "Mark" and Q cover the same ground, he carefully combines, or, as scholars say, conflates them, unlike Luke who occasionally does this as regards narrative but never as regards teaching, and who often sets aside "Mark" altogether where the same ground is covered in another source. Good instances of such conflation are the account of John the Baptist (III. 1–12), where Matthew gives us both Mark's and Luke's (i.e. the Q) account, the missionary charge to the Twelve (X. 1–27), which combines Mark's charge to the Twelve, Luke's charge to the Seventy, and apparently a third source and the Beelzebub controversy (XII. 24–30), where "Mark" and Q (=Luke) are combined.

(4) The teaching is arranged according to subject-matter. This involves taking sayings on the same subject which appear

in quite different places in "Luke", so that the original order of
Q largely disappears. Short sayings are of course less common
in "Mark"; but some of them are transferred to go with similar
subject-matter; for example, the Sermon on the Mount contains the saying on salt (Mt. v. 13), and on the lamp under a
bushel (Mt. v. 15=Mk. iv. 21), and at the end of the Lord's
Prayer we have Mark's saying on forgiveness (Mt. vi. 14–15=
Mk. xi. 25–26).

(5) The teaching is arranged in five great blocks; the
significance of this will be discussed later.

M

The bulk of the matter appearing in this Gospel which is
derived neither from "Mark" nor Q is teaching. But, owing to
the compiler's method of conflating teaching on the same
subject from whatever source it is derived, if there was a second
source for the teaching comparable to Q, we cannot expect to
find solid blocks taken from this source like the blocks of
narrative taken from "Mark". Streeter's view that such a source
exists has been widely accepted. The Sermon on the Mount
in "Matthew" is far longer than the similar Sermon on the Plain
in "Luke", and though some of the additional material is
taken from other parts of "Luke" the bulk is not. Even the
blessings at the beginning do not all appear in "Luke", so it
looks as if this other document, which Streeter calls M, contained blessings, some of which were very likely identical.
After the Marcan sayings on salt and the lamp comes a long
section on the greater demands of the new than of the old law
(Mt. v. 17–48), which is in its main construction not Q, though
vv. 25–26, 39, 42 and 44–48 have been gathered out of Q,
while v. 32 on divorce differs both from Q (Luke) and "Mark"
in making an exception to the rule ("saving for the cause of
fornication"), which suggests that it appeared in M in this
different form. Then comes a section on the chief religious
acts, almsgiving, prayer, and fasting (Mt. vi. 1–18), which
appear to be M, save for the Marcan saying on forgiveness
(Mt. vi. 14–15); in it is included the Lord's Prayer in a form
which, till "Luke" was altered to bring it into greater conformity

with "Matthew", was so different that presumably Matthew is using M here. (Whether it appeared at all in Q, and, if so, whether Matthew has conflated the two cannot be known.) Then Matthew returns to Q, apparently conflating in vv. 19–23, and then using Q except for a few verses (Mt. vi. 34, vii. 6, 14, 15, 19–21), which of course Luke may have omitted. The charge to the Twelve (Mt. x. 5–12) contains so much matter additional to Q and "Mark" that it is presumably a conflation of Q and "Mark" with M: "Matthew" xi. 29–30 ("Come unto me all ye that labour . . .") is also not Lucan. Introduced into a Marcan setting are detached sayings (Mt. xii. 5–7, 11–12). A longer passage is Mt. xviii. 13–22, on forgiveness and on settlement of disputes by "the church", conceived as a local congregation; and a still longer passage is the denunciation of the Scribes and Pharisees (xxiii. 1–26), which contains Luke's similar Q passage, but is much longer, and presumably conflated with M. We have included no parables, since it cannot be proved that M contained any and Q certainly did not.

The proof that these passages, or the bulk of them, come from a single document is that they possess features in common which appear nowhere else in the Gospels. They are eminently Judaistic and, even where there is nothing Judaistic, they are concerned with the relation of Our Lord's teaching to the Jewish Law.

(1) They command the observance not only of the whole law, but even of the "tradition of the elders" by Christians. "Think not that I came to destroy the law or the prophets: I came not to destroy, but to fulfil. For verily I say unto you, Till heaven and earth pass away, one jot or one tittle shall in no wise pass away from the law, till all things be accomplished. Whosoever therefore shall break one of these least commandments, and shall teach men so, shall be called least in the kingdom of heaven" (Mt. v. 17–19); this is the initial proclamation of the right attitude of Christians to the Law. It is clearly contrary to the whole teaching of Paul and the whole practice of Gentile Christianity. "The scribes and the Pharisees sit on Moses' seat: all things therefore whatsoever they bid you, these do and observe: but do not ye after their works; for they say, and do not"

(xxiii. 2–3) goes further, and is contrary to Mark's express statements about the traditions of the elders being often contrary to the Law itself.

(2) No attempt is to be made to convert the Gentiles. "Go not into any way of the Gentiles, and enter not into any city of the Samaritans: but go rather to the lost sheep of the house of Israel" (Mt. x. 5–6). "But, when they persecute you in this city, flee into the next: for verily I say unto you, Ye shall not have gone through the cities of Israel, till the Son of man be come" (Mt. x. 23). Obviously this last verse could not have been part of a charge delivered to the Twelve at the start of a single preaching tour from which they returned according to plan. The address had therefore changed its character in time and come to be regarded as a charge to the Apostles about their work after His departure, so that it has become an attack on the Gentile mission.

(3) The difference between the Jewish and Christian attitude to the Law has changed. In all other accounts formalism is subordinated to adherence to the two cardinal principles of loving God with the whole heart and loving one's neighbour as oneself, whereas in M the Christian's "righteousness is to exceed the righteousness of the scribes and Pharisees" in its rigour. The attacks on them are not for demanding too much but for practising too little. The criticism of them in "Mark" and Q appeals to us as a great advance; the added attacks in M strike us as unfair.

(4) The passage on bringing disputes before "the church" suggests, not a late development, where the Church is a universal body composed of Christians throughout the world, to whatever local church they belong, but a small body, capable by its size of dealing with personal disputes, and the close is significant: "If he refuse to hear the church also, let him be unto thee as the Gentile [the Authorized Version has 'heathen man'] and the publican" (Mt. xviii. 17). In other words it is the Jewish-Christian community in Jerusalem, organized as a Jewish synagogue and exercising similar functions. "The friend of publicans and sinners" was unlikely to have uttered such a statement; and, for that matter, Matthew was hardly

likely to have repeated it, which makes it unlikely that Matthew
was the author of M, and consequently more likely that he was
the author of Q.

Throughout, therefore, M clearly represents the extreme
Judaizing party at Jerusalem who are usually associated with
James "the Lord's brother" but, so far as we can gather from
Paul's Epistles, went considerably beyond him.

How then did the compiler come to include two such
opposite accounts of Our Lord's teaching in one Gospel? He
omits nothing of the pro-Gentile elements in "Mark" and Q,
even where they are expressly opposed to M. Nor does he
himself seem to side with M, in spite of his obviously Jewish outlook; for it is he and he only who records the famous saying,
"Thou art Peter; and upon this rock I will build my church;
and the gates of Hades shall not prevail against it" (Mt. xvi.
18). That something of this kind must really have been said is
rendered probable by Peter's name; Peter is a Greek translation
of Cephas, which means "rock", and his real name was Simon:
the very fact that it was translated shows the importance
attached to the name long before his death. But, in recording
it, the compiler can only mean that James was not to be
accounted the Christian leader, as his followers for several
generations after his death claimed him to be. Christianity was
not a hereditary monarchy, to which James succeeded, as these
people averred. There is no other claimant against whom
Peter's claim could be directed; certainly not Paul, who
indignantly rejects the pretensions of a Pauline party (as of a
party of Peter or of Apollos) at Corinth.

Once more then, how came the compiler to include the
Judaizing assertions of M? The only answer which seems at all
satisfactory is that M had considerable weight behind it, which
would be true if it represented the version of Christ's teaching
current in Jerusalem (very much of it is similar to Q), and
that the compiler was a man who was very careful to include all
which he finds in his authorities, as his treatment of "Mark"
and Q shows that he was, but, while painstaking in describing
the trees, was unable to see the wood. Like most adherents of
the letter, he lacked what we should call common sense, as his

interpretation of many Old Testament quotations as Messianic, which no modern writer would ever dream of so interpreting, shows. He has wonderful literary gifts, and his grouping of the teaching to produce an effect is masterly, but his mind is essentially that of a scribe.

Other Sources

A marked feature of the Gospel is the large number of Old Testament quotations which are woven into the narrative. They may be divided into two groups:

(1) those quoted by Jesus in the course of His ministry. They are common to the three Synoptic Gospels and are based on the Septuagint Version.

(2) those introduced by the compiler, each being prefaced by the words, "that it might be fulfilled which was spoken by the prophet", or their equivalent (I. 22–23, II. 5–6, 17–18, 23, IV. 14–16, VIII. 17, XII. 17–21, XIII. 35, XXI. 4–5, XXVII. 9–10). They are all peculiar to the Gospel and seem to be based on the Hebrew version.

The quotation from II. 23 does not occur in any book of the Old Testament, while that from XXVII. 9–10 is said to be taken from "Jeremiah", whereas it seems rather to correspond to "Zechariah" (XI. 13).

These considerations suggest that the quotations are an independent translation of an Aramaic original. It is possible, therefore, that the author used a "Book of Testimonies".

There are several parables peculiar to Matthew, namely, Tares, Hid Treasure, Pearl of Great Price, Draw-net, Unmerciful Servant, Labourers in the Vineyard, Two Sons, Marriage of the King's Son, Ten Virgins, Sheep and Goats, and probably the parables, which are also in "Luke", but in a somewhat different form, namely, Lost Sheep, Marriage, Talents.

We have already left open the question whether there existed written collections of parables, when dealing with "Mark".

The remainder of the material peculiar to "Matthew" consists of the following narratives:

(1) the Stories of the Nativity: the Genealogy (i. 1–17), the Birth of Jesus (i. 18–25), the Visit of the Wise Men (ii. 1–12), the Flight into Egypt and the Massacre of the Innocents (ii. 13–18), the Return to Nazareth (ii. 19–23).

(2) John's hesitation at the Baptism of Jesus (iii. 14–15), Peter walking on the Water (xiv. 28–31), the Coin in the Fish's Mouth (xvii. 24–27).

(3) stories connected with the Passion and Resurrection: Judas and the Thirty Pieces of Silver (xxvi. 14–16), the Death of Judas (xxvii. 3–10), Pilate's Wife's Dream (xxvii. 19), Pilate Washing his Hands (xxvii. 24–25), the Earthquake and the Resurrection of the Saints (xxvii. 51–53), the Watch at the Tomb (xxvii. 62–66), the Rolling away of the Stone at the Tomb (xxviii. 2–4), the Bribing of the Guards (xxviii. 11–15).

These narratives probably belonged to a cycle of tradition current in the church in which the Gospel was written, since they have certain characteristics in common. They are marked by a similarity of style. For example, the phrase "in a dream" occurs in several of the narratives and is found nowhere else in the New Testament. Stress is laid on the fulfilment of prophecy, as in the stories connected with the Nativity, the preaching of John the Baptist, and the treachery and death of Judas. Such accounts as those of Peter walking on the water, the resurrection of the saints on the day of the Crucifixion, and the angel at the empty tomb, with his appearance "as lightning and his raiment white as snow", suggest a desire to heighten the miraculous element. There is also an evident attempt to justify the primitive tradition of the Christian Church. The doubts of those who questioned the truth of the royal descent of Jesus or of the Resurrection, would be dispelled by the Genealogy and by the account of the Guard at the tomb who became "as dead men" and were afterwards bribed to spread the story that the body of Jesus had been stolen while they slept. The hesitation of John in baptizing Jesus would satisfy those who found it difficult to understand the necessity for the baptism of the Son of God, since He was sinless and it was a baptism "unto the remission of sins".

The editor has shown great editorial skill in the way in which he has fused into a coherent whole the material of his sources. The resultant work is not a disjointed narrative but a new literary creation.

Aim

The need of the Church for written records of the teaching of Jesus was partially met by the appearance of several collections of sayings of Jesus, notably that of Q, and the "Gospel of Mark". The latter as a life was unsatisfactory owing to its many omissions: it presupposed a considerable knowledge of the background of the ministry of Jesus and supplied little of His teaching. There was a need for a more comprehensive account which should unite the events of His life and His teaching in a coherent whole. This task was undertaken by the author of the first Gospel who combined "Mark" and Q, at the same time adding material from other sources.

The Church expanded so rapidly that it was not long before it included peoples of different races and cultures. It was unlikely that a Gospel like "Mark", written at Rome primarily for Gentiles, would satisfy Christian communities in other parts of the Empire, like the provinces of Palestine, Syria, and Asia. Gentiles generally and Jews would look at the Christian religion from different points of view. The former would be specially interested in Jesus as the Saviour of the world, while the latter would be chiefly concerned with His Messiahship, the coming of the Kingdom of God, the Final Judgment, and the relation of Christianity to Judaism. More than one Gospel was necessary if the needs of the various peoples, which constituted the Church, were to be satisfied. Where there was a mixed community of Christians, a Gospel which reflected a purely Jewish or a purely Gentile point of view, would be unlikely to meet with general approval. The "Gospel of Matthew" was written for a mixed church and was intended as a synthesis, on which both Jews and Gentiles should be agreed. The compiler was a

Jew, with a Jewish outlook, but was not necessarily a Judaizer. That his Gospel has a strong Jewish colouring may be judged by the following evidence:

(1) he proves that Jesus is of Davidic descent by tracing His legal descent back through David to Abraham, and by stressing the fact that He is the Son of David and a King. Whereas in "Mark" the title, Son of David, is given only once to Jesus, namely by Bartimaeus, in the first Gospel He is described as such by the Canaanitish woman (xv. 22), the multitudes (xxi. 9), and the children in the Temple (xxi. 15). As regards the title of King, the wise men came from the East seeking Him, "that is born king of the Jews" (ii. 2), and having found Jesus they "fell down and worshipped him" (ii. 11). The advent of His kingdom is announced both by John the Baptist (iii. 2), and by the King Himself (iv. 17). In His triumphal entry into Jerusalem Jesus is represented as coming to claim His kingdom (xxi. 1–11), and in His discourse on the Last Judgment as judging all nations as their King (xxv. 32). Even the title on the cross bears witness to His kingship (xxvii. 37).

(2) he shows that Jesus is the fulfilment of Messianic prophecy. Quotations from the Old Testament are far more numerous than in "Mark" and "Luke" put together. Among the many prophecies quoted are those which foretell the birth of Jesus (i. 23), the return of Joseph and Mary from Egypt (ii. 15), the murder of the innocents (ii. 18), the preaching of John the Baptist (iii. 3), the triumphal entry into Jerusalem (xxi. 5), the rejection of Jesus by the Jews (xxi. 42), and the purchase of the potter's field (xxvii. 9–10).

(3) he emphasizes the relation of Christianity to the Law. It is a new Law, promulgated on Mount Sinai by divine authority. Jesus has come, not to destroy the Law but to fulfil it (v. 17). The most trivial detail in it can never be changed (v. 18). His followers must render such obedience to it that their righteousness shall exceed that of the Scribes

and Pharisees, otherwise they "shall in no wise enter into the kingdom of heaven" (v. 20). He who breaks the least commandment and teaches men so is least in the kingdom (v. 19). The old law is valid but the new both completes and transcends it.

(4) he represents Jesus as saying, "I was not sent but unto the lost sheep of the house of Israel" (xv. 24), and as commanding His disciples to confine their ministry of preaching and healing to these lost sheep (x. 6).

(5) he makes frequent allusions to Jewish customs, without explaining them, assuming that his readers, being chiefly Jews, would be familiar with them.

There are certain passages, however, which have a worldwide implication. Stress is laid on the Jews' rejection of Jesus who is reported as saying, "The kingdom of God shall be taken away from you, and shall be given to a nation bringing forth the fruits thereof" (xxi. 43). The Pharisees are denounced in a series of woes (xxiii). "Many shall come from the east and the west, and shall sit down with Abraham, and Isaac, and Jacob, in the kingdom of heaven: but the sons of the kingdom shall be cast forth into the outer darkness" (viii. 11–12). The Gospel is to be preached to the whole world (xxiv. 14), and disciples are to be made of all the nations (xxviii. 19). The compiler wishes to show that the rule of the Messiah is to be universal, embracing both Jews and Gentiles.

Characteristics

Love of Order. The material of the Gospel is arranged in an orderly manner. Teaching given on different occasions is brought together and arranged in five large blocks, which are inserted at intervals in the Marcan narrative. These five blocks are as follows:

1. The Sermon on the Mount (v–vii).
2. The Directions to the Disciples (x).
3. The Parables of the Kingdom (xiii).
4. Sayings on Greatness and Forgiveness (xviii).
5. Sayings and Parables on the Last Things (xxiv, xxv).

Most of the material of these five blocks comes from the document Q, or M, except the parables, which are partly from "Mark" and partly from unknown sources, and is joined to the Marcan narrative by a formula of transition which closes each of the five groups (VII. 28, XI. 1, XIII. 53, XIX. 1, XXVI. 1): "And it came to pass, when Jesus had ended these words . . ." In arranging his material the author probably had in mind the five books of the Pentateuch, the five books of the Psalms, the five Megilloth, and other similar groups. It is hard to believe that it was mere coincidence.

The Gospel shows a fondness for the numbers 3 and 7. The genealogy of Jesus falls into three groups of fourteen names (2 × 7), and is perhaps an acrostic on the name of David, the letters of which in Hebrew add up to 14. An angel of the Lord appears on three different occasions to Joseph (I. 20, II. 13, II. 19); Peter denies his Master three times (XXVI. 69–75); in the garden of Gethsemane Jesus leaves His disciples to pray a third time (XXVI. 44); at the Crucifixion there is darkness over all the land for three hours (XXVII. 45). The teaching of Jesus on fasting, prayer, and almsgiving is arranged in three units, each of which is built on the same plan. Similarly Jesus feeds four thousand people with seven loaves and a few fish (XV. 36), while a brother must forgive not seven times but until seventy times seven (XVIII. 22). There are seven parables in Chapter XIII. and seven woes in Chapter XXIII.

The same orderly tendency is seen in the recurrence of certain formulae and favourite catchwords. Not only do the five main blocks of teaching end with a formula, but paragraphs are almost invariably joined together by the word "then". Six times we meet with the stereotyped formula, "The kingdom of heaven is like . . .", and six times with the words, "There shall be wailing and gnashing of teeth". The orderly arrangement of the Gospel suggests that it was specially written for liturgical purposes.

The Apocalyptic Element. He expands Mark's Apocalyptic by the transfer of various Q passages, which thus acquires a more definite apocalyptic flavour, and by adding the Parables of the Virgins and the Talents, and the picture of the Judgment of those who had, or had not, assisted "the least of these my brethren", thus making it one of the most prominent sections in the Gospel, while he carefully omits from the Q passages, which he includes, the key opening, "The kingdom of God cometh not with observation". In the parables of the kingdom, in the place of the seed growing secretly, with its opposite tenor, he has the Parable of the Wheat and the Tares, which is accorded a full interpretation in apocalyptic terms, no explanation being accorded to the Parables of the Leaven and the Mustard Seed which represent the coming of the kingdom as a growth.

Ecclesiastical Interests of the Author. Matthew's Gospel alone uses the word "Church" to express what is elsewhere called the "Kingdom". It seems to be used in his M source in the sense of the local Christian community of Jerusalem, organized as a Jewish synagogue. But, in the commission to Peter, it is clearly used in the sense of the whole body of Christians throughout the world—the Pauline sense—where it is taken from the word "congregation" used in the Old Testament of Israel and implies that Christians are the true Israel. To Peter are given "the keys of the kingdom of heaven: and whatsoever thou shalt bind on earth shall be bound in heaven: and whatsoever thou shalt loose on earth shall be loosed in heaven" (Mt. xvi. 19), thus conferring on him the power given in M to the Jerusalemite congregation (Mt. xviii. 18). We have shown that this was probably intended to rule out the powers claimed for James by his extreme supporters and very likely represents the attitude of mind of the mixed church in Antioch-in-Syria; but it goes far beyond any powers which we find Peter exercising in "Acts", where the decision to admit the Gentiles without requiring them to keep the ceremonial law was made by certain of the Apostles and the elders of the Church in Jerusalem, and, though the decision was approved, if not actually proposed by Peter, it was in no sense his personal decision.

The other notable case where this Gospel breathes the atmosphere of a later time is the concluding charge (xxviii. 18–20) to preach to all nations and to baptize them in the name of the Father, and of the Son, and of the Holy Spirit. The compiler thus finally shows that, despite anything in M, he is a full believer in the Gentile mission, and believes it to have been directly commanded by Our Lord Himself, whereas elsewhere it is implied in many parables and sayings, but nowhere stated in this direct form. Nor have we the baptismal formula elsewhere in the Gospels; it is uncertain whether originally baptism was not in the name of Jesus.

Style. The style of the Gospel is clear, smooth, and concise. His fondness for stereotyped formulae and catchwords has already been mentioned. Many of Mark's picturesque details are omitted and his redundances cut out. For example, we are not told that Jesus took the children in His arms to bless them or that the man with his sight partially restored saw men "as trees walking", or that Jesus was with the wild beasts in the desert. Mark's words, "And at even, when the sun did set" (Mk. I. 32) become, "And when even was come" (Mt. VIII. 16); the words, "And the wind ceased, and there was a great calm" (Mk. IV. 39), become "And there was a great calm" (Mt. VIII. 26); while the words, "And straightway the leprosy departed from him, and he was made clean" (Mk. I. 42), become, "And straightway his leprosy was cleansed" (Mt. VIII. 3). If, however, the style has not the artlessness, colour, and vigour of that of Mark's Gospel, it is calmer and more restrained than the latter.

The author of the Gospel preserves the poetic parallelism of the sayings of Jesus more faithfully than the other two synoptic writers. The Sermon on the Mount provides many examples of this poetic form of speech, of which the following may be cited:

"Blessed are ye when men shall reproach you, and persecute you, and say all manner of evil against you falsely, for my sake" (v. 11).

"Be not anxious for your life, what ye shall eat, or what ye shall drink; nor yet for your body, what ye shall put on. Is not the life more than the food, and the body than the raiment" (VI. 25).

"Enter ye in by the narrow gate: for wide is the gate, and

broad is the way, that leadeth to destruction, and many be they that enter in thereby. For narrow is the gate, and straitened the way, that leadeth unto life, and few be they that find it" (VII. 13).

The author takes care to preserve the literary devices of contrast and repetition which give impressiveness to the sayings of Jesus. Notice how, by these devices, the corruptibility of the treasures of earth and the incorruptibility of the treasures of heaven are impressed upon the mind in the following passage:

"Lay not up for yourselves treasures upon the earth, where moth and rust doth consume, and where thieves break through and steal: but lay up for yourselves treasures in heaven, where neither moth nor rust doth consume, and where thieves do not break through nor steal: for where thy treasure is, there will thy heart be also" (VI. 19–21).

Similarly the vulnerability of the house built upon the sand and the invulnerability of that built upon the rocks, to the assaults of flood and wind, are driven home in the following words:

"And the rain descended, and the floods came, and the winds blew, and beat upon that house; and it fell not: for it was founded upon the rock" (VII. 25).

"And the rain descended, and the floods came, and the winds blew, and smote upon that house; and it fell: and great was the fall thereof" (VII. 27).

Certain passages, especially parts of the Sermon on the Mount (v., VI., VII.), the descriptions of the woes pronounced against the Pharisees (XXIII.), and of the Great Judgment (XXV.), together with some of the parables, are of unsurpassed beauty and charm, and are worthy to be reckoned among the great literature of the world.

Of course, it should not be forgotten that the poetic form of the sayings, which gives them their beauty and charm, was not the creation of the author but of Jesus Himself; nevertheless credit is due to Matthew for his share in preserving their perfect balance and symmetry.

Historical Value

Judged by either ancient or modern standards of historical criticism, the author of the first Gospel cannot be ranked among the great historians. He has not the impartiality of Mark, or the accuracy, historical perspective and literary skill of Luke, or the profound spiritual insight of John. Credit must be given to him for his recognition of the importance of "Mark" and the document Q, and for the skilful way in which he has fused the two together to form a coherent whole. His Gospel preserves for all time the fullest record we possess of the teaching of Jesus which is as valid to-day as when it was first delivered. Soon after its appearance it became the most popular Gospel in the early Church, and was the most widely read and most often quoted.

The form in which the sayings of Jesus was cast has not been entirely beneficial. The arrangement of the sayings according to the subject-matter, such as duty to one's neighbour, forgiveness, and the right use of riches, has led to a clearer understanding of their comprehensiveness and of the unity of His teaching. At the same time, however, it has led to serious consequences, for it has tended to create the false impression that He delivered a number of set discourses and formulated a code of ethics for the regulation of mankind, whereas His teaching was largely occasional, and consisted of the enunciation of a few general principles by which all the problems of life might be solved.

The first Gospel played an important part in helping to preserve the unity of the early Church. The majority of its members accepted the teaching of the Gospel as the standard of orthodoxy, to which it appealed in its successful struggle against heretics who began to appear towards the close of the first century. The Antinomians claimed to be exempt from the obligation to observe the moral law, since, according to Paul, the just were saved by faith alone. The Gnostics held that man was saved by the possession of a secret knowledge, supposed to have been given privately by Jesus to His twelve disciples: they also destroyed the historical foundations of the Church by their denial of the God of the Old Testament, and of the reality of the Incarnation. The Montanists claimed to be instruments of a new revelation by the Holy Spirit. The leaders of the Church, taking their stand on this Gospel, could claim that Christianity was a new Law of Righteousness to which all men owed allegiance; that in the Gospels alone, especially the first, was to be found a complete record of the teaching of Jesus; that Jesus was a real historical figure who had lived, died, and been raised from the dead; that Christianity was the continuation and consummation of Judaism, and that the Church, as the Kingdom of God, was the sole channel of divine revelation.

The first Gospel not only served as a bulwark against heresy, but also provided a model for the organization, government, and discipline of the developing Church. Those whose duty it was to build the superstructure of the Church, the foundations of which were laid in Christ, were strongly influenced by the legalistic and ecclesiastical conceptions of Christianity as revealed in this Gospel, with the result that the primitive Church, consisting of many scattered communities loosely joined together, was gradually transformed into a firmly united and powerful institution, claiming apostolic foundation, the right to be considered the sole repository and guardian of the truth, and the right to exercise absolute authority over all men, whether in Church or State.

The stress laid on the Messiahship of Jesus helped to demonstrate the truth of Christianity as a historical religion, ordained of God, and with its roots deep in the past. To the modern mind the argument from prophecy may seem unscientific and unconvincing, but it has, nevertheless, shown that the appearance of Jesus on the stage of history was not a mere accident or divine whim, but was in accordance with the eternal purposes of God.

CHAPTER VIII

THE GOSPEL ACCORDING TO LUKE

Authorship

The unanimous tradition of the early Church in the second century of our era attributes the third Gospel to Luke. Irenaeus states that "Luke, the follower of Paul, recorded in a book the Gospel that was preached by him." The Muratorian Fragment (*c.* A.D. 170), which gives a list of the New Testament books, attributes it to "Luke, that physician", who after the Ascension of Christ, when Paul had taken him with him as companion on his journey, composed it in his own name on the basis of report. It was the only Gospel recognized by the heretical teacher Marcion (*c.* 140), just as Paul's were the only Epistles he recognized, though he cut certain passages from the Gospel which conflicted with his views; its Gentile and Pauline character was thus seen early, for it was that character which attracted Marcion.

This evidence for Lucan authorship from a second-century tradition is further strengthened by the fact that the dedicatory preface to the Gospel makes it practically certain that the author was known in the early Church, and that his name was first attached to the original roll of manuscript. There is also overwhelming evidence for believing that the third Gospel and "Acts" were written by the same person, that the writer was a companion of Paul, and that it was the Luke who is mentioned in the Epistles and called "the beloved physician" (Col. IV. 14). (For proof of this see Chapter XI.)

Sources

Main Sources. In the dedicatory preface to the third Gospel we learn that Luke had made careful investigation of his sources, both oral and written, and that he had decided to write a connected and systematic account of the life and teaching of Christ. We may infer, too, that he was not an eye-witness of the events which he recorded, and that he must, therefore, have obtained his information at second hand. We can trace in his Gospel four main sources, namely:

(1) the Gospel of Mark.
(2) the collection of sayings of the Lord, called Q.
(3) a special source, commonly called L, comprising mainly the Travel Document (ix. 51–xviii. 14), and the non-Marcan portions of the narratives of the Passion and the post-Resurrection appearances (xxii. 14–xxiv.).
(4) Birth and Infancy narratives.

Stages of Composition. The Gospel bears clear marks of having been composed in stages. Chapter iii., beginning with an elaborate dating, and continuing with the ministry of John the Baptist, which was the recognized beginning of the ministry (Acts x. 37–38), and with the genealogy, bears all the marks of being the original beginning; for, if the narrative of the birth had already been written, we should expect the dating and genealogy to have been included in it.

Streeter has put forward a further theory, that this original draft did not include the parts taken from "Mark", on the ground that in several cases where a narrative of the same events, or events similar to incidents recorded in "Mark", is included, no trace of Mark's account is found in "Luke" (e.g. the work of John the Baptist, the call of Peter, and the anointing by a woman), and that even the Passion narrative is mainly non-Marcan. He shows that, if we omit all the Marcan matter, it remains a complete Gospel, beginning with the teaching of the Baptist and ending with the Passion and Resurrection, and containing the bulk of the teaching, a large number of incidents, the call and names of the Twelve, in fact all which is needed to satisfy his own account of Peter's summary in "Acts" x. 37–42. This view has met with wide acceptance. Streeter admits that it is hard to prove that both this original draft, which he calls "Proto-Luke", and the Gospel as we now have it were the work of Luke, but makes it the most probable hypothesis.

The Marcan sections are arranged in large blocks by themselves, except in the Passion narrative, where this was obviously impossible (IV. 31–44, V. 12–VI. 11, VIII. 4–IX. 50, XVIII. 15–43, XIX. 29–36, XIX. 45–46, XX. 1–XXI. 11, XXII. 1–13). At least half of Mark's Gospel is included, apart from parts of the Passion narrative. There are one long omission (Mk. VI. 45–VIII. 26), which is probably due to a mutilation in the copy of "Mark" which he used, since it seems both to begin and end in the middle of a narrative, several omissions of matters of which he has given a different account, occasional omissions of verses which reflect unfavourably on the Twelve (e.g. the request of James and John to sit on Jesus' right hand and left), and considerable shortening in the wording. Mark's order is preserved far more than in Matthew's Gospel. We may reasonably assume that a similar treatment is accorded to Q, though here the omissions may be fewer, as in several cases Q accounts have been preferred to Mark's accounts.

Sources other than Mark and Q. The question thus arises how Luke obtained the information not gained from "Mark" or Q. The Passion narrative has already been discussed in the chapters on "Mark" and "Matthew". Luke's parables are amongst the best-known portions of his Gospel (e.g. the Good Samaritan and the Prodigal Son); but we are in the same doubt whether written collections of parables existed as in connection with Mark's and Matthew's parables.

Chapters IX. 51–XVIII. 14 are the longest section of non-Marcan matter. As this section is placed after the Marcan account of the Transfiguration it is often assumed that Luke thought of all that is recorded in it as belonging to the last journey from Galilee to Jerusalem, but, as over half of it is teaching derived from Q and there are numerous parables, it would not seem to be Luke's intention to assign any particular time to it. It represents the bulk of the matter obtained before "Mark" was added. But the portions which are neither Q nor parables come from an eyewitness. They show strong sympathy with women and with Samaritans, and like several passages in other parts of the Gospel reveal an intimate knowledge of incidents connected with Herod's court (Lk. III. 1–19,

VIII. 3, IX. 7–9, XIII. 31, XXIII. 7–12). To account for these characteristics we need a Christian Jew of Palestine, a companion of Christ during His journey to Jerusalem, and one who had dealings with the Samaritans and was acquainted with Herod's court. Joanna fulfils the conditions. She was one of the women who accompanied Christ and His disciples on their travels and "ministered unto them of their substance", and was married to Chuza, Herod's steward (VIII. 3). Since it is practically certain that the document Q contained no narratives of the Passion and the post-Resurrection appearances, and the arraignment before Herod (XXIII. 7–12) is usually assigned to Joanna, it is possible that other parts of the Passion narrative may be due to her or to other of these women too. Other possible sources of information are Philip the Evangelist and his four daughters, and Manaen, "the foster-brother of Herod the tetrarch" (Acts XIII. 1). As Luke had ample opportunities of getting first-hand information from all these persons during Paul's imprisonment at Caesarea, it is unnecessary to suppose that they were taken from a written document.

The three hymns in the Birth and Infancy narratives, namely the "Magnificat", the "Benedictus", and the "Nunc Dimittis", must have been originally written in Hebrew or Aramaic, as they contain phrases which could never have occurred to anyone writing in Greek but are quite natural in a Semitic language. The song of Hannah in "Samuel" is their model. It is quite probable that they were in use for Christian worship in the church at Jerusalem and that Luke thus obtained a translation.

Aim

The Gospel is dedicated to Theophilus, who was probably a Roman official of high rank and a convert to the Christian faith, and was written in particular to provide him with historical evidence for the Christian instruction which he had received orally. It was, however, not intended for him alone, but also for Gentile converts generally, as may be seen from the following facts:

(1) Jewish words and customs are explained for the benefit of Gentiles who could not understand them. "Master" is substituted for "Rabbi", "lawyer" for "scribe", and "verily" for "Amen". The "Sea of Galilee" is described as the "Lake of Gennesaret", "Capernaum" as "a city of Galilee", and "the feast of unleavened bread" as the "Passover".

(2) the Gospel is comparatively free from Old Testament quotations and makes little use of argument from prophecy.

(3) the descent of Jesus is traced from Adam and not from Abraham as in Matthew's Gospel, with the evident intention of showing His significance for all mankind.

(4) Jesus is not only the Messiah of Jewish expectation, but also the Saviour of the whole human race. The message of the angelic host is, "Glory to God in the highest, And on earth peace among men in whom he is well pleased" (II. 14). The child Jesus is to be "a light for revelation to the Gentiles" as well as "the glory of thy people Israel" (II. 32). Luke alone adds the quotation from Isaiah, respecting the mission of John the Baptist, the words, "And all flesh shall see the salvation of God" (III. 6). In the story of Christ's rejection at Nazareth there is a clear indication that the Gospel is for the Gentiles. He reminds His hearers that of all the widows in Israel during the great famine in the days of Elijah, the prophet was sent to none of them but only to a heathen woman of Zarephath; and that of all the lepers in the land in the time of Elisha no one was cleansed but Naaman the Syrian (IV. 25–27). The Samaritans, who were despised as aliens by the Jews, are prominent in the Gospel. Christ rebukes James and John for desiring Him to destroy the inhabitants of a Samaritan village who refuse to receive Him (IX. 51–56): the chief figure in one of the best-known parables is a good Samaritan (X. 30–37), while of the ten lepers who are healed by Christ only one returns to express his gratitude, and he is a Samaritan (XVII. 11–19). The Gentile convert, whose servant is healed, is commended as one who "loveth our nation, and himself built us our synagogue" and as having greater faith than

is to be found in Israel (VII. 1–10). Gentiles shall come from the east and west, and from the north and south, and shall sit down in the kingdom of God (XIII. 29). Before His Ascension Christ commands His disciples to preach repentance and remission of sins "unto all the nations, beginning from Jerusalem" (XXIV. 47).

A third aim of the Gospel is to commend Christianity to the Imperial Government, showing that a Roman official had considered it to be a harmless religion and had treated its Founder with fairness and tolerance. When Jesus is brought before Pilate and charged with being an impostor, with sedition, and with being "Christ, a king", the procurator, after examination, finds Him innocent, and proposes to release Him. To the insistent demands of His enemies that He shall be crucified, Pilate answers, "Why, what evil hath this man done? I have found no cause of death in him: I will therefore chastise him and release him" (XXIII. 22). Finally, however, the voices of His enemies prevail and the procurator delivers Him up to their will. The responsibility for the death of Jesus is thus laid upon the Jews.

Language

Luke was probably a Gentile who wrote his Gospel in Greek. There is no evidence that he was acquainted with either Aramaic or Hebrew. He did not employ one uniform style throughout, but varied it according as his source was oral or written, Hebrew or Greek. The dedicatory preface (I. 1–4) is written in the conventional polished literary style of contemporary writers, while the Birth and Infancy narratives (I. 5–11) are an excellent imitation of the Greek of the Old Testament. The remainder of the book is written in easy, fluent, Hellenistic Greek. In some of the sayings from Q there is evidence of an underlying Semitic language, while the use of the Septuagint for the Old Testament quotations colours the whole book, "giving it an archaic, Semitic tinge, which Luke no doubt thought more suitable than the artificial rhetorical Greek of the period (this is found only in I. 1–4), for the narratives of the Lord's words and deeds, which were as sacred as the Old Testament, and required a biblical style".[1]

Place and Date of Composition

A very old tradition associates Luke with Antioch-in-Syria, His vivid accounts of the church in that city are the work of an eyewitness. If we accept the Western Text, we have confirmation of his close association with that church in the words "and there was much rejoicing, and when we had been in conversation together, one of them named Agabus, stood up", etc. (Acts XI. 28). The use of the first person "we" implies his presence at Antioch-in-Syria about A.D. 45. In the "Monarchian Prologue" to the Gospel he is described as "Luke, a Syrian of Antioch by nation", and in the "Ecclesiastical History" of Eusebius as "Luke, by birth one of the people of Antioch". This tradition is carried on by Jerome. But even if he was a native of Antioch, it does not necessarily follow that he wrote his Gospel there. "The fact that the connection of Peter with Antioch—the proudest boast of that church—is completely ignored is fatal to the theory of some modern scholars that the book was written in and for that church."[2] According to the "Monarchian Prologue" to the Gospel the scene of Luke's literary labours was "in the parts of Achaia". Now the Gospel is dedicated to the "most excellent Theophilus", who was probably a Roman official of high rank. The two had met each other when Theophilus was perhaps governor of a province. If that province was Achaia, then his headquarters must have been at Corinth where there was a flourishing Christian church. Luke was with Paul on the latter's last visit to Jerusalem and during his two years at Caesarea, where, we may assume, he would have ample opportunity to collect material and to start writing his Gospel, the first draft of which he would finish there or during his two years' residence at Rome. Subsequently he would enlarge his original draft by additions from "Mark" and send a copy to Theophilus to whom it was dedicated.

[1] McNeile, *An Introduction to the Study of the New Testament*, 1927, p. 44.
[2] Streeter, *The Four Gospels*, 1930, p. 533.

The question of the date of the Gospel involves the date of "Acts", since the preface to "Acts" refers to the Gospel as "the former treatise". Writers who think that "Acts" must have been written immediately after the two years' imprisonment of Paul, which is the last event recorded, are obliged to date the Gospel some years before Nero's persecution; but this involves too early a date for "Mark" and is not necessary to explain any reference in "Acts" to Paul's subsequent fate, as will be shown in the chapter on "Acts". Those who think that Luke must be dependent on Josephus for information on the various risings against the Romans mentioned by Gamaliel in "Acts", are compelled on the other hand to strive for a late date, nearer to A.D. 100; but here again, as we shall see, Luke's account of Gamaliel's speech is evidence rather that he had not read Josephus than that he had, as he makes mistakes about dates, which would be easy if he were writing from a vague general knowledge of Jewish history, but not at all after Luke's careful manner if he had access to a written authority. The best date, therefore, is within the period A.D. 75–85 on the ground that, in Mark's apocalyptic discourse, he omits the reference to the Abomination standing in the Temple, as this was obviously impossible now that the Temple was destroyed, and substitutes a prophecy of the Fall of Jerusalem.[1]

Characteristics

The Gospel of the Poor and the Outcast. It is the Gospel of the poor and the outcast. The "Magnificat" sounds a note that is heard throughout the book: "He hath put down princes from their thrones, And hath exalted them of low degree. The hungry he hath filled with good things; And the rich he hath sent empty away" (i. 52–53). The child Jesus is born in a manger (ii. 7), and tidings of His birth are given by an angelic host to shepherds in the field (ii. 8–12). The publicans are warned against

---

[1] Luke has not only recorded a prophecy of the Fall of Jerusalem, which he found in an Aramaic or Hebrew original (Luke xxi. 20–24), but has also taken his account of the relation between the destruction of Jerusalem and the End (Luke xxi. 25–36) from "Daniel" ix. 24–27. These prophecies seem to be the natural sequence of the beginning of Mark's chapter, where the discourse arises out of a prophecy of the destruction of the Temple.

extortion and soldiers against violence and discontent (III. 12–14). The disciples of John the Baptist are bidden by Christ to tell their master that the poor have good tidings preached to them (VII. 18–22). The followers of Christ are commanded to give alms to the poor. "Howbeit give for alms those things which are within; and behold, all things are clean unto you" (XI. 41), and again, "Sell that ye have, and give alms" (XII. 33).

Emphasis is laid upon the perils of wealth. It is called the "mammon of unrighteousness" (XVI. 9), and men are warned that they cannot serve "God and mammon" (XVI. 13). The Pharisees are described as lovers of money (XVI. 14) and woe is pronounced against those who are rich and full (VI. 24–25). Christ refuses to judge between men in respect of property (XII. 13–14): the rich man is punished in the next life because in his own comfortable state he has taken no notice of the beggar at his gate, while the poor beggar has his reward (XVI. 19–31). Men must learn to put the "treasures of heaven" before the "treasures of earth", for "a man's life consisteth not in the abundance of the things which he possesseth" (XII. 15). In the parable of the Rich Fool we are shown the folly of the man who trusts in his riches and is not rich towards God (XII. 16–21). Luke is sympathetic towards those who make a right use of their riches. He seems to commend the women who ministered to Christ and His disciples (VIII. 3): he has sympathy for Zacchaeus, the rich publican (XIX. 1–10) and describes Joseph of Arimathaea as a "good man and a righteous", and one "who was looking for the kingdom of God" (XXIII. 50).

Emphasis is laid upon Christ's sympathy with the outcast. "The Son of man came to seek and to save that which was lost" (XIX. 10). The despised Samaritans are within the embrace of the love of God (IX. 51–56, X. 30–37, XVII. 11–19): the publicans and sinners draw near to hear Him, but the Pharisees and the scribes murmur, saying, "This man receiveth sinners, and eateth with them" (XV. 1–2). The woman "which was in the city, a sinner" is forgiven because of her faith and her great love (VII. 36–50): the father rejoices at the return of the prodigal son from the far country (XV. 11–32), and the penitent thief is comforted with the words, "To-day shalt thou be with me in Paradise" (XXIII. 43).

The Gospel of Womanhood. It is especially the Gospel of womanhood. Women occupied an inferior position in society and were generally disparaged or ignored. Luke, however, is deeply sympathetic towards them: he sympathizes with their religious aspirations and recognizes that they no less than men have a place in the Kingdom. It is in this Gospel alone that we read of the widow Anna (II. 36), of the widow of Nain whose only son Christ raises from the dead (VII. 11–15), of the nameless penitent in the house of Simon (VII. 36–50), of the band of women who follow Christ and His disciples and minister unto them of their substance (VIII. 3), of Mary choosing the good part and Martha cumbered with much serving (x. 38–42), of the woman with the spirit of infirmity (XIII. 10–13), of the daughters of Jerusalem who follow Christ to the cross weeping (XXIII. 27–31), and of the parables of the Woman and the Lost Coin (XV. 8–10), and the Widow and the Unmerciful Judge (XVIII. 1–8).

The Gospel of Tolerance. Mark gives one instance of Jesus rebuking intolerance. When John informs Him that they had forbidden a person whom they had seen casting out devils in His name, because he was not one of His followers, He rebukes him with the words, "Forbid him not: for he that is not against you is for you" (Lk. IX. 49–50=Mk. IX. 38–40); but soon after Luke adds a second, when He rebukes James and John for wishing Him to destroy the inhabitants of a Samaritan village because they had refused to receive Him, as "his face was as though he were going to Jerusalem" (IX. 51–56). The grateful leper who returns to thank Christ for healing him is a Samaritan (XVII. 15–16), while it is the good Samaritan rather than the callous priest or Levite who is chosen as the type of charitable service (x. 30–37).

The Gospel of Prayer. Special prominence is given to prayer in the Gospel. It is recorded that Christ prayed on several occasions. In Luke's account of the descent of the Holy Spirit at Jesus' baptism, Luke adds to the words "Jesus also having been baptized", the words "and praying" (III. 21), not found in

"Mark" or "Matthew". After the cleansing of a leper, great multitudes come to hear Him, but He retires to the desert and prays (v. 16): before choosing the twelve disciples He goes to a mountain and continues all night in prayer to God (vi. 12). This again is not in the accounts in "Mark" or "Matthew", and a similar addition is made to the account of the Transfiguration that He "went up into the mountain to pray. And as he was praying, the fashion of his countenance was altered, and his raiment became white and dazzling" (ix. 28–29): on the return of the seventy missionaries He rejoices in the Holy Spirit and gives thanks to the Father (x. 21). He prays for Simon that his faith may not fail (xxii. 31–32): on the cross He prays that His enemies may be forgiven (xxiii. 34), and with His last breath commends His spirit to God (xxiii. 46).

Not only do we find in this Gospel instances of Christ at prayer, but also His teaching about prayer. The Lord's Prayer, which He gives as a model for all Christians, is probably not derived from Q, as Luke's form, before it had been assimilated in many manuscripts to Matthew's, contained such substantial differences that it is unlikely that they were taken from the same source. In the Parables of the Importunate Friend (xi. 5–8) and the Unjust Judge (xviii. 1–8) stress is laid upon persevering prayer. These instances are peculiar to "Luke" and are in addition to the teaching drived from Q which is given in xi. 11–13.

The Gospel of Joy. The note of joy sounds through the whole of the Gospel. Of the birth of John the Baptist it is said, "Thou shalt call his name John. And thou shalt have joy and gladness; and many shall rejoice at his birth" (i. 13–14). The "Magnificat" (i. 46–55), the "Benedictus" (i. 68–79), and the "Nunc Dimittis" (ii. 29–32), are hymns of joy and thanksgiving. After the raising from the dead of the widow's son at Nain, fear takes hold of all who see it, and they glorify God, saying, "A great prophet is arisen among us: and, God hath visited his people" (vii. 11–16). The seventy missionaries return with joy from their mission, and on hearing their report Jesus rejoices in the Holy Spirit (x. 17–21): after the healing of the woman with the spirit of infirmity, all the multitude rejoice for all the glorious things that are done by Him (xiii. 10–17). He adds to Mark's account of the healing of blind Bartimaeus the words "and all the people, when they saw it, gave praise unto God" (xviii. 43); and to the account of the Triumphal Entry into Jerusalem he adds that "the whole multitude of the disciples began to rejoice and praise God with a loud voice for all the mighty works which they had seen" (xix. 37). The centurion at the foot of the cross glorifies God when he sees what is done, and says, "Certainly this was a righteous man" (xxiii. 47). After His Ascension the disciples return to Jerusalem with great joy, and are continually in the Temple, blessing God (xxiv. 52–53).

Of all the Gospels this one is most truly "good tidings of great joy". Luke is overjoyed at the thought that Jesus is not only the Messiah of Jewish expectation, but also the Saviour of all mankind. His joyous faith may be expressed in the words, "My soul doth magnify the Lord, And my spirit hath rejoiced in God my Saviour" (i. 46–47).

The Gospel of the Holy Spirit. Stress is laid in the Gospel on the work of the Holy Spirit. John the Baptist is to be filled with the Holy Spirit from his mother's womb (i. 15). The Virgin Mary receives the Holy Spirit and the power of the Most High overshadows her (i. 35): when she visits Elizabeth the latter is inspired by the Holy Spirit to recognize in Mary the mother of the Lord (i. 43). Zacharias is filled with the Holy Spirit and prophecies (i. 67): the Holy Spirit is upon Simeon and leads him to the Temple to welcome the child Jesus as the Messiah (ii. 25–28). In the account of the Baptism and Temptation Luke follows his sources in recounting the descent of the Holy Spirit and that it was the Spirit who led Him into the wilderness, but it is his own addition that He "returned in the power of the Spirit" (iv. 14). On the return of the seventy missionaries, He rejoices in the Holy Spirit (x. 21); the Holy Spirit will be given in answer to prayer (xi. 13); the disciples are to remain at Jerusalem until they are clothed with power from on high (xxiv. 49). The Holy Spirit is so prominent in the book that it has been called, "The Gospel of the Holy Spirit".

The Gospel of the Home. Though Luke stresses the universality of the Gospel, he does not forget that Christ moved among the common ways of life. There is a charming domestic note about his Gospel. During Christ's ministry we catch glimpses of Him being entertained as a guest in the houses of Simon (vii. 36–50), of Zacchaeus (xix. 1–10) and of Mary and Martha (x. 38–42): we see Him sitting down to supper with the two disciples at Emmaus, and blessing and breaking the bread (xxiv. 30). Luke, with his deep humanitarian sympathies is interested, too, in the lives of the people—in their homes, their food and clothing, their occupations, their feasts, their social customs, and the relations between masters and servants. There are many pictures of domestic life in his Gospel, as for example, in addition to the many instances derived from "Mark" and Q, those of Zacharias asking for a writing tablet (1. 63), of the good Samaritan paying his host at the inn two pence (x. 35), and of the man rousing his friend at midnight to borrow three loaves (xi. 5). The Evangelist sees in Christ, not only the Saviour of the world, but also the friend of man.

Style

Of the three synoptic authors, Luke is the only one who can be called a stylist, having a command over language and a power of using it which entitle him to be ranked among the great writers of the world. We have already shown his ability to vary his style at will, but no matter whether he employs the polished rhetorical Greek of contemporary literature, or the vernacular of the Mediterranean world, or imitates the archaic style of the Septuagint, he shows complete mastery of his art.

He is the first Christian hymnologist. The Birth and Infancy narratives may have been derived ultimately from an Aramaic or a Hebrew original, but, nevertheless, in his hands they became new literary creations, the work of a conscious literary artist. The confident faith, tenderness, and poetic charm of the three great hymns—the "Benedictus", the "Magnificat", and the "Nunc Dimittis"—were soon recognized, and it was not long before they became part of the liturgy of the Gentile churches to which they could presumably have become known only through his Gospel.

He excels in the art of pictorial description. His accounts of the Nativity (I. 5–11), of the Widow's Son at Nain (VII. 11–17), of Mary and Martha (x. 38–42), and of the journey to Emmaus (XXIV. 13–32), and the Parables of the Good Shepherd (xv. 3–7), the Good Samaritan (x. 30–37), and the Prodigal Son (xv. 11–32), are superb examples of his narrative power. It is a noteworthy fact that many of the scenes only portrayed in his Gospel have been favourite subjects of artists.

He has also the power of vivid portraiture. In a few words he suggests the essential characteristics of persons—Simeon, "righteous and devout, looking for the consolation of Israel" (II. 25); Anna, a prophetess who "departed not from the temple, worshipping with fastings and supplications night and day" (II. 37); the woman at Nain, mourning the loss of her only son (VII. 12); Peter, James, and John, their eyes "heavy with sleep" on the Mount of Transfiguration (IX. 32); James and John, the sons of thunder, wishing to call down fire from heaven upon the inhabitants of a Samaritan village (IX. 54); Zacchaeus who "sought to see Jesus who he was; and could not for the crowd, because he was little of stature "(XIX. 3); Joseph of Arimathaea, "a councillor, a good man and a righteous" (XXIII. 50); and the two disciples on the road to Emmaus, whose hearts burned within them as He spoke to them in the way (XXIV. 32).

Frequent use is made of light and shade by the device of contrast. The self-righteous Pharisee is contrasted with the woman who is a sinner (VII. 37), the good Samaritan with the callous priest and Levite (x. 30–37), the busy, bustling Martha with the quiet, contemplative Mary (x. 38–42), the rich man with the beggar Lazarus (XVI. 19–31), the boastful Pharisee with the humble, penitent publican (XVIII. 9–14), and the penitent thief with the reviling robber (XXIII. 39–40).

Historical Value

The Gospel of Luke is a valuable contribution to our knowledge and understanding of the ministry of Christ. It is the most comprehensive of the four Gospels, since Luke is more consciously a historian and biographer than the other three Evangelists. By rescuing from oblivion and recreating the Birth and Infancy narratives, parables like those of the Good Shepherd, the Good Samaritan, and the Prodigal Son, and incidents like those of the raising of the widow's son at Nain, of Christ in the house of Simon the Pharisee, and of the journey to Emmaus, he has not only given us a deeper knowledge and clearer understanding of the Gospel message, but has also enriched the liturgy of the Church and the literature and art of the world. The Gospel of the love and mercy of God and of the brotherhood of man, proclaimed by Luke, "the beloved physician", has made a deep appeal to people throughout the ages and has been an unfailing source of inspiration to poets, painters, sculptors, and musicians. The content of the Gospel and the charm of its style entitle it to be called, in the words of Renan, "the most beautiful book in the world".

CHAPTER IX

THE GOSPEL ACCORDING TO JOHN

Authorship

Traditional View. The ultimate tradition was unanimous in attributing the Gospel to the Apostle John, the son of Zebedee. This attribution first appears in a statement attached to the Gospel itself. "This is the disciple which beareth witness of these things, and wrote these things: and we know that his witness is true" (XXI. 24). This "beloved disciple", whom they claim is the author, is mentioned in the Gospel itself as present at the Last Supper (XIII. 23), the Crucifixion (XIX. 26–27), and on the shores of the Sea of Tiberias (XXI. 7), and has been generally identified with the other disciple of John the Baptist who with Andrew follows Jesus (I. 35–36), who gains admission for Peter to the house of the High Priest (XVIII. 15–16), and who goes with Peter to the Tomb (XX. 3), though none of these three identifications is certain. It can be taken as almost certain that the writers of the ascription intended it to refer to the Apostle John, as, of the three Apostles who in the Synoptic narratives form an inner band, Peter is ruled out by being mentioned along with the "beloved disciple" and James as already dead. For the same reasons it is probable that the writer of the Gospel himself intended the "beloved disciple" to be the Apostle John.

But who were these persons—"we" implies a number of persons who authorize the statement, though "I" in the following verse (XXI. 25) implies that some one person is writing on their behalf—and why do they think it necessary to append this note? No such statement is appended to any of the other Gospels or to "Acts": Luke writes in the first person, though he does not give his name; no accompanying preface or epilogue appears in the Gospels of Mark or Matthew. It is perhaps of help to seeing a reason why such a note was added to the

Fourth Gospel to ask why no such note was added to any of the others. In the case of Luke's two works they are formally addressed to Theophilus, and there must have been a correspondence between Luke and Theophilus, who thereby knew who was writing to him: but in the other two cases, the reason appears to be that each was published by a church (Rome and Antioch), and regarded rather as the work of that church than of an independent author. But the persons who speak as "we" clearly regard an acceptance of the Fourth Gospel as in a large measure depending on the identity of its author. Why this difference? The easiest answer is that on various points the Fourth Gospel seeks to correct statements in the Synoptics and that the general impression which it gives is different; the claim to a higher authority than that of the three accepted Gospels could only be justified if the author was in a better position to know. Evidently the ascribers were conscious of an unwillingness to accept the new Gospel.

Two possible sets of persons have been suggested as putting forward the attestation—the presbytery of the church of Ephesus, where the Gospel was almost certainly written, and the authorities of some other church which decided to accept it. The second hypothesis seems to us the more probable. People in Ephesus would themselves know the author: if the statement is true, it would not be needed: if it is false, it would not be accepted. But the acceptance by some other church would be strongly helped if the authorities of that church could state that they had gone into the question of authorship and were convinced that it was the work of an Apostle and was therefore reliable.

The first mention of John the Apostle by name as the author is probably that of the Muratorian Fragment (c. A.D. 170) which states: "The Fourth Gospel is that of John, one of his disciples. When his fellow disciples and bishops intreated him, he said: 'Fast ye now with me for the space of three days, and let us recount to each other whatever may be revealed to each of us.' On the same night it was revealed to Andrew, one of the Apostles, that John should narrate all things in his own name as they called them to mind. And hence, although different points are taught us in the separate books of the Gospels, there is no difference as regards the faith of believers, since by the one sovereign spirit all of them give all the details concerning the Lord's Nativity, His Passion, His Resurrection, His conversation with His disciples, and His twofold advent—the first in the humiliation of rejection, which is now past, and the second in the glory of royal power, which is yet in the future." This account is obviously impossible, as the whole body of Apostles were together only in the very early days of the Church, and it would necessitate making it the earliest of the four Gospels, whereas all tradition and all evidence, external and internal, make it the last. But the second part clearly suggests that some persons did find differences between it and the Synoptic Gospels, which made it hard for them to accept both.

The view which ultimately became universal that it was written at Ephesus is first found in Irenaeus (c. A.D. 180), who asserts that "John the disciple of the Lord who leaned upon His breast himself set forth the Gospel while dwelling at Ephesus in Asia". Similar testimony is given by Tertullian, Clement of Alexandria, Origen, and later writers. The place of its origin would almost certainly be generally known, and Ephesus is accepted by most modern critics. It was also recognized generally to have been the last of the four Gospels, and this carried the implication that the Apostle John, to be the author, must have lived to an advanced age.

Passing to internal evidence, we may safely conclude that the author was a Palestinian Jew and had seen and heard Jesus. On this second point the Gospel itself is indecisive, as in Chapter I. 14 ("we beheld his glory") "we" might refer to the earliest Christians in general, but in the First Epistle, which is generally accepted as a work of the same author, Chapter I. 1–3 is decisive. The writer believed in Jesus from personal evidence. But we must not assume that he had seen or heard everything recounted in the Gospel, and no claim to be an Apostle is implied. Any of the five hundred persons to whom Our Lord appeared after His Resurrection could justifiably write in this strain. The evidence that the writer was a Palestinian Jew appears throughout the Gospel.

(1) The style of the Gospel has an Aramaic colouring. Some of the quotations from the Old Testament are taken from the Hebrew version as well as from the Septuagint. The writer, therefore, must have known both Hebrew and Greek.

(2) He is familiar with:

(a) Jewish festivals. He refers to the Feast of the Passover (II. 13, VI. 4, XII. 1), the Feast of Tabernacles (VII. 2), and the Feast of Dedication (X. 22).

(b) Jewish Messianic ideas (I. 19–27, IV. 25, VII. 25–30, 40–42, XII. 34).

(c) the Jewish customs of purifying (II. 6), of excommunicating (IX. 35), of preparing the Passover (XIX. 14), and of embalming (XIX. 39–40).

(d) Rabbinical ideas, such as those on Sabbath observance (V. 10, VII. 23, IX. 16), and pre-natal sin (IX. 2–3).

(e) the geography of Palestine. Mention is made of "Bethany beyond Jordan" (I. 28), "Cana of Galilee" (II. 1), "a city of Samaria, called Sychar" (IV. 5), "Aenon near to Salim" (III. 23), and "a city called Ephraim" (XI. 54).

(f) the city of Jerusalem. He refers to a pool by the sheep-gate, "which is called in Hebrew, Bethesda, having five porches" (V. 2), "the treasury" in the Temple (VIII. 20), "the pool of Siloam" (IX. 7), "the brook Kidron" (XVIII. 1), and "a place called The Pavement, but in Hebrew, Gabbatha" (XIX. 13).

(g) on certain points, as we shall see, such as the duration of Jesus' ministry, the number of visits to Jerusalem, and the date of the Last Supper, the author's knowledge seems superior to that of the Synoptists.

Opposition to Traditional View. Many competent critics deny Johannine authorship, mainly on the following grounds:

(1) There is evidence for believing that the Apostle John was martyred with his brother James in Jerusalem many years

before the Fourth Gospel is supposed to have been written. The passage in "Mark" x. 39, predicting the death of James and John, is only intelligible on the assumption that the latter had died before the Gospel was written. In a seventh- or eighth-century Epitome of the History of Philip of Side, a Church historian of the fifth century (c. A.D. 410), we read: "Papias in his second book says that John the Divine and James his brother were killed by the Jews." George Hamartolus, a ninth-century chronographer, quotes Papias as saying that John "was killed by the Jews, thus plainly fulfilling along with his brother the prophecy of Christ concerning them and their own confession and common agreement concerning him". A Syriac Calendar (c. A.D. 410) commemorates the death of James and John on the same day—December 27th. A Latin Calendar of Carthage (early ninth century) has for December 27th, the Feast of "St. John the Baptist and of St. James whom Herod slew". It is probable that the Feast was originally that of St. John and St. James, since the Baptist had his own separate feast in the same Calendar on December 24th.

The evidence for John's early death is considerable but not conclusive. The passage in "Mark" x. 39 has undergone certain modifications in the Synoptic Gospels: Matthew makes no mention of the "baptism" while Luke omits the incident altogether. Papias has probably been wrongly reported for Philip of Side was a notoriously inaccurate historian. The martyrologies belong to a time when all the Apostles were supposed to have suffered martyrdom and are therefore of little value. John at any rate was not killed at the same time as his brother James, since Paul mentions him as alive in "Galatians" II. 9, but Papias' alleged statement does not necessarily mean that their martyrdom was simultaneous.

(2) The tradition that John resided at Ephesus and lived there to an advanced age has no foundation in fact. "Acts" is silent on the subject. Paul, in his farewell speech to the Ephesian elders, warns them that after his departure

"grievous wolves shall enter in among you, not sparing the flock" (Acts xx. 29). The Apostle would hardly have used such words had he known that John was residing at Ephesus. Clement of Rome intervened in the affairs of the church at Corinth, when Ephesus was nearer and apparently had an important leader of the Church residing there. Ignatius of Antioch, in a letter to the Ephesian Christians, reminds them of what Paul had done for them but makes no allusion to John. The silence of Ignatius suggests that the only John residing at Ephesus was John the Elder.

The evidence adduced against the tradition of John's residence at Ephesus though not negligible, is not conclusive. The fact of his residence there is attested by at least five different writers of the second century—Irenaeus, Clement of Alexandria, Hegesippus, Polycrates, and the author of the Muratorian Fragment. The tradition is so strong and widespread that it cannot be ignored; but it may well be that it arose from a confusion between John the Apostle and John the Elder, and may all be derived from a common source. No writer later than Papias actually met John the Apostle, even if Papias did, and we have no record of any person who met him at Ephesus.

(3) A study of contemporary writings, such as those of Ignatius of Antioch, Polycarp, and Justin Martyr, show that the Fourth Gospel was known and used quite early in the second century but without authentication of authorship. The fact that it was not fully recognized as of apostolic origin until about A.D. 170 suggests that doubts had been cast upon its apostolicity from the beginning. The view that the Johannine authorship was acknowledged from about A.D. 170 by practically the whole of the Church cannot be accepted. The reference to the Gospel in the Muratorian Fragment is strongly apologetic and reads like a defence of the Gospel against the charge that it could not be of apostolic origin on account of its wide divergence from the other Gospels. About A.D. 175 there existed in

Rome a small sect, called the "Alogi", the members of which refused to accept the Logos doctrine of John and rejected his Gospel, attributing it to the Gnostic Cerinthus. Hippolytus, a Roman theologian (c. A.D. 190–235), wrote a "Defence of the Gospel and Apocalypse of John", in answer to an attack made on the two books by the presbyter Gaius. The opposition had come, not from heretics outside the Church but from orthodox circles in Rome.

(4) From Mark's Gospel we get a very strong impression that John the Apostle was a Galilean, and in "Acts" Luke affirms this of all the Apostles (II. 7). But the fact that all the incidents mentioned in "John", which are not taken from "Mark", except the Marriage at Cana, took place in or near Jerusalem, and the writer's detailed knowledge of Jerusalem and the area immediately round it, combined with the absence of any such knowledge of Galilee, suggest that the writer was a Jew who had lived his early life in Jerusalem.

Summing up we conclude that the cumulative effect of all the evidence adduced to prove (1) that John did not reside at Ephesus, (2) that he did not live to an advanced age, and (3) that he did not write the Gospel attributed to him, is considerable but not decisive.

A Modern View. There is to-day a wide acceptance of the view that the Gospel was written by John the Elder of Ephesus. It is practically certain that the three Epistles of John are written by the same author. In the second and third Epistles the author calls himself the "Elder". Irenaeus tells us that in his youth in Asia Minor he used to listen to Polycarp, Bishop of Smyrna, who described his relations "with John and others who had seen the Lord". Irenaeus identifies John with the Apostle, and states that he survived in Ephesus until after the accession of the Emperor Trajan (A.D. 98). It is thought that he confused John the Elder, who wrote the Gospel, with the Apostle, and that this mistake accounts for the early Church tradition.

The authorship of the Gospel cannot be proved, but if an author must be named, we incline to the view that it was written by John the Elder, a disciple of John, or by a group of his disciples in Ephesus.

Comparison of the Fourth and Synoptic Gospels

A comparison of the Fourth Gospel with the Synoptic Gospels reveals both similarities and differences. Some of the differences can be harmonized, but when such reconciliation is impossible we must recognize that one or the other statement must be inaccurate, but at the same time we must not assume that the Synoptics must necessarily be correct and the Fourth Gospel wrong.

Similarities. The Fourth Gospel reproduces the main features of the Synoptic record. We have the story of John the Baptist, the Cleansing of the Temple, the Healing of the Nobleman's Son, the beginning of a period of controversy between Jesus and His enemies, the Feeding of the Five Thousand, the Walking on the Sea, the Anointing by a Woman, the Triumphal Entry into Jerusalem, the Passion, and the Resurrection. It is generally agreed that John was familiar with "Mark", for in his Gospel he reproduces a number of his peculiar phrases. This dependence may be seen by comparing Jn. v. 8–9 with Mk. ii. 11–12; Jn. vi. 7 with Mk. vi. 37; Jn. xii. 3–5 with Mk. xiv. 3 and 5; Jn. xiv. 31 with Mk. xiv. 42; Jn. xviii. 18 with Mk. xiv. 54; Jn. xviii. 39 with Mk. xv. 9. Where there is a verbal variation John usually agrees with "Mark" as against "Matthew" and "Luke". We may reasonably assume that John was familiar with "Luke" because of the close similarity between the two Gospels of the accounts of Martha and Mary, and of the Passion, and because of the fact that both Gospels place the post-Resurrection appearances to the disciples at Jerusalem, not as do Mark and Matthew, in Galilee. The evidence for John's use of "Matthew" is inconclusive: there are a few minor agreements of "Matthew" and "John", but they have no significance. The probability is that he either had no knowledge of it or ignored it on account of the Judaistic and Apocalyptic outlook.

Differences

These may be considered under the two headings of (1) differences regarding particular events, and (2) what is more important, differences of representation of Christ's person and teaching. The importance to the critic of deciding on the author's correctness regarding particular events is that it is easier to come to an unbiased conclusion on the reliability of his information on such matters: if he is reliable on them, we must take more seriously the likelihood of his reliability on the more important matters.

1. (*a*) *The Baptist's Ministry.* According to the Synoptic Gospels the Baptist's ministry is ended before Jesus' Ministry begins, whereas in "John" they overlap. John has modified the Synoptic narrative in order to emphasize the passing over of the disciples from the Baptist to Jesus. On the trustworthiness of this account we must remember that Matthew and Luke are merely repeating "Mark" and that Mark's account of the ministry begins with the call of Peter. What is definitely stated is that the Galilean ministry began after the arrest of the Baptist and a previous Judaean ministry is highly probable. It is very reasonable to assume that the first disciples had become acquainted with Jesus before their call, so that John's representation of them as followers of the Baptist is most probable. But John is clearly wrong in assuming that they recognized Him as the Messiah: on that point Peter must surely be right that his confession shortly before the Transfiguration was the first such confession. On the other hand, the idea may have occurred to them as a possibility.

(*b*) *Scene of Jesus' Ministry.* The Synoptic Gospels place Jesus' ministry chiefly in Galilee, with a few journeys outside the district and with the last week in Jerusalem, while the incidents and teaching which John records are mainly in and about Jerusalem and took place when Jesus visited Jerusalem for feasts. By recording the occasion of every such visit, John virtually accepts the Synoptists' view that the greater part of the ministry was in Galilee, but he records little of it. There are, however, indications in the other Gospels that Jesus had visited Judaea and Jerusalem before His last visit at the close of His ministry. In "Luke" IV. 44 we read that He went preaching through the synagogues of Judaea;[1] the scribes and the Pharisees would not have travelled from Judaea to Galilee had He not taught in Jerusalem. We infer from His lament over the city that He had visited it many times, and from His triumphal entry that He was well known there. The two accounts are therefore complementary, not contradictory, and can best be explained by the place of origin of the writers. The Synoptic accounts go back to Peter, a Galilean, who probably did not accompany Jesus on these visits to feasts, since he seems to have been unacquainted with His friends there—the man who was to lend the ass (Mk. XI. 2–5) and the owner of the upper room (Mk. XIV. 13–15). The author of the "Gospel according to John" was probably an inhabitant of Jerusalem who could have been little more than a boy at the time, and saw and heard Jesus only on the occasions of His visits to the Holy City.

(c) *Duration of Jesus' Ministry.* It is often thought that the Synoptic Gospels assume a ministry of not more than a year, while in John it includes three Passovers (II. 13, VI. 4, XII. 1) and must have lasted over two years. In fact the Synoptic Gospels are quite silent on the point; it probably never occurred to them to inquire. Chronology is considered by the professional historian as essential to History; but neither Peter nor Mark was a trained historian. There are hints, however, in the Synoptic accounts that the ministry lasted longer than a year. In "Mark" II. 33 the mention of the cornfields shows that the time is early summer, but in "Mark" VI. 39 the reference to the "green grass" shows that it is the spring of the following year. A two and a half years' Ministry would agree better with the chronology of the life of Christ, who was born in the reign of Herod the Great (d. 4 B.C.), was about thirty years old when He began to preach (Luke III. 23), and was crucified about A.D. 29 or 30 (according to patristic tradition and modern reckoning).

[1] The Authorized and Revised Versions of the Bible describe Jesus as preaching in the synagogues of Galilee; but some of the best MSS., including B, ℵ, and C, read "of Judaea", and these are followed by Weymouth in his *New Testament in Modern Speech*, and by Moffatt in *A New Translation of the Bible*. See McNeile, *Introduction to the New Testament*, 1927, p. 258.

(d) *Date of Last Supper.* According to the Synoptic Gospels the Last Supper is the Passover Meal, while John puts it on the eve of the Passover. Here we have a definite contradiction and John is probably correct. The Paschal lambs would be slain on the afternoon of the 14th of the month Nisam, that they might be eaten after sunset the same evening, after which all Jews would keep the next twenty-four hours with Sabbatical rigour. It is unlikely that the arrest, trial, and crucifixion of Jesus would have taken place within that period. The correctness of the date is indirectly confirmed by Paul's representation of Christ as the Passover (1 Cor. v. 7).

(e) *Date of Cleansing of the Temple.* The Synoptic Gospels place the Cleansing of the Temple at the close of the Ministry, and make it the immediate cause of the arrest of Jesus: in the Fourth Gospel it is placed at the commencement of the Ministry, and its place is taken by the Raising of Lazarus, which rouses the authorities to take action. Here it is impossible to decide which is right. On the one hand the Synoptists may have been led, through their belief that there was no Jerusalem ministry prior to the last week, to place both the Cleansing of the Temple and the Teaching given in "Mark" XI. 27–XII. 44 in the last week because they took place in Jerusalem: on the other hand John may have been influenced by his desire to secure a suitable introduction to his theme that the new Gospel is to supersede the old religion typified by the Temple. It is to be noted that John denies that Jesus did any public teaching during the last week (XI. 54–57), and must be assumed to be deliberately correcting Mark when he makes this assertion.

(f) *Omissions.* The Fourth Gospel is silent on certain incidents mentioned in the other Gospels. There is, for example, no mention of the Virgin Birth, the Baptism, the Temptation, the Transfiguration, the Institution of the Lord's Supper, the Agony in the Garden, and the Ascension. There is no reference to the Virgin Birth because Jesus is the Logos incarnate. "The Evangelist shrank from any theory of His origin that might impair the central idea of full activity, from the beginning of His work to the end."[1] The Baptism, Temptation, and Agony

---

[1] E. F. Scott, *The Fourth Gospel*, 1908, p. 187.

might be interpreted as weakness or subordination in Jesus who was the Eternal Son of God: the Transfiguration is omitted because His whole life was a continual transfiguration. The omission of the Institution of the Lord's Supper may have been due to two reasons. The Evangelist had already given His teaching on the Sacrament as a sequel to the Feeding of the Five Thousand: but by substituting the Feet-Washing he wishes to show that the last bequest of Jesus to His disciples was not a ritual observance but an exhortation to mutual love and service. There is no Ascension because Jesus had never ceased to be the Son of God and therefore had no need of a return to the Father.

(g) *Additions.* There are several incidents in the Fourth Gospel which have no parallels in the other Gospels. The latter make no mention of the Miracle at Cana (II. 1–11), the Conversation with Nicodemus (III. 1–21) and the Woman of Samaria (IV. 1–29), the Healing of the Paralytic at the Pool of Bethesda (V. 1–15), the Man Born Blind (IX. 1–38), and the Raising of Lazarus (XI. 1–44). It may be, however, that some of them are connected. The story of Nicodemus may be another version of the Rich Young Ruler (Mk. x. 17–22), the Paralytic of the Pool of Bethesda may be identified with the Paralytic of Capernaum (Mk. II. 1–12), and the Man Born Blind with Bartimaeus (Mk. x. 46–52), while the Miracle of Cana may have some connection with the words of Jesus in "Mark" II. 19: "Can the sons of the bride-chamber fast, while the bridegroom is with them? as long as they have the bridegroom with them, they cannot fast."

(h) *Controversy with the Jews.* According to the Synoptic Gospels the chief enemies of Christ are the scribes and Pharisees who object to His attitude towards the Law and to His Messianic claims. In the Fourth Gospel the opposition comes from the Jews as a whole, while controversy rages round the questions of His unity with God, His pre-existence, the partaking of His flesh and blood, and the apparent failure of His mission. The conditions described by the Fourth Evangelist are not those which prevailed during the Lord's earthly Ministry, but those which existed at the time when he wrote his

Gospel. It is a picture of the conflict of the Christian Church of his own day with Judaism.

2. We turn now to the differences of representation of the person and teaching of Jesus.

(a) *The Person of Jesus*. The person of Jesus portrayed in the Fourth Gospel is apparently quite different from that portrayed in the other Gospels. In the latter He is set forth as a great prophet, and teacher, the friend of publicans and sinners: in the former He is still human—He sits weary by the well (IV. 6), weeps by the grave of Lazarus (XI. 35), is troubled in soul (XII. 27), is distressed by the treachery of His false disciple (XIII. 21), and thirsts on the cross (XIX. 28)—but His humanity is not stressed. He is an aloof, austere, and somewhat inhuman figure. There are no Birth and Infancy narratives; He does not increase in wisdom and stature, nor does He submit to the baptism of repentence for the remission of sins. He experiences no temptation in the wilderness, and instead of disclaiming the appellation of "good" challenges His opponents with the words: "Which of you convicteth me of sin?" (VIII. 46). He does not seek strength and guidance in prayer. Judas is chosen, not because He considers him suitable for the work of an apostle, but in order that he might betray Him: in the Garden of Gethsemane there is no cry of agony but only the quiet recognition that His hour has come. He is portrayed, not as the human Jesus of the Synoptic Gospels, but in His eternal character as the Son of God. "Before Abraham was," He says, "I am" (VIII. 58). In Him the "Logos" has become flesh (I. 14); He is sent by the Father to be the Saviour of the world (VIII. 16); to see the Son is to see the Father (XIV. 9), and to know the Son is to know the Father also (XIV. 7). He is the Source and Giver of life eternal (V. 40, VI. 33, X. 28), the true Bread from heaven, giving life to the world (VI. 32, 51). He is the proper object of worship; to refuse to honour the Son is to refuse to honour the Father which sent Him (V. 23). He is subject to no external force; He chooses His own time and lays down His life of His own accord. "Therefore doth the Father love me, because I lay down my life, that I may take it again. No one taketh it away from me, but I lay it down of myself.

I have power to lay it down, and I have power to take it again" (x. 17–18). The cry, "It is finished", signalizes the triumphant accomplishment of His work on earth (xix. 30).

In considering the wide divergence between the Synoptic Gospels and the Fourth Gospel as regards the character of Jesus, we must not forget that His character is too great for any one person to comprehend. Writers may show us different aspects of His character, but the resultant portrait will only be a partial revelation of Him in whom "dwelleth all the fulness of the Godhead bodily" (Col. ii. 9). Just as Plato saw in Socrates what was invisible to Xenophon, so John, after years of meditation discovered and revealed a side of the character of Jesus which the Synoptists either ignored or but dimly apprehended owing to their lack of spiritual insight. The Synoptists are largely chroniclers of events in the life of Jesus, while John is the historian of His inner consciousness. There may be chronological differences in the two accounts, as for example in the time of the Cleansing of the Temple and the date of the Crucifixion, but there are no essential differences in the portrayal of His character. The Jesus of John is not the creation of his imagination, but the same historical figure which the Synoptists portray in their Gospels, but while the latter see Him as a great prophet, teacher, healer, and friend of man, the former is lost in wonder at the glory of Him whom he now recognizes as "the only begotten from the Father, full of grace and truth" (i. 14). He who in the Synoptic Gospels is portrayed as the friend of children, of the poor, and of the outcast, who gives us the Parables of the Prodigal Son and the Good Samaritan, is fundamentally the same person as He who in the Fourth Gospel sits weary on the well at Sychar and says to the woman of Samaria, "If thou knewest the gift of God, and who it is that saith to thee, Give me to drink; thou wouldest have asked of him, and he would have given thee living water" (iv. 10); and who says to His disciples: "Ye are my friends, if ye do the things which I command you. No longer do I call you servants; for the servant knoweth not what his lord doeth: but I have called you friends; for all things that I heard from my Father I have made known unto you" (xv. 14–15).

When we read in the Synoptic Gospels of Him who spoke with authority, healed the sick, and cast out devils, we know that it is the same person who in the Fourth Gospel is described as the "Word" made flesh, the Source and Giver of all life (I. 1–4), the Light of the World (IX. 5), the Truth and the Way to the Father (XIV. 6).

(b) *The Teaching of Jesus.* We find a striking difference in the content of the teaching of Jesus. In the Synoptic Gospels the chief themes are the Kingdom of God, the forgiveness of sin, and the relation of man to God and to his fellow men. In the Fourth Gospel He does not deal with the Kingdom of God, but is represented as being absorbed in philosophical and theological problems dealing especially with the nature of His own person and with His relationship to the Father. The Evangelist was no doubt familiar with the simpler and more popular teaching of Jesus as recorded in the Synoptic Gospels, but omitted it in order to concentrate upon His divinity. After many years of meditation and communion with his Master, he saw with a clearer vision the deep spiritual significance of certain aspects of His teaching which the other Evangelists had ignored or barely touched upon. The doctrine of the divinity of Jesus is not the invention of John; it is found in the Synoptic Gospels though it is not stressed. Jesus speaks with authority, has power over nature, disease, and death, and claims to forgive sins, to heal all the woes of the world, and to be the final judge of mankind. In the Temptation, quoted by Matthew and Luke, the repetition of the words, "If thou art the Son of God" (Mt. IV., Lk. IV.), shows that He is conscious of His unique filial relationship to the Father, while the whole of the Christology of the Fourth Gospel is summed up in the words: "All things have been delivered unto me of my Father: and no one knoweth the Son, save the Father; neither doth any know the Father, save the Son, and he to whomsoever the Son willeth to reveal him" (Mt. XI. 27).

Miracles. In his attitude to Miracles John presents an interesting contrast to the Synoptists. To reveal the miraculous power of Jesus he prefers miracles which seem to present peculiar difficulties, such as nature miracles like those of turning water into wine, feeding the multitude, and walking on the sea. To heighten the miraculous elements he mentions those which make the performance of the miracle more difficult. The paralytic has been ill thirty-eight years, the blind man has been blind from his birth, and Lazarus has been in the grave four days. The miracles in the Synoptic Gospels are works of mercy, while in John they are not only works of mercy but also signs of the divine nature of Jesus. The Feeding of the Five Thousand is a sign of the spiritual food which Jesus gives to men; the Healing of the Cripple on the Sabbath Day at Jerusalem is not only an act of mercy, but a sign that He is at work in the world, and that He must do the works of the Father who sent Him. The Healing of the Blind Man is a sign that He is the light of the world, while the Raising of Lazarus is a manifestation of the. principle that He is the Resurrection and the Life. In almost every case the account of the miracle is followed by a discourse expounding the spiritual truth of which the miracle is the outward and visible sign.

Historically, we feel that the Synoptists must be right. The disciples were so overwhelmed by wonder at Jesus' powers that they could never have attributed to Him the statement that "no sign shall be given to this generation" or have regarded the idea of His casting Himself from the pinnacle of the Temple as an evil suggestion of the devil, if that had not been Jesus' own attitude. To Jesus the miracles were works of mercy, not "signs", as John calls them. There is, however, nothing wrong in using them as illustrations, or, as it were, as texts for sermons, as John does, if we regard the Gospel, not as a new biography but as a meditation on the existing biographies.

Parables. In the Synoptic Gospels Jesus speaks with a wealth of parables, but in the Fourth Gospel they are absent, and their place is taken by allegories like those of the Good Shepherd (x. 7–16) and the Vine (xv. 1–8). The Evangelist omits the parables because he believes that they were intended to veil the true meaning of Jesus, while he himself wrote to discover the truth. "These things have I spoken unto you in proverbs: the hour cometh, when I shall no more speak unto you in proverbs, but shall tell you plainly of the Father" (xvi. 25).

The Messianic Claim. Another important difference is that in the Synoptic Gospels Peter is the first human being to recognize Jesus' Messiahship, just before the Transfiguration, whereas in "John", Jesus claims it from the very first and the Apostles recognize it. He certainly gives the impression of intending to correct the Synoptists on this point.

The matter is much more intricate than either John or readers of the New Testament till recent times had realized. The fusion of the ideas "Messiah", "Son of man", "Son of God", and "Suffering Servant", was so complete in Christian minds by the time John wrote that to assert any one of these claims was to assert all; and so it has remained to modern times, when the discovery of extra-canonical apocalyptic literature and a changed attitude towards the interpretation of Old Testament prophecy has made us realize that to Jesus' Jewish contemporaries each of these titles had a somewhat different meaning, and in particular that the Suffering Servant was never identified with any of the others. What the Synoptists assert is that Jesus regularly used the title of the "Son of man",[1] that at the Baptism and Transfiguration God called Him His Son, but that He did not assert His Messiahship even to the

[1] The term "Son of man" is usually supposed by experts on Jewish apocalyptic literature to betoken a pre-existent heavenly being, who would introduce the final rule of the saints. This, of course, is a misunderstanding of the meaning of the phrase in "Daniel" VII. 18, where "like a son of man" is merely a contrast to the previous rulers who are represented as like beasts (lion, bear, leopard), and stands for Israel, as the beasts do for Babylon and the other empires which succeeded it. The Apocalyptic view is exhibited most fully in the so-called "Book of Enoch".

Professor T. W. Manson is alone in supposing that in the Gospels it is used, not of an individual but of a community, even if that community is best represented by an individual. He has considerably modified his views; his latest presentation is in *The Bulletin of the Rylands Library*, vol. XXXII (1949–50), pp. 171–93. His main position is that Jesus knew the phrase only in "Daniel", and was unaware of "Enoch", and used the phrase in Daniel's original sense. It is very hard to believe that Jesus was unaware of the widespread interest in Apocalyptic in the religious thought of His time, and of the ideas expressed in "Enoch", even if He had not actually read the book, especially as it is known to several New Testament writers (1 Peter III. 19–20, Jude 14–15, Rev. 1. 14. "His head and his hair were white as wool" is part of Enoch's actual account of the "Son of man"). As the phrase is also frequently used in the Old Testament to denote merely "a man", Jesus may have sometimes used it in this sense, where the Evangelists assume that He is using it in the technical sense; but, as the phrase in this latter sense is in the New Testament only used in the discourses of Jesus Himself, it is clear that it was not a phrase of later Christianity which was falsely attributed to Jesus, since later Christianity fully identified the "Son of man" with the "Messiah", whereas in the Synoptic Gospels Jesus is represented as using the phrase the "Son of man" but not publicly proclaiming His Messiahship till the end.

Twelve till just before the Transfiguration or publicly till His trial. This account is quite intelligible because the ordinary idea of the Messiah was of a conquering earthly monarch and, in the account of the Temptation, Jesus is said to have considered this idea and set it aside as a temptation of the devil. From the moment Jesus accepts the title from Peter He teaches the identity of the Messiah with the servant who was to suffer. If then we do not think of words but of meaning, John, when he recounts how the multitude, after the miraculous feeding, wished to make Jesus a king and He refused, is in effect stating that He denied Messiahship in the sense in which it was popularly understood; while the Synoptists acknowledge that the reply to the messengers of the Baptist who asked whether He was "He that should come" is a virtual acceptance of Messiahship in a sense in which He interprets Old Testament prophecy. John then is not putting forward a different view as regards what Jesus claimed, though he is mistaken as regards the actual language in which He claimed it.

Form of the Teaching. The language of Jesus in the Synoptic Gospels is simple, clear, vivid, and challenging, while in the Fourth Gospel we have long discourses in a style that closely resembles that of the author himself. Other characters like Nathanael, Nicodemus, Martha, and Mary speak in the same strain. These discourses are sometimes described as the free inventions of the author or as authentic utterances derived from a source now lost to us; but it is best to regard them as developments of sayings of Jesus preserved in the Synoptics. They are the fruit of many years of meditation and deep religious experience, but meditations and sayings are so intermingled that it is impossible to separate them, though at times we can hear the authentic words of Jesus Himself, as in the following: "Except a man be born anew, he cannot see the kingdom of God" (III. 3); "I am the bread of life" (VI. 35); "I am the light of the world" (IX. 5); "He that loveth his life loseth it; and he that hateth his life in this world shall keep it unto life eternal" (XII. 25). The discourses may be likened to the Targums-Aramaic translations of the Hebrew Scriptures and a running commentary upon them.

CHAPTER X

THE GOSPEL ACCORDING TO JOHN
(continued)
Aims

Interpretative. The Fourth Gospel was written to interpret Christianity to a changing world. It appeared at a critical period in the history of the Christian Church. The original Apostles and the first converts had passed or were passing away, and their places had been taken by men generally inferior in intellect, in powers of leadership, and in spirituality. The hope of a speedy return of Christ to inaugurate His kingdom on the earth had practically vanished, and men realized that they would have to live in the world as it was. The first wave of enthusiasm, roused at Pentecost, had spent its force, and the quickening power of the Holy Spirit was no longer experienced as in the early days. The Church was engaged in the task of organization, and what had been a living faith was beginning to harden into formalism and to show signs of degenerating into superstition. Finally the figure of Christ had become a dim memory, and there was a danger that Christianity might in time become separated from its Founder and sink into a barren philosophy or a lifeless tradition, without any power to influence the world.

The author of the Fourth Gospel, realizing that Christianity could not survive as a living power without the inspiration of the personality of its Founder at the centre of it, called the Church of his own day back to the Jesus of history, who had actually lived and died among men and over whom Death had no dominion. That same historical figure was not only the Messiah of Jewish expectation, but also the glorified Christ of religious experience with whom they could enjoy a closer fellowship than was possible in the days of His flesh. So he writes: "Many other signs therefore did Jesus in the presence of the disciples, which are not written in this book: but these are written, that ye may believe that Jesus is the Christ, the Son of God; and that believing ye may have life in his name" (xx. 30–31).

John interprets Christianity in the light of Paul's teaching. This is not surprising, since Paul's influence was strong in the Christian Church; and Ephesus, from which the Gospel emanated, had been one of his chief centres of missionary activity. The author borrows most of his main conceptions from Paul and develops or modifies them in the light of his own religious experience. He shares with Paul the belief in the love of God, in the glorified Christ of religious experience, in union with Christ, in the spiritual freedom of all believers, and in the universality of the Gospel. Primitive Christian views on the Second Coming, the Resurrection, and the Judgment, accepted by the Synoptists and described by Paul in the traditional language of Apocalyptic, are spiritualized. The Second Coming is identified with the coming of the Holy Spirit into the hearts of men. "Nevertheless I tell you the truth; It is expedient for you that I go away: for if I go not away, the Comforter will not come unto you; but if I go, I will send him unto you" (xvi. 7). The Resurrection takes place when a man is "born again" and passes from death to life: the Judgment is not an event in time but a process continually going on here and now as men accept or reject Christ. His judgment is involuntary, for men by their attitude to Him are compelled to pass judgment upon themselves. "This is the judgement, that the light is come into the world, and men loved the darkness rather than the light; for their works were evil" (iii. 19). Though he has grasped the conception of a spiritual Resurrection and Judgment in the present, yet, strange to say, he retains his belief in a literal Resurrection and final Judgment at the "last day". For the Christian the "end" of all things will mean the completion of that which in principle he already possesses in this life. "Verily, verily, I say unto you, The hour cometh, and now is, when the dead shall hear the voice of the Son of God; and they that hear shall live. For as the Father hath life in himself, even so gave he to the Son also to have life in himself: and he gave him authority to execute judgement, because he is the Son of man.

164

Marvel not at this: for the hour cometh, in which all that are in the tombs shall hear his voice, and shall come forth; they that have done good, unto the resurrection of life; and they that have done ill, unto the resurrection of judgement" (v. 25–29). The language of the Fourth Gospel is sometimes reminiscent of that of Paul. In Chapter VIII. 33–39 we have a number of ideas obviously derived from Paul. The sayings, "Every one that committeth sin is the bondservant of sin. And the bondservant abideth not in the house for ever: the son abideth for ever"; and, "If therefore the Son shall make you free, ye shall be free indeed", have their parallels in the Epistles. (Cf. Rom. VI. 16–23; Gal. IV. 30–31, V. 1.)

A comparison of the two types of teaching reveal differences as well as similarities. The two Apostles, for example, hold different views on the meaning of sin, faith, and the cross, but after allowing for such differences, we may say that John builds on the foundations laid by Paul.

Finally John seeks to interpret Christianity in terms which the Graeco-Roman world could understand. Hitherto the Gospel had been presented in terms which were fundamentally Jewish. Even Paul's system, in spite of the fact that he used terms drawn from Greek philosophy and the Mystery Religions, is based on Judaism. To the Greek world John's message is that Christianity is the one true philosophy. The Jewish Messianic idea is replaced by that of the "Logos", a Stoic conception, utilized by Philo, the Jewish philosopher of Alexandria, as a means of effecting a synthesis between the Jewish conception of God as personal and transcendant with the Greek idea of a universal reason diffused through all things. The conception of the incarnate "Logos" would satisfy the Greek mind, while the Jew would find it possible to differentiate between God and the "Logos" within the limits of monotheism (see pp. 174–5 on the "Logos"). "John's great achievement was to transplant the Gospel of Jesus into a new soil before its roots had time to wither."[1]

Polemical Aims. Its hostility to the Jews is one of the most marked features of the Gospel. By the end of the first century

[1] W. Manson, *The Incarnate Glory*, p. 37.

Christianity and Judaism were in open conflict with each other. No opportunity was lost by the orthodox Jews in their endeavour to undermine the Christian Church. Any Jew who expressed the belief that Jesus was the Messiah was excommunicated, and a prayer against those who became Christians was introduced into the Synagogue worship. The orthodox Jews declared that the worship of Jesus meant the worship of two Gods; so far from being divine He was an ignorant man from an obscure village in Galilee. His vaunted miracles had been performed before an ignorant and credulous peasantry. He made little impression during His lifetime, and what followers He made were drawn from the ignorant multitude. He, who claimed to be the Messiah, had been betrayed by one of His own followers and had been condemned to death, not only by the Jewish Sanhedrin, but also by the impartial court of the Roman procurator.

A large section of the Fourth Gospel (v.–xii.) is taken up with the conflict of Jesus with the unbelieving Jews, whose presence is felt throughout the book. John is at pains to defend Jesus from their misrepresentations. Stress is laid upon His "oneness" with the Father. He was not an unknown, ignorant man who took advantage of the credulity of the Galilean peasants, but a well-known teacher who had taught in Jerusalem, the headquarters of the national religion. The action of Judas was due to the fact that Jesus fore-knew and permitted the betrayal. Pilate, so far from condemning Him, had declared Him to be innocent. His death on the cross was a self-determined act, necessary to His glorification.

It is possible that the Gospel is also a defence of Christianity against the followers of John the Baptist. The author deliberately subordinates the Baptist to Jesus. In the Synoptic Gospels the former is a religious reformer and a preacher of righteousness and of good works; but in the Fourth Gospel he is merely a witness of the "Light", and having borne his witness he is content to disappear. He acknowledges his own inferiority in the words: "He must increase, but I must decrease" (iii. 30). We learn from "Acts" xviii. 25, and xix. 3–4, that there was a party of the Baptist at Ephesus, while in the

"Clementine Recognitions", which dates perhaps from the early third century, we read, "Some even of the disciples of John, who seem to be great ones, have separated themselves and proclaimed their own master as Christ".

John also is attempting to counteract certain materialistic views connected with the sacraments of Baptism and the Lord's Supper, which had been brought into the Church by converts from the Mystery Religions, which had become very popular in the Graeco-Roman Empire. Each Mystery Cult had a redeemer god in whose name candidates were admitted after a solemn ceremony of initiation, which included baptism and participation in a sacred meal, after which they were reborn into eternal life. The virtue of the rite lay, not in the spiritual reality of which the symbol was merely the outward and visible sign, but in the symbol itself, while its validity depended, not on the receptivity of the worshipper, but on the correct performance of the ritual. These Mystery Religions were crudely materialistic and appealed to men of that day who could not conceive of a religion without magical rites.

To John Christianity is also a sacramental religion, salvation depending upon the observance of the ordinances of Baptism and the Lord's Supper. It is, however, the spiritual reality of the sacrament that is of supreme importance and not the outward rite. In the conversation of Jesus with Nicodemus, John guards against the materialistic view of Baptism. Both "Water" and "Spirit" are necessary to the efficacy of the sacrament, but it is the "Spirit" that is the regenerating power in the soul. "Except a man be born of water and the Spirit, he cannot enter into the kingdom of God" (III. 5). Similarly in the discourse on the "Bread of Life" the teaching is that it is necessary to eat the flesh and drink the blood of the Son of man in order to gain Life. Jesus is represented as saying, "Except ye eat the flesh of the Son of man and drink his blood, ye have not life in yourselves. He that eateth my flesh and drinketh my blood hath eternal life" (VI. 53–54). We are, however, not to interpret the words in a literal and material sense, for "It is the spirit that quickeneth; the flesh profiteth nothing: the words that I have spoken unto you are spirit, and are life" (VI. 63).

"The power that works in the Sacrament does not reside in the flesh, in the material bread, but in the Spirit of the Risen Christ. Spirit alone can communicate life. The weak and transient 'flesh' is incapable of doing it. Christ is the bread. He is not the wafer. He is present in the heart of the communicant, not in the material bread."[1]

The Fourth Gospel is to some extent a protest against the Gnostic heresy. Gnosticism was divided into many sects and presented a great variety of forms. Perhaps its main conception was the inherent evil of the world, including man. Since the world was evil the creator could not have been the "good God", but an inferior and imperfect being—the demi-urge. This being was the God of the Old Testament and was therefore to be rejected. A "good God" could not enter into relations with man who was evil: they therefore set up a whole hierarchy of semi-divine mediators between God and man. Since the body was evil, Christ could not have had a real incarnation: His body was either the temporary instrument of a Divine Spirit which left it before death, or a mere illusion. Salvation depended upon the possession of a secret knowledge, supposed to have been imparted by Christ to the Apostles, and passed on to their more intimate disciples. The spiritual enlightenment which would follow would bring them into communion with the "good God". Salvation was the exclusive privilege of an intellectual minority.

John, with his sharp division between good and evil, the flesh and the spirit, with his insistence on the necessity of knowing God, and with a certain intellectualism in his conception of faith, was to some extent sympathetic towards Gnosticism. He was, however, opposed to its fundamental conceptions. He stresses the creation of the world by the divine "Word", and the reality of the incarnation. He accepts the Father of Jesus Christ as the God of Israel, reverences the prophets, and accepts their witness. No reference is made to the spiritual agencies which play an essential part in Gnosticism. Salvation is for all men and does not depend upon the possession of esoteric knowledge. To all men is given "the right

[1] McConnachie, *The Gospel of Life*, p. 71.

168

to become children of God" (I. 12). He carefully avoids the words "Wisdom", "Faith", and "Knowledge", except in their verbal forms, because of their Gnostic import.

Ecclesiastical Aims. The Church as an institution made a deep appeal to the Fourth Evangelist, and though he never mentions the word, it was never for long absent from his thoughts. His Gospel is in one aspect of it a protest against the conditions which prevailed in the Church in his own day and a vision of what might be. He seeks to extend its bounds, to spiritualize its worship and its doctrinal conceptions, to inspire its leaders with a nobler ideal, and altogether to deepen its spiritual life. Speaking as its representative he lays down the principles of the common faith, which have the sanction of the elders of Ephesus or perhaps of the members of the Johannine circle there. He conceives of the Church as a community of redeemed men and women, who are in the world but separate from it. The work of Christ is "to draw to Himself certain disciples out of the unbelieving mass and to consecrate them as a people apart—different in aims and character and destiny from their fellow men. They have special ties binding them to each other in which the world claims no part. The revelation made to them is unintelligible to the world. They exist in the world but are radically separate from it."[1]

Though the Church is a separate community it is universal in its scope. To those who receive Christ and believe on His name, He gives the right to become children of God (I. 12). Christ's preaching to the despised Samaritans (IV. 39–42) and His meeting with certain Greeks at Jerusalem are to John a foreshadowing of the time when the whole of mankind will acknowledge Him as Saviour. The time is ripe for a great ingathering of people of all nations into the Church. "Lift up your eyes, and look on the fields, that they are white already unto harvest" (IV. 35). By narrating the incidents of the Cleansing of the Temple and the Conversation with the Woman of Samaria, the Evangelist seeks to stress the spirituality of worship. The "Father's house" is not to be made a house of merchandise (II. 16): true worship is independent of time, or

[1] E. F. Scott, *The Fourth Gospel*, 1908, pp. 114 f.

place, or ritual. "Woman, believe me, the hour cometh, when neither in this mountain, nor in Jerusalem, shall ye worship the Father. Ye worship that which ye know not: we worship that which we know: for salvation is from the Jews. But the hour cometh, and now is, when the true worshippers shall worship the Father in spirit and truth" (IV. 21–23). He acknowledges the efficacy of the Sacraments of Baptism and the Lord's Supper, but teaches that the outward rites have no virtue in themselves but are merely symbols of an inner spiritual reality. Similarly the prevailing conceptions of the Second Coming, the Resurrection, and the Judgment are spiritualized. Finally, Christ is represented as denouncing unworthy leaders in the Church and as setting before them the example of the Good Shepherd (x. 1–16).

Language

The Gospel is written in correct Greek, but the style is not that of one who is writing his native tongue. Its limited vocabulary, poetic parallelisms, and especially its many Aramaisms, show it to be the work of a Jew who has not gained complete mastery over the Greek language. Like Mark he evidently thought in Aramaic and wrote in Greek. Owing to the strong Semitic colouring, Dr. Burney concludes that the Gospel is a Greek translation of an Aramaic original. In support of his argument he points, not only to its numerous Aramaisms, but also to several passages which are difficult or obscure in the Greek but which become perfectly intelligible on the assumption that they are mistranslations of an Aramaic original (e.g. I. 29, VII. 37–38, VIII. 56, XX. 2).[1] This theory, however, has not met with wide acceptance. The Gospel's dependence on the Greek Gospel of Mark would seem to weigh against the theory that it was originally written in Aramaic. Moreover, many of the Aramaisms can be otherwise explained. Some are constructions which are actually found in classical Greek, or were making their way into Hellenistic Greek, while certain of the mistranslations depend upon uncertain interpretations of the passages. Aramaisms occur

[1] C. C. Burney, *The Aramaic Origin of the Fourth Gospel*, 1922.

more frequently in the discourses than in the narrative portions, which suggest either that Our Lord's words were misunderstood by His hearers, or that the writer made use of an Aramaic collection of sayings.

Place and Date of Composition

Place. Tradition is practically unanimous that the Fourth Gospel was written at Ephesus. It must have emanated from some centre of learning where the members of the Church were familiar with Hellenic and Greek modes of thought. Most, if not all, of the traces of its existence are connected with Asia. The school of Christian thought that produced the Apocalypse, the Fourth Gospel, and the Johannine Epistles, had its home in Asia Minor. After the Fall of Jerusalem (A.D. 70) Ephesus became the centre of Christian life and activity. Dr. Burney suggests that it was written at Antioch-in-Syria, where there was a flourishing church, consisting of both Jews and Gentiles, and where the Apostle John is supposed to have resided before finally settling down at Ephesus.

Date. Since John made use of "Mark" (*c.* A.D. 65) and "Luke" (*c.* A.D. 75–85), the earliest date for the composition of the Fourth Gospel must be after the publication of "Luke". Ignatius does not actually quote from it but he was familiar with its characteristic ideas. "His whole outlook", says Canon Streeter, "and his theology have been profoundly influenced by the study of this Gospel."[1] Such being the case, the date cannot be later than about A.D. 115. The earliest evidence for the existence of the Gospel is probably to be found in a papyrus fragment in the John Rylands Library, Manchester, which was discovered in Egypt in 1920 and edited by C. H. Roberts in 1935. This contains parts of "John" xviii. 31–33, 37–38, and is claimed to be a fragment of a copy of the Gospel made between A.D. 130 and 150. Since some considerable time must have elapsed before it reached Egypt from Ephesus, it could hardly have been written later than about A.D. 110. We shall probably be safe in fixing the date of its composition within the period A.D. 90–110.

---

[1] Streeter, *The Four Gospels*, 1930, p. 455.

Characteristics

Son of God. The title "Son of God" or the "Son" is employed
in the Fourth Gospel to describe a unique relationship which
exists between Jesus and God. In the Synoptic Gospels stress is
laid upon the Fatherhood of God. He is not only the sovereign
ruler of mankind, demanding complete obedience to His will,
but also a loving Father who cares for all men. Jesus is not
concerned with His own "Sonship", but with God's Fatherhood and with its demand upon Him for the complete surrender
of His own will. His one great desire is that all men through
Him shall attain to a knowledge of the Father. Of the titles
which He uses or accepts for Himself, that of the "Son of God"
is to Him a synonym of the title Messiah as He conceived
Messiahship, that is, as excluding the popular idea of an earthly
conqueror, and adds nothing to what is involved in that title.
The only exception to this statement occurs in the passage:
"All things have been delivered unto me of my Father: and no
one knoweth the Son, save the Father; neither doth any know
the Father, save the Son, and he to whomsoever the Son
willeth to reveal him" (Mt. xi. 27=Lk. x. 22). Here we appear
to have a distinct claim to "Sonship" based on the assurance of
God's Fatherhood.

In the Fourth Gospel stress is laid upon the "Sonship" of
Jesus. He is the "Son of God" because He shares the divine
nature, being "the only begotten Son, which is in the bosom of
the Father" (i. 18). His life on earth is only a continuation of
a "Sonship" which has existed from all eternity (i. 1–2).
Though He has become "flesh", He is still omnipotent and
omniscient and claims from men the obedience due to God. He
is the complete revelation of the Father, "If ye had known me,
ye would have known my Father also: from henceforth ye know
him, and have seen him" (xiv. 7). While He is on the earth
His disciples cannot attain to a full knowledge of Him—but
when He returns in the Spirit, He will show them plainly the
Father (xvi. 25). Experience of the Fatherhood of God can
only be realized through union with the Son. "But as many as
received him, to them gave he the right to become children
of God, even to them that believe on his name" (i. 12).

"Sonship" implies complete obedience and surrender to the will of the Father. "I can of myself do nothing: as I hear, I judge: and my judgement is righteous; because I seek not mine own will, but the will of him that sent me" (v. 30).

Witness. Throughout the Gospel the claim of Jesus to "Sonship" is supported by the evidence of certain witnesses. The first witness of whom we read is John the Baptist who is sent from God "that he might bear witness of the light, that all might believe through him" (i. 7). His work consists in recognizing Jesus as the "Son of God" (i. 34). Since he is held in high esteem both by his own disciples and by the Jewish people, his testimony is valuable, but it is, after all, only that of a man. Jesus has greater evidence than that of John (v. 36).

There is the witness of the followers of Jesus. Andrew, after spending a day with Him, finds his brother Peter and says: "We have found the Messiah" (i. 41). When Jesus invites the Twelve to declare their loyalty after many disciples had deserted Him, Peter answers, "Lord, to whom shall we go? thou hast the words of eternal life. And we have believed and know that thou art the Holy One of God" (vi. 68–69). Thomas, convinced at last that Jesus has risen from the dead, exclaims: "My Lord and my God" (xx. 28). Though His disciples have misunderstood Him, Jesus says to them: "And ye also bear witness, because ye have been with me from the beginning" (xv. 27).

The Scriptures also bear witness to Jesus, as the "Son of God". To the Jews He declares: "Ye search the Scriptures, because ye think that in them ye have eternal life; and these are they which bear witness of me" (v. 39). Moses, their pride and hope, is on His side and accuses them. "For if ye believed Moses, ye would believe me; for he wrote of me. But if ye believe not his writings, how shall ye believe my words?" (v. 46).

The works of Jesus, which consist not only of His miracles but also of His manifold activities on earth, are convincing proof of His "Sonship". "The works that I do in my Father's name, these bear witness of me" (x. 25). Faith, elicited by works, is not the highest kind of evidence. Jesus complains that the people will not believe except on the evidence of signs and wonders (IV. 48). Greater than the witness of His works is the witness He bears to Himself by virtue of His own person. This is the highest witness of all. It is true that He says: "If I bear witness of myself, my witness is not true" (v. 31), but He implies that His self-witness does not stand alone: behind Him is the Father who will bear witness to Him. Elsewhere He declares: "Even if I bear witness of myself, my witness is true; for I know whence I came, and whither I go" (VIII. 14). "He Himself in His whole personality is the true evidence and confirmation of His supreme claims."[1]

The witness of Jesus to Himself is supported by that of the Father. "I am he that beareth witness of myself, and the Father that sent me beareth witness of me" (VIII. 18). The witness of the Father is the immediate sense of a divine power apprehending us through Jesus Christ. "No man can come to me, except the Father which sent me draw him" (VI. 44). This witness will become clearer and fuller in the experience of the saint. "But when the Comforter is come, whom I will send unto you from the Father, even the Spirit of truth, which proceedeth from the Father, he shall bear witness of me . . . he shall guide you into all the truth" (xv. 26, xvi. 13).

The Logos. The word "Logos" was a popular term understood by well-educated men of the age, just as terms like "evolution", "relativity", and "life-force", are familiar to-day. The doctrine of the "Logos" was first expounded by the Greek philosopher Heraclitus (c. 500 B.C.–450 B.C.) and was later adopted by the Stoics. Among the latter it stood for the universal reason that pervades all things, including man. The virtuous man was one who was guided by reason, and who was striving to enter into harmony with the immanent reason of the universe and to co-operate with it in shaping all things towards perfection.

The Jews conceived of God as transcendant, dwelling apart "in the light which no man can approach unto" (1 Tim. VI. 16), and so they felt the necessity for an intermediary between God and man; hence they tended to personify certain qualities and attributes of the deity, such as His Spirit, His Word, and His

[1] E. F. Scott, *The Fourth Gospel*, 1908, p. 199.

Wisdom. Before the creation of the world "the spirit of God moved upon the face of the waters" (Gen. I. 2): it was by His Word that He made the heavens and the earth and revealed Himself to His prophets. The Word is God's instrument of deliverance in Psalm CVII. 20. His Wisdom is personified in the Books of "Job" (e.g. XXVIII. 12–28), of "Proverbs" (e.g. VIII. 22–30), of "Ecclesiasticus" (e.g. I. 1–20), and of the "Wisdom of Solomon" (e.g. VII.–X.). In the "Targums", which are Aramaic translations of the Old Testament, there is a tendency to attribute all the actions of God to the Memra (Word). Thus we read: "They heard the voice of the Memra of the Lord God walking in the Garden."

Philo, the Jewish philosopher of Alexandria (c. 20 B.C.– A.D. 50), took over the term Logos, combining the Stoic conception of the immanent reason, the Platonic idea of the ultimate Good, and the Hebrew thought of the Word. For Philo the Logos signifies the sum of all the divine activities in the world: through it God is revealed and man can attain to the higher life, so that it is not only the agent in creation but also in salvation. His belief in Monotheism prevented him from identifying the Logos with the Deity Himself: he therefore uses such terms as "a second God", "first-born son", and "image of God".

John took over the term Logos and used it to interpret Christ to the Graeco-Roman world. To the Jew it would signify the creative activity of God, while to the Greek it would suggest the ultimate good and the immanent reason of the universe. The Evangelist, however, is not concerned with a philosophical principle but with a historical figure. Christ is all that men had imperfectly conceived in the Logos, and infinitely more. He is, in fact, the incarnate Logos. "And the Word became flesh, and dwelt among us (and we beheld his glory, glory as of the only begotten from the Father), full of grace and truth" (I. 14).

Truth. The word "truth" is one of the characteristic words of the Fourth Gospel. As conceived by John it corresponds to what is known in philosophy as ultimate reality and in theology as the divine nature. The ultimate truth is in God, and all things are true or real as they reflect His thoughts and purposes.

This conception goes back to the Platonic doctrine of "ideas" or "forms", according to which all material things are but imperfect copies or pale shadows of the realities laid up in heaven. Christ is one with God and is Himself the truth. "I am the way, and the truth, and the life" (xiv. 6). His great mission in life is to declare the truth. "To this end have I been born, and to this end am I come into the world, that I should bear witness unto the truth" (xviii. 37). It is knowledge of the truth that makes men free. "And ye shall know the truth, and the truth shall make you free" (viii. 32). The function of the Holy Spirit is to guide men into the truth. "Howbeit when he, the Spirit of truth, is come, he shall guide you into all the truth" (xvi. 13).

Light. "Light", as conceived by John, is practically identical with "truth". The Logos (i.e. God), as the "truth", the agent of creation, and the source of all life, has always been seeking from the beginning of time to manifest Himself to His creatures. He is, therefore, not only "truth" but "light". The Evangelist uses the term "light" for the divine revelation because it is "the immemorial symbol of all that is divine and holy: it suggests gladness, security, quickening and illumination."[1] Even before the Incarnation He was quickening the conscience of men lost in moral and spiritual darkness, but they lacked the spiritual perception to recognize Him. In the conflict with the moral and spiritual darkness of the world the light had never been conquered (i. 1–11).

The chief function of John the Baptist was to bear witness to the coming of Christ, the Logos incarnate. "There came a man, sent from God, whose name was John. The same came for witness, that he might bear witness of the light, that all might believe through him" (i. 6–7). As one who in His own person reveals divine truth and banishes the moral and spiritual darkness of the world, Christ is the light of the world. "I am the light of the world: he that followeth me shall not walk in the darkness, but shall have the light of life" (viii. 12). He, who is the light, came not to execute judgment upon men but to save them. Men pass judgment upon themselves

[1] E. F. Scott, *The Fourth Gospel*, 1908, p. 254.

according as they accept or reject Him. "I am come a light into the world, that whosoever believeth on me may not abide in the darkness. And if any man hear my sayings, and keep them not, I judge him not: for I came not to judge the world, but to save the world. He that rejecteth me, and receiveth not my sayings, hath one that judgeth him: the word that I spake, the same shall judge him in the last day" (xii. 46–48).

Life. We read that the Gospel was written that we might have life in His name (xx. 31). In God and in the Logos, who is one with Him, there is a divine life which is different in kind from that in man. It belongs to the higher, eternal world, and man by his own striving cannot attain to it. Christ, as the incarnation of the Logos, partakes of this divine life. "For as the Father hath life in himself, even so gave he to the Son also to have life in himself" (v. 26). He has come to impart His life to man. "I came that they may have life, and may have it abundantly" (x. 10). To possess this life man must attain to a knowledge of God as revealed in Christ (xvii. 3): such knowledge involves, not merely intellectual assent, but complete understanding, confidence, submission, and love. This life is sometimes called "eternal life", the word "eternal" suggesting the quality of life rather than its duration. To the Evangelist the Resurrection is not the beginning of a new life but the fulfilment and confirmation of a life already begun on earth. The real Resurrection takes place when a man is "born again" and makes the great transition from death to life. "Christ had made Himself flesh in order that in this world of time, amidst the limitations of the earthly conditions, we might become partakers of the eternal life."[1]

Historical Value

Its documentary value. Opinions differ as to the value of the Fourth Gospel as a historical document. Some hold that it has no value, being merely an allegory or fictitious narrative intended to convey spiritual truth. Not only every incident but every detail, such as names of places, numbers, lengths of periods, and seasons, have their allegorical interpretations. For

[1] E. F. Scott, *The Fourth Gospel*, 1908, p. 247.

example, the Woman of Samaria (IV. 1–42) stands for the Samaritan community, the Impotent Man at the Pool of Bethesda (v. 1–9) for sinful Israel, the five porches of the pool for the Pentateuch, and the thirty-eight years of sickness for the wanderings of the Israelites in the wilderness. The one hundred and fifty-three fish, mentioned in Chapter XXI. 1–11, are a symbol of the ten Commandments and the seven gifts of the Spirit, because, as St. Augustine argues, $1+2+3 \ldots 17 = 153$, and $10+7=17$. But, had the Evangelist intended his work to be an allegory, he would surely have attached the meanings to it. Whenever he uses the allegorical method—and he frequently does—he suggests the meaning by the teaching recorded more or less in connection with the fact. The Feeding of the Five Thousand symbolizes the bread of life which Christ gives to men; the Healing of the Blind Man is a sign that He is the light of the world; and the Raising of Lazarus is a manifestation of the principle that He is the Resurrection and the Life. Moreover the allegories are not fictitious but are based upon historical facts. It is not the allegory that makes the story but the story the allegory. Since, according to the Evangelist, the Word became "flesh", he is bound to emphasize the historical character of the events which he describes. As Canon Streeter says: "John may have been mistaken about his facts, but to him it is as important to emphasize the historical as to see in the historical the symbol of the Eternal. But he was interested in these stories, not so much because they were marvellous, as because they seem to him to embody eternal truth. To him fact and meaning are related as flesh to spirit— the flesh is a necessary vehicle, but it is spirit which really counts."[1]

Some acknowledge that the Fourth Gospel is a quasi-historical document but attach little or no value to it: for an authentic account we must turn to the Synoptic Gospels. This view is based on the grounds of its wide divergence from the earlier Gospels and on the supposed greater accuracy of the latter. The Fourth Evangelist, it is alleged, was a mystic whose chief interest lay in the spiritual interpretation of events, so that

[1] Streeter, *The Four Gospels*, 1930, p. 389.

it is unlikely that he could have been a careful and accurate historian. He wrote many years after the time of Christ, when memories of the past had become dimmed by time and meditation had distorted his view. His Gospel is largely a work of the imagination, consisting of his own reflections mingled with a few historical incidents, some of which are of doubtful accuracy. The Synoptists, on the other hand, were mainly concerned with the chronicling of events, and wrote nearer the time of Christ when memories of the past were still fresh in their minds: imagination and reflection played little or no part in the composition of their works. Their simple, unadorned descriptions of events create a greater impression of accuracy than the long philosophical and theological discourses of the mystic.

It is true that John was a mystic whose chief concern was the spiritual interpretation of events, but he was nevertheless interested in the actual life and teaching of Christ, as we have already shown. One of his chief aims in writing his Gospel was to bring home to the Church of his own day the fact that the Christian religion had its origin in a real historical figure. There is evidence that he was possessed of trustworthy information over and above that derived from the Synoptic Gospels. He would surely not have recorded any incident which he did not believe to have actually occurred. He may have been mistaken on certain matters, but there may be inaccuracies in the other Gospels as well, for all men are liable to error, even when writing under inspiration. When he differs from the Synoptics "he is not flying in the face of a universal tradition embodied in three separate Gospels", but is in fact differing from only one Gospel, namely "Mark", on which the other two depend.[1] If at times the Fourth Gospel is inferior in historical accuracy to the Synoptics, there are also times when it is superior to them. It is a mistake to suppose that because the Synoptic Gospels were written some years before the Fourth Gospel that they must necessarily be the best interpreters. The true historian must possess, not only knowledge, but also the power of interpretation. An ordinary man may produce an

[1] Streeter, *The Four Gospels*, 1930, p. 418.

accurate record of the events of an age, but it requires a man
with imagination and insight to reveal their relative value and
significance. The Synoptists could chronicle the events in the
life of Christ, but they could only dimly apprehend their
spiritual significance: they could portray the "outer life" of
Christ as it was revealed in His works, but of His "inner life"
they knew little. The Fourth Evangelist was a man of profound
spiritual insight who had meditated for years on the life and
teaching of Christ. From the vantage-point of age he could
now perceive the spiritual significance of events and penetrate
into the inner consciousness of his Master. "In history, as in
religion, it is the spirit that quickens, and unless we can
penetrate the spirit of great historical transactions, interpret
the principles out of which they spring, and throw ourselves
with sympathetic imagination into the passions which animated
the great human drama, we miss the only truth that is worth
receiving."[1]

In the light of the above facts, the Gospel cannot be dismissed
as mere fiction. Though it may not be as authoritative as the
Synoptic Gospels, it is nevertheless a valuable contribution to
our understanding of the life and teaching of Christ, and is
therefore an important historical document.

Religious value. The Fourth Gospel is valuable as a supplement to the Synoptics. Sometimes it corrects them, as on the
question of the date of the Crucifixion, while occasionally it
supplies fresh information such as that which is included in the
Passion narrative. Sometimes it develops doctrines which are
found in embryo in the Synoptics, such as that of the Sonship
of Christ. It also supplements them by revealing the spiritual
significance of events and the deeper secrets of Christ's
personality.

It was an important factor in promoting the spread of
Christianity. By the close of the first century Christianity was
established in Syria, Asia Minor, Macedonia, Greece, Rome
and perhaps Egypt. It had extended very slightly, if at all, to
the more western portion of the Empire. It was, however, still

---

[1] Drummond, *An Enquiry into the Character and Authorship of the Fourth Gospel*,
1903, p. 29.

confined to a minority of the people of the Empire, having appealed largely to the uneducated masses. It was as true then as in Paul's day that "not many wise after the flesh, not many mighty, not many noble" were called (1 Cor. 1. 26). Unless it could make its appeal to all classes of society, there was a danger that it might linger on as one of the many insignificant religions of the Empire or wither and eventually die out altogether. The Fourth Evangelist interpreted the Gospel in Greek modes of thought and thus made it intelligible and more acceptable to the cultured pagans of the Graeco-Roman world.

It has been a powerful influence in preserving the memory of Christ in the Church. There has always been a tendency to accept His teaching and to ignore His life. By the end of the first century His name was becoming a dim memory, and Christians hardly realized that the glorified Christ, who was the object of their worship, had once lived among men. The Fourth Evangelist saw clearly that the Church could not survive as a living power, once it was separated from its historical origins. Christianity was not a system of ethics but belief in a Person. He therefore recalled the Christians of his own day back to the Jesus of history, who was the source of all life, and thus saved Christianity from becoming a mere system of ethics, or a barren philosophy, or a lifeless tradition.

Finally it has brought inspiration, strength, comfort, joy and peace to successive generations of Christians and has thus deepened the spiritual life of the Church. By its assurance of the Fatherhood of God and of the possibility of fellowship with Christ, by its revelation of the eternal truth behind the transient event, by the promise of a more abundant life, of a joy that the world can neither give nor take away, and of a peace that passeth knowledge, it has satisfied the deepest needs of the soul. Age after age, men, in their search for satisfaction, have discovered how true are the words of Peter, "Lord, to whom shall we go? thou hast the words of eternal life" (vi. 68).

CHAPTER XI

ACTS

Authorship

External Evidence. Early Christian writers are unanimous in ascribing the authorship of "Acts" to Luke, the writer of the Third Gospel and the companion of Paul. Towards the close of the second century A.D., Clement of Alexandria, Irenaeus, and Tertullian, accept Lucan authorship without question. Eusebius (*c.* A.D. 325), the best historian of the early Church, refers to the author as "Luke, by race a native of Antioch, by profession a physician".

Internal Evidence. The confirmation of Lucan authorship from internal evidence involves three propositions—namely, (1) that "Acts" was written by the same author as the third Gospel, (2) that the writer was a contemporary of Paul, (3) that it was Luke who is mentioned in the Epistles and is called "the beloved physician" (Col. IV. 14).

Common Authorship. The third Gospel opens with a preface and dedication to the "most excellent Theophilus", who was probably a Roman official of high rank. "Theophilus" was a Greek word meaning "God-lover", and was probably not his real name but a prudential pseudonym by which he was known among his Christian friends. "Acts" also opens with a preface and dedication to the same "excellent" person, in which reference is made to a "former treatise", embodying "all that Jesus began both to do and to teach" (I. 1)—a clear reference to the third Gospel.

The two books are in fact one. The third Gospel is a record of what Jesus "began both to do and to teach" during His earthly ministry, while "Acts" is concerned with the continuation of that work and teaching after His Ascension through the instrumentality of His disciples, inspired by His Spirit.

There is a close connection between the closing words of the third Gospel and the opening words of "Acts". In the former

182

Our Lord's prophecy that the Gospel should be preached to all nations, "beginning from Jerusalem", is repeated in almost identical words in the latter: in each case the disciples are commanded to stay at Jerusalem until they have received the gift of the Holy Spirit (cf. Lk. xxiv. 49; Acts i. 4).

Both books are characterized by a universal outlook. In the third Gospel Jesus is to be, not only the glory of His people Israel, but also a "light for revelation to the Gentiles" (Lk. ii. 32). In "Acts" the disciples are to be His witnesses "both in Jerusalem, and in all Judaea and Samaria, and unto the uttermost part of the earth" (i. 8). Paul is commanded to preach the Gospel to the heathen. "Depart," says the Lord to him, "for I will send thee forth far hence unto the Gentiles" (xxii. 21).

The style of the third Gospel and "Acts" is very similar. Each has a special vocabulary of its own, which is due partly to the difference of subject-matter and partly to the author's mastery of the Greek language. Taking the books together, they contain some seven hundred words which are found nowhere else in the New Testament, and of these about fifty-seven occur in both works. There are differences, it is true, in the two vocabularies and in grammatical usage, but the similarities far outnumber the differences. In both books also, we find the same mastery of the succinct phrase, and the same power of graphic description and of vivid portraiture.

The Author a Contemporary. "Acts" is generally written in the third person, but there are four passages in which the narrator uses the first person plural, and which record journeys or parts of journeys: (*a*) from Troas to Philippi (xvi. 10–17); (*b*) from Philippi to Miletus (xx. 5–15); (*c*) from Miletus to Jerusalem (xxi. 1–18); and (*d*) from Caesarea to Rome (xxvii. 1– xxviii. 16). They are known as the "We" sections, and, by reason of their detail, suggest that they are extracts from a travel-diary kept by an actual companion of Paul. If the writer of the diary is the author of the whole book, then the author of "Acts" was a contemporary and eyewitness of these parts of Paul's missionary journeys. Hawkins and Harnack have subjected the style and vocabulary of the Lucan writings to an exhaustive analysis, and have proved conclusively the identity of both style and vocabulary in the "We" sections and the rest of the book. The somewhat fantastic suggestion that the author of the rest of the book might have rewritten the "We" sections in his own style but left the first persons unchanged is quite out of keeping with the way in which he has dealt with "Mark" in his first volume. Moreover, there are cross references from the "We" sections to other parts of the book. Thus in Chapter xxi. 8 there is a reference to the fact that Philip was one of the Seven, while in Chapter vi. 1–6 we have an account of their appointment and are told that Philip was one of them. Paul's purpose on passing through Macedonia and Achaia on his way to Jerusalem is mentioned in Chapter xix. 21, which is outside the "We" sections.

The Contemporary was probably Luke. Paul calls Luke "the beloved physician". In both the Third Gospel and "Acts" we have the frequent use of medical terms; this may be seen in the cases of the healing of the man at the Beautiful Gate of the Temple, Elymas at Paphos, the cripple at Lystra, and the father of Publius at Melita. While such use is not conclusive proof that the author of the two books is a doctor, since medical phraseology was to some extent the common property of cultured men of those days, such as Lucian and Plutarch, it does, at least, point in that direction. The references in "Acts" to miraculous cures, magic, and sorcery, also suggest that the author took a professional interest in the treatment of disease.

The identity of the author can be established with some degree of probability by adopting a process of elimination. If the author was a travelling companion of Paul and an eye-witness of the events which he described, then from the list of Paul's companions we can eliminate Timothy, Aristarchus, and Trophimus, who are mentioned by the writer and are therefore different from him; Mark, who had ceased to be his companion; and Demas, who had deserted him. We are thus left with four—namely, Crescens, Justus, Titus, and Luke. The two former are of little importance and have no special connection with Paul, and so the choice is between Titus and Luke. Neither of the two is mentioned in "Acts", and there is nothing in the tradition of the early Church to suggest that Titus might be the author. We know that Luke was with Paul during his imprisonment at Rome, and he is, therefore, the likely author of the "We" sections.

Arguments against Lucan Authorship. This view that Luke was the author, which had been accepted till the early years of the nineteenth century and has now been rehabilitated, did not pass unchallenged during the middle of the nineteenth century, when the Tübingen school launched an attack on the authenticity of the history presented in "Acts", by representing it as a second-century work, written to cover up a controversy between Jewish and Pauline Christianity which, it was alleged, divided the whole of the early Church. It alleged that the book represented a second-century, not a first-century, outlook, and that the political and geographical facts were true for the second century only. Investigation has now completely refuted the theory. The famous English archaeologist, Sir William Ramsay, after his excavations in Asia Minor, turned to the study of "Acts" to see what light it threw on the state of that district. Beginning with the assumption that the book was a second-century production, he was gradually forced to the conclusion that it must have been written in the first century, with admirable knowledge. In fact its contemporary allusions, where first and second centuries differ, are always to the state of things existing in the first century, never to those existing in the second.

Nevertheless arguments against Lucan authorship are still used, but they amount to little. The argument that the author must have obtained his information concerning the rebellions of Theudas and Judas (v. 36–37) from Josephus' *Antiquities*, published about A.D. 93, is refuted by the fact that he reverses Josephus' order for the two rebellions, which suggests that he was drawing from a vague general knowledge of Jewish history and not from a written source at all. Another objection, that a companion of the Apostle would have used his Epistles in the composition of "Acts", is a transference of modern ideas on the composition of history to ancient times; the more the writer had had personal contact with the subject of his biography, the

185

less he would have recourse to what he had written. Allied with the last objection are others, which hold that the narrative in "Acts" is in various ways contradictory to the Epistles. Doubtless, "Acts" emphasizes Paul's conformity to the Jewish Law, whereas the Epistles, being written to Gentile converts, emphasize that that Law is not binding on them; but Paul himself at times in his Epistles emphasizes his own personal Jewish status. And again, there are a few minor differences as regards facts, but they are mainly of omission; the only serious difference, on the number of his visits to Jerusalem, is discussed in the chapter on "Galatians". A supposed difference in the picture of Paul as given in "Acts" with that which modern readers derive from the Epistles, amounts to no more than that Luke is interested in Paul's achievements rather than in describing his personality, while the latter's own writings incidentally reveal more of his personality.

The Growth of the Book

The book then grew out of the diary. Chapters xvi.-xxviii. (almost half of the whole) are composed of the diary, the events intervening between those recorded in the diary, and a series of speeches by Paul presenting the case for Christianity to Jews and Gentiles. What this section now records is the big expansion of Christianity into the Gentile world—into Macedonia, Greece (Achaia), the province of "Asia" (the thickly populated Greek coast-line of Western Asia Minor), and finally Rome, the capital of the civilized world. What it aims at is clearly so to present the account of this expansion and the nature of the Christian message as to attract educated Gentiles to the faith. It is propaganda, but propaganda based on full conviction. The writer is not distorting history, but presenting the history he had witnessed, because he believed it would have the same effect on others that it had had on himself.

But clearly a history of Christianity which began with Paul's crossing from Asia to Europe would be unintelligible without an account of the earlier stages. Of these stages, Luke was in a better position to speak of Paul's ministry from his first departure from Antioch-in-Syria to convert Asia Minor than of the earlier events. The "Western" manuscripts introduce "We" clauses into the account of the decision at Antioch-in-Syria to send Barnabas and Paul on this mission (XIII. 1–4), and some little confirmation of this is obtained from Eusebius' statement that Luke was a native of Antioch-in-Syria. If Eusebius derived this information from other sources, it makes the "Western" reading highly probable; if, on the other hand, it is an inference drawn by Eusebius from the "Western" reading, it shows that he had that reading before him. If then the "Western" reading is right, we may extend the original section of the book back to Chapter XIII. Even if it is not, Luke must have obtained the information in Chapters XIII.–XV. from Paul himself, and they form a natural addition to Chapters XVI.–XXVIII.

For events before that, except Paul's conversion, Luke had to depend on research. The difference is that for the second half of "Acts" Luke already had the information and therefore began to write, whereas for the Gospel and the first half of "Acts", before he began to write he had to collect information.

The contents of the first half of "Acts" suggests that the process of collecting information went on largely at Caesarea during the two years of Paul's imprisonment there, when Luke had less preaching to do than before or after. Philip the deacon, who lived at Caesarea with his daughters, is more prominent than any of the Twelve save Peter; and Peter's recorded activities are largely in the hinterland of Caesarea, that is in the towns of Lydda and Joppa and the country of Samaria. Moreover, Luke records how, on a journey from Caesarea to Jerusalem he met one Mnason, "an original disciple" (XXI. 16), an incident which must have had some special interest to make him record it, which may well be information which he obtained from him. It is at this period too when he must have had most opportunity for contact with the Christians of Jerusalem, from whom he must have obtained much of the information contained in his Gospel, especially that from the women who followed Our Lord, and possibly the hymns which appear in its early chapters.

In the light of these facts we can approach more easily the difficult problem of the date of "Acts".

Date of Composition

In modern times the date of a book has a clear meaning; it means the date at which it was first printed. Successive editions mean successive printings with alterations. Before the invention of printing the date of a book had no such clear meaning. The author wrote a single manuscript which he could keep by him, and expand and alter at will for an indefinite period. The unusual number of differences between the "Western" text of "Acts" and the other texts suggests that this actually happened to "Acts", and, as most of the changes seem to make for greater clearness, that the "Western" text was taken from a later stage of the manuscript. What then we mean by the date of "Acts" can only be the date at which a copy of the manuscript was sent to Theophilus, and we have to allow for the possibility that Luke went on adding to his own copy later, and that our versions are derived from Luke's own copy, not from that sent to Theophilus.

One fact only is clearly stated by Luke himself, that he sent the Gospel to Theophilus before he sent "Acts", because he speaks of the Gospel as "the former treatise" (1. 1). We have no means of knowing how far the composition of either Gospel or "Acts" had proceeded before Luke went with Paul to Rome. We do, however, know that no ancient writer states that either was written at Rome, and that some assert that they were written in Achaia (Greece). The second statement may be a guess; but it is most unlikely that, if either had been first known to others besides the author in Rome, the fact would not have been recorded. It is clear, too, that Luke had no access to Mark personally after he had incorporated Mark's Gospel in his own, otherwise he would have been able to supply whatever was contained in the missing end of that Gospel. Hence we reach one important conclusion about the date at which both were sent to Theophilus, namely, that it was after Luke had left Rome, that is, after Paul's death. But we must be very careful to keep in mind that this date in no way determines the period at which the bulk of "Acts" was written, and gives us only the earliest date of the incorporation of "Mark" in "Proto-Luke" as regards the Gospel, but no date for the composition of "Proto-Luke" itself.

One school of thought consequently thinks that "Acts" had practically assumed its present shape at the end of Paul's two-year imprisonment at Rome (A.D. 64) and was not brought up to date when it was sent to Theophilus. What strikes the modern reader most is that the book should end without stating whether Paul was acquitted or convicted. But Luke's silence goes beyond this; there is no mention of any event after A.D. 64 of the Neronian persecution (A.D. 64-68), of the Fall of Jerusalem (A.D. 70), of the increasing bitterness between Jews and Christians after that event, or of subsequent Church history and development. Paul, in his farewell speech to the Ephesian elders, declares that they will see his face no more (xx. 25). This may imply that Paul was already dead when Luke wrote this. The idea that Paul subsequently visited Asia Minor is derived from the Pastoral Epistles; but, if these are made up of fragments written at different times, they prove nothing. These arguments possess great weight, though we shall show in the section on the purpose of the book that Luke deliberately refrained from adding anything later with a definite object.

As regards the date at which Luke sent his manuscript to Theophilus, "Acts", as we have seen, was sent later than the Gospel, and the Gospel, as has been shown in Chapter VIII, was probably sent after the Fall of Jerusalem, in view of Luke's changes in Mark's Apocalypse in the light of that event.[1] How much later we have no means of judging, if once we refuse to accept the idea that information is derived from Josephus' *Antiquities*. But Luke's age would make it difficult to assume a much later date, so that we are fairly safe in placing it between A.D. 75 and A.D. 85.

[1] Professor Dodd has shown that the prophecy which Luke inserts was a general prophecy of the Fall of Jerusalem, written before the event and containing no specific references to incidents in its destruction; but Luke's dropping of the prediction of Antichrist in the Temple in favour of this other prophecy requires explanation, as it had been a part of the accepted apocalyptic beliefs. The natural explanation is that Luke saw the impossibility in view of the destruction of the Temple. It is strange that Matthew did not.

Purpose

Assuming the growth of "Acts" to have been, as outlined in the preceding paragraphs, from a narrative of Paul's later missionary work, based on Luke's own diary and information derived from the Apostle till it assumed its present form, we can deduce its purpose from what is added, from what is omitted, and from the point at which it ends.

1. *To defend Christianity against Opponents.* The additions clearly show the purpose of defending Christianity against opponents, both pagan and Jewish. Speech after speech is added to the narrative of events in the second half, and several appear in the first half in which Paul in the second half, Peter and Stephen in the first half, set forth the teaching of Christianity and the arguments for accepting it. But, apart from the positive arguments in its favour, we can see clearly that Luke is also meeting two of the main arguments which were brought against Christianity, namely (*a*) that it was hostile to Roman authority, (*b*) that it was based on Judaism yet rejected by the legitimate Jewish exponents of their own religion.

(*a*) The Roman Government tolerated all religions, unless they were clearly immoral or revolutionary. They tried, however, to secure loyalty by enforcing divine honours to the genius of Rome and the Emperor, which could be added to all forms of paganism; and, in the case of the Jews, who could not pay such honours, were even content that they should pray for the Emperor instead of praying to him. As long as Christianity was regarded as a branch of Judaism it was therefore a lawful religion. But, when it became recognized as a separate religion, it became highly unpopular with the followers of the old religions because, unlike other creeds, it tried to destroy all religions but itself. Nero was the first persecutor on a large scale through his desire to divert from himself the odium of having caused the great fire of A.D. 64, but it was not officially declared an illegal association till the reign of Trajan (A.D. 98–117), that is, after Luke's death.

In the light of this attitude of the Roman government, we can see why so much stress is laid in the later portion of "Acts" on the attitude of Roman governors to Paul and of Paul to the Roman government, to the authorities at Philippi, Thessalonica, and Ephesus, to Gallio, Felix, and Festus, and finally to the central government at Rome itself. In every case, the Roman authorities though incited to persecution, at the end of their investigation decide that Paul is not preaching anything hostile to Roman authority, and in every case Paul acts as a loyal Roman citizen, proud of his citizenship. We now see the full significance of the resonant lines (as they are in the original Greek) with which the book closes, "preaching the kingdom of God and teaching the facts about the Lord Jesus Christ with complete liberty of speech and without prohibition" (xxviii. 31). In other words, Nero himself did not interfere till he had a motive, which was not based on the nature of Christianity but was akin to his whole career of wickedness. The book really closes with an appeal to Rome to return to the policy that had been followed till A.D. 64 and to ignore the acts of the Neronian terror. It closes in A.D. 64 because what follows is not the action of Rome but of the tyranny which had engulfed Rome.

(b) Against the argument that the Jewish authorities ought to understand their own religion better than these "unlearned" amateurs, Luke is not content with arguing that Christianity fulfils Old Testament prophecy, but is constantly reiterating Old Testament assertions that the Jews had always rejected God's messengers, even Moses, still more the prophets, and would continue to do so, with the implication that the rejection of Christianity was to be expected and was no argument against its truth.

2. *To trace the Progress of the Gospel.* The selective character of the narrative is easily apparent, especially in the earlier part. In spite of the name, "Acts of the Apostles", by which we commonly know the work, Peter is the only one of the Twelve who is prominent. John is mentioned in connection with him three times; of John's brother James only his martyrdom is recorded, while the rest are never mentioned individually. No reference is made to the spread of the Gospel to Alexandria, or to Babylon and the East. What is recorded follows the programme of Chapter i. 8, "Ye shall be my witnesses both in

Jerusalem, and in all Judaea and Samaria, and unto the uttermost part of the earth". In short, the narrative traces the development of Christianity from being a Jewish sect to being a world-wide religion; Chapters I.–v. deal with the Jerusalem phase; Chapters VI.–VII. centre round Stephen with the centre of gravity tending to the Greek-speaking Jews and proselytes; Chapter VIII. shows the extension to Samaria and centres round Philip; Chapters IX.–XII. tell of the first extension to the Gentiles, with two outstanding events, the conversion of Paul and the admission of the Gentile Cornelius to the Church by Peter; Chapters XIII.–XV. record the first large-scale admission of Gentiles and the official determination that Gentiles may become Christians without becoming Jews. After that the narrative turns westward and traces the spread of the Gospel through the Graeco-Roman world to Rome, the capital. The East is left behind; even Antioch falls out of the story. Here clearly we have a narrative so chosen and so told as to support the argument of the speeches. Ever since Luke wrote, his view of the sequence of events has to such a degree become accepted history that it is hard to think of it as having ever been a novelty. Time has shown that what Luke thought important *was* important, and was lasting. But it is utterly remote from the thought of the Jerusalemite Christians.

(3) *To show the Holy Spirit at Work in the Church.* A third purpose is to show that Christ is still present in His Church, inspiring and guiding it in all its undertakings through the power of the Holy Spirit. Immediately before His Ascension He promises His disciples that they will receive power when the Holy Spirit falls upon them (I. 8): the promise is fulfilled at Pentecost, and Peter promises his hearers that they, too, will receive the gift of the Holy Spirit if they repent and are baptized (II. 38). When, after his healing of the cripple at the Beautiful Gate of the Temple and his speech in Solomon's porch, he is brought before the Sanhedrin, he is filled with the Spirit to make his defence (IV. 8); and when, on his release, he rejoins the brethren, they are all filled with the Holy Spirit and speak the word of God with boldness (IV. 31). Stephen (VII. 55) and Barnabas (XI. 24) are described as being "full of the Holy

Ghost", even as Jesus was anointed "with the Holy Ghost and with power" (x. 38). Philip the Evangelist is instructed by the Spirit to accost the Ethiopian eunuch, and after the interview with him is ended he is led away by the Spirit to another place (VIII. 26–40). Peter is directed by the Spirit to accept the invitation of Cornelius and to go to Caesarea with the messengers whom the latter has sent (x. 19–20). The Holy Spirit falls upon the Samaritan converts (VIII. 14–17), Cornelius and his household (x. 44–48), and the disciples of John at Ephesus (XIX. 6–7). It is the Holy Spirit that separates Barnabas and Saul for missionary work (XIII. 2), guides the Church at the Council of Jerusalem (xv. 28), forbids Paul and his companions to speak the word in Asia (xvi. 6), makes the Ephesian elders "bishops to feed the church of God" (xx. 28), and warns Paul of the bonds and afflictions which await him at Jerusalem (xx. 23). The presence and power of the Spirit are so manifest throughout the book that it has been aptly called the "Acts of the Holy Spirit".

Sources

Second Part of "Acts". It is not difficult to conjecture what sources must have been used in the composition of the second part of "Acts" (xv. 36–xxvIII. 31). For the "We" sections he evidently relied on his own notes or personal recollections of his travels. It is probable that he was also present on other occasions, not mentioned in the "We" sections, for certain passages, such as those dealing with Paul's arrest and imprisonment at Philippi (xvi. 18–40), his farewell meeting with the Ephesian elders at Miletus (xx. 17–38), and some of those dealing with the Apostle's imprisonment in Jerusalem and Caesarea (xxi. 18–xxvi. 32), give the impression of being the work of an eyewitness, though they are not written in the first person. The rest of the material found in the second part of "Acts" must have come from Paul himself or from the Apostle's companions, such as John Mark, Timothy, Silas, Gaius, Aristarchus, and Aquila and Priscilla.

First part of "Acts". As regards the first half it is fairly obvious that Chapters vi.–xii., except Paul's conversion, consist of information derived at Caesarea and largely from Philip. Lydda, Joppa, and Samaria are all in the hinterland of Caesarea, and Herod's speech took place there. But we are in ignorance of the exact sources for Chapters i.–v., of which the historical accuracy appears to be less than in the rest of the book, as will be shown in a later section; and it is probable that they were gathered from different informants at Jerusalem, whose divergent accounts have not always been successfully blended. Several theories of written sources have been put forward, but they are quite unconvincing.

Speeches. The important part played by the speeches in presenting the case for Christianity has already been noted. It was a convention among Greek historians to present the aims, policy, and outlook of public men in the form of speeches. It was never supposed that a speech in those words had been delivered; at the same time such speeches cannot be called imaginary so much as composite photographs, to use a metaphor, of the sayings of the public men at various times. Luke must have often heard Paul speak and the speeches may be trusted to give a substantial picture of his arguments; but the style is Luke's. Luke may never have heard Peter and certainly had not heard Stephen, but he knew the teaching of early Christianity; and it is that teaching which these speeches embody.

Letters. We should probably be right in assuming that the two letters, namely, that to "the brethren which are of the Gentiles in Antioch and Syria and Cilicia", acquainting them with the decisions of the Council of Jerusalem (xv. 23–29), and that of Claudius Lysias to Felix, giving an account of Paul's arrest and imprisonment (xxiii. 26–30), are similarly to be understood as giving the substance of the communications, thrown into the form of letters in accordance with the same convention, for Greek writers never give summaries as such.

Historical Value

1. *Alleged Inaccuracy.* We have already dealt with the Tübingen theory, which denies historical value to "Acts", and shown it to be groundless. "Acts" is a genuine first-century writing, and the facts, in so far as they came within Luke's personal knowledge,

are as accurate as those of any contemporary writer in ancient times. Charges of inaccuracy must be limited, first, to statements in the first part of the book derived by Luke from others, and, secondly, to any which arise out of bias or presupposition in any part of the work. The chief of these may be stated.

(a) The account of the death of Judas (i. 18–19) differs from "Matthew" xxvii. 3–8, and Matthew's account looks to be the more probable. The substantial facts, however, the death of Judas and some connection between him and the potter's field, are common to both accounts and are all which the writers considered essential as fulfilling, to the minds of early Christians, Old Testament prophecy.

(b) Harnack believes that there are two accounts of the giving of the Holy Spirit, one in Chapter ii. 1–4, and the other in Chapter iv. 31. This seems unnecessary, as the giving of the Holy Spirit by outward signs is mentioned both in connection with the conversion of the Samaritans (viii. 17–19) and of Cornelius (x. 44–46) and is not treated by Luke as peculiar to the Day of Pentecost.

(c) Similarly the two appearances before the Sanhedrin recounted in Chapters iv. and v. are by some regarded as duplicates of the same event. This can neither be proved nor disproved.

(d) Luke attributes to Gamaliel a reference to the rebellion of Theudas, which, according to Josephus, took place in A.D. 44–45, over ten years after Gamaliel spoke. Here a clear mistake is made, but on a point plainly irrelevant to the argument. The argument is simply that all previous Messianic and nationalist movements—and they had been many—had failed. Luke illustrates by mentioning two in particular which he knew of, but, owing to the absence of any history of the period before Josephus wrote, had no means of dating. It does not, however, affect the argument.

(e) It is pointed out that the gift of tongues, as practised in many congregations of the early Church, consisted in unintelligible utterances which required an interpreter, whereas Luke in the account of Pentecost represents these utterances as given in recognized languages and intelligible to those who spoke them. Presumably Luke regarded the normal "speaking with tongues" as speech in a foreign language: the phrase suggests that such was the general belief, though no one who understood that language might be present, but the emphasis laid on it in the account of Pentecost is due to a Jewish belief that the commandments were given at Sinai in such a way as to be intelligible to all nations in their own language, and Pentecost is turned into a second Sinai, the place of the foundation of the Christian Church, as Sinai was of the Jewish Church. But here we have a mistaken interpretation, not an invention of facts. "Speaking with tongues" was an undoubted fact common in the early Church.

(f) The number of Paul's visits to Jerusalem is discussed in the chapter on "Galatians". Other supposed discrepancies with Paul's Epistles amount to little. Paul states that no human being had a share in his conversion (Gal. i. 12); this is not really inconsistent with the part played by Ananias in Luke's account (Acts ix. 10–19, xxii. 12–16), since Paul is thinking of the mental processes which led him to accept Christianity and of those only. Luke undoubtedly omits Paul's three years' stay in "Arabia" (Gal. i. 17–18); but ignorance on a fact like this is no evidence of incompetence as a historian. "Galatians" says that Paul escaped from Damascus because "the governor under Aretas the king" sought to arrest him (2 Cor. xi. 32–33) whereas in "Acts" he fled because the Jews formed a plot to kill him; but we can imagine no other motive for the governor's action except incitement from the Jews.

2. *Alleged Prejudice.* As regards the charge of showing prejudice, Luke undoubtedly composed "Acts" with the purpose of defending and commending Christianity, but it does not follow that he must have deliberately suppressed information or falsified facts. A man may indulge quite sincerely in propaganda without doing either. "Acts" is not a dull catalogue of events but a well-planned and artistically arranged whole. From the material at his disposal Luke made a careful selection of incidents, and arranged them in such a manner as to produce a certain definite impression. Many incidents were omitted, not because he wished to distort the truth, but because he considered

them to be superfluous or irrelevant to the purpose which he had in view. The only serious charge brought against Luke is that he has deliberately omitted to give a full and true account of the internal dispute in the Church concerning the admission of Gentile converts. He mentions the dispute but leaves us with the impression that it was settled amicably by means of a compromise. The dispute, however, was not between Paul and the Twelve with Peter at their head, as the Tübingen critics assert, but between Paul and certain persons who regarded themselves as followers of James. Peter was not a party to the dispute but a would-be mediator. To the Gentile Luke, this deprived the controversy of much of its significance. He is at pains to show that Paul was willing to conciliate the Jewish party too, and therein he is doubtless correct. The Tübingen theory cannot be dismissed hastily as absolutely false, but the importance of the controversy has been exaggerated.

3. *Alleged Credulity.* To one school of modern writers "Acts" cannot be historical because it is full of miracles. But the Epistles equally assume gifts of healing to have been normal in the early Church, and modern opinion recognizes the power of mind in curing disease to an extent which is opposed to the medical views of fifty years ago. It seems to us quite impossible to escape from the evidence in favour of such cures in face of the combined evidence of Paul and the other contemporary witnesses. Nevertheless it is probably true that Luke, having witnessed many such cures, which as a doctor he knew not to be explicable on purely medical grounds, is inclined to assume a miracle as the easiest explanation of certain cases where modern readers, whose tendency is to reduce the miraculous as far as possible, would seek other explanations. Ananias and Sapphira may have died of shock; Eutychus may only have been stunned; it may be true that the snakes in Malta are not poisonous; but, after all, it is on Luke's own accounts of the facts that these hypotheses are based. Interpretations must be distinguished from facts, and an author's interpretations are necessarily those of his own age and environment.

Luke's Accuracy. We can now turn to the obvious accuracy of Luke's picture as a whole. He shows a good understanding of the development of the early Church and of the conditions existing in Palestine and in the Graeco-Roman world generally. He knows the origin and composition of the primitive Christian community, and is acquainted with the controversy which existed between the Hellenists and the Palestinian Jews: he is aware of the communistic basis of the Church and gives a perfectly natural account of the spread of the Gospel to the Gentiles. He understands the relations which existed between the Church and the Jewish parties in the state. Sadducees, not the Pharisees, as in the Gospel, now stand out as the chief opponents of the Christian community. In addition, he is familiar with the synagogue, the Temple and its guard, the Jewish Sanhedrin, the Herodian régime, and the Roman procurator and his court. Luke was a Gentile, and there was nothing in his own experience which would have enabled him to describe the early history of the Church so naturally. In spite of occasional inaccuracies, he must have had access to reliable sources of information.

When he comes to describe the wider world of the Empire he is equally accurate. Historical research has proved that in his accounts of Paul's missionary journeys his geographical and topographical references are correct. He knew, for example, that Lystra and Derbe were cities of Lycaonia and that Iconium was not. In his account of his voyage to Rome he shows, not only knowledge of seamanship and seafaring life, but also of localities. He displays a like accuracy in his references to the Roman administration of the provinces. Owing to the frequent interchange of provinces between the Emperor and the Senate, and the great variety of local customs, laws, and institutions, which existed in the Empire, the official titles of magistrates varied from time to time and from place to place, so that it was not an easy matter for a writer to be strictly accurate, but Luke apparently makes no mistake. He is correct in describing the Roman governors of Cyprus and Achaia as "proconsuls", Philippi as a Roman "colony" with its praetors and lictors, the magistrates of Thessalonica as "politarchs", and the official of Melita as "first man". In some cases where the author's statements have been impugned, he has been proved to be correct. Inscriptions discovered at Thessalonica and on the island of Melita (Malta), for example, show that the magistrates were called by the titles given to them in "Acts".

Luke's wide human sympathies led him to study the lives of the people among whom he moved. The picture which he gives of life in the Graeco-Roman world of the time has been proved to be true in every detail. We see the proud, haughty Romans, who hold the Mediterranean peoples in subjection and are intent upon maintaining peace and order; the fanatical Jews, living among the Gentiles, whom they despise and by whom they are hated in return; the ignorant Lycaonians preparing to offer sacrifices to Paul and Barnabas (xiv. 12–13); the little band of devoted women assembled for worship at a quiet spot beside a river at Philippi (xvi. 13); a number of "loafers" gathering a crowd and causing an uproar in Thessalonica (xvii. 5); the Athenians, who spend their time "in nothing else, but either to tell or to hear some new thing" (xvii. 21); the excitable and superstitious Ephesians shouting for about two hours, "Great is Diana of the Ephesians" (xix. 34); the fashionable Tyrannus in his lecture room (xix. 9); the Roman advocate, Tertullus, trying to win the favour of Felix by his blandishments (xxiv. 1–4); the disciplined Roman commanders, Claudius Lysias and Julius, strict in the performance of their duties (xxi.–xxiii., xxvii.); the sailors undergirding the ship and throwing the freight overboard (xxvii. 17–18); and the little group of earnest Christians setting out from Rome to welcome Paul, who is about to enter the city as a prisoner (xxviii. 15).

The value of "Acts" is enormous. It is the only history of the growth of Christianity which we possess till Eusebius almost three hundred years later, and without it Eusebius would be almost impossible. From the Epistles, were they not illuminated by "Acts", we could deduce little. Rarely did an ancient historian so completely agree with modern opinion as regards what was important in contemporary history and what was not. It is hard to realize that Luke's selection was made by a contemporary of Paul and not by a contemporary of Constantine.

The contrast between Luke and the writers of the second-century apocryphal "Acts" of various Apostles is the difference between the historian and the romancer. Only two Greek historians of their own times are greater as historians than Luke —Thucydides and Polybius. It is by comparison with Greek historians, not with modern historians, with their access to libraries and museums, to shorthand reports and collections of letters, that Luke must be judged. So judged, "Acts" proves to be a work of art. The writer has a clear purpose, which he accomplishes: each act in the drama fits into its place in the whole; the decisive events stand out in clear relief; events and speeches combine to produce the desired impression; its persuasive power is obtained not by distorting history, but by presenting it; its biographical character does not narrow its historical outlook but emphasizes it; nothing irrelevant is recorded. Unconsciously it becomes the best picture of provincial life in the first century A.D. which we possess.

PART IV

PAUL'S EPISTLES

CHAPTER XII

INTRODUCTION TO PAUL'S EPISTLES

Origin

The work of Paul as a missionary was not confined to preaching the Gospel. Like a wise master-builder he thought about the future of his new converts, as there was a very real danger that, living in isolation, they might find the demands of the Christian life too great for them and that they might be tempted to revert to paganism. Hence he organized them in communities in which they could find fellowship with one another and could be built up in the Christian faith. He claimed no "lordship" over them, but encouraged them to govern themselves, he himself being content with a general oversight, which entailed a heavy responsibility, so that he could truthfully say: "Beside those things that are without, there is that which presseth upon me daily, anxiety for all the churches" (2 Cor. xi. 28). The mission field was so vast in extent, embracing the provinces of Galatia, Asia, Macedonia, and Achaia, that he could pay the local churches only occasional visits, but he endeavoured to keep in touch with them as far as possible, sometimes sending one of his assistants, such as Timothy or Titus, to visit them, and sometimes communicating with them by letter. Not all his letters, however, were addressed to local churches or even to churches at all. "Romans" is addressed to a church which he had not founded and over which he could claim no authority, "Colossians" to a church which had been founded by one or more of his converts and over which he could only claim authority indirectly, and "Philemon" to a friend, on behalf of a runaway slave.

Their Relation to Contemporary Letters

The letter was not a new literary form in Paul's day. The art of letter-writing was a favourite form of diversion among the Greeks and the Romans long before the beginning of the Christian era. By the time of Demetrius of Phalerum, librarian to Ptolemy I (320–285 B.C.), it had reached such a stage of development that he could classify letters under twenty-one heads. The foundation of the Roman Empire, with its peaceful organization and uniform system of administration, its excellent means of communication, and its army of educated officials, often separated from the capital and from one another by great distances, gave a great impetus to the art. The innumerable official communications were dispatched by the imperial post, while private letters were entrusted to friends and couriers who were able to pass safely and quickly from one district to another. The art was also promoted by the increased cultivation of the papyrus plant in Egypt, which ensured a plentiful supply of writing material. Letter-writing attained such proportions that it almost became a craze. "From the end of the Republic every wealthy Roman, among his regular paraphernalia of opulence, kept a staff of letter-carriers, who came and went among his friends. The messenger who brought a letter would wait for an answer; the recipient of a chatty budget might be called upon to leave his present avocations and toss off an adequate reply, or at least a few elegant, if vacuous, lines, literally by return of post. Loud were the complaints if a courier came back empty-handed, and there are signs that the habit of instructing a messenger not to return without a reply might cause annoyance comparable to what is sometimes occasioned in our own day by the telephone."[1]

The letters of the ancient world may be divided roughly into two categories, namely (1) the literary, and (2) the non-literary. The literary letter was a carefully prepared work, written with a view to publication: it was addressed to no one in particular and so lacked the note of personal intimacy, the letter form being adopted merely to create the impression of informality. When completed it was reduplicated by slaves and sold in the shops of the great cities of the Empire, just like a book. Of these literary productions some were fictitious like the "Epistles of Phalaris", while others, like the Epistles of

---

[1] Brooke, *Private Letters, Pagan and Christian,* 1929, p. 21.

Horace and Ovid, were genuine. This literary form was familiar not only to the Greeks and the Romans, but also to the Jews, as is shown by the "Epistle of Jeremiah" appended to the "Book of Baruch" and the Epistles at the beginning of 2 "Maccabees". It is customary to style this kind of letter "Epistle", which may be defined as a literary composition, cast in the form of a letter and expressly intended for publication.

The non-literary letter was an informal communication, written more or less hurriedly without much concern for style and addressed to a particular person or particular persons. Since it is not the product of conscious art, it is more spontaneous and more personal than the Epistle. Of recent years there have been recovered from the sands of Egypt many such letters, which are invaluable for the light they shed on the lives of the common people during the Ptolemaic and Roman periods.[1]

Opinions differ as to which of the above categories Paul's letters belong; but since they combine elements of the Epistle and the ordinary private letter, they cannot strictly be said to belong to either of them. In the depth of their thought and their literary finish they are akin to the Epistle, and are far removed from the simple, unstudied letters discovered in the sands of Egypt. Even Paul's enemies in the church at Corinth recognized their superiority over the ordinary letters with which they were familiar, as is shown by their words: "For, His letters ... are weighty and strong; but his bodily presence is weak, and his speech of no account" (2 Cor. x. 10). The author of 2 "Peter" also realized the depth of their thought, when he wrote that in the Epistles of "our beloved brother Paul" there are "some things hard to be understood" (2 Peter iii. 15–16). His letter to the "Romans", for example, is more of a theological treatise than a letter and was probably the result of many years of meditation.

It is true that Paul's letters were dictated to an amanuensis, but it does not necessarily follow, as some critics assert, that they were ephemeral productions, composed without much

[1] Deissman, *Light from the Ancient East*, 1927.

thought and effort. With the exception of "Philemon" they were all written to be read aloud in the church-meeting. Some of them, like 1 and 2 "Thessalonians" and "Philippians", are addressed to particular churches; "Galatians" is addressed "to the churches of Galatia"; "Colossians" is to be sent on to Laodicea, and a letter to Laodicea is to be forwarded to Colossae (Col. iv. 16). Since Paul knew that his letters would be given wide publicity, we may be sure that he would not send a carelessly composed manuscript: he would naturally be concerned, not only for the thought of his letters, but also for their style. Some of the noblest passages in his writings (cf. 1 Cor. xiii., xv.) are composed with such consummate literary skill that it is impossible to believe that they were thrown off on the spur of the moment.

On the other hand, Paul's letters have much in common with the ordinary, non-literary letters of the age. They were generally dictated to an amanuensis, the Apostle himself adding at the end his signature and a few words of personal greeting: in this he was following the practice of the times, for in many of the recently discovered papyri the signature is in a different hand from the body of the letter. In the matter of structure they are modelled on that of the private letter, which included opening greeting, thanksgiving and prayer, special contents, salutation, and valediction. As regards subject-matter, they undoubtedly contain a certain amount of doctrine and exhortation, but they are, nevertheless, neither theological treatises nor sermons, but real letters, every one of which is written to meet an immediate need, such as to correct an erroneous impression derived from a previous letter, as in 2 "Thessalonians", or to combat heresy, as in "Colossians". When we study the style, we find that it is not uniform throughout, but that it adapts itself according to the mood called forth by the situation in which the Apostle finds himself. It can be smooth and calm, as when he is pursuing an argument, abrupt and impassioned, abounding in interrogations, anacolutha, and other irregularities, as when he is defending himself and his Gospel against his enemies, or lofty and sublime, as when he is dealing with the question of the resurrection of the dead. As his readers are for the most part uneducated he frequently employs the phraseology of the non-literary letter—a phraseology which had evidently become stereotyped by long usage. Paul's letters, therefore, have something of the freedom, the intimacy, and the warmth of feeling of the private letter. We may say that he took as his model the private letter of the times, adopted its structure and and to some extent its phraseology, enlarged its scope, polished it, and employed it as a means of communication between himself and various churches scattered throughout the mission-field.

Date

Paul's letters are the earliest New Testament documents that have come down to us. Their chronology cannot be accurately determined, but on the hypothesis that "Galatians" was written immediately before the Council of Jerusalem (c. A.D. 49) and that the Captivity Epistles belong to the period of the Apostle's two years' imprisonment at Rome (c. A.D. 59–61) they must have been written at various dates within the period A.D. 48–61. They are earlier than the Gospels which, though they occupy first place in the New Testament Canon, belong to the period c. A.D. 65–110; earlier than "Acts", which records the life of Paul down to within two years or so of his death; and earlier than the rest of the New Testament writings, which, it is generally agreed, fall outside the Apostle's lifetime.

Collection

We do not know by whom or how Paul's letters were first collected or the exact date of their publication. It is certain that Paul could not have published them himself in his own life-time as they were not written for publication, and he probably had no idea that he was producing works which one day would be placed on a level with the Scriptures. His greatness as a missionary and the "weightiness" of his letters were recognized even during his lifetime, while after his death his name was held in increasing veneration and his letters soon came to be regarded as an authoritative source and standard of Christian teaching. It would not be long, therefore, before there would be a widespread desire for a collection of his letters, which were known to be preserved and treasured by various Christian communities. Since all his letters, with the exception of "Romans", were addressed to churches or individuals in the provinces of Galatia, Asia, Macedonia, and Achaia, it is possible that some prominent Christian or group of Christians in one of the influential churches of these provinces, like Ephesus or Corinth, may have borrowed the letters (originals or copies) from the archives of local churches or from private persons; but it is more likely that Paul kept copies, at least of his most important letters, and that on his death they passed into the custody of the Church, and were in due course published, perhaps at Rome, in order to satisfy a widespread demand for them. There is some reason for thinking that a collection of Paul's letters were circulating throughout the Church towards the close of the first century. Clement of Rome (c. A.D. 96), writing over thirty years after the Apostle's death, assumes in his first letter to the Corinthian church that its members were familiar with 1 "Corinthians", for he bids them turn to the letter which the "blessed apostle Paul" wrote to them "when he began to spread the Gospel". His letter shows that he himself was acquainted, not only with 1 "Corinthians", but also with "Romans". The letters of Ignatius and Polycarp, which probably belong to the first quarter of the second century, reveal such an intimate knowledge of the thought and language of the Pauline letters, that it is evident that they must have been in possession of a collection almost identical with our own. It is not, however, until the beginning of the fourth decade of the same century that we have definite evidence for the existence of a Pauline collection. The heretic Marcion (c. A.D. 140), rejecting the Jewish Scriptures, published his own Canon of the New Testament, consisting of a mutilated version of Luke's Gospel, together with a collection of ten Pauline letters (the three Pastoral Letters and "Hebrews" being omitted). Since there is no evidence that Marcion made the collection himself, we may assume that he made use of one which was already in existence in the Church.

Paul's Contribution to the Canon

Of the twenty-seven books of the New Testament, twenty-one are letters, and of these fourteen are traditionally ascribed to Paul. Of these fourteen, "Hebrews" is now almost universally rejected as being non-Pauline, while there is wide acceptance of the view that the three Pastoral Letters are pseudonymous works, embodying genuine fragments of the Apostle's correspondence. The four "principal Epistles", namely, "Galatians", 1 and 2 "Corinthians", and "Romans" are indisputably genuine, while objections have been raised by some critics to the authenticity of 2 "Thessalonians" and "Ephesians", but the balance of the argument is in favour of the traditional view. We are thus left with ten letters, which may, with reasonable certainty, be ascribed to Paul. They are "Galatians", 1 and 2 "Thessalonians", 1 and 2 "Corinthians", "Romans", "Ephesians", "Colossians", "Philemon", and "Philippians".

Lost Letters

It would appear that not all Paul's letters have been preserved. His earliest writings were "Galatians" and 1 and 2 "Thessalonians", but the final greeting in 2 "Thessalonians" —"The salutation of me Paul with mine own hand, which is the token in every epistle: so I write" (III. 17)—suggests that during the early period of his missionary career, he wrote other letters besides the three which we now possess. References are made to lost letters in 1 "Corinthians" V. 9 and 2 "Corinthians" II. 4, VII. 8, but portions of these may be preserved in the sections, 2 "Corinthians" VI. 14–VII. 1, and 2 "Corinthians" X.–XIII. respectively. It is probable that "Romans" XVI. 1–23 is a fragment of a letter originally sent to Ephesus, and that only fragments of several of Paul's notes are embedded in the Pastoral Letters. We may safely assume that the Apostle wrote many letters of which only a few have survived the centuries.

Historical Value

The Epistles are valuable historical documents because they add considerably to our knowledge of the life, teaching, and character of Paul derived from "Acts", which is our sole authority for the history of the early Church from the Ascension to the arrival of Paul at Rome. As a historian, the author of "Acts" is chiefly concerned with the foundation of churches, not with the work of consolidation. Such matters as the organization, administration, doctrine, and worship of the Church are omitted or rarely touched upon, his chief aim being to show the progress of the Gospel from Palestine, through Gentile lands to Rome. Without the Epistles, for example, we should not know that Paul was responsible for the pastoral oversight of the churches which he had founded, and that he communicated with them partly by means of letters, nor that some of his converts were little more than nominal Christians, unworthy of their high calling, that his authority was not always recognized, and that on more than one occasion he was called upon to meet a dangerous situation. We should know nothing of the activities of the Judaizers in the Galatian churches, of the views of the Thessalonian Christians concerning the Second Advent, of the disorders in the Corinthian church, of the measures taken to raise money to help the poor Christians at Jerusalem, of the growth of heresy in the churches at Ephesus and Colossae, of Paul's endeavours to win the support of the church at Rome for his projected mission to Spain, or of the generosity of the Philippian Christians.

Paul's Epistles must rank as at least equal to his missionary labours as the source of his influence on the development of Christianity. His missionary labours covered Cilicia, Cyprus, the interior of Asia Minor, Macedonia, and Greece; but he was not the founder of the churches in Antioch, Alexandria, Rome, or North Africa. Ephesus became more famous as the supposed home of John and the actual source of the Johannine literature than as a scene of Paul's labours. But his Epistles were read everywhere, and contain his interpretation of the Gospel which has had a profound influence on Christian thought throughout the centuries.

Finally, in the Epistles Paul unconsciously reveals himself in all the richness of his personality. "Thus every letter is a picture of Paul, and therein lies the unique value of the letters as sources for a historical account of this author. There can be but few Christians of later days for whose inner lives we have such thoroughly undesigned sources of information. Even the 'Confessions' of Augustine with their literary appeal to the public cannot stand comparison with Paul's letters. And there are probably exceedingly few people of the Imperial Age of Rome whom we can study so exactly as we can Paul through his letters."[1]

Chronology of Paul's Life and Epistles

Differences of two or three years exist in the dating given by various writers to events in Paul's life; the following table is therefore only approximate. The only Epistle on which there is a serious difference of opinion as regards the period of his life at which it was written is "Galatians", though some few writers place the "Captivity Epistles" earlier.

	A.D.
Conversion of Paul	32
First visit to Jerusalem	35
Second visit to Jerusalem	46
First missionary journey	47–48
"Galatians"	48 or 49
Third visit to Jerusalem	49
Council of Jerusalem	49
Second missionary journey	49–52
1 and 2 "Thessalonians"	50–51
Fourth visit to Jerusalem	52
Third missionary journey	52–56
All letters to Corinthians, "Romans"	55–56
Fifth visit to Jerusalem	56
Paul's arrest and imprisonment at Caesarea	56–58
Appeal and voyage to Rome	59
Imprisonment at Rome	59–61
"Captivity Epistles" ("Colossians", "Philemon", "Ephesians", "Philippians")	59–61
Paul's execution	64

[1] Deissman, *Paul, a Study in Social and Religious History*, 1926, p. 25.

CHAPTER XIII

THE EPISTLE TO THE GALATIANS

Galatia

Galatia was a district in the centre of Asia Minor, bounded roughly on the north by Bithynia and Pontus, on the south by Lycaonia, on the east by Cappadocia, and on the west by Phrygia. From the third century B.C. onward it was inhabited by Keltic tribes which had conquered the original natives who were of Phrygian stock. Their chief cities were Ancyrus, Tavium, and Pessinus. In 189 B.C. they were defeated by the Romans but were allowed to retain their independence under the protection of Rome. When Pompey reorganized the East in A.D. 64, Galatia became a client state of Rome, and from this time onward it was ruled, first by three chiefs with the status of tetrarchs, and finally by a single ruler with the title of king. On the death of King Amyntas in 25 B.C. his dominions were formed into a province of the Roman Empire and called "Galatia". It comprised the original kingdom, and in the south, Pisidia and parts of Phrygia and Lycaonia. Thus, in the time of Paul the cities of Antioch-in-Pisidia, Iconium, Lystra, and Derbe, were all in the Roman province of Galatia.

Recipients

It is impossible to state definitely the persons to whom the Epistle is addressed, owing to the ambiguity of the term "Galatia" or "Galatians". The North-Galatian theory takes Galatia to mean the original pre-Roman kingdom, and maintains that the Epistle was written to churches founded by Paul on his second missionary journey (Acts XVI. 6), and revisited by him on his third missionary journey as recorded in "Acts" XVIII. 23. The South-Galatian theory, on the other hand, takes Galatia to mean the Roman province of that name, in the south of which lay the cities of Antioch-in-Pisidia, Iconium,

Lystra, and Derbe, and maintains that the Epistle was addressed to the churches founded by Paul in these cities on his first missionary journey (Acts XIII. 13–XIV.) and revisited by him on his second missionary journey (Acts XVI. 6). Until recently the North-Galatian theory was generally taken for granted, but the South-Galatian theory is now widely but not universally accepted on the following grounds.

1. The evidence that Paul ever visited Galatia proper is derived from the two phrases recorded in "Acts" in which we read that on his second missionary journey he passed through "the region of Phrygia and Galatia" and finally reached Troas (XVI. 6–8), and that on his third missionary tour he passed through "the region of Galatia and Phrygia" on his way to Ephesus (XVIII. 23, XIX. 1). Both statements, however, probably refer to the same district, namely the Phrygian region in the south of the Roman province of Galatia. Moreover, Galatia proper would be entirely in the wrong direction for Paul, since his intention was to preach in Asia until he was forbidden by the Holy Spirit (Acts XVI. 6), and also in the wrong direction for arriving "over against Mysia" (Acts XVI. 7). The implication of "Acts", too, is that he travelled from Iconium to Troas without preaching on the way.

2. It is contended that only the inhabitants of Galatia proper could have been called "Galatians". But Paul, in speaking of the churches which he had founded, was accustomed to employ the names of Roman provinces: thus he speaks of "Asia", "Macedonia", and "Achaia", so it is reasonable to assume that he spoke of "Galatia" in the same sense.

3. The repeated mention of Barnabas (Gal. II. 1, 9, 13) implies that he was personally known to the Galatians; but he did not accompany Paul on his second missionary journey, when the latter is supposed to have evangelized them. There was therefore no point in mentioning him, since they would have no interest in his activities.

4. In 1 "Corinthians" XVI. 1–4, we read that the churches of Galatia took part in the collection made by Paul for the poor Christians at Jerusalem. Delegates from all the provinces which he had visited accompanied him on his journey to

Jerusalem, but none was sent from Galatia proper, whereas Gaius and Timothy, who were delegates (Acts xx. 4), came from Derbe and Lystra respectively.

5. In "Galatians" IV. 13 Paul says, "But ye know that because of an infirmity of the flesh I preached the Gospel unto you the first time," from which we infer that his visit to the Galatians was the result of an illness. It is unlikely that under the circumstances he should have made a long and hazardous journey to Galatia proper. Probably on his first missionary journey he left the enervating climate of the lowlands of Perga for the more bracing climate of the highlands of Antioch-in-Pisidia.

6. A letter to the important cities of Antioch-in-Pisidia, Iconium, Lystra, and Derbe, is much more likely than to the scattered rural population of Galatia proper, for it was always Paul's policy to plant Christianity in the chief centres of population from which it could spread to the surrounding districts.

7. It is unlikely that the Judaizers should have passed by the cities of South Galatia, in which Paul had conducted a highly successful mission, and begun their campaign in the unimportant churches of a remote district in the north of the province.

8. The words: "But ye received me as an angel of God, even as Christ Jesus" (Gal. IV. 14), are perhaps a reference to the incident at Lystra when Paul was mistaken for Mercury, while the words: "For I bear branded on my body the marks of Jesus" (Gal. VI. 17), may be an allusion to the stoning of the Apostle at the same place.

Purpose

In the course of his first missionary journey Paul had preached the Gospel at Antioch-in-Pisidia, Iconium, Lystra, and Derbe, establishing churches which were predominantly Gentile, and appointing officials to supervise them. Gentile converts had been admitted to the Church without having to submit to the rite of circumcision, which imposed the obligation to observe the Law. In spite of his bodily infirmity, the inhabitants had welcomed him with great enthusiasm; they had received him as an angel of God, and would have plucked out their eyes for him (IV. 14–15). The Apostle felt that they had made a promising start in the Christian life (v. 7), strengthened as they were by the gift of the Holy Spirit, whose presence was manifested among them in works of power (III. 1–5). Shortly after his departure, certain Judaizers, with a prominent and evidently powerful person at their head, appeared among them, determined to undo the Apostle's work. They insisted upon the necessity of obedience to the Law, declaring that Paul's Gospel was incomplete and needed supplementing by external observance and ritualism, and even by circumcision. Recognizing that his authority and personal influence were an obstacle to their success, they adopted the policy of denying his apostolic authority and the validity of his Gospel, and by attributing his preaching to unworthy motives. He was a second-rate preacher who had derived his authority from the original Apostles. All that was common in his teaching and their own he had derived from the Twelve, while that which was new and distinctive was no part of the true Gospel. In his desire to please men he had been guilty of inconsistency, now opposing circumcision and now teaching it (I. 6–10).

The Judaizers seem to have been men of importance, at least in the eyes of the Galatians, over whom they soon acquired considerable influence. By the use of flattery and fair speech they had so bewitched the Galatians that some of them had submitted to the rite of circumcision and had begun to observe "days, and months, and seasons, and years" (IV. 10), and to take upon them the yoke of the Law with all its burdens.

When Paul heard of their sudden defection he was both alarmed and indignant, for he saw clearly that it meant, not only the undermining of his own authority and personal influence among the Galatians, but also the substitution of the doctrine of justification by the works of the Law for the great truth, which he had taught them, of justification by faith alone (for the meaning of this doctrine see Chapter XVI on "Romans"), and the destruction of all hope that Christianity would become a universal religion. As he was unable for some reason to visit the Galatians, he wrote his Epistle to defend his apostolic authority and the validity of his Gospel, to vindicate his character against the accusations of his enemies, to point out to the Galatians the fatal consequences of their error in believing the Gospel of the Judaizers, and to recall them to the Gospel of liberty which he had made known to them.

Contents

Apologetic. After a short introduction Paul vindicates the independence of his apostolic authority. He received his commission as an Apostle and his Gospel, not from men but by direct revelation from Christ. Before his conversion he was a zealous Jew and a fierce persecutor of the Christian Church. Immediately after his conversion he did not resort to the original Apostles for instruction in the Christian faith, but instead went into Arabia and thence returned to Damascus. It was not till three years after his conversion that he visited Jerusalem, when of the Apostles he saw only Peter and James. Afterwards he travelled to Syria and Cilicia, and was unknown by sight to the brethren of Judaea (I. 1–24).

Fourteen years later he revisited Jerusalem and discussed the Gospel privately with the leaders of the Church. He made no concession to the Judaizers, not even when the question of the circumcision of Titus was raised: on the contrary the leaders treated him as an equal, and recognized that he had a sphere of labour among the Gentiles as truly as Peter had among the Jews (II. 1–10). Later, at Antioch, he publicly rebuked Peter for his inconsistency in breaking the Law himself, while at the same time desiring to enforce its observance upon Gentile converts (II. 11–21).

Doctrinal. The Galatians must be bewitched since they have turned their hearts away from the Gospel of a crucified Saviour. He asks them when they received the Holy Spirit—clearly this was an outward event, as it was with the Apostles at Pentecost, or with the Samaritans, Cornelius, and others—when they came to believe in Christ or when they began to keep the Law (III. 1–2). (The historical answer is, of course, "When they came to believe in Christ," and this must be the doctrinal answer, too.) The Jews base their claims on being the descendants of Abraham. But the Old Testament itself asserts that "Abraham

believed God, and it was reckoned unto him for righteousness"
(III. 6), and that all nations should be blessed in him (III. 8), thus
proclaiming the justification of the Gentiles by faith (III. 9); and
this promise could not be abrogated by the Law, which was
given four hundred and thirty years later (III. 15–18). So belief
produces a blessing (III. 8) whereas the Law produces a curse,
since no man can completely fulfil it; this curse Christ removes
(III. 10–14). Why then was the Law given? The Law was given
as a temporary measure until Christ came, its object being to
make men realize their sinfulness and their need of a Saviour.
It was given through the mediator, Moses, and the angels;
but the promise of God was far stronger because its continuance
depended on Him alone (III. 19–22).

The Law is like the slave who takes children to school—it
looked after men while it led them to the true teacher, Christ,
that they might be accounted righteous on the score of faith
(III. 23–26). Those who are united with Christ are members of
a kingdom in which all distinctions of race, condition, and
class are obliterated (III. 27–29).

He contrasts their pupilage and subjection under the Law
with their spiritual freedom as sons of God, and appeals to them
as his spiritual children not to relapse into slavery (IV. 1–20).

He gives an allegorical interpretation of the story of Sarah
and Hagar to prove that those who believe in salvation by
faith in Christ (the descendants of the freewoman, Sarah) are
the true sons of Abraham and spiritually free, whereas those
who believe in salvation by the works of the Law (the descendants of the bondwoman, Hagar) are spiritually in bondage
(IV. 21–31).

He exhorts them to stand fast in their Christian liberty which
Christ has won for them. Circumcision involves the keeping of
the Law and their separation from Christ: if they are united
with Him, circumcision is of no importance (V. 1–12). Freedom
must not be confused with licence: true freedom will manifest
itself, not in selfish indulgence, but in service to others. The
works of the flesh are contrasted with the fruits of the Spirit
(V. 13–26).

Practical. He exhorts them to exercise forbearance towards their erring brethren, to be humble, to support their teachers, to realize their responsibilities to themselves and to others, and to continue in well-doing (vi. 1–5).

In the concluding words, written in his own bold hand-writing, he condemns once more the false teachers, and sums up the main points of his Epistle, closing with a final bene-diction (vi. 6–18).

Place and Date of Composition

The place and date of composition cannot be fixed with any certainty. On the North-Galatian theory, the Epistle must have been written in the course of Paul's third missionary journey, after his second visit to Galatia (Acts xviii. 23), either on his way from Galatia to Ephesus, or at Ephesus (Acts xix. 1–41), or during his journey via Macedonia to Corinth (Acts xx. 1), or at Corinth (Acts xx. 2–3). Bishop Lightfoot, basing his argument on the close affinity of "Galatians" with 1 and 2 "Corinthians" and "Romans", contends that the four Epistles belong to the same period in Paul's life, and that "Galatians" was written in Macedonia after 2 "Corinthians" and rather earlier than "Romans".

The South-Galatian theory admits of two dates. Those who think that two visits are implied in "Galatians" iv. 13, and that they can only be those recorded in "Acts" xiii. 13–xiv., and xvi. 1–6, hold that the Epistle must have been written during the second missionary journey after Galatia had been traversed or after the Apostle's return from it, and that it may therefore have been composed in Macedonia, Athens, Corinth, or Antioch-in-Syria. Probably, however, the Greek of "Galatians" iv. 13 does not imply two visits, but merely a comparison of his original preaching with his present attitude. Even if it does imply two visits, in a letter written shortly after leaving the province, the outward journey and the return journey (as far as Lystra, Iconium, and Antioch-in-Pisidia, the towns at which the incidents referred to in the Epistle occurred, were concerned), would naturally be treated as two visits, since the time between them might be longer than between the second and the writing of the Epistle. It is therefore more probable that the Epistle was written at Antioch-in-Syria shortly after Paul's return from his first missionary journey and before the Council of Jerusalem. This theory is supported by the following facts.

1. The traditional view which identifies Paul's second visit to Jerusalem, recorded in "Galatians" II. 1–10, with the third visit in "Acts" xv., is probably wrong: the second visit in "Galatians" corresponds, not with the third visit in "Acts", but with the second (Acts XI. 27–30). It may be noted that the apostolic letter from the Council of Jerusalem in "Acts" xv. 23–29, is addressed to the churches in Syria and Cilicia, of which Antioch-in-Syria and Tarsus were respectively the chief, not to those in Galatia. This shows that the Council was not summoned on account of Paul's first missionary journey but because of previous work. The history of the development of events may be reconstructed thus. Paul and Barnabas spent about twelve months conducting a missionary campaign in Antioch-in-Syria, in the course of which the question of the relation of Gentile converts to the Law arose and caused a certain amount of trouble in the local church. When the two Apostles were appointed to take relief to the poor Christians at Jerusalem (Acts XI. 27–30), Paul consented to undertake the task, partly because he was keenly interested in the material welfare of the poor, but mainly because he wished to discuss his Gospel with the recognized leaders of the Church. In a private interview he succeeded in gaining recognition for his teaching and work among the Gentiles, while at the same time assuring them of his determination to minister to the needs of the poor (Gal. II. 10). The amicable settlement, however, apparently did not satisfy the Judaizers. Later, on the return of the Apostles from their first missionary journey, Judaizers from Jerusalem appeared at Antioch-in-Syria, demanding that the admission of Gentile converts should be made conditional upon their submission to the rite of circumcision. They also sent emissaries to the Galatian churches, which Paul and Barnabas had founded, to persuade the new converts to accept all the obligations of the Law. On hearing of the success of these Judaizing emissaries and of the sudden defection of some

of the Galatian converts, Paul wrote his Epistle in a white heat of indignation. So serious was the trouble at Antioch-in-Syria that it was thought advisable to convene a Council at Jerusalem to settle the question. The result was a triumph for Paul and the upholders of Gentile liberty (Acts xv.). On his second missionary tour Paul announced as the agreed policy of the leaders of the Church what he had already urged in his Epistle.

2. The omission of any reference to the decrees of the Council of Jerusalem can be explained if the Epistle was written before it took place.

3. If the original "Romans" was a circular letter, it also might have been written before the Council of Jerusalem.

On the supposition that "Galatians" was written before the Council of Jerusalem, it may be dated about the year A.D. 48 or 49, and is the earliest of Paul's letters which we possess.

Authenticity

External Evidence. The Epistle is sufficiently alluded to or quoted to prove that the early patristic writers were acquainted with it. It was known to Polycarp, Ignatius, and Justin Martyr, and was included in Marcion's Canon, the Muratorian Fragment, and the Old Latin and Syriac Versions of the New Testament. Irenaeus, Clement of Alexandria, and Tertullian recognized it as a genuine work of Paul, while according to Origen "Galatians" vi. 14 was the only passage from Paul's Epistles which the anti-Christian writer, Celsus, quoted. In recent times, the Tübingen school of critics recognized its genuineness, and employed it, together with 1 and 2 "Corinthians" and "Romans", as a basis for their attack on the other Epistles attributed to Paul.

Internal Evidence. The Epistle deals with a question which belongs to an early stage in the history of the Church. By the Fall of Jerusalem in A.D. 70 the controversy concerning the relation of Gentiles to the Law had become a thing of the past, and consequently the Epistle must have been written during Paul's lifetime. There is nothing in it which might be considered a motive for forgery.

In subject-matter and style it is in harmony with the other

Pauline Epistles. Most of the Apostle's doctrines, notably those of the righteousness of God, of justification by faith in a crucified Redeemer, of reconciliation with God through Christ, of sanctification by His Spirit, and of the freedom and universality of the Gospel, are indicated in the Epistle, though they are not completely worked out as they are in "Romans". The style, with its apt metaphors and rhetorical devices, its vigour and bursts of eloquence, its condensation of thought and keen logic, its rabbinical method of reasoning and unconscious delineation of character, are typically Pauline, and stamp the Epistle as indisputably the work of Paul. No better verification of the maxim, "the style is the man", could be found in all literature; it is, in fact, so characteristic of the Apostle that no forger could possibly have imitated it so successfully as to deceive generations of readers.

Historical Value

"Galatians" has been called the Magna Charta of Christian freedom. Paul's opponents in the Galatian churches were not orthodox Jews; they were Jewish Christians who, while accepting Jesus as Christ and Lord, taught that salvation depended upon the strict observance of the Law. The Apostle lost no time in combating this dangerous doctrine with all the force at his command, for he saw clearly that nothing less than the truth of the Gospel was at stake. His efforts were evidently successful for we hear no more of the controversy in the Galatian churches. He thus saved Christianity, which was a world religion, from becoming an obscure Jewish sect probably doomed to ultimate extinction.

Paul's great doctrine of justification by faith has inspired men throughout the ages to resist all attacks on the liberty and truth of the Gospel. His rabbinical method of reasoning has doubtless lost its appeal, but the ultimate basis of the doctrine rests, not on arguments drawn from the Old Testament, but on his own personal experience of the inadequacy of the Law as a method of attaining to righteousness, and of the new power and sense of peace which come to a man who lives by faith in Christ.

CHAPTER XIV

THE FIRST AND SECOND EPISTLES TO THE THESSALONIANS

I THESSALONIANS

Thessalonica

Thessalonica was an important commercial city, situated at the head of the Thermaic Gulf and on the Egnatian Way, which crossed the Balkan Peninsula, forming a link between Italy and the East. It was the capital of the province of Macedonia and a "free city", ruled by its own magistrates or "politarchs" and popular assembly. There was a colony of Jews in the city, as is shown by the presence of a synagogue there: attached to this synagogue were many God-fearers who had been drawn to Judaism by its sublime monotheism and its stern moral code (Acts XVII. 4).

Foundation of Local Church

On his second missionary journey Paul, with his companions, came to Thessalonica and on three successive sabbaths reasoned in the synagogue, making some converts among the Jews but many more among the "devout Greeks". The Evangelists continued their campaign until they were finally driven out by the intrigues of the orthodox Jews, who indirectly raised a tumult in the city and laid a charge of sedition and treason against them before the local magistrates (Acts XVII. 5–7). Before their departure, however, they had founded a church, composed largely of Gentiles, while the central position of Thessalonica on the Thermaic Gulf and the Egnatian Way offered a splendid opportunity for the spread of the Gospel to the surrounding districts (1 Thess. I. 7, IV. 10).

Purpose, Place, and Date of Composition

Leaving Thessalonica the Evangelists travelled westward to Beroea, where they preached the Gospel with great success until their work was again interrupted by the arrival of Jews from Thessalonica, intent on fomenting trouble. Paul therefore withdrew to Athens where he was joined by Timothy and Silas (Acts XVII. 10–15). The Apostle no doubt heard that the Thessalonian converts were suffering persecution at the hands of their fellow countrymen (1 Thess. II. 14) and longed to revisit them but Satan, he says, hindered him (1 Thess. II. 18). Though he dreaded being left alone at Athens, he at last sent Timothy back to Thessalonica to strengthen their faith and to report (1 Thess. III. 1–5), and it would seem that Silas was sent on another mission, perhaps to Philippi (cf. Acts XVIII. 5; Phil. IV. 15). Meanwhile Paul moved on to Corinth where Timothy found him and made his report (Acts XVIII. 5; 1 Thess. III. 6), which was, on the whole, reassuring. There had been persecution but the Thessalonians had stood firm, so much so that they had set a fine example to all the Christians in the provinces of Macedonia and Achaia (1 Thess. I. 7). The rest of the news was not so satisfactory. There appear to have been division between the Jewish and Gentile sections of the church, and a tendency to laxity of morals. Paul's enemies were trying to discredit him by casting doubts upon his motives and conduct, while some of the converts, taking advantage of the communal spirit in the church, had ceased to work and were looking to their fellow Christians to support them in idleness. During his mission to the Thessalonians, the Apostle had apparently taught that the Lord would soon return to establish His kingdom on the earth and that they would survive to see Him coming in His glory. They were, therefore, naturally concerned about the fate of those of their number who had already died. Paul, therefore, wrote his first Epistle to the Thessalonians to encourage them to stand firm under persecution, to vindicate his character, to warn them against the temptation to immorality and idleness, and to relieve them of their anxieties touching the fate of their friends who had been removed by death. It was written from Corinth about A.D. 50.

Contents

After sending greetings Paul thanks God for the courage and

devotion of the Thessalonians, who have passed completely from their former idolatrous worship to the service of a "living and true God", and have become a worthy example to all the Christians throughout the provinces of Macedonia and Achaia (I. 1–10).

They can surely have no doubt about the purity of his motives when they recall his courage in preaching the Gospel in face of opposition, his absence of all self-seeking, his voluntary independence, his blameless life, and his tender solicitude for them (II. 1–12).

He thanks God that they have responded nobly to his teaching, accepting his message as the word of God, and enduring persecution which is the common heritage of the Christian Church (II. 13–16).

Timothy, whom he had sent to build up their church, has returned bringing "glad tidings" of their faith and love. The Apostle prays that he may soon be able to revisit them, and that they may continue to progress in love and holiness (II. 17–20, III. 1–13).

He urges upon them the necessity of chastity, brotherly love, and the diligent performance of their daily duties (IV. 1–12).

Death will not exclude the Christian from the triumph of the Second Coming (IV. 13–18).

The Coming of Christ is certain, but of "the times and the seasons" no man knows. Christians must so live as to be prepared for His Coming at any moment (V. 1–11).

The Epistle closes with a series of short exhortations, a prayer for their complete sanctification, a command that the Epistle is to be read to the whole church, and a final benediction (IV. 12–28).

Authenticity

External Evidence. The external evidence for Pauline authorship is strong. There are possible allusions to it in the works of Ignatius and Hermas: it is included in the Pauline collection of Marcion (*c.* 140) and in the Muratorian Fragment (*c.* 170).

Irenaeus is the first to quote from it, and later allusions to it by Clement of Alexandria and Tertullian make it clear that it was accepted as a genuine epistle of Paul. It is also contained in the Syriac and Old Latin Versions of the New Testament.

Internal Evidence. The internal evidence is equally strong. The affectionate and confident tone of the Epistle, the judicious combination of reproof and exhortation, and the vigorous style are typically Pauline. No forger, writing after Paul's death, would have represented him as expecting to survive until the Second Coming (VI. 15–17), since he would have known that his anticipation of survival had been falsified by the event. The difficulty created in the minds of the Thessalonian converts by the death of some of their number before the Second Coming clearly belongs to an early stage in the development of the Christian Church. No motive has ever been advanced for the forgery of such a letter in Paul's name.

Arguments against Pauline Authorship. A few objections have, however, been made.

(1) It is alleged that Acts XVII. 4 implies that, apart from a nucleus of Jews, the bulk of Thessalonian Christians were "God-fearers", whereas the Epistle (I. 9, II. 14, IV. 1–5) treats them as former idolaters with pagan morals. But "God-fearers" had been brought up as pagans.

(2) It is also objected that Acts XVII. 2 states that Paul preached "for three sabbaths" in the synagogue, whereas the Epistle implies a stay of some length. But there is no contradiction here; Paul always began by preaching to the Jews, and the three weeks are only concerned with this stage.

(3) Again, "but the wrath is come upon them to the uttermost" (1 Thess. II. 16), is alleged to refer to the Fall of Jerusalem. Actually it is a quotation from "The Testament of Levi" (VI. 11), which Paul thinks to be applicable to his statement about the treatment accorded by the Jews, first to Jesus and subsequently to His followers. The words translated, "to the uttermost", mean either, "to the end", or "to a completion", and have reference to the preceding words, "to fill up their sins alway"; and the meaning is that God has, in His anger against their treatment of Jesus, allowed the Jews to go on sinning (cf. 2 Thess. II. 11).

(4) An argument that the Epistle contains none of the

characteristic Pauline doctrines is alleged against several of the Epistles as well as against 1 "Thessalonians", but is equally beside the point in all cases, as it is based on a complete ignoring of the function of a letter, which is to deal with the circumstances of the moment.

2 THESSALONIANS

Purpose, Place, and Date of Composition

The second Epistle to the Thessalonians was occasioned by the report of further trouble which had arisen concerning the Second Coming. Apparently Paul's teaching had been misunderstood or misrepresented, so that certain teachers were proclaiming that the Day of the Lord was already at the door (II. 2).

The excitement and unrest, caused by this teaching, were increased by alleged revelations of the Spirit, by the interpretation of Scripture, and by the production of a letter, purporting to come from Paul, in support of such a belief (II. 1–2). Members of the church had begun to doubt whether their sufferings were reconcilable with the just judgments of God (I. 3–6). The Apostle, therefore, wrote his second Epistle to the Thessalonians to correct the erroneous teaching, and to comfort and strengthen them in their afflictions. It was written from Corinth some months after his first Epistle and may be dated early in A.D. 51.

Contents

After the opening salutation Paul declares that it is his duty to thank God for their increasing faith and brotherly love. Their endurance and faith amid all their persecutions are a demonstration of the righteous judgment of God, who at the last day will give them rest and drive for ever from His presence all those who refuse to accept the Gospel (I. 1–12).

He implores them not to be troubled by prophetic inspiration or by arguments from Scripture, or by any letter purporting to come from him, to the effect that the "Day of the Lord" has already come. Before His Coming the "Man of Sin", the embodiment of wickedness and claiming to be divine, must first appear. At present there is a restraining force holding him in check, but when this is removed he will be revealed and destroyed (II. 1-12).

He thanks God for their election to salvation, and urges them to remain steadfast in the "traditions" which they have received (II. 13-17).

He solicits their prayers for himself that he may be delivered from his enemies, and prays that they may remain loyal to his teaching (III. 1-5).

He admonishes those who are neglecting their daily work and living on charity, and advises them to live in accordance with his teaching and example (III. 6-15).

The letter closes with a greeting, in Paul's own characteristic style of writing, and a final benediction (III. 16-17).

Apocalyptic Teaching

This is the only letter of Paul in which elements of Jewish Apocalyptic, other than the Second Coming of Christ and the general Resurrection and Judgment, appear. "Apocalyptic" is the name given to a large class of Jewish literature, which appeared in the last two centuries B.C. and the first century A.D., in which the catastrophic end of the present dispensation, the triumph of "the saints", and the punishment of their persecutors, are described in terms of strange symbolic imagery, the prophecies being attributed to some well-known character of the past. Though a few apocalyptic passages have found their way into several of the prophetic books of the Old Testament, "Daniel" is the only complete Apocalypse which was accepted in the Old Testament Canon, and it is to the "Book of Daniel" that we must trace back most of the features which, with many variations of detail, reappear time after time in all these works. The part of the "Book of Daniel" which lay at the root of most of these descriptions is Chapter VII., in which, after four world empires have been described under the symbolism of four beasts (the last with ten horns), a little horn springs up "speaking great things", but it is destroyed by the Ancient of Days, and one like a Son of Man is given the dominion. This little horn developed in later literature into the Antichrist, while the figure like a Son of Man became identified with the Messiah. In the New Testament this tradition is christianized in the short Apocalypse in "Mark" (XIII. 3–37) and in the "Apocalypse (Revelation) of John". The Antichrist appears in "Mark" as the "abomination of desolation" of "Daniel" IX. 27, turned into a person, who takes his stand in the Temple (cf. Mk. XIII. 14 with Mt. XXIV. 15), and in "The Revelation" as "the great beast" (XIX. 19–21). The writer of the "First Epistle of John" assumes that his readers are familiar with the idea of the Antichrist (II. 18) but regards the Antichrist as a class of false teachers rather than as a single person. Whether Paul continued to accept a personal Antichrist all his life it is impossible to say, but he makes no mention of him in his later letters; in this Epistle, however, he accepts the idea in all its fullness, his appearance in the Temple, and his destruction at the coming of the Messiah. The only new feature is the hindrance (II. 6, 7) which prevents his final appearance, though the tendencies making for him are already at work. The only explanation which has been found for this passage is that the tendencies are the Jewish persecution of Christianity, and the hindering force is the attitude of the Roman authority, which had recently, in the person of Gallio, supported Paul against Jewish persecution.

Authenticity

External Evidence. The external evidence for 2 "Thessalonians" is equally as strong as for 1 "Thessalonians". It was apparently known to Polycarp, Ignatius, and Justin Martyr, and was included in Marcion's Canon and in the Muratorian Fragment. Direct quotations from it are found in the works of Tertullian, Irenaeus, and Clement of Alexandria.

Internal Evidence. In spite of the tradition of Pauline authorship serious objections have been raised against the authenticity, and these require a brief examination.

(1) The close similarity of much of the Epistle to 1 "Thessalonians" is said to suggest a copyist, but is easily explained if we assume that Paul re-read his first letter before he wrote the second.

(2) It is said to be Jewish in character, whereas the first Epistle is clearly written chiefly with Gentiles in mind. But the use of Apocalyptic is no proof that it was intended for Jews, as "Mark" is eminently a Gentile Gospel, and the seven churches to which the "Revelation" was written must have been mainly Gentile.

(3) It is suggested that the apparent change of attitude to the nearness of the Second Coming betokens either an attempt of a later writer to defend Paul from a charge of being wrong in his prediction of the nearness of the Coming, or else an attempt to make it appear that extreme apocalyptic views were held by Paul, who, according to this theory, did not really hold them. But the views will not hold their ground, since after Paul's time the Antichrist became identified with the Roman Empire, as we see throughout "Revelation". The Apocalyptic of 1 and 2 "Thessalonians", on the other hand, is exactly that of the short Apocalypse embodied in "Mark", which is, of course, much older than the Gospel itself, not that of the post-persecution Apocalypses.

Historical Value of 1 and 2 Thessalonians

The two Epistles are among the earliest Christian writings which we possess. They furnish us with a clear picture of an early Christian community, the members of which have just emerged from paganism. It is by no means a perfect picture. Paul is not entirely satisfied with their spiritual condition, though he is pleased with the progress they are making. They have completely abandoned idolatry and are enthusiastic in their devotion to the new faith. They live in a state of unnatural excitement, caused by the expectation of the immediate return of the Lord, and are distressed lest those of their number who have died might not share in the joys of the coming kingdom. Apart from their interest in the Second Coming they are apparently unconcerned about doctrine. The question of the relation of Gentile converts to the Mosaic Law, which had caused so much trouble in the Christian Church, has not arisen among them. They are, in fact, "babes in Christ" who need instruction in the rudiments of the Christian faith. Some of

229

them do not realize that Christianity and morality are one and cannot be separated, and that the thought of the Second Coming should inspire them to greater efforts; hence they fail to exercise moral restraint, neglect their daily work, and wrong their fellow men. They are loyal to the founders of their church, but are not disposed to obey the officers who have been placed over them.

The content of Paul's preaching to a pagan audience is shown in the two Epistles. Christianity means belief in the one true God, the risen Christ, the Second Coming, and the final Judgment. His message to pagan converts is summed up in the words: "Ye turned unto God from idols, to serve a living and true God, and to wait for his Son from heaven, whom he raised from the dead, even Jesus, which delivereth us from the wrath to come" (1 Thess. 1. 9–10).

The two Epistles supplement our knowledge of the founding of the Thessalonian church, given to us in "Acts". They afford additional information concerning the duration of Paul's mission to the Thessalonians, his relations with the local church after his departure, the composition of that church, and the moral and spiritual life of its members.

Finally, the two Epistles throw light on the personality of Paul. They reveal him, not as a theologian concerned with the formulation of a doctrinal system, but as a pastor intensely interested in the spiritual life of the church which he has founded. We see his devotion to the cause of Christ, his kindly treatment of new converts, his gentle dealing with human weaknesses, and his deep yearning for the salvation of men.

CHAPTER XV

THE FIRST AND SECOND EPISTLES
TO THE CORINTHIANS

I CORINTHIANS

Corinth

Corinth was a wealthy commercial city on the narrow isthmus connecting the Peloponnesus with the mainland of Greece. Situated on a trade-route between East and West, it was one of the most important cities of the Empire: merchandise from Italy, Sicily, and Spain passed through its western harbour Lechaeum on the Corinthian Gulf, and that from Egypt, Phoenicia, Syria, and Asia Minor, through Cenchreae on the Saronic Gulf. In New Testament times it was a comparatively modern city, the original city having been destroyed by the Romans in 146 B.C. When it was refounded as a colony by Julius Caesar in 46 B.C. it was settled with Roman veterans from Italy. Its growth was so rapid that in the time of Paul it had perhaps 500,000 inhabitants. They were a heterogeneous people consisting chiefly of Romans, Greeks, who greatly outnumbered the Roman element, Jews and Asiatics.

The city was famous, not only as a commercial centre, but also for the production of pottery and bronze ware, which were well known throughout the Mediterranean world. In a plain near by were held the Isthmian games which attracted a large concourse of strangers. The Corinthians professed a great love of learning, but no distinguished name in art, literature, and philosophy is associated with the city except that of Diogenes the Cynic. The influx of foreigners for purposes of trade, bringing with them their vices as well as their virtues, and the acquisition of wealth, led to deterioration of character. The people, too, were devoted to the worship of Aphrodite, which sanctioned gross immorality. The moral corruption of the city was a byword to contemporary writers, so that "to live like a Corinthian" was a proverbial expression for a profligate life.

In sympathies and organization it was more Roman than Greek. Of the inscriptions from Corinth belonging to the first century A.D., most of them are in Latin, the official language of the government. The Roman strain in the citizens may be seen in their delight in gladiatorial combats in the amphitheatre; it was one of the few Greek cities where such cruel spectacles were tolerated. Corinth was the political capital of the senatorial province of Achaia and the headquarters of the proconsul.

The Founding of the Church

Paul, on his second missionary journey, came from Athens to Corinth and lodged with Aquila and Priscilla, who had been expelled from Rome by an imperial edict under which all Jews were to leave the city. During the week the Apostle supported himself by his trade of tent-making, and on the Sabbath reasoned in the synagogue in an attempt to convince Jews, proselytes, and God-fearers of the truth of the Gospel (Acts xviii. 1-4). Encouraged by the arrival of Silas and Timothy, he turned to his work with renewed enthusiasm, becoming wholly absorbed in the word and testifying to the Jews that Jesus was the Christ. Finally, in spite of the conversion of Crispus, the chief ruler of the synagogue, with all his household, he was driven out of the synagogue, but pursued his task from the house belonging to Titus Justus, who lived close by. His work among the Gentiles now began to bear fruit, and many were converted, among whom were Erastus, the treasurer of the city, Gaius, and the household of Stephanas, described by Paul as "the first-fruits of Achaia" (1 Cor. xvi. 15).

We read in 1 "Corinthians" ii. 3, that Paul was with them "in weakness, and in fear, and in much trembling:" but strengthened by a vision of the night, in which the Lord assured him of his personal safety and promised him great success in his labours, he continued to work in Corinth for eighteen months, "teaching the word of God among them" (Acts xviii. 11). Angered by his activities and by his success, the orthodox Jews brought him before the court of the proconsul, Gallio, on a charge of preaching an illegal religion; but as soon as Gallio recognized that it was a purely religious dispute, he dismissed the case on the ground that he had no jurisdiction in such matters. Henceforth Paul was able to preach the Gospel without molestation, with the result that he succeeded, not only in establishing a Christian Church at Corinth, but also in evangelizing to some extent the whole of the province of Achaia (2 Cor. 1. 1).

Purpose

After a stay of eighteen months he crossed the Aegean Sea to Ephesus, accompanied by Aquila and Priscilla, whom he left there while he himself went on to Jerusalem and Antioch-in-Syria (Acts XVIII. 18–22). After Paul's departure Apollos, an eloquent Alexandrian Jew, arrived at Ephesus, and after receiving further instruction in the Christian faith from Aquila and Priscilla, was commended by the brethren to the Corinthian Church, where he continued the Apostle's work and publicly refuted the Jews, "shewing by the scriptures that Jesus was the Christ" (Acts XVIII. 24–28). Some unhappy incident, however, made him leave Corinth and return to Ephesus, where he met Paul, who was now on his third missionary journey (1 Cor. XVI. 12). The latter made Ephesus his headquarters for over two years, and preached the Gospel with such enthusiasm that we read that "all they which dwelt in Asia heard the word of the Lord, both Jews and Greeks" (Acts XIX. 10).

There are reasons for thinking that Paul wrote six letters to the Church at Corinth.[1] Some time after his arrival at Ephesus he received information from a source unknown to us that the Corinthian Christians were associating with persons guilty of immorality. He therefore wrote his first letter, commanding them not to keep company with fornicators (1 Cor. v. 9).

From members of the household of Chloe, who probably had connections with both Corinth and Ephesus, he received

[1] The six are (1) the letter mentioned in 1 Cor. v. 9, (2) our 1 Cor., (3) the lost letter, (4) the letter of defence, (5) the letter of reconciliation, (6) the letter about the collection for the poor saints at Jerusalem. Fragments of nos. 1, 4, 5 and 6 are embodied in our 2 Cor. See pp. 233–4, 239–45.

disquieting information concerning the factious spirit and the moral laxity of the Corinthian Christians (1 Cor. 1. 11). He perhaps learnt from the same source, or from Apollos, or from Stephanas, Fortunatus, and Achaicus (1 Cor. xvi. 17) of a case of incest (1 Cor. v. 1), and of the practice of bringing Christian lawsuits before pagan courts (1 Cor. vi. 1). The Corinthians, too, sent a reply to his first letter, pointing out an ambiguity in his instructions regarding their association with immoral persons, and raising a number of points on questions of doctrine, discipline, and worship, and requesting his decisions upon them.

On hearing of the disorders in the church, he dispatched Timothy to Corinth, to remind them of the teaching which he had given them (1 Cor. iv. 17). This would appear to be the same mission as that mentioned in "Acts" xix. 22, where it says that he had sent Timothy and Erastus to Macedonia. Since, however, a communication by sea would reach Corinth before Timothy, who was travelling by the overland route, he wrote his second letter (our 1 "Corinthians"), his object in writing being to correct the ambiguity of his first letter (1 Cor. v. 9), to restore order in the church, and to answer the questions on which they had sought his guidance. We are not told that Timothy ever reached Corinth; all we know is that he was in Macedonia when Paul wrote 2 "Corinthians", for he is joined with the Apostle in the opening salutation (2 Cor. 1. 1).

Place and Date of Composition

The Epistle was written at Ephesus. This is shown in 1 "Corinthians" xvi. 7–9, in which Paul, after declaring his intention of visiting Corinth, adds: "But I will tarry at Ephesus until Pentecost; for a great door and effectual is opened unto me, and there are many adversaries." Moreover, he sends salutations from "the churches of Asia" (xvi. 19), and from Aquila and Priscilla who were residing at Ephesus at the time (Acts xviii. 26).

It was written towards the close of Paul's long visit to Ephesus on this third missionary journey (Acts xix. 1–10, xx. 31) and shortly before his departure for Greece (Acts xx.

1–2). The exact date is doubtful, but it was probably written early in A.D. 55.

Contents

The Epistle, like all Paul's letters, is not logically arranged, though we can always see how each section suggests the next. After the introduction (1. 1–9) we can trace two main strands, namely (1) dealing with complaints against himself and disorders in the church, and (2) questions raised by members, together with cognate matters suggested by these questions. It is easier to understand the drift of the Epistle if these matters are sorted out, rather than by taking the sections of the letter in the order in which they appear.

1. *Complaints against himself.* It is clear from 2 "Corinthians" that there was a section of the Corinthian Church opposed to Paul, and one special leader of that section, whose name never appears. In this Epistle there is less defence of himself than in 2 "Corinthians", but we can see that the complaints are troubling him.

(a) The more definitely Greek section complains that his teaching is lacking in the qualities which all Greeks looked for in their teachers, namely, rhetoric and philosophy. This, he says, is as great a stumbling-block to the Greeks as the apparently self-contradictory idea of a crucified Messiah is to the Jews. To the Jews it is the humiliating aspect which is the obstacle, to the Greeks the lack of intellectual meaning. There is, too, a suspicion of the Gospel because few persons of learning, rank, or influence, have become converts (1. 17b–31). His reply is that to the Christian the Crucifixion is not a sign of human weakness but the source of a Divine Power, not a sordid piece of human folly but a source of Divine Wisdom: to the complaint of the ignorance and poverty of the converts, he replies that God shows His power all the more by choosing the weak, ignorant, and poor, to confound the strong, the learned, and the rich. But he goes on to modify what he has said on the unphilosophic character of Christianity (II.). Christianity, it is true, does not depend on any philosophy which can be reasoned out by human logic, but it is based on the hidden plan of the

Divine Mind which is revealed by the Divine Spirit to the developed Christian—not to Christian beginners, "the babes in Christ", who are still thinking in human terms, as he is afraid they are.

(b) Some definitely challenge his position as an Apostle (ix. 1–2) and apparently bring up the fact of his living by his own labour and not on the support of the Corinthian converts like his opponents, as a proof that he did not make the same claims to be an Apostle as they did. He meets this by emphasizing most vigorously his right to such sustenance (ix. 3–14), but declaring that it was because it was part of his universal policy of being "all things to all men" that he might by all means save some, that he had not exercised that right (ix. 15–27).

Charges against the Corinthian Church. (a) The first, which is closely connected with the attacks on himself, is the formation of parties—of Paul, Peter (Cephas), and Apollos, and another which claimed to be specifically of Christ (i. 10–17a). He returns to this question in Chapter iii., where he points out that Paul, Apollos, or any other preacher plays but a subordinate part. This he shows by two comparisons—with a building and with a garden. The building is the Christian community; the foundation is Christ; on this foundation every preacher must build, and be judged by the success of his building. The garden was planted by himself (Paul), and watered by Apollos, but the real work is that of God, who gives the growth.

(b) He deals with an incestuous marriage. The offender should be excluded from the fellowship of the church until he renounces his sin and in penitence seeks readmission (v. 1–8).

(c) They go to law with one another before pagan law courts. In case of a dispute they should choose a "wise man" as arbiter; but no Christian ought to give occasion for a lawsuit. It is better to suffer injustice than to bring the church into public disgrace (vi. 1–8).

(d) He complains of unseemly behaviour at the Lord's Supper, including the common meal, which sometimes preceded and sometimes followed the actual administration. The rich come early and eat and drink, even to excess, while the poor come late and go hungry. He reminds them of the institution of the Lord's Supper and of its solemn meaning. In partaking of the bread and wine they are commemorating the Lord's death; to eat and drink unworthily is to share the guilt of those who crucified Him (XI. 17–34).

(e) Of a less definite kind are his censures on their boastfulness which are closely connected with their contempt of himself as an Apostle (IV.), and on the confusion of Christian liberty with licence, which led especially to sexual immorality, against which Paul protests on the ground that the body is God's temple and to defile it is to desecrate His temple (VI. 9–20). Later on he warns his readers that on several occasions the Israelites, who had been delivered from Egypt, had experienced a figurative baptism in the waters of the Red Sea, and had been fed with heavenly food, but had sinned in spite of all these favours and had been punished with death (X. 1–15).

(f) Finally, he deals with the denial of the resurrection, apparently not of Christ's resurrection, but of the possibility of a future resurrection of mankind. This leads to an important passage, because it gives us the earliest evidence of Christ's resurrection, concerning which Paul had doubtless made careful inquiries both before and after his conversion, as he mentions only appearances to persons whom, or some of whom, he knew—to Peter, to the Twelve, to five hundred brethren, to James, and to all the Apostles (XV. 1–11)—and from it he works on to the resurrection of all believers (XV. 12–28). It is because he is so certain of the resurrection that he gladly endures hardships, otherwise it would be better to seek the pleasures of this life, and he uses it as the ground of an appeal for righteousness (XV. 29–34). But he goes on to meet their genuine difficulties in a passage which is of special interest because their difficulties are precisely those which are often felt to-day. The resurrection body will not be material—"flesh and blood cannot inherit the kingdom of God"—but it will be real and individual; to express its nature he has recourse to an expression, "spiritual body", which, though in form paradoxical, conveys to us his meaning as far as it can be conveyed. He uses the analogy of the growth of a plant from a seed to show what development is possible even in the physical world: with regard to those who are alive at the Second Coming, there will be a sudden transformation of the material into the spiritual body (xv. 35–58).

2. *Answers to Questions.* Answers are given to five questions which had apparently been raised by members of the Corinthian church, namely (*a*) on the relation of Christians to immoral persons, (*b*) on marriage, (*c*) on the eating of food offered to idols, (*d*) on the veiling of women in public worship, and (*e*) on spiritual gifts.

(*a*) In a previous letter the Apostle had commanded them not to keep company with persons found guilty of immorality. He now repeats his command, making it clear, however, that he means unchaste Christians, not pagans (v. 9–13).

(*b*) In Paul's private opinion celibacy is preferable, but marriage is sometimes expedient to avoid the temptation to impurity. Divorce is strictly forbidden by Christ's command. A marriage between a believer and an unbeliever should not be broken, unless the unbeliever breaks it by desertion, when the believer is released from the bond. As a general rule a man should be content to remain in the condition in which he was when he became a Christian. Virgins may marry without sin, though they do better to remain unmarried. A widow is free to marry provided her second husband is a Christian, but a second marriage is not recommended (vii.).

(*c*) Food offered to idols may be bought in the market-place and eaten without question; but the strong should abstain rather than cause offence to weaker brethren. The Christian should not attend heathen sacrificial banquets, for to share in an idolatrous feast is to have communion with devils. If the Christian accepts a heathen's invitation to a private meal where food from the market-place is provided, he may eat it without question; but if anyone informs him that the food has been offered to idols, he should abstain out of consideration for the informer. The Christian is free in his actions as far as he himself is concerned, but in his relations with others he is bound by the law of love (viii. 1–13, x. 14–33).

238

(*d*) He condemns those women of the Corinthian church who have asserted their equality with men by taking part in public worship with their heads uncovered. The covered head is a Christian convention which they would do well to observe (XI. 1–16).

(*e*) All spiritual gifts are from God and should be exercised for the good of the whole Church. No one has all the gifts, but each should desire the greater gifts, especially that of Love which transcends all the others. The gift of "prophecy", which may edify the Church and lead to the conversion of the stranger, is to be preferred to that of "speaking with tongues", which may rouse emotion but is otherwise of no value. Public worship should be conducted "decently and in order" (XII.–XIV. 40).

Conclusion. He gives directions for the collection for the saints at Jerusalem, speaks of the future plans of himself, Timothy, and Apollos, sends greetings from himself and others, and closes with a final benediction (XVI.).

2 CORINTHIANS

Purpose, Date, and Place of Composition

Paul's second letter (1 Cor.) was presumably taken by Titus (2 Cor. XII. 18) who, finding the Corinthian Christians were in open revolt against the Apostle's authority, returned to Ephesus to report on the serious nature of the situation. Dean suggests that at this juncture Paul wrote a third letter (wholly lost) in which he proposed to visit Corinth twice, once on his way to Macedonia and a second time on his way back (2 Cor. I. 13–16). The mention of "writing" in verse 13 is most easily explained on the supposition that he had sent them a letter. This new proposal cancels that of 1 "Corinthians" XVI. 5.[1] Later, however, he changed his plan.

Alarmed by the news of the revolt, Paul paid a visit to Corinth, which is not recorded in "Acts", for he says in 2 "Corinthians" XII. 14, "Behold, this is the third time I am ready to come to you", and in 2 "Corinthians" XIII. 1, "This is the third time I am coming to you."

[1] Dean, *St. Paul and Corinth*, 1947, p. 12.

From 2 "Corinthians" we can form some idea of the nature of the trouble at Corinth. Shortly after Paul's first departure from the city (Acts XVIII. 18) a party of Jewish agitators arrived there with credentials from some quarter or other. Bitterly hostile to Paul, they set to work to undo his work and to undermine his authority and influence. They prided themselves on being pure Jews nurtured in the atmosphere of the Holy Land, while Paul was a Hellenist born and bred at Tarsus in Cilicia and tainted with a pagan environment (2 Cor. XI. 21–22). They taught a different Gospel, cultivated a different spirit, and preached another Jesus (2 Cor. XI. 4). Paul calls them false apostles, deceitful workers, ministers of Satan, (2 Cor. XI. 13–15). They repudiated his authority on the ground that he had never known Christ, nor had he received his commission to preach the Gospel from Him. The fact that, unlike the other Apostles, he supported himself by his own labours, was really an acknowledgment on his part that he lacked apostolic authority. They insinuated that his refusal to demand maintenance from the Corinthian church was a slight upon it. His refusal, in fact, was merely a crafty trick, for through his agents he made money out of the collection for the relief of the poor Christians at Jerusalem (XII. 14–18). In the furtherance of their plan to destroy his authority and influence, they cast aspersions on his person and character. His personality was unimpressive and his delivery beneath contempt (2 Cor. X. 10). He suffered from a physical infirmity which rendered him unacceptable as a preacher (2 Cor. XII. 7). However brave he might be when writing a letter at a distance, he was a coward at close quarters (2 Cor. X. 8). He was inconsistent, making promises only to break them, boastful, and a fool (2 Cor. I. 15–18, III. 1, XI. 16).

Some scholars hold that these agitators were Judaizers, who taught the doctrine of salvation by the works of the Law as opposed to Paul's doctrine of justification by faith in Christ. The advocates of this view argue that although the former doctrine is not definitely stated in the Epistle, it is implied. Paul, for example, refers to the false apostles as "ministers of righteousness" (2 Cor. XI. 15) who preach a different Gospel from his own (2 Cor. xi. 4), and contrasts the New Covenant with the Old Covenant, the glory of the Gospel with the bondage of the Law (2 Cor. iii. 4–18). Others are of the opinion that they were Jews of an ultra-liberal type who emphasized the gift of inspiration. They claimed to have received visions and revelations (2 Cor. xii. 1–4) denied to Paul, and were therefore his superior in spirituality and authority. Believing that they had completely emancipated themselves from the Law, they reckoned that they were living on a higher plane than the Apostle, who, by his insistence on obedience to a Christian code of ethics, was walking "according to the flesh" (x. 3).

Paul's visit caused him great grief, for he met with serious opposition from the anti-Pauline party under the leadership of one particular, unnamed individual. Instead of carrying out his original intention of proceeding to Macedonia and visiting Corinth again on his return journey (2 Cor. i. 15–16) he returned to Ephesus and wrote a "Letter of Defence" or "Severe Letter", "out of much affliction and anguish of heart .. with many tears "(2 Cor. ii. 4). Evidence for the writing of this letter is also to be found in 2 "Corinthians" vii. 8, which reads, "For though I made you sorry with my epistle, I do not regret it, though I did regret". It was apparently conveyed by Titus with orders to exert his influence to bring about a reconciliation.

After Demetrius' riot Paul left Ephesus and travelled northward, hoping to meet Titus at Troas but, as the latter did not arrive, he crossed the sea to Macedonia (2 Cor. ii. 12–13). There he met Titus with the good news that the Corinthian Christians had repented and returned to their allegiance to him (2 Cor. vii. 5–7). In a spirit of profound thankfulness Paul now wrote his fifth letter (our 2 "Corinthians") designed to end the controversy and to arrange for the collection for the relief of the poor saints at Jerusalem. It was probably written late in A.D. 55.

The Unity of the Epistle

It is generally agreed that 2 "Corinthians" is a composite work, consisting of portions of Paul's letters preserved in the

16   241

files of the Corinthian church and brought together by an editor after the apostle's death.

(1) It is almost certain that 2 "Corinthians" VI. 14–VII. 1 is part of a letter which Paul sent to Corinth after his arrival at Ephesus, warning them not to associate with those of their number who were found guilty of immorality. The reason for thinking so is that in its present position the passage has no connection with its context. If it is removed, however, there is no break in the sequence of thought between VI. 13, "Be ye also enlarged", and VII. 2, "Open your hearts to us".

(2) There is wide acceptance of the view that part of the "Letter of Defence" or "Severe Letter" is preserved in 2 "Corinthians" X.–XIII. on the following grounds:

(a) There is a marked change of tone between 2 "Corinthians" I.–IX. and 2 "Corinthians" X.–XIII. In Chapters I.–IX. the breach between Paul and the Corinthians seems to be completely healed. The section abounds in expressions of thanksgiving, love, and confidence, and is evidently written with the express purpose of removing all bitterness caused by past recriminations. In Chapters X.–XIII., however, it is evident that the controversy is still raging: the Apostle, writing in a spirit of hot indignation, attacks those whose aim is to undermine his authority and influence. It is unlikely that he would close a letter of reconciliation with a stern rebuke, biting sarcasm, and threats, for such utterances would renew the former agony of suspense and perhaps rouse the old controversy.

(b) In 2 "Corinthians" I.–IX. there are several references to a former letter apparently severe in tone. Paul says that it was written "out of much affliction and anguish of heart . . . with many tears" (II. 4). After dispatching it he expressed sorrow for his action (VII. 8): in 2 "Corinthians" III. 1, he says, "Are we beginning again to commend ourselves?" implying that in a previous letter there had been an element of self-commendation. At the time he was contemplating a visit to deal sharply with them, but which, however, he did not pay (2 Cor. I. 23, II. 1). These points exactly describe Chapters x.–xiii., and apply to no other letter of Paul.

(c) In 2 "Corinthians" vii. 8, Paul says, "Though I made you sorry with my epistle, I do not regret it, though I did regret; for I see that that epistle made you sorry, though but for a season". It is unlikely that Paul would be so tactless and unsympathetic as to write a severe letter, then repent that he had sent it, and then, when reconciliation had taken place, write another equally or even more severe.

(d) In 2 "Corinthians" i.–ix. there are allusions to matters mentioned in 2 "Corinthians" x.–xiii., which imply that the latter section was written first. Examples of such allusions can best be shown in parallel columns, thus:

2 "Corinthians" i.–ix.	2 "Corinthians" x.–xiii.
To spare you I forbare to come unto Corinth (i. 23).	If I come again, I will not spare (xiii. 2).
And I wrote this very thing, lest, when I came, I should have sorrow from them of whom I ought to rejoice (ii. 3).	For this cause I write these things while absent, that I may not when present deal sharply (xiii. 10).
For to this end also did I write, that I might know the proof of you, whether ye are obedient in all things (ii. 9).	Being in readiness to avenge all disobedience, when your obedience shall be fulfilled (x. 6).

It is evident that in each pair of parallel passages we have an allusion to the same thing in 2 "Corinthians" i.–ix. in the Past Tense and in 2 "Corinthians" x.–xiii. in the Future Tense.

(e) We know that Chapters i.–ix. were written from Macedonia (ii. 13, vii. 5, ix. 2), but Paul's words in Chapter x. 16, indicate that the geographical position of the writer was on the east of Corinth rather than on the north, thus suggesting that Chapters x.–xiii. were written from Ephesus. This affords another hint of identification between Chapters x.–xiii. and the "Severe Letter".

(*f*) The view that 1 "Corinthians" is the "Severe Letter" is open to the objection that Paul could not have been so anxious about the effects of such a moderate letter, nor would he have written the stern passages of Chapters x.–xiii. afterwards.

(*g*) It has been suggested that Paul in 2 "Corinthians" x.–xiii. is addressing a rebellious minority, but it would not have been wise to isolate a minority and thereby to imply that they were excluded from the scope of the doxologies in 2 "Corinthians" i. 3–11, and ii. 14–17.

(3) According to Dr. Dean, fragments of the "Letter of Defence", or "Severe Letter" are also preserved in 2 Cor. ii. 14–vi. 13, and vii. 2–4, his reason for this conclusion being that the section is a defence of the Gospel and of his apostolic ministry. The argument against this view is that Paul twice asks if he is commending himself to them again (2 Cor. iii. 1, v. 12). It is not unnatural that even in the "Letter of Reconciliation" he should revert to defence, though he does so in a kindlier way.

(4) Dr. Dean also thinks that Chapter ix. is a further letter to the Corinthian church, for he finds "a note of anxiety and urgency" in Chapter ix. which is absent from Chapter viii. "We get the impression that he finds it necessary to urge them to greater liberality than they were showing." This view depends wholly upon the impression which the chapter makes upon us.

Contents

Adopting Dr. Dean's analysis of the letter, we may divide the contents thus:

(1) The Letter of Defence (2 Cor. x.–xii., ii. 14–vi. 13, vii. 2–4, xiii. 1–10).

(2) The Letter of Reconciliation (2 Cor. i.–ii. 13, vii. 5–viii. 24, xiii. 11–14).

(3) Sixth Letter (2 Cor. ix.).

(4) Fragment of Letter mentioned in 1 Cor. v. 9, and embodied in 2 Cor. vi. 14–vii. 1.

(1) *The Letter of Defence.* Paul, replying to the charge that he is courageous at a distance but meek enough at Corinth, declares that he is armed, not with bodily weapons like his enemies, but with spiritual weapons, which he will use "to avenge all disobedience". Those who claim to belong in a special way to Christ should realize that he, too, is as truly Christ's as any of them, and that when he comes to Corinth, he will speak no less strongly than he writes, though his bodily presence is weak, and his delivery beneath contempt (X. 1–11).

He is prepared to face his opponents, not in a spirit of self-glorification, but in the light of his work for God in the field of labour appointed to him (X. 12–18).

He is afraid that they may be beguiled by his opponents who preach another Jesus, and a different Gospel from his own. He is in no way inferior to the superlative apostles who have come among them; they may be more eloquent but they have not more knowledge of the truth (XI. 1–6).

If he refused to accept maintenance, it was from no sense of unworthiness. He put them to no expense: he intends to carry on the practice of supporting himself in order to discomfit his opponents who masquerade as ministers of Christ (XI. 7–15).

He is compelled to boast owing to the attacks made upon him. He adduces the purity of his lineage, the hardships which he has endured, his visions and revelations, and the miracles which he has performed, to prove that he, more than any of them, is a member of Christ. Even a physical infirmity from which he suffers is by the grace of God a source, not of weakness but of power (XI. 16–XII. 12).

The Corinthian church is not inferior to the rest of the churches, except that it has not been asked to contribute to his support. He repudiates the suggestion that he has taken money from them through his agents by craft (XII. 13–21).

He thanks God who leads him in His triumphal procession, and who through him wafts the fragrance of His knowledge abroad. The fragrance gives life to all who welcome it and death to those who scorn it (II. 14–17).

He is not praising himself. They are his letters of commendation written, not with ink, but with the spirit of the living God, who has made him a minister of the New Covenant. It is a ministry, not of the written law which kills, but of the Spirit which gives life. If the giving of the Law which condemns man was invested with a brief and transient glory, the glory which invests the New Covenant must be greater and more lasting. As a minister he is given great boldness of speech, and, unlike Moses, freedom of unveiled access to God. Satan has blinded those who are perishing so that they cannot see Christ. He preaches Christ and presents himself only as their servant, for it is God who enlightens their hearts to know His glory as revealed in Christ (III.–IV. 6).

Though a preacher of the Gospel, he has this treasure in a frail body, to show that the power of his message comes from God. His afflictions, however, are only temporary; if his earthly body is broken up he has an imperishable home, built by God, eternal in the heavens. He would prefer to be with the Lord, but whether in this life or in the next, his aim must be to please Him, before whose judgment-seat all must appear (IV. 7–V. 10).

He is not commending himself but giving them an opportunity to defend him against his opponents. God will decide whether he is mad or not, but at least he is sane in his zeal for them. As an ambassador of Christ, he pleads with them to be reconciled to God and to live up to the grace of God given to them, for these are the days in which to obtain salvation. He strives to prove himself a faithful minister, being patient in tribulation and cultivating all the Christian graces (V. 11–VI. 10).

He pleads with them to make room for him in their hearts, for he has wronged none of them (VI. 11–13, VII. 2–4).

He refers to a third visit and warns them that he will not spare the wrongdoers: this will prove that he is the spokesman of Christ. He hopes that he will not have to deal sharply with them, so that his apostolic authority may be used for edification, not destruction (XIII. 1–10).

(2) *The Letter of Reconciliation.* After the formal greetings, Paul

246

gives thanks to God for the comfort granted to him under his sufferings for Christ, assures them that in all his dealings with them he has acted in holiness and sincerity, and hopes that at the Second Coming they will be able to have pride in him and he to feel pride in them (I. 1–14).

He repudiates the charge of inconsistency in failing to keep his promise to visit them, declaring that he had changed his mind because he wished to spare them pain (I. 15–II. 4).

Referring to a guilty person upon whom some form of discipline had been exercised, the Apostle thinks that the punishment is sufficient and pleads with them to forgive him for the sake of Christ (II. 5–11).

He expresses his relief and joy in hearing from Titus of the good news of their repentance, their longing for reconciliation, and their zeal for him. He has boasted about them to Titus and his boasts have been justified. Now he need have no further anxiety about their future welfare (II. 12–13, VII. 5–16).

The collection for the saints at Jerusalem has been such a great success that he is sending Titus and two other brethren to Corinth to complete the collection there. It is not a command but is requested as a token of Christian love. Jesus is their example, who for their sakes became poor. Each should give according to his ability: the object in giving is not to ease one at the expense of another but to equalize resources (VIII.).

The Epistle closes with words of comfort from the Apostle, salutations from the brethren, and a final benediction (XIII. 11–14).

(3) *Sixth Letter.* He has held them up as an example to the Macedonians and hopes that they will not put him to shame by their remissness. He urges them to give liberally and ungrudgingly and not under pressure. The money will supply the needs of the saints, show that they are Christ's disciples, unite Jew and Gentile, and make all thank God for His unspeakable gift (IX.).

(4) *Fragment of First Letter.* They must separate themselves from the heathen, and especially from idolatrous practices (VI. 14–VII. 1).

1 and 2 CORINTHIANS

Authenticity

External Evidence. The external evidence for 1 and 2 "Corinthians" is especially strong. As regards the first Epistle, Clement of Rome, writing to the Corinthian church (*c.* A.D. 96), tells them to "take up the letters of the blessed Paul the Apostle in which he wrote to you about himself and Cephas and Apollos, because even then ye had made yourselves parties". It was known to Ignatius and to Polycarp, whose writings are so saturated with its thought and language, that he must have known it almost by heart. It is included in Marcion's Canon and the Muratorian Fragment, and is cited by Irenaeus, Tertullian, and Clement of Alexandria.

As regards 2 "Corinthians", the external evidence does not begin quite so early as that for 1 "Corinthians". It was probably unknown to Clement of Rome. Like the first Epistle, however, it appears in Marcion's Canon and the Muratorian Fragment, and was familiar to Irenaeus, Tertullian, and Clement of Alexandria.

In the nineteenth century the two Epistles were among the four "principal" Epistles—the other two being "Romans" and "Galatians"—which were accepted by the Tübingen school of critics as genuine works of Paul.

Internal Evidence. The internal evidence for both Epistles is equally strong. They reveal such an intimate knowledge of conditions as they existed in an early Christian community, that it is inconceivable they could be the product of invention. The similarities between the Epistles and "Romans" and "Galatians", together with the fact that they are saturated with the characteristic ideas of Paul, preclude the possibility of a forgery, as do also the autobiographical details, and the style which is beyond question that of the Apostle. Finally, in comparing the two Epistles with "Acts", we find "such combination of agreement in essentials and discrepancy in detail as we expect from honest witnesses".[1]

[1] Bacon, *Introduction to the New Testament*, 1900, p. 56.

Historical Value

Christian Conduct and Worship. The two Epistles are our chief documents for the study of the conduct and worship of an early Christian community, and of the conflict of the new faith with paganism. The church at Corinth was predominantly Gentile, but there were apparently some Jews (1 Cor. XII. 2, VIII. 8). Most of its members appear to have belonged to the poorer classes, but it would be a mistake to infer from this that they were all illiterate or unintelligent, for some of them were interested in rhetoric and philosophy. We notice, among matters which appear in the other Epistles, too, the particular difficulties of Jews and Greeks, the tendency of the former to revert to legalism and the latter to pagan morals, and the perversion of the idea of Christian liberty into licence. Among matters which are peculiar or almost peculiar to the letter, we notice the divisions, the demand for rhetoric and philosophy the litigiousness, the disorders in public worship and the form which Paul would have it assume, and the dangers inheren' in the gift of "speaking with tongues".

Doctrine. The two Epistles are valuable for their exposition of Pauline doctrines chiefly those (1) of Christ, (2) of the Church, (3) of Baptism, (4) of the Lord's Supper, and (5) of the Resurrection.

(1) Christ is the Son of God (1 Cor. I. 9; 2 Cor. I. 19) and it is in Him that all Christians live (2 Cor. I. 21, II. 14, 17, V. 17, etc.). For our sakes He became poor (2 Cor. VIII. 9), and died and rose again from the dead, that through Him God might reconcile us to Himself (2 Cor. v. 14–19).

(2) The Christian is not called to live in isolation from his fellow men. He is a member of a fellowship—the Church (1 Cor. XII. 27), which the Apostle describes as the "Body of Christ", symbolizing, "the inherent relation of the several members to one another, the reciprocal relation of the head to the members, the phenomena of nourishment and growth".[1] Within its fellowship all distinctions of race and class have vanished (1 Cor. XII. 13; cf. Gal. III. 28): no man, however degraded he may be, is excluded provided he repents and is

[1] C. A. Scott, *Christianity in the Light of Modern Knowledge*, 1929, p. 372.

baptized in the name of Jesus Christ. Many of the Corinthian converts before their conversion had been guilty of immorality, idolatry, theft, covetousness, drunkenness, revelry, and extortion, but they had been justified "in the name of the Lord Jesus Christ, and in the Spirit of our God" (1 Cor. VI. 11; cf. Acts II. 38). Christians form a distinct community; the world for them is divided into Jews, Gentiles, and the Church of God (1 Cor. X. 32). Everyone must regard any gift he might have as a trust from God and must use it for the good of the Church (1 Cor. XII. 27–31).

(3) Baptism is the symbol of the believer's incorporation into the Church, which is the "body of Christ" (1 Cor. XII. 13). The rite of itself does not ensure salvation. Paul illustrates this from history. The Israelites in passing through the Red Sea underwent an experience analogous to baptism, but in consequence of their sin they perished in the wilderness (1 Cor. X. 1–10). The Apostle apparently approves of vicarious baptism, that is, the practice of living persons being baptized for the dead (1 Cor. XV. 29).

(4) The Lord's Supper is a memorial of the death of Christ and must be observed in the Church "till he come" (1 Cor. XI. 26). It is also a symbol of the communion and unity of all who partake of the "cup of blessing which we bless" and the "bread which we break" (1 Cor. X. 16). While we partake of the symbols, we have communion with the living Christ who is spiritually present. To fail to realize the solemn significance of the rite—the reality of Christian fellowship and of communion with Christ—is to eat the bread and to drink the wine unworthily and to share in the guilt of those who crucified Him (1 Cor. XI. 27). Participation in the Lord's Supper does not ensure salvation. The Israelites, after their deliverance from Egypt, ate manna, a spiritual food, and drank of the spiritual rock, which is Christ, but they sinned and "were overthrown in the wilderness" (1 Cor. X. 1–5).

(5) The church at Corinth consisted of both Greeks and Jews. To many Greek philosophers death meant extinction; the Stoics taught that at death the body perished, while the oul was reabsorbed into the universal reason of which it

formed a part, with the consequent loss of personal identity. The Jews, on the other hand, believed in a physical resurrection and a materialistic paradise to be won by merit. It would appear that the Greek Christians accepted the fact of the resurrection of Christ but denied the possibility of the resurrection of mankind. Paul, who is fighting on "two fronts", rejects the views of those who denied the resurrection of the dead and also the views of those who believed in a physical resurrection. The resurrection of Christ is the pledge of the resurrection of all believers (1 Cor. xv. 20). The body raised from the dead will be a spiritual body not the natural body revivified, for "flesh and blood cannot inherit the kingdom of God" (1 Cor. xv. 50). A marked change, however, took place in Paul's views on the Resurrection in the interval between the writing of the two letters. He came to believe that there would be no interruption of the communion with Christ. At death the body will perish but the soul will receive a heavenly and spiritual body, or in modern speech, the personality will be perfected, and we shall be "at home with the Lord" (2 Cor. v. 1–10). Some scholars, however, hold that there is really no change in Paul's views, and that the words express the Apostle's hope that he will survive till the Second Coming and thus escape death.

Christian Ethics. The two Epistles mark the beginning of Christian ethics, that is, the application of Christian principles to human conduct and worship. Paul saw clearly that Christianity was not a national cult but a world religion, and that the principles of the Gospel teaching were as applicable to a great commercial city like Corinth as to a simple form of society like that which existed in Palestine in the days of Christ. Throughout the centuries the Church has turned to these Epistles for guidance in matters of behaviour and public worship.

Christian Evidence. The two Epistles rank among the most valuable of the New Testament books for Christian evidence. The two accounts of the Lord's Supper (1 Cor. xi. 23–26) and of the Resurrection (1 Cor. xv. 3–9) were written only about twenty-five years after the Crucifixion, and about ten years before the publication of "Mark", the earliest Gospel. They afford therefore the earliest evidence we possess for the institution of the Lord's Supper and for the Resurrection. They also show that the great doctrines of the Christian faith were not a later growth but had existed from the very first.

Confirmatory of, and Supplementary to, Acts. The two Epistles confirm the information supplied by "Acts". Timothy and Silas are fellow‚workers with Paul at Corinth (cf. Acts XVIII. 5 and 2 Cor. I. 19). Aquila and Priscilla have friends at Corinth and are now residing at Ephesus (cf. Acts XVIII. 19 and 1 Cor. XVI. 19). Crispus, the ruler of the synagogue is one of the few converts whom Paul baptized (cf. Acts XVIII. 8 and 1 Cor. I. 14). Apollos has visited Corinth where he has conducted a successful mission (cf. Acts XVIII. 27–28 and 1 Cor. III. 6). On the other hand the Epistles give us further information concerning Paul's relations with Corinth. We learn that Paul first visited the city "in weakness, and in fear, and in much trembling" (1 Cor. II. 3). It is clear, too, that he revisited the city more often than "Acts" tells us. One visit was evidently humiliating in the extreme to himself and painful to all concerned (2 Cor. II. 4, VII. 8). The Epistles deal with the conduct and worship of the Corinthian Christians and with the problems confronting them, subjects on which "Acts" is silent, for it was the author's chief aim to trace the expansion of the Gospel from Jerusalem to Rome, not to give a detailed study of local churches. The Epistles supplement our knowledge of the character of Paul, derived from "Acts", for "it is quite obvious that a man who, as a contemporary and occasional companion of Paul, describes the Apostle from the outside, could not reach the truth that Paul reaches as unconsciously in his letters he draws a picture of himself".[1]

The two Epistles, especially the first, are valuable as works of art. They contain several sublime passages, notably those on "Love" (1 Cor. XIII.) and on the "Resurrection" (1 Cor. XV.) which entitle them to be ranked among the world's great literature.

[1] Deissmann, *Paul, a Study in Social and Religious History*, 1926, p. 25.

THE EPISTLE TO THE ROMANS

The Roman Church

Its Origin. The origin of the Church at Rome is lost in obscurity. According to tradition, it was founded by Peter, who became its first bishop (*c*. A.D. 42), holding office till his martyrdom twenty-five years later; but in the earliest form of tradition Peter and Paul are always named as joint founders. It is difficult, however, to bring Peter to Rome before *c*. A.D. 49, for he was imprisoned by Herod Agrippa I shortly before that king's death (A.D. 44) and was present at the Council of Jerusalem (*c*. A.D. 49). In "Galatians" and 2 "Corinthians", Paul seems to take it for granted that Peter was one of the leaders of the church in Palestine. Had the church at Rome been founded by the latter, Paul would surely have mentioned him in his letter and sent him greetings. On the other hand there is no reason for doubting the early tradition that both the Apostles suffered martyrdom at Rome in the Neronian persecution (A.D. 64–68).

The church at Rome probably owes its origin to the colony of Jews there. Their synagogues had attracted a large number of God-fearers, drawn by the sublime monotheism and austere morality of Judaism. It is recorded in "Acts" II. 10, that in the crowd addressed by Peter on the Day of Pentecost were "sojourners from Rome, both Jews and proselytes". Some of these were probably converted and returned home, taking the Christian faith with them; later they would be joined by refugees who fled from Palestine during the persecution which followed the martyrdom of Stephen. Apart from pilgrims and refugees, many Christians would probably travel between Palestine and Rome for business purposes, for there were safe and rapid means of communication both by land and sea between the imperial capital and the provinces. There is a possibility, too, that friends and converts of Paul were among the earliest Christians in Rome. If Chapter XVI. is really part of the Epistle, which, as we shall see later, there is reason to doubt, then the description of Mary as one "who bestowed much labour on you" (Rom. XVI. 6), and of Andronicus and Junias as "my kinsmen, and my fellow-prisoners, who are of note among the apostles, who also have been in Christ before me" (Rom. XVI. 7), may mean that they had taken part in the founding of the church. The sense of unity and the spirit of fellowship would in time induce all these Christians to form a local church.

In *c.* A.D. 50 the Jews were expelled from Rome by a decree of the Emperor Claudius in consequence, according to the historian Suetonius, of riots instigated by "one Chrestus". The name "Chrestus" is probably a mis-spelling of the name "Christus". It is almost certain, therefore, that by this time a Christian community had grown up under the shadow of the synagogue, and that disputes between Christians and orthodox Jews had arisen in the colony. On the accession of Nero (A.D. 54) the Jews were allowed to return, and for several years we hear of no persecution of Christians. The moral corruption of the time gave the Roman church a better opportunity of winning adherents in the capital, for men, tired of vice and licentiousness, were longing for a nobler way of life, which only Christianity could provide. By the time Paul wrote his "Epistle to the Romans" a flourishing church existed in the imperial city, for he writes as if it was firmly established and had become famous among the Christian communities of the Empire. He tells them that their "faith is proclaimed throughout the whole world" (I. 8), and that he had proposed to come to them but had been prevented (I. 13).

Its Composition. Opinion is divided on the question of the composition of the Roman church, but the weight of evidence supports the view that it consisted mainly of Gentiles with a minority of Jews. There are passages which appear to be addressed to Jewish readers. Thus, he addresses them as men who "know the law" (VII. 1) and have now "been discharged from the law, having died to that wherein we were holden"

(VII. 6); and again he writes, "But if thou bearest the name of a Jew . . ." (II. 17). He refers to "Abraham our forefather, according to the flesh" (IV. 1), and to "our father Isaac" (IX. 10). In addition to these direct quotations a considerable portion of the Epistle is taken up with the discussion of the Law and the rejection of Israel, which would have a special interest for Jews: the Epistle presupposes a knowledge of the Old Testament, from which more than sixty quotations, found in the former, are taken.

On the other hand it is equally clear from certain passages in the Epistle that the church was predominantly Gentile. In introducing himself to his readers he speaks of his apostleship among all the nations, "among whom are ye also" (I. 5-6), and wishes to have fruit of them "even as in the rest of the Gentiles" (I. 13). The reason for his desire to preach the Gospel in Rome is that he is "debtor both to Greeks and to Barbarians" (I. 14). In Chapter XI. 13-14, he calls his readers Gentiles and proceeds in a way applicable only to Gentiles, while in his closing address (XV. 15-16) he speaks of himself as "a minister of Christ Jesus unto the Gentiles, ministering the gospel of God, that the offering up of the Gentiles might be made acceptable, being sanctified by the Holy Ghost". Some of the passages which are supposed to have been addressed to Jews may have been meant for Gentiles as well, for they can be paralleled from other Pauline Epistles, which were written to predominantly Gentile churches. For example, in 1 "Corinthians" the Apostle speaks of the Israelites in the wilderness as "our fathers" (X. 1): in "Galatians" he presupposes a knowledge of the Law in his readers, and expresses the idea that they have been emancipated from bondage to it (cf. IV. 1-9). Finally, many of the members of the Roman church had probably been either proselytes to Judaism or God-fearers before their conversion and would, therefore, be acquainted with the Jewish Scriptures and have some knowledge of the Law.

Purpose

At the time of writing the Epistle, Paul had reached a turning-point in his career. In the course of some twenty years of missionary activity he had preached the Gospel of Christ "from Jerusalem, and round about even unto Illyricum" (xv. 19), establishing churches in the provinces of Galatia, Asia, Macedonia, and Achaia. The controversy with the Church at Corinth was ended, cordial relations had been established, and his authority recognized. The collection for the poor Christians at Jerusalem was completed, and nothing further remained to be done except to convey the money to its destination. It might well have appeared to the Apostle that his pioneering work in the East was finished, and that others could now build upon the foundations which he had laid. He was not a man, however, to relax his efforts or to relinquish a task to which he had dedicated his life. His great ambition was to evangelize the whole world, which to him was synonymous with the Empire. He was, in fact, the first to recognize the importance of the Empire in the spread of the Gospel. As a Hellenistic Jew and as a traveller, he had had ample opportunity of studying the imperial system of administration at work and had been greatly impressed by it. It had brought peace, order, security, and prosperity, to a distracted world. Thanks to the excellent facilities for communication which it had provided, he and his fellow missionaries had been able to travel quickly and safely, both by land and sea, from one place to another. As a Roman citizen he had received the protection of the State in time of danger. Roman officials had saved him from infuriated mobs and had refused to prevent him from preaching the Gospel. It is probable that the idea of an Empire, embracing all the peoples of the civilized world, with one system of administration, and under one ruler, suggested to him the idea of one Church, conterminous with it, with one system of organization, and under one head—Christ.

His new plan was to evangelize the West, using Rome as a base of operations. For a long time he had cherished the idea of visiting the imperial capital, but so far his missionary labours among the Gentiles had prevented him (Acts xix. 21; Rom. i. 13). When he had conveyed the money collected from the churches of Macedonia and Achaia to Jerusalem, he would at last be free to pay his long-intended visit. He needed the co-operation of the Roman church in his missionary campaign in the West, but the question was how to secure it. As it had not been founded by himself he could not claim jurisdiction over it; its members were unacquainted with the Gospel which he preached, except perhaps by report. The majority of them were unknown to him and so he could not be sure of a warm welcome from them. Since he had no claim upon their sympathy and support, the most that he could do was to appeal to them as an approved minister of Christ. He therefore wrote a letter to introduce himself to them, and to enlist their co-operation in his projected missionary campaign in the West.

The fact that the Epistle is largely a systematic exposition of certain phases of Christian doctrine rather than a personal letter, suggests that the Apostle had other reasons for writing. He was fully aware of the fact that he had many enemies within the Church whose main object was to drive him out of the mission field. The emissaries of the Judaizers had pursued him from place to place, determined to wreck his work and to destroy his influence, by denying his Gospel, rejecting his authority, and casting aspersions upon his character. They had caused trouble in the other parts of the mission field and no doubt had their sympathizers and supporters in the Roman church, where their presence would not make for peace, since they believed that Gentile converts should render strict obedience to the Law. Further, we infer from the Epistle that the Gentiles were inclined to despise their Jewish brethren. The Apostle, therefore, wrote his Epistle, setting forth the essentials of the Christian faith as he understood them, not only in order to give them an idea of what he stood for and what they would be committing themselves to if they decided to support him, but also to answer any objections which might be raised against the Gospel which he preached, to remove any suspicions which might have been roused by his opponents and by those who were inclined to distrust him, and to bring about a reconciliation between Jews and Gentiles. As he had not been previously engaged in any controversy with the Church, and wished to create a good impression and so win the co-operation of all its members in his projected mission, he wrote in a conciliatory spirit, reasoning calmly and persuasively, with none of the heat and passion which characterized his letter to the Galatians and his second letter to the Corinthians.

It is sometimes urged that Paul, having a presentiment of his approaching death, wrote a compendium of Christian doctrine as a kind of "Last Will and Testament" for future generations, and that he entrusted it to the Roman church as the most suitable of all the Christian communities. Rome was the capital of the Empire and a letter addressed to the Church there would carry weight and be preserved for posterity. This view, however, cannot be maintained, since the Epistle does not contain the whole of Paul's teaching: there is no exposition, for example, of the doctrines of the Church, of the Lord's Supper, of the Resurrection, and of the Second Coming. He did not write as though his work was now finished, and he must bequeath to future generations of Christians a systematic treatise on Christian doctrine as he conceived it: on the contrary he believed that there was still more work for him to do, and he was making plans to carry the Gospel to the West. Moreover, he made it quite clear in his Epistle that he was writing to the members of the Roman church to introduce himself and to secure their co-operation in his projected mission.

Place and Date of Composition

Place. From certain allusions in the Epistle we infer that the Epistle was probably written at Corinth. In it Paul refers to his approaching visit to Jerusalem with the money collected from the churches of Macedonia and Achaia for the relief of the poor Christians in that city. "But now, I say, I go unto Jerusalem, ministering unto the saints. For it hath been the good pleasure of Macedonia and Achaia to make a certain contribution for the poor among the saints that are at Jerusalem" (Rom. xv. 25–26). We hear also of Paul's visit to Jerusalem for the same purpose from "Acts" and the two letters to the Corinthians (Acts xix. 21, xxi. 17, xxiv. 17; 1 Cor. xvi. 1–6; 2 Cor. viii. 1–6, ix. 1–5). When he wrote his letter to the

Romans, the collection seems to have been completed and he was on the eve of his departure to Jerusalem with the money. The letter, therefore, must have been written at that point in Paul's missionary journey mentioned in "Acts" xx. 2–3, that is, during his three months' stay in Achaia after leaving Macedonia. It is reasonable to assume that the exact place of composition was Corinth, where there existed a flourishing church, founded by himself.

In Chapter xvi. 1, Phoebe, a member of the church at Cenchreae, the eastern port of Corinth, is prominently mentioned and, if this chapter is really part of the letter, was probably the bearer of the letter. Among those who send greetings are Gaius, Paul's host (xvi. 23), who was one of the few whom Paul baptized at Corinth (1 Cor. i. 14); Erastus (xvi. 23), the treasurer of the city where the latter was written and who stayed on at Corinth (2 Tim. iv. 20); and Timothy and Sosipater, who were with the Apostle at this period (xvi. 21). This chapter was certainly written at Corinth, but if we decide that it is not an organic part of the Epistle but a fragment of a separate document, then the evidence which it affords is invalid. Still, even without it, the evidence is sufficient to warrant the assumption that the Epistle was probably composed at Corinth.

Date. The date of "Romans", like those of the other Pauline Epistles, depends upon the chronology of Paul's life, which is uncertain. On his third missionary journey, the Apostle, after the riot at Ephesus, proceeded first to Macedonia and thence to Achaia, where he stayed three months (Acts xx. 1–3). As we have already shown, it was during this period that the Epistle was written. At the end of the period he decided to sail to Syria, but on discovering a plot to kill him, he changed his plan and went by the overland route by way of Macedonia (Acts xx. 3) hoping to arrive at Jerusalem in time for the Feast of Pentecost (Acts xx. 16). Since the Mediterranean Sea was practically closed to navigation from early November to the end of March, and the Apostle hoped to keep the Feast of Pentecost at Jerusalem, the Epistle must have been written late in A.D. 55 or early in A.D. 56.

Contents

We have already shown that Paul's primary object in writing the Epistle is to secure the co-operation of the Roman church in his projected missionary campaign in the West, and that to further his purpose he answers objections which might be raised against Christianity (as he conceived it). After the introduction, in which he emphasizes his apostolic authority and expresses his earnest desire to visit Rome (I. 1–17), the Epistle becomes, therefore, an apology for Christianity, though by the order and otherwise, it does not take that form. It is further concealed from us by the alternation of "kerygma" and "didache", universal in epistles, the "kerygma" in this case being the defence, and the "didache", as always, exhortation, moral advice, and appeals to the religious instincts of the readers.

Re-arranging the Epistle so as to bring this out, we find that he meets four main attacks on Christianity, or at least Pauline Christianity, namely:

(1) Christianity claims to be based on the Old Testament, nevertheless it rejects the Law which is the heart of the Old Testament.

(2) It is rejected by the Jewish authorities, who should understand their own religion.

(3) By rejecting the Law it is antinomian and allows men to do whatever they like.

(4) It rejects the civil authority and is therefore revolutionary.

(1) *Kerygma.* Abraham was called before the Law was given and was justified by faith: the rite of circumcision had only been the confirmation of his faith. The promise of inheriting the earth was given to him apart from the Law, and the seed to whom the promise descends are the faithful who follow their spiritual ancestor in believing God, even against nature, as Abraham and Sarah believed Him (IV. 1–25).

Jews and Gentiles are equal in the sight of God, and His judgment will fall equally on all, irrespective of nationality. The Jews, with their greater privileges and knowledge of God, are all the more culpable if they transgress His laws.

Circumcision is of no avail, for God judges not by the flesh, but by the spirit (II. 11–29).

The only superiority of the Jews lay in the fact that they were entrusted with the Scriptures (III. 1–4); but, equally with the Gentiles, they are guilty of sin and need redemption by faith in Christ. Faith does not cancel the Law but upholds it (III. 9–31).

Didache. The "didache" on this (v.) is an exhortation on the blessed state of the believer. Faith gives him a new life, which carries with it the right of free access to God, peace of heart, patient endurance of tribulation, hope, and the assurance of final salvation. Life has come to all by one man (Christ) even as in the Old Testament death came to all by one man (Adam).

(2) *Kerygma.* It is stated in the Old Testament, time after time, that only a remnant of the Jews would be saved. There is still a remnant which, through God's grace, has believed and has been accepted (XI. 1–10).

There has been from the first an element of selectiveness. The blessing was not given to all the children of Abraham but to one line only. This selection by God in advance does not imply injustice on His part. From people who have sinned and deserved punishment He chooses His "Israel", including, as Hosea and Isaiah foretold, Gentiles as well as Jews (IX. 6–29).

God's purpose throughout has been ultimately to admit all nations to the blessing, and this has been rendered possible by the disbelief of the Jews which brought about their own rejection (x).

He expects that, when this admission of the Gentiles has been accomplished, the Jews will come in (XI. 11–36).

Didache. The "didache" on this (XII.) is an appeal to believers to dedicate their lives to the service of God, to use their spiritual gifts for the good of the whole Christian community, which is one, as the human body with all its diversity of parts is one, and to live in charity with all men, even with their persecutors (the Jews).

(3) *Kerygma.* Christians are dead to sin in Christ's death and alive to Christ through His resurrection: those who sin are

slaves to sin, but Christians are free (VI. 1–23). Christians, through Christ's redemption, are dead to the Law, which has no power over the dead (VII. 1–6). This does not mean that the Law is identical with sin: the Law reveals the true nature of sin, because no man can obey the Law owing to the inner conflict (VII. 7–25). Christians have a law of the Spirit, which sets them free from the law of sin and death. No man belongs to Christ who has not the Spirit, giving him life (VIII. 1–17).

Passing from defence to attack, he warns them against imitating the pagan world. Pagans have shut their eyes to the revelation of God in Nature, preferring vain speculation, which has led them into idolatry and immorality; so they have sunk, men and women alike, to the lowest depths of moral degradation. The Jews are guilty of the offences which they condemn in others: they mistake God's forbearance for indifference, not realizing that His kindness is leading them to repentance. He will judge all men according to their works (I. 18–II. 10).

Didache. The "didache" on this (VIII. 18–39) is on the Christian's confident outlook. The whole creation is looking forward to the regeneration begun in them (18–23); the Spirit is pleading for them (26–27); God's elect cannot be separated from Him by any earthly circumstance (28–39).

(4) *Kerygma.* Christians must obey the civil power because all authority is derived ultimately from God, and to resist authority is to resist God's order. They must render to everyone his due, whether it be tribute, tax, reverence, or honour. The Christian, who acts in the spirit of love, fulfils the Law, for he will never injure his neighbour (XIII. 1–10).

Didache. The "didache" on this (XIII. 11–XV. 13) becomes a didache on the whole Epistle. Christians are exhorted to be steadfast, owing to the nearer approach of the Second Coming. The strong must bear with those weak in faith, whom they must not offend in matters touching the eating of food, and the observance of holy days. All must preserve a sense of mutual responsibility, taking Christ as their example.

(In Chapter XV. 14–33 the Apostle speaks of his projected visit to Rome *en route* for Spain, after he has conveyed to

Jerusalem the contributions collected from the churches of Macedonia and Achaia for the relief of the poor Christians in that city, asks for their prayers for his safety and for the acceptance of his offerings, and ends with a benediction.)

Note. Chapter XVI. 1–23, as we shall show, is probably a fragment of a letter written to the church at Ephesus. The Doxology (25–27), too, is probably the work of a later writer. In this chapter the Apostle sends greetings to numerous friends and to the church as a whole, warns them against false teachers, and closes with a Doxology.

Authenticity

External Evidence. The external evidence for the genuineness of the greater part of the Epistle is particularly strong. Traces of it are found in 1 "Peter", and probably "Hebrews" and "James". It was evidently known to Clement of Rome, Polycarp, and Justin Martyr. Marcion includes it in his collection of Pauline Epistles, placing it fourth on the list. It appears in the Muratorian Fragment, being the last of the seven Epistles addressed to the Churches, and is cited by Irenaeus, Clement of Alexandria, and Tertullian. By the end of the second century it was used freely and was generally recognized as having apostolic authority.

Internal Evidence. The internal evidence for the Epistle is practically irrefutable. Its contents, style, and vocabulary, are so characteristically Pauline that very few scholars have ever questioned its genuineness. In it we find many of the Pauline doctrines, such as those of justification by faith, of union with Christ, and of the universality of the Gospel. As regards its style, one has only to compare it with those of "Galatians" and 1 and 2 "Corinthians" to realize that all four have the same stylistic features and must have come from the same hand. The vocabulary, too, is typical of this group of Epistles; for example, the word "nomos" (law) occurs seven times in "Romans", thirty-two times in "Galatians", and eight times in 1 "Corinthians". Though the Epistle is more of a theological treatise than a personal letter, it nevertheless unconsciously reveals the character of the author, which is clearly recognizable as that of Paul. It is, in fact, so characteristic of the Apostle's genius that it has been called "the most Pauline" of all his writings.

Integrity

Although very few critics have ever denied the authenticity of the Epistle, there are certain textual phenomena, connected with Chapters xv. and xvi., which make it doubtful whether we have it as it was originally written by the Apostle.

(1) One MS., written in both Latin and Greek, omits the phrase "in Rome" in Chapter i. 7, 15.
(2) The position of the Doxology (xvi. 25–27) varies in different MSS. In the best MSS. it is found at the end of the Epistle, but in the majority of them it appears at the end of Chapter xiv. Some give it at both places and two or three omit it altogether. The Chester Beatty papyrus, which dates from about A.D. 200, places it at the end of Chapter xv.
(3) Certain MSS. of the Latin translation, known as the Vulgate, divide the Epistle into fifty-one "breves" or sections, of which the fiftieth covers Chapter xiv. 15–23, while the fifty-first corresponds to Chapter xvi. 25–27. Chapters xv.–xvi. 23 are thus omitted. (In Revised Version verse 24 forms part of verse 20.)
(4) It is almost certain that Marcion, who made the first collection of Paul's Epistles, left out altogether the last two chapters.
(5) Early writers of the second and third centuries (e.g. Irenaeus, Tertullian, and Cyprian), who cite "Romans" freely, never quote from the last two chapters.

Various attempts have been made to solve the problem presented by the last two chapters. It has been suggested that they are both spurious. As regards Chapter xv., it has been argued that the information supplied in verses 19–28 is inconsistent with what we know of Paul's movements from "Acts", and that the Apostle would never have called Christ "a minister of the circumcision" (verse 8). Such a view, however, is untenable. None of the details in verses 19–28 is contradicted by "Acts", while some of them are confirmed by 1 and 2 "Corinthians". The journey to Spain is only a plan and may not have been carried out. The words of verse 8 closely resemble those of "Galatians" IV. 4–5 which read: "But when the fulness of the time came, God sent forth his Son, born of a woman, born under the law, that he might redeem them which were under the law, that we might receive the adoption of sons." Moreover, the first thirteen verses of Chapter XV. continue the argument of the preceding one, while there is nothing in the chapter as a whole, either in contents or in style, which might be justly regarded as un-Pauline.

As regards Chapter XVI. the personal greetings are so characteristically Pauline, that it is difficult to see how any forger could have compiled them or what purpose they could have served. It is probable, however, that the Doxology (XVI. 25–27) is the work of a later hand, since its thought and language are different from the rest of the Epistle and closely resemble those of "Ephesians" and the Pastoral Epistles. There is no manuscript evidence for separating this chapter from the one preceding it, since it forms an integral part of every extant manuscript. Nevertheless there is wide acceptance of the view that while Chapter XVI. (excluding the Doxology) is the work of Paul, it is not an organic part of the Epistle, but a fragment of a letter which he wrote to the church at Ephesus, recommending it to Phoebe, a Christian woman of Cenchreae. The following are the reasons for this view:

(1) It contains a long list of greetings from Paul to friends at the destination to which he is writing, and reveals an intimate knowledge of their circumstances, their family relationships, and their work. It is unlikely that he could have had so many friends in a distant city which he had never visited.

(2) Among those to whom he sends greetings are Prisca and Aquila who had laboured with Paul during the greater part of his stay at Ephesus. The Apostle refers to the church

in their house, both in this chapter (XVI.) and in 1 "Corinthians" XVI. 19. This suggests that in both cases the reference is to the same church and house at Ephesus. At a later date they are found again at Ephesus (2 Tim. IV. 19).

(3) The allusion to Epaenetus as "the firstfruits of Asia unto Christ" (XVI. 5) naturally suggests Ephesus.

(4) Most of the names are of Greek rather than of Roman origin.

(5) The warning against false teachers who "are causing the divisions and occasions of stumbling" (XVI. 17) is surprising in a letter written to a church which he had never visited and over which he had no authority. Such a warning would be more suitable for the church of Ephesus than that of Rome.

(6) The words of Chapter XV. 33: "Now the God of peace be with you all. Amen"—read like the conclusion of a letter.

On the other hand it may be argued that:

(1) There was constant communication between Rome and the provinces, and that many of Paul's friends might have found their way to Rome and joined the local church.

(2) It was not Paul's practice to send personal greetings to members of churches which he knew well, but since he was a stranger to Rome, he might well have thought it advisable to make as many personal contacts as possible.

(3) Most of the names mentioned in the chapter can be found in inscriptions from Roman sepulchres.

(4) There is no definite evidence that the warning against false teachers was not just as applicable to Rome as to Ephesus.

(5) The concluding words of Chapter XV. are unlike those of the last chapters of the rest of Paul's Epistles.

Summing up, we may say that the balance of probability is in favour of the theory that Chapter XVI. (excluding the Doxology) is a fragment of a letter, originally sent to Ephesus.

Texts of the Epistle

Considerable difficulty has been caused by the diversity oi early texts as regards Chapters xv. and xvi., and the position of the Doxology, which in our Bibles appears at the end of Chapter xvi. Both chapters are missing in some texts; and the Doxology sometimes appears at the end of Chapter xiv., sometimes at the end of Chapter xvi., occasionally in both places, and in the Chester Beatty papyrus (our earliest manuscript), at the end of Chapter xv.

This has led to a theory that the bulk of the Epistle was written by Paul as an exposition of Christianity without any view of its destination, and that when he determined to include it in a letter to the church at Rome, he added to it the matter suitable for such a letter in Chapter xv. Whether he further added Chapter xvi. later, or whether that is a fragment of a separate letter altogether, is not determined by this theory. The main objection to this theory is that the doctrinal portion does not end at the end of Chapter xiv. but at Chapter xv. 13, where the personal matter suitable to a letter begins.

Another theory is that in copies of the Epistle made up for use in public worship, the purely private parts were omitted as having no obvious religious value. This theory admits of two interpretations of the position of the Doxology; one, that it is a genuine part of the Epistle, composed for its end, and that it was felt that, even if the private letter was omitted, this Doxology must still be put in at the end of what was retained; the other, that it is not the work of Paul at all, but was composed for use when the Epistle was used in public worship, like the Gloria traditionally used at the end of each psalm when used in Christian worship. There is no fatal argument against this theory, though that is no proof that it is true.

The most significant fact seems to be that in the Chester Beatty papyrus, the oldest manuscript, it should appear at the end of Chapter xv., even though no other manuscript follows it. This suggests that such was its original position, and that Chapter xvi. was not from the beginning included in the Epistle, since it could have been transferred for liturgical reasons both to the end of Chapter xiv. or to that of

Chapter xvi., but could not reasonably have been transferred to any other position than the end.

Historical Value

"Romans", which contains the essentials of Pauline Christianity, has exercised a profound influence on theologians belonging to different schools of thought, notably Augustine, Anselm, Luther, Calvin, and John Wesley. Among the doctrines expounded are those (1) of the Atonement, (2) of Justification by Faith, (3) of Sanctification, and (4) of Election.

(1) In formulating his doctrine of the Atonement Paul starts from the fact of the universality of sin. "All have sinned, and fall short of the glory of God" (Rom. iii. 23). There is, in human nature, an inevitable tendency to sin. "For I know that in me, that is, in my flesh, dwelleth no good thing" (vii. 18, viii. 8). Sin came into the world by one man (Adam) and death by sin, and so death spread to all men, since all men have sinned (v. 12). There is a law of sin and death, and once it is set in motion, its consequences inevitably follow, "For the wages of sin is death" (vi. 23). Man cannot escape from the power of sin, either by cultivating the wisdom of the Greek or by the zealous observance of the Mosaic Law.

Men thus labour under a sense of guilt and are estranged from God. By no possible efforts of their own can they attain to righteousness; but, now, into a world in which all men have sinned, salvation has come. The sacrificial death of Christ is the means which God, in His mercy, has provided to reconcile men to Himself. God's righteousness is now offered freely to all who have faith in Christ. All who believe are delivered from the bondage of sin and the sense of guilt, are accounted righteous before God and reconciled to Him, and enter upon a new life in Christ (cf. iii. 21–26, v. 1–11, viii. 1–11).

(2) Paul teaches that complete righteousness before God can be attained through Christ alone, apart from the works of the Law. Since there has been much misunderstanding of the phrase, "justification by faith", it is important that we should have a clear idea of the terms "justification" and "faith". The Greek word, translated "to justify", is a forensic word and

means "to account or to pronounce righteous" or "to acquit" not "to make righteous". The sinner, therefore, who is justified before God's tribunal, is accounted righteous or acquitted. He need do nothing to secure acquittal for it is secured, not on the ground of merit, but by the grace of God. As regards the term "faith" it is, in English, frequently regarded as synonymous with the term "belief", but strictly speaking, it is not so. We believe in a proposition but we have faith in a person. The difference in the two terms is well illustrated in a passage from the "Epistle of James": "Thou believest that God is one; thou doest well: the devils also believe, and shudder" (II. 19). Here it is a question of intellectual assent only and not of faith; their belief does not bring them into any personal relation to God and has no effect on their characters. Belief is a purely intellectual matter and has no driving power. "Faith", as interpreted by Paul, means more than intellectual assent: it involves an attitude of dependence, trust, and love towards God and a desire to serve Him. There is an emotional response to God who is the object of "faith", and this issues in a new kind of life. Paul's faith "working through love" is a kind of attempt to supply the emotional power to that which starts by being purely intellectual. It is not a chance phrase, for the idea appears again in 1 "Corinthians": "And if I have all faith, so as to remove mountains, but have not love, I am nothing" (XIII. 2). He never, however, explains how belief can produce love, unless we assume that his view is that belief is followed by the gift of the Holy Spirit which produces love. We should perhaps say that it is the contemplation of the life, character, work and death of Christ which produces love, and that belief is a kind of switch which turns on the current.

(3) Those who are in Christ Jesus are no longer under the control of the flesh but of the Spirit (VIII. 1–4). Anyone who does not possess the Spirit of Christ does not belong to Him (VIII. 9), but in response to faith the Spirit is given. He comes to dwell with us, assisting us in our weakness and interceding for us "with sighs that are beyond words" (VIII. 26). The sons of God are those who are guided by the Spirit of God, and when we cry, "Abba, Father", it is the Spirit confirming the

witness of our spirits that we are the children of God; "and if children, then heirs; heirs of God, and joint-heirs with Christ" (VIII. 15–16). By faith, and under the sanctifying power of the Spirit, we enter into an ever-deepening communion with Christ, so that we identify ourselves with Him and share mystical union with Him, going through, in our own experience, a similar process of crucifixion and resurrection, dying to sin and living to God in Christ Jesus our Lord (VI. 1–11). He, who raised up Christ from the dead, shall also, by the working of His indwelling Spirit in our lives, give life again even to our bodies, though now they are subject to death (VIII. 11).

Paul speaks of the "Spirit of God", the "Spirit of Christ", "Christ", and the "Spirit of Him that raised up Christ", as if they were identical. The action of one involves all. "God is inseparably one in His being and in His action. If the Father creates, He creates through the Son and by the Spirit. If the Son redeems, the redemption proceeds from the Father and is effected in the Spirit. If the Spirit sanctifies it is from and in the Father and the Son."[1]

(4) Paul teaches that both individuals and nations are elected according to God's eternal purpose. He is, however, concerned primarily, not with the ultimate destiny of the individual but with the Divine ordering of History. His Jewish opponents argued that God could not reject His chosen people, but Paul answers that God is free to elect or reject individuals and nations as He desires. The rejection does not mean that God has broken His promise, for the previous history of the nation shows that individual descendants were elected or rejected according to God's free choice (IX. 1–16). The history of Pharaoh shows that God hardens "whom he will"; the potter has the right from the same lump of clay "to make one part a vessel unto honour, and another unto dishonour" (IX. 17–21). His absolute freedom of election, however, is not unjust, but is used in abundant mercy (IX. 22–29). Having shown the absolute sovereignty of God, the Apostle now becomes inconsistent, and explains that the Jews have failed to realize that the coming of Christ has meant the abolition of the Law, and

[1] Gore, *The Epistle to the Romans*, 1899, p. 286.

have refused to accept the Gospel, not through ignorance but through disobedience and obstinacy; hence they are morally responsible for their own rejection. But God has not cast them off for ever; their unbelief will continue until the Gentiles as a whole are brought in, when all Israel will be saved (x.-xi.).

A Missionary Manifesto. The Epistle is a call to missionary enterprise. The Church finds in it, not only proof that it is under an obligation to evangelize the heathen, but also inspiration for the task. The Apostle was first and foremost a missionary, whose sole ambition was the redemption of all mankind. He believed that it was the purpose of God that he should preach the Gospel to the Gentiles (Gal. i. 15–16). To the Corinthians he wrote: "For necessity is laid upon me; for woe is unto me, if I preach not the Gospel" (1 Cor. ix. 16). Though his own fellow countrymen had persecuted him, he longed for their salvation. "For I could wish that I myself were anathema from Christ, for my brethren's sake, my kinsmen according to the flesh" (Rom. ix. 3). In his letter to the Roman church he sought to rouse in its members a sense of their responsibility for those who had never heard the Gospel. He stresses the fact that there is no distinction between Jew and Gentile (ii. 11, iii. 29); "The same Lord is Lord of all, and is rich unto all that call upon him" (x. 12). All men have fundamentally the same nature and all have need of salvation. The Gospel is sufficient to meet all their needs, being "the power of God unto salvation to every one that believeth" (i. 16). Through faith in Christ they can find, not only release from the bondage of sin and the sense of guilt, but also a new life of freedom and of heightened energy, and the joy and peace that come from an ever-deepening fellowship with Christ. Those who accept the Gospel are under an obligation to communicate it to others; he himself feels that he owes a duty both to Greeks and to Barbarians, both to the wise and to the foolish (i. 14).

Its Spiritual Influence. The Epistle has exercised a profound influence on mankind by its enunciation of principles upon which alone a true manhood and a worthy civilization can be built. Of all the Apostles, Paul was the only one who really understood the mind of Christ and had the ability to interpret it in terms which men could understand. When men relegate God to a distant heaven and believe that He is indifferent to their needs, the Epistle gives them the assurance that the universe is in the hands of a loving God, who has revealed Himself in Christ, and from whose love nothing in heaven or in earth can ever separate them (VIII. 35–38). When amid their projects for social reconstruction they fail to take into account the sinfulness of human nature, it proclaims the great fact of sin, whose wages is death (VI. 23). When they become slaves of sin, it shows them how they can, by God's grace, escape from its bondage, and pass into the service of righteousness (VI. 18), presenting their bodies "a living sacrifice, holy, acceptable to God" (XII. 1). When they desire to take vengeance on their enemies, it exhorts them to overcome evil with good, remembering that vengeance belongeth to God (XII. 19–20). When they make God a national God and erect barriers of race, class, or creed, it declares that "the same Lord is Lord of all" (X. 12), that with Him there is no respect of persons (II. 11), and that they are all "one body in Christ, and severally members one of another" (XII. 5). When they refuse to recognize their obligation to their fellow men, it reminds them that they owe a debt to humanity, and that all men are brothers, "for whom Christ died" (XIV. 15). When they seek to save themselves by such means as the acquisition of knowledge, or obedience to a written code, or education, or legislation, it teaches them that salvation can only be obtained through faith in Christ (I. 16–17). Moral and spiritual regeneration has always come when men have listened to Paul, as he speaks to them in the pages of his "Epistle to the Romans".

CHAPTER XVII

THE CAPTIVITY EPISTLES

Place of Composition

Written in Prison. The Epistles to the Colossians, to Philemon, to the Ephesians, and to the Philippians are called the "Captivity Epistles". That they were written from prison is clearly indicated in the following passages embodied in them:

(*a*) "Continue stedfastly in prayer, watching therein with thanksgiving; withal praying for us also, that God may open unto us a door for the word, to speak the mystery of Christ, for which I am also in bonds" (Col. IV. 2–3).

(*b*) "The salutation of me Paul with mine own hand. Remember my bonds" (Col. IV. 18).

(*c*) "Paul, a prisoner of Christ Jesus, and Timothy our brother, to Philemon our beloved and fellow-worker" (Philem. 1).

(*d*) "Yet for love's sake I rather beseech, being such a one as Paul the aged, and now a prisoner also of Christ Jesus" (Philem. 9).

(*e*) "For this cause I Paul, the prisoner of Christ Jesus in behalf of you Gentiles" (Eph. III. 1).

(*f*) "For which I am an ambassador in chains; that in it I may speak boldly, as I ought to speak" (Eph. VI. 20).

It must be noted at once, in order to understand what follows, that the so-called "Epistle to the Ephesians" has no claim to that title. In the two best manuscripts its dedication is "to the saints which are . . ." followed by a blank; and, as we shall see in the chapter on the Epistle, it is now generally considered that it was a circular letter, in which the ideas expressed in "Colossians" are more fully worked out, and that the different destinations were added in the blanks on the various copies.

Unfortunately, though the Apostle makes it quite clear that

he is "in bonds", he nowhere mentions the place of his imprisonment, so that the place and date of composition of the Epistles are in dispute. Apart from the short imprisonment at Philippi, "Acts" mentions only the long imprisonment which began at Caesarea and ended in two years' captivity in Rome. But in 2 "Corinthians" xi. 23 (part of the "Letter of Defence", written from Ephesus), Paul exclaims: "Are they ministers of Christ? . . . I more; in labours more abundantly, in prisons more abundantly, in stripes above measure, in deaths oft." This was written before the imprisonment in Caesarea and Rome; hence we conclude that there were many imprisonments, unmentioned in "Acts". At the same time it is reasonable to assume that they were not of great length, otherwise they were hardly likely to pass unnoticed, at least if they occurred within the period of Paul's missionary work with which Luke was closely connected.

The traditional and still the commonest view is that they were written during the two years' imprisonment at Rome, recorded in "Acts" xxviii. 30. Two other views, however, have been put forward; the earlier, that they were written during the imprisonment at Caesarea; and a later, advanced quite recently, that they date from a hypothetical imprisonment at Ephesus.

The Caesarean Theory. The Caesarean view may easily be dismissed on the ground that Paul is expecting a speedy release (Philem. 22: "But withal prepare me also a lodging: for I hope that through your prayers I shall be granted unto you"; Philippians ii. 24: "But I trust in the Lord that I myself also shall come shortly"). As he had himself "appealed unto Caesar" he could not possibly have expected a release at Caesarea.

The Ephesian Theory. The view that the four letters were written during an imprisonment at Ephesus has far more serious claims for consideration, although we have no evidence for such an imprisonment.[1] The evidence on which we must rely is entirely internal; the statement in the "Monarchian Prologue" that "Colossians" was written from Ephesus is valueless in so far as it would separate this Epistle from the others.

[1] Duncan, *St. Paul's Ephesian Ministry*, 1929.

Ephesus is geographically well situated, not only for Asia but also for Macedonia. It was for some time Paul's headquarters; the surrounding churches, even when he had not visited them personally, were founded by his helpers. "Colossians", the lost letter to the Laodiceans (Col. IV. 16), and the circular letter which we wrongly called "Ephesians", represent clearly a systematic attempt to reach the churches of Asia, while Philippi in Macedonia is only half the distance from Ephesus that it is from Rome.

But the most attractive part of the theory is the way it fits in with certain statements in "Acts" and I "Corinthians". For in "Acts" XIX. 21–22 we are told that Paul sent Timothy through Macedonia (which almost inevitably would mean through Philippi) to Corinth, intending to follow himself, and in I "Corinthians" Timothy's visit to Corinth (IV. 17) and his own intention to visit Corinth after passing through Macedonia (XVI. 5) are both mentioned. Now this is exactly the position described in "Philippians"; he intends to send Timothy (II. 19) and hopes to follow himself (II. 24). The resemblance is not quite complete; in "Acts" Erastus goes with Timothy; in the greetings of persons with Paul, Erastus is not mentioned in any of the four Epistles. He does appear in Romans XVI. 23; but, as we have seen, that chapter may be part of a letter from Rome to Ephesus or of the letter to Rome: we cannot, therefore, argue from it with any certainty. The absence of any mention of Epaphroditus' preliminary visit to Philippi (Phil. II. 25–30) in I "Corinthians" may be due to his going to Macedonia only.

The subsidiary arguments in favour of this theory have less weight. Among them is urged the statement that the Philippians had not been able to send him a contribution because they lacked opportunity (Phil. IV. 10), which would be perfectly true if the letter were written from Ephesus; for since leaving Corinth Paul had visited Palestine and Syria, and had traversed the regions of Galatia and Phrygia (Acts XVIII. 18–23). But, if he wrote from Rome, they could have sent him a contribution during his three months' stay in Corinth (Acts XX. 2–3). (It must be noticed that this is a private contribution and has nothing to do with the collection for the Christians of Jerusalem.)

275

The argument, however, is not conclusive. Paul had visited Philippi after his stay in Corinth (Acts xx. 6); and the lack of opportunity could perfectly well refer to the time of his imprisonment at Caesarea and the voyage to Rome.

Other arguments are:

(1) That it was unlikely that Paul would have so many friends who followed him to Rome, as are mentioned in the greetings. But, apart from Aristarchus and Luke, and possibly Epaphroditus, there is no reason to suppose that the others were not in Rome independently; in the case of Mark, for instance, there is no evidence that he accompanied Paul at any time since he left him on his first journey.

(2) That Onesimus, the runaway slave from Colossae, would be more likely to take refuge in the comparatively near town of Ephesus than in distant Rome. It could equally well be argued that a runaway slave would be less likely to be detected the farther he got away from those who knew him, and that it was easier to hide in the vast city of Rome without inquiries being made into his identity than anywhere else.

(3) At the time when "Romans" was written, Paul regarded his work in the East as completed, and is contemplating a visit to Rome (Acts xix. 21; Rom. i. 10–15) and a missionary campaign in Spain (Rom. xv. 19–25), whereas in these Epistles he is still proposing visits to the Aegean. To this it may be replied that the visit to Rome had been accomplished, if these Epistles were written from that city, though otherwise than as he planned, and it cannot surely be held that he ever contemplated finally leaving the Greek-speaking world. The imprisonment would necessarily change his plans.

(4) In "Philippians" we learn that there had been frequent communications between Philippi and Paul's place of imprisonment. News had been taken to Philippi of Paul's arrival; they had sent a contribution by the hand of Epaphroditus; they had subsequently heard of Epaphroditus' illness; Epaphroditus had learned of their receiving this news. It is urged that, as Philippi is only half the distance from Ephesus that it is from Rome, this tells in favour of Ephesus. But against place must be set time. In "Acts" xix. 10, two years is stated as the length of Paul's

preaching in Ephesus; this may be only up to the riot, but, as Luke clearly thinks he left shortly after the riot, he probably means it to represent Paul's whole stay. If so, any imprisonment at Ephesus must have been short, whereas the two years' imprisonment at Rome gives ample time for all these communications. This argument, which has been put forward for Ephesus, may be held to tell even more in favour of Rome.

The Roman Theory. We now turn to the arguments for Rome.

(1) At one time the references to the "praetorian guard" (Phil. I. 13) and to the saints "that are of Caesar's household" (IV. 22) were supposed to point indisputably to Rome. Since then, however, inscriptions at Ephesus have shown that soldiers of the praetorian guard were stationed there, and that imperial slaves and freedmen were sufficiently numerous there to form burial clubs.[1] It is even argued that the small number of the guard at Ephesus would make it possible for his imprisonment and its cause to be known "throughout the whole praetorian guard", which would be difficult in the large force at Rome. But surely this is to take a natural expression of speech too literally; when we say that "everybody knows", we never mean it to be taken of every single individual. It still remains true that, though there may have been plenty of imperial slaves in Ephesus, they would be scattered among the general population, and only at Rome would they form a group in some measure isolated, and necessarily sharing their interests and information.

(2) At one time great stress was laid on the supposed difference between the theology of the Captivity Epistles and that of "Romans", "Corinthians", and "Galatians", which were supposed to represent the real Pauline Christianity. German critics in the last century largely denied the Pauline origin of the Captivity Epistles altogether, and regarded them as second-century products, designed to support the theology of their own age by foisting it on to Paul. Although it has been shown that no belief can be found in these Epistles which is not to be found, though only in brief references, in the admittedly "Pauline" group, there still survives a trace of this

[1] McNeile, *Introduction to the New Testament*, 1927, p. 170.

view that the Captivity Epistles show a sufficient change of interest and stress to demand some interval of time, whereas the Ephesian view would make them contemporary. Our own belief is that a difference of six to eight years at a late stage in Paul's career is unlikely to have substantially altered his theology. He had been a Christian many years before even the earliest Epistle was written. The differences of stress are to be accounted for by the circumstances of the churches to which he is writing. "Colossians" and "Ephesians" (there is little special theology in "Philippians") are clearly written to meet a type of theosophy which anticipated the widespread Gnosticism of the second century, in which the chief feature was the belief in a number of intermediate beings between God and man, who were neither gods nor men, to whom the believer should pray, as God was too far removed to be approached immediately. The reply is to present Christ as the only mediator between God and man, and that because he is both God and man. Hence the stress on the pre-existence and divinity of Christ. The supposed specific "Pauline" doctrines of justification by faith and of election are equally replies to the difficulties felt in other churches. It is therefore dangerous to attempt to date Paul's Epistles by their theology.

(3) By far the strongest argument for a Roman origin is to be found in the statements about his imprisonment and expectations of release contained in "Philippians". He is clearly awaiting a decision—release or death (Phil. 1. 19–26); he does not know which is better, but he is inclined to think it will be release. The same expectation of release is found in "Philemon" 22. Meanwhile the Gospel is making great progress where he is (Phil. 1. 12–18); and it is obvious that he is allowed full liberty to write, and to send his messengers everywhere. All this corresponds exactly to what we know of the Roman imprisonment. It does not correspond with what we should expect of an imprisonment at Ephesus. He mentions risk of life at Ephesus in the "Letter of Reconciliation", written to the Corinthians from Macedonia shortly after leaving Ephesus (2 Cor. 1. 8–10), but surely his fear in Ephesus had been of mob violence—and we may assume that it was in the same mob violence that

Priscilla and Aquila "who for my life laid down their own necks" (Rom. XVI. 3), since it is hard to see how anyone could risk his life to secure Paul's acquittal by a court. An imprisonment is indeed suggested by his calling Andronicus and Junias his "fellow-prisoners" (Rom. XVI. 7); but it must have differed in two important respects from the Roman imprisonment. First, it is difficult to see what capital charge could have been brought, and if it had been, it must have resulted in an acquittal. Now Luke is always looking out for acquittals by the Roman government, and would almost certainly have recorded such an instance. Second, the whole object of the Ephesian persecution was to stop the preaching of Christianity, and no such liberty as he was enjoying is likely; whereas at Rome his imprisonment was only detention pending trial, and the authorities were not interested in preventing his missionary efforts.

We feel, therefore, that the balance of the argument is in favour of Rome, though the evidence is not conclusive. It does not appear that hitherto any attempt has been made to separate "Philippians" from the other three Epistles and assign it to Rome and the other three to Ephesus, though it would be difficult to refute such a theory conclusively.

Date of Composition

Three of the Epistles, namely, "Colossians", "Philemon", and "Ephesians", are closely connected with one another. They were written at or about the same time, while the first two, and probably the third also, were carried to their destination by the same messenger, Tychicus, who was accompanied by the runaway slave Onesimus. If Rome is their place of origin, then they were probably written in the early part of Paul's two years' imprisonment there, that is, about A.D. 60. "Philippians" stands apart from the other three Epistles. It was written at a different time, addressed to readers in a different locality, and carried by a different messenger—Epaphroditus. If it, too, was written from Rome, then it must almost certainly be assigned to the closing period of the imprisonment, that is, about A.D. 61, for he is expecting a speedy decision of the court in his favour and hopes to visit Philippi again on his liberation. Moreover, the numerous communications between Rome and Philippi, which are implied, demand a considerable lapse of time between the Apostle's arrival at Rome and the dispatch of the Epistle.

If, on the other hand, it is assumed that Ephesus is the place of origin of the Epistles, then they must have been written during his long sojourn in that city on his third missionary journey. This would mean that they were written in close conjunction with 1 "Corinthians" and the "Letter of Defence" (in 2 Cor.), and a short time before the "Letter of Reconciliation" (in 2 Cor.) and "Romans", that is, about A.D. 55.

CHAPTER XVIII

THE EPISTLES TO THE COLOSSIANS AND TO PHILEMON

COLOSSIANS

Colossae

Colossae was a small city in the valley of the Lycus, a tributary of the Maeander, and distant about ten miles from Laodicea and thirteen miles from Hierapolis. The three cities were in Phrygia, but in New Testament times they were included in the Roman province of Asia. Commanding the approaches to a pass in the Cadmus range and situated on a great trade route between Ephesus and the Euphrates, it had once been an important commercial centre. It is spoken of by the Greek historians, Herodotus (c. 484–425 B.C.) and Xenophon (c. 426–359 B.C.), as a great city, but it had gradually declined as Laodicea prospered, probably because of the latter's more advantageous position on the trade route. The Greek historian, Strabo (63 B.C.–A.D. 24), refers to it as a small city, and when Paul wrote it was an insignificant place in process of decay. It had a mixed population of Phrygians, Greeks, and Jews. Antiochus the Great (223–187 B.C.) transplanted two thousand Jewish families from Babylonia and Mesopotamia to Lydia and Phrygia, and some of these probably settled at Colossae. They multiplied and prospered to such an extent that, in 62 B.C., their annual tribute of a half-shekel to the Temple at Jerusalem amounted to so large a sum that the Roman proconsul, Flaccus, alarmed at its exportation, seized twenty pounds' weight of gold, representing more than 11,000 inhabitants, exclusive of the women, children, and slaves of the households. In the year A.D. 61 the greater part of the region was devastated by an earthquake, and according to the Church historian, Eusebius,

Colossae was overwhelmed in the disaster. It was probably a short time before the earthquake that Paul wrote his letter to the Colossians.

Founding of the Church

For our knowledge of the origin and history of the church at Colossae, we rely solely on Paul's letter to its members. Though he regards them as his spiritual children, he makes no claim to be the founder of the church; in fact he expressly states that they were personally unacquainted with him (II. 1). There is no mention in "Acts" of any visit that he ever paid to the valley of the Lycus. On his second missionary journey, he was "forbidden of the Holy Ghost to speak the word in Asia" (Acts XVI. 6), while on his third missionary tour he reached Ephesus by way of "the upper country" (Acts XIX. 1), from which we infer that he took the less-frequented mountain road, though it is possible that he travelled along the main road through the valley of the Lycus, without stopping to preach on the way. During his long sojourn of over two years at Ephesus he preached the Gospel, not only in the city, but also in the surrounding district, so that the word of the Lord grew mightily (Acts XIX. 20) and spread throughout the Roman province of Asia (Acts XIX. 10). One of his converts was Epaphras, who returned to his home in Colossae, where he founded a church; he also founded churches in the neighbouring cities of Laodicea and Hierapolis. His zeal in the work of evangelization earned the praise of Paul who describes him as "our beloved fellow-servant, who is a faithful minister of Christ on our behalf" (Col. I. 7), and as one who "hath much labour for you, and for them in Laodicea and for them in Hierapolis" (IV. 13). In addition, Paul converted Philemon and his wife Apphia, and also Archippus who was probably their son. Since they also lived at Colossae, they no doubt assisted Epaphras in the work of spreading the Gospel, for the Apostle sends greetings to "Philemon our beloved and fellow-worker, and to Apphia our sister, and to Archippus our fellow-soldier, and to the church in thy house" (Philem. 1–2). The church at Colossae was predominantly Gentile (cf. Col. I. 21–22, II. 13) but it probably contained also a Jewish element, since so many Jews lived in the neighbourhood.

Purpose

Some time after the founding of the church at Colossae, Epaphras visited Paul in the place of his imprisonment. The reason for his visit is not mentioned, but he doubtless reported on the internal condition of the church, for the Apostle reckoned it as one of the churches for whose spiritual welfare he himself was responsible, although he was not its founder, while the Colossians, in their turn, recognized his authority over them. In some respects his report of the church seems to have been satisfactory, for he praised its members for their faith and love (Col. 1. 4); but at the same time he must have expressed his anxiety at the appearance among them of a dangerous form of false teaching, which he probably felt only Paul could combat with any hope of success. Had the heresy been allowed to develop unchecked, it would have ultimately led to the subversion of Christianity, for it meant the depreciation of the person and work of Christ. The Apostle, alive to the danger of the situation and perhaps prompted by Epaphras, wrote his "Epistle to the Colossians", to refute the false doctrine, which was being propagated among them, and to exhort them to remain steadfast in the faith. At the same time he took the opportunity to enlarge upon the bonds which should unite the various members of a Christian household, the subject being probably suggested to him by the fact that he was about to send back the runaway slave, Onesimus, to his master Philemon, who was a member of the church at Colossae, and to plead with him to receive Onesimus "no longer as a servant, but more than a servant, a brother beloved" (Philem. 16).

The Colossian Heresy

We know nothing of this heresy apart from what can be inferred from Paul's letter. It would appear to have been an amalgam of Christianity, Jewish ritualism, and Greek philosophy. The Colossians were apparently being taught that faith in Christ as the sole condition of salvation was insufficient.

Men must also observe the Jewish ceremonial law, which included circumcision (II. 11), the keeping of "a feast day or a new moon or a sabbath day" (II. 16) and the avoidance of unclean food (II. 21), worship angels (II. 18), practise asceticism (II. 21–23), and be initiated into a secret wisdom (II. 2–3). The heretical teachers called their doctrine a theosophy or philosophy (II. 8), and employed technical terms borrowed from the pagan cults.

Their teaching was based on the false philosophical theory of the dualism of matter and spirit. There was a spiritual world, which was essentially good, and a material world, which was essentially evil. Since there could be no contact between a holy, absolute, and unapproachable God and a world of evil, man could not enter into communication with Him except through a hierarchy of angelic beings, who were regarded as Emanations of the "fulness of Deity". Christ, therefore, was only one of the many mediators that bridged the gulf between God and man. It was necessary to conciliate these angelic beings by the performance of magical rites and by mortifying the body to rid it of the pollution of matter. Some men, however, believed that since matter and spirit were separate domains and material things might be disregarded by the spiritual man, he was therefore free to indulge his lower nature without restraint. Thus the belief that the body was essentially evil could lead either to asceticism or Antinomianism.

Paul's Refutation of the Heresy

In refuting this heresy Paul seeks to establish the all-sufficiency of Christ in the divine plan of salvation. The so-called "Philosophy" is of human origin and is nothing but an empty delusion (II. 8). The true knowledge, contained in the Gospel, as preached to them by Epaphras, is of divine origin, for before it was disclosed to the saints of God, it had been hidden in the divine mind "from all ages and generations" (I. 26). This knowledge is to be obtained by faith in Christ, in whom are hidden "all the treasures of wisdom and knowledge" (II. 3). Christ is the incarnate Son of God in whom the divine Fulness willed to settle "without limit". He is superior to and sovereign over the universe, the Church, and all angelic beings. He does not share his work of universal redemption and of reconciliation with anyone: by His death on the cross He is the sole redeemer of sinful man and the sole reconciler of all things to God (i. 13–21). Since Christ is pre-eminent in all things, it follows that: (1) He is an all-sufficient Saviour, (2) He is the only mediator between God and man, and (3) man need no longer fear the angelic powers and seek to conciliate them. As for the ceremonial law, it had never been more than a foreshadowing of better things to come which had been realized in Christ. By His death on the cross Christ had abolished the Law and triumphed over all angelic powers (ii. 13–17). Ascetic practices are of no value against carnal indulgence (ii. 20–23). The way to holiness is not by mortifying the body, but by putting away its base passions and living a new life of the spirit by faith in Christ, in an endeavour to be conformed to the image of God after whom all the children of men are created (iii. 1–11).

This theme is repeated by Paul himself in "Ephesians" on the same lines; but it is also the basis of "Hebrews", by an unknown author, whose aim is to show the superiority of Christ to the angels and to the Aaronite priesthood, and the supersession of the ceremonial system, which was only a foreshadowing. This unknown author deals with the theme in his individual way, with far more quotations from the Old Testament, but in essence the theme is the same.

Contents

After sending greetings from Timothy and himself, Paul thanks God for their faith and love and prays that they may be filled with spiritual wisdom and understanding, so that they may be worthy of Him who has rescued them from the power of the Darkness and transferred them into the kingdom of His beloved Son (i. 1–13).

Christ, the sole redeemer of mankind, is the image of the unseen God; by Him all things were created, both visible and invisible. He is prior to all things, and in Him all things cohere. He is supreme over the whole of the universe, the

Church, and all angelic powers. It was the good pleasure of the Father that the fulness of the Deity should dwell in Him without limit, and that He should reconcile all things to God in a peace made by His atoning death on the cross. Now by His death they can stand in God's presence, pure and unashamed, provided they remain loyal to the Gospel (i. 14–23).

The Apostle's mission is to proclaim that open secret, unknown to past ages but now disclosed to the saints of God—a secret which holds glorious wealth for the Gentiles in the fact of Christ's presence among them as their hope and glory (i. 24–29).

In Christ are hidden all God's treasures of wisdom and knowledge. They should not allow themselves to be misled by plausible arguments and vain speculation, which is of human origin. It is in Christ that they reach their full life (ii. 1–10).

There is the true spiritual circumcision, which came in through baptism, when they were buried with Christ and were raised to life with Him. He has forgiven their sins, cancelled the Law, and vanquished the angelic powers (ii. 11–15).

They should allow no one to criticize them on questions relating to food and drink, and to the observance of festivals and holy days. Such things are merely foreshadowings of Christ. Nor should anyone be allowed to prescribe rules for them regarding fasting and the cult of angels, presuming on his visions and inflated by his sensuous notions, instead of keeping, as a member of the Church, in touch with its Head (ii. 16–19).

Christ has set them free from subjection to elemental spirits, so there is now no need to submit to human ordinances concerning things which have no permanent religious significance. Such ordinances have a show of wisdom, self-imposed worship, humility, and ascetic vigour, but they possess no value for combating the lower nature (ii. 20–23).

Now that they are risen with Christ, they should fix their thoughts on things of heaven where Christ reigns, killing all evil desires and sensual passions which incur the wrath of God on those who disobey Him. Since they have freed themselves from their old nature and are living in union with Christ, they should put on the new nature, which is continually growing nearer to the pattern of Him who created it. In that new life all distinctions which divide men vanish, and Christ is all in all (III. 1–11).

As God's chosen people, they should be sympathetic, kind, humble, gentle, forbearing, forgiving, and above all loving, for love is the bond which binds all men together in Christian perfection, and allow the peace of God to rule in their hearts and to fill them with thanksgiving. The Christian message should be so implanted in their minds that they will teach and train one another, expressing their thanksgiving in psalms, hymns, and spiritual songs. Everything should be done in Christ's name (II. 12–17).

The Apostle urges wives to obey their husbands, children their parents, and slaves their masters, while husbands are to love their wives, parents to avoid discouraging their children by bad temper, and masters to render just and equal treatment to their slaves (III. 18–IV. 1).

He exhorts them to constancy in prayer and thanksgiving, mentions Tychicus and Onesimus who will give them fuller information, sends greetings from his companions and from himself, gives instructions for exchanging letters with the church at Laodicea, urges Archippus to be diligent in his ministry, reminds them that he is a prisoner, and closes with a benediction (IV. 2–18).

Elemental Spirits in the Pauline Epistles

Meaning of "Elements". It is quite clear from his Epistles that Paul accepts the existence of the "Elements" or "Universe-Rulers" (cf. 1 Cor. II. 6–8; Gal. IV. 9; Col. II. 8–10, 14–18; Eph. II. 1–2, III. 8–11, VI. 12). In his references to them three words stand out, namely: (1) elements, (2) rules(i. e. rulers), and (3) authority. The meaning of the last two is obvious, but the first needs examination. Originally it meant a letter of the alphabet or one of the forms of matter supposed to be basic; then it came to be applied to the sun, moon, and five planets. Apparently its subsequent progress was to the spirits supposed to inhabit and control these and perhaps other phenomena of the visible heavens, till finally it is used in these Epistles of evil spirits in them. Outside the Epistles it is found in an apocryphal work attributed to Solomon which speaks of "the elements, the world-rulers" (see Eph. VI. 12 for this latter phrase). We notice that the "rulers" and "authorities" are spoken of as "of this world" or "age", and as dwelling "in heavenly places" and their chief as the "prince of the power of the air" (Eph. II. 2).

Origin of the Idea. Though the notion of spirits below the rank of gods but above that of men was readily accepted by peoples who had come to be theoretic monotheists but hankered after their former paganism, it is probable that the form of it which we have here, and which associates them with the objects in the visible heavens, is derived in all cases from Persian Zoroastrianism—in Judaism by direct contact under Persian rule, in the Roman Empire generally through Mithraism, and very probably in other parts of Asia besides Palestine by direct contact, as all the provinces subsequently Roman had at one time been Persian.

In Judaism there are two sides to the Persian influence, the belief in angels of various ranks and the belief in the devil and his subordinates. The seven archangels of post-exilic Judaism are the Persian beings, presumably gods degraded to a lower rank, of the sun, moon, and five known planets; even in the New Testament in the book of "Revelation" we find the angel that dwells in the sun. The Persian religion was dualistic and had an evil god as well as the good god, independent of him though somewhat weaker; in Judaism he becomes a fallen angel, the devil or Satan, and is supplied with a host of subordinates, just as God has a number of subordinates (some like cherubim and seraphim pre-Persian, others of Persian origin). Orthodox Judaism did not worship angels, but the pagan adopters of the idea would be under no bar such as was set for the Jew by the first and second commandments.

Although we know this much of the growth of beliefs about angels and devils in general, we know nothing of the particular form of these beliefs which Paul confronted and attacked than what we gather from the Epistles themselves. They are associated with the keeping of Jewish feasts, which shows that they were in some measure associated with Judaism, but as we have seen, it cannot have been with orthodox Judaism; this means that they were what is called syncretistic, that is to say, formed by taking features from more than one religion. From "Galatians" IV. 10, we gather that they had been held by his converts before they became Christians, and these converts must have been pagans. They are associated with food restrictions, that is asceticism, on the one hand, but also with disregard of moral standards on the other. The reply, insisting on Christ Jesus as the one mediator between God and man, together with reference to the worship of angels, shows that these powers, call them elements, rulers, authorities, or what not, were regarded by the heretics as good powers and as intermediaries for the man with God (Col. II. 14–23).

Paul's Contact with the Idea. This is bound up with the question of the geographical limits of this teaching. It is at once noticed that, though the "rulers of this world" (or "Age") are mentioned in the quotation from 1 "Corinthians" as bad, there is nothing to suggest that Paul had come across any belief at Corinth that they were good, and they are not mentioned in any other of the letters to European churches, while they are mentioned in all three letters to Asiatic churches ("Galatians", "Colossians" and what we wrongly term "Ephesians", which was probably addressed to churches near Colossae). But all three Epistles are addressed to churches in what may be called the Phrygian interior of Asia Minor, which was more primitively pagan than Greek; and there is nothing in the Epistles to tell us whether they were also to be found in the churches of the Aegean seaboard such as Ephesus, or in Tarsus, Paul's original home. The statement in "Revelation" that the author wished to worship the angel but was forbidden by the angel himself, may be introduced to prohibit such a practice, in which case it must have been known in the churches of the Aegean seaboard, but this is a hazardous hypothesis.

Paul may therefore have first met the belief in Tarsus or in his visit to the churches of South Galatia. What we have to remember is that, wherever he learnt of the ideas, he accepted the existence of these powers but regarded them as evil.

Paul's own views. Why did he accept them at all? It is not easy to answer this question. His acceptance is thorough-going and is worked into his whole theological system. These beings he conceives as extraordinarily powerful, constituting a kingdom warring against God and against the members of the Christian Church. They were responsible for the Crucifixion, but did not realize who it was they were crucifying (1 Cor. 11. 8); and the Crucifixion potentially destroyed their power (Col. 11. 15). They are responsible for human ill-doing (Eph. 11. 2), and a danger even to Christians (Eph. vi. 12). The whole plan of redemption was devised by God from eternity with reference to them (Eph. 111. 11). His views on this subject are a part of the philosophy which he reserves for mature Christians (1 Cor. 11. 6) in a passage written before he was called on to deal with the Colossian heresy, a philosophy which is absent from all the books of the New Testament written by other writers (though approached by the author of "Hebrews") and is more fitly called Pauline Christianity than many of the views to which this title is given.

The first point in answering the question is that Paul was intensely conscious of the power of evil. Probably no one can reach the intensity of Paul's religious fervour without the urge which comes from the awareness of moral or social evil. This feeling is obvious in Our Lord Himself and in most of the New Testament writers. But in Paul's case it became more personal and intense by his horror of the astounding criminality of the Crucifixion, which arose from the feeling that he himself would have been among the authors of the crime had he had the opportunity, and that by taking a leading part in the martyrdom of Stephen he had, as it were, made himself a participator. He could only explain his own malignity by supposing himself to be under the direction of some overwhelming evil influence.

The belief in the army of evil under the devil was part of the belief of all the original Christians and is attributed in many passages in the Gospels to Jesus Himself. But this does not explain the identification of the evil powers with the rulers and authorities of the astral bodies, which is one of Paul's special beliefs. It is hard to believe that he first formed this hypothesis on his missionary journey to the cities of southern Galatia: had he come across the view so late, it could hardly have entered so completely into his being. At least he must have formed it during the period, of which we have no account in "Acts", when soon after his conversion he was teaching in his native land of Cilicia with its capital, Tarsus. But may it not have been part of the Judaism in which he was brought up? The mention of "elements" as "universe-rulers" in pseudo-"Solomon" suggests that it was a part of the beliefs of some Jewish school. Paul treats the Graeco-Roman gods as "devils"; may that not be because he had throughout treated the astral powers of Zoroastrianism and Mithraism as such? His horror of the Crucifixion passed into an explanation of it; so stupendous an event as the sacrifice of the Son of God was explicable only as God's method of defeating these superhuman powers which, as it were, had made themselves masters of God's universe, not merely as a result of human sin.

It is perhaps necessary to notice that the Apocalypse may imply an identification of the devil and his angels with astral powers, when it describes the war in heaven in which they were thrown out of heaven to the earth (Rev. xii. 7-9), which is treated as a future event; but, throughout the rest of the book, God's angels appear to be in control of sun and sky. The Gospels, with their many references to the devil and to demons, never connect them with astral powers; sun and sky, the phenomena of the heavenly bodies, and the weather, are all under God's immediate control: this represents the earliest form of Christianity. Nor is there any suggestion of the identification in the Johannine writings, the final form which Christian theology took in the New Testament. It seems unfortunate that Paul should have approached even so near as he did to the view of the material universe as evil by admitting an evil control of important parts of it. In the long run the Gospels won; but traces of the other view both in heresies and even in doctrines of the Atonement can be found for long after apostolic times.

Authenticity

External Evidence. The authenticity of "Colossians" has been accepted by the majority of New Testament scholars. The external evidence is reasonably good. Traces of the Epistle are probably to be found in the works of Clement of Rome, Ignatius, Barnabas, and Justin Martyr. The fact that it is included in Marcion's Canon shows that by about A.D. 140 it was well known and was accepted at Rome. It is mentioned in the Muratorian Fragment, and is cited by Irenaeus, Tertullian, and Clement of Alexandria. Until the rise of the Tübingen school of critics in the nineteenth century its genuineness was never doubted.

Internal Evidence. The Tübingen school of critics denied the authenticity of the Epistle on the grounds that: (1) the doctrines which it attacks are those of second-century Gnosticism, and therefore it must be the work of a later writer, and (2) it differs in style, language, and thought from the earlier Pauline Epistles. The first objection cannot be maintained, since subsequent research has proved that the terms of Gnosticism can be found in various movements, dating back to at least the early years of the first century, especially in places where the streams of Jewish, Greek, and Oriental thought met, as in Asia Minor. The style is doubtless different from that of Paul's earlier Epistles, the sentences being longer and more involved, the movement of thought slower, and the tone loftier; but this may be accounted for by a difference in subject and by the lack of urgency, due to the absence of any personal opponent. Many of Paul's characteristic words are found in the text, while some of them, like "fullness", "spiritual", "wisdom", "knowledge", and "perfect", which are not so, are technical terms borrowed from the terminology of the heretical teachers. It is true that several of the Apostle's characteristic words are absent from the Epistle, but some of them are also absent from his earlier Epistles. As regards the thought, it may be granted that it does show an advance on that of the earlier Epistles, but this is due, partly to a development in his own ideas on the person and work of Christ, and partly to the fact that in his desire to emphasize the completeness of His redemptive work he makes explicit what is implicit in his other writings (cf. 1 Cor. VIII. 6 and Col. I. 15–20; 1 Cor. II. 6–8 and Col. II. 15). There is, in fact, nothing in the thought, style, and language which would warrant our attributing it to any other writer than Paul. It may be added that a recent theory of the origin of "Hebrews" holds that it, too, was written to the Asiatic Christians who were in contact with this syncretistic teaching, and that Paul had it before him when he wrote this Epistle and was influenced by it.

Historical Value

"Colossians" is important for its exposition of the doctrine of the person and work of Christ. In his criticism of the new religion, expounded by the heretical teachers, Paul was compelled to grapple with the question of the significance of Christ in creation. By his insistence on the exalted nature of Christ and on the completeness of His work of redemption and reconciliation, he exercised a powerful influence in preserving the identity of Christianity as an independent religion and in preventing it from degenerating into a mere speculative philosophy. The Church came to regard the Epistle as a form of orthodoxy, touching the person and work of Christ, and found in it a powerful argument in its struggle against second-century Gnosticism. More than ever before, it was realized that faith in Christ was the sole condition of salvation, and that Christianity was the one true religion.

The Epistle is also of value for the light it sheds on the syncretistic movement which was characteristic of the age. Greeks and Romans, especially the more educated classes, had lost faith in their ancestral gods, while some of the more thoughtful among them had turned to philosophy, which professed, not only to explain the mysteries of the universe, but also to provide a way of life. Many in their search for spiritual satisfaction had flocked into the Mystery Cults which had entered the Graeco-Roman world from the East. The foundation of the Empire had led to the fusion of the races and to the growth of internationalism. Men, more conscious than ever before of the unity of mankind, dreamt of a universal religion, which should both serve as a bond of union and satisfy their spiritual aspirations. It seemed to them that the ideal religion would be one which combined the finest elements in the various cults with Greek philosophical ideas. In "Colossians" we see the beginnings of religious syncretism, or the blending of religions, within the Christian Church. The movement, however, was older than Christianity and widespread. In the second century, those "theosophies" which made use of Christian primitive beliefs were collectively called Gnosticism, because those who had been initiated into them claimed to be in possession of "gnosis" or supernatural knowledge. It threatened the very existence of Christianity, being all the more dangerous since it was represented by some of the keenest minds in the Church, and was only vanquished after a long and bitter struggle.

PHILEMON

Purpose

The Epistle was written to Philemon, one of Paul's converts, who was a leading member of the church at Colossae (cf. Col. IV. 9, 17). That he was a man in prosperous circumstances may be judged by the fact that he possessed slaves, had a house large enough to be the meeting-place of a church, and was given to hospitality (Philem. 1–7, 15–16). His slave, Onesimus, a name frequently borne by slaves, after having apparently robbed him sought refuge presumably at Rome, where he was converted under Paul's teaching and attached himself to the Apostle as his personal attendant, in which capacity he performed his duties with such zeal and diligence as to win the approbation of his new master for his usefulness and helpfulness. Paul came to regard him with such warm affection that he called him "a brother beloved" (Philem. 16) and felt that to part with him would be like parting with his "very heart" (Philem. 12). But Philemon had a prior claim to him, and it was obviously the Apostle's duty to restore him to his lawful master. When Onesimus heard of his intention he must have been filled with fear, for return meant, if not crucifixion or torture, at least being branded as a runaway slave and as a thief. He must, however, have agreed to return, and probably travelled with Tychicus who was carrying a letter from the Apostle to the church at Colossae. With Tychicus or Onesimus Paul sent this short letter to Philemon, pleading with him to forgive the fugitive slave and to receive him, no longer as a slave but as something more than a slave—"a brother beloved" (Philem. 16).

Contents

After a salutation from himself and Timothy, the Apostle thanks God for the love and faith which Philemon has shown towards the Lord and his fellow church members (1-7). In the request he is about to make, he would be quite free to order him to do his duty, but prefers to appeal to him on grounds of love. As an old man and as a prisoner for Christ, he appeals on behalf of his spiritual son, Onesimus. Despite his name (worth), he was once a worthless character but is now worth something to both of them. He is sending him back, though it is like parting with his own soul. He would like to keep him as Philemon's deputy, but he will do nothing without his friend's consent, so that his kindness may be a free act, without any appearance of compulsion (8-14). Perhaps the slave was parted from him that he might receive him back, no longer as a mere slave but as a beloved brother. If the slave has defrauded him, the Apostle will repay the debt, but if it comes to speaking of debt, Philemon owes him a larger debt—his very soul. He believes that Philemon will do even beyond what he asks. After expressing the hope that he may soon be able to visit him, he sends greetings from Mark, Aristarchus, Demas, and Luke, and concludes with a benediction (15-24).

Authenticity

External Evidence. The Epistle is included in Marcion's Canon and is mentioned in the Muratorian Fragment. At the beginning of the third century it is quoted by Origen, its first commentator, as Pauline, but in the following century it was rejected by many Christians on account of its triviality and its unedifying character. Jerome in his preface (A.D. 380) thought fit to vindicate its apostolic worthiness and religious helpfulness against its many detractors.

Internal Evidence. In modern times the German critic, Baur, while acknowledging that it is infused with the purest Christian feeling, denied its authenticity chiefly because he rejected "Colossians" with which it is closely associated. In style and spirit it is so characteristic of Paul's genius that it is now almost universally recognized as his work. "This short letter", says Sabatier, "is so intensely original, so entirely innocent of dogmatic preoccupation, and Paul's mind has left its impress so clearly and so indelibly upon it, that it can only be set aside by an act of sheer violence."[1]

Historical Value

"Philemon" is important for its treatment of the question of slavery, on which the whole of the economic structure of the ancient world was based. The Apostle has often been condemned because he did not attack the iniquitous system, which was fundamentally opposed to the principles of the Gospel which he preached. Instead of denouncing it and advocating its abolition, he accepted it as part of the existing order. Christian slaves were not to trouble about their servitude, but were to be content with their lot, and to perform their duties faithfully as unto the Lord (cf. 1 Cor. vii. 21–24; Col. iii. 22–24; Eph. vi. 5–9). He has a great deal to say about the spiritual freedom of men and their equality before God, but nothing about their political freedom and their equality before the law. But, if Paul did not denounce slavery, neither did any other writers of the New Testament; nor is there any sign in the Gospels that Christ ever alluded to it, though slavery in Palestine, with its injustice and inhumanity, could not have escaped His notice.

It would have been foolish and even criminal to have pressed for the immediate abolition of slavery, for there was an enormous number of slaves in the Empire, whose release would have resulted in unemployment on a vast scale, widespread poverty, and misery, and would probably have culminated in all the horrors of civil war. Had Paul advocated their emancipation, he might have incited them to revolt and thus laid himself open to the charge of propagating a revolutionary religion—a charge which he was always anxious to avoid. As

[1] Sabatier, *The Apostle Paul*, 1891, p. 227.

a missionary, whose sole ambition was the salvation of mankind, he was primarily concerned with the transformation of individuals, not with the reconstruction of society, with spiritual freedom not with political freedom. Moreover, he was expecting the speedy return of Christ, when the existing order of things would pass away and the Kingdom of God would be established on earth. It must, therefore, have seemed to him a waste of time and energy to advocate the abolition of a system, which, in the ordering of Providence, was already doomed. It was more important that men should be engaged in the perfecting of their characters in expectation of the return of their Lord.

The abolition of slavery could only come by the gradual penetration of the principles of the Gospel among the nations. "The kingdom of heaven", says Christ, "is like unto leaven, which a woman took, and hid in three measures of meal, till it was all leavened" (Mt. XIII. 33). Though Paul did not denounce slavery, by the proclamation of the great truths of the Fatherhood of God and the Brotherhood of Man, he brought about a gradual revolution, leading first to the more humane treatment of slaves, then to their frequent manumission and ultimately to their complete emancipation.

The Epistle is also important for the light it sheds on the personality of Paul. It could only have been written by one who was deeply imbued with the true Christian spirit. In his other Epistles he is the missionary, organizer, theologian, pastor, or controversialist, but here we see him in the role of a friend— understanding, tactful, kind, gentle, courteous, and loving, and with a touch of humour. He had changed since the time when he stood by, consenting to Stephen's death, and breathed "threatening and slaughter against the disciples of the Lord" (Acts IX. 1). From the day of his vision on the Damascus road, his life had been a continual pressing on "toward the goal unto the prize of the high calling of God in Christ Jesus" (Phil. III. 14). As we read this brief personal letter, we understand more clearly how it was that he won the loyalty and affection of all who knew him.

CHAPTER XIX

THE EPISTLE TO THE EPHESIANS

Recipients

To whom the Epistle is addressed is unknown, but it is practically certain that it was not intended for the church at Ephesus alone. In two of the oldest and best manuscripts (Codex Vaticanus and Codex Sinaiticus) the words "at Ephesus" (i. 1) are missing, while without them the translation, "who are also faithful" or "who are also believers", does not make good sense. Marcion's copy evidently lacked the words, for it is styled the "Epistle to the Laodiceans". In the following age Tertullian accused Marcion of altering the title and departing from the tradition of the Church, from which it would seem that neither of them had the words in the Epistle itself. In the third century Origen had access to a copy from which they were absent, while in the fourth century Basil states that they were not known in the most ancient copies.

The Epistle has not the character of one addressed to readers with whom the writer is acquainted. Paul had spent more than two years at Ephesus where he had founded an important church (Acts xix.) and if the last chapter of "Romans" (xvi. 1–23) is a portion of a letter sent to Ephesus, he must have made many friends there. On his last journey to Jerusalem the leaders of the church met him at Miletus and parted from him with every sign of affection (Acts xx. 17–38). Yet in the Epistle he sends no greetings to his friends, makes no reference to his work in the city, and implies that he knew them and they knew him only by hearsay. He speaks of their faith without any indication that they are his converts (i. 15), and apparently doubts if they have heard that he had been commissioned by God to preach the Gospel to the Gentiles (iii. 2).

There is wide acceptance among those who accept the Epistle as a genuine work of Paul, of the view that it is a circular letter addressed to a group of churches in the province of Asia, and that a blank was left to be filled in with the name of each church to which Tychicus was to deliver a copy. This would explain the impersonal nature of the Epistle—the absence of personal greetings and of any clear traces of special local problems. In "Colossians" IV. 16, Paul directs that the Epistle "be read also in the church of the Laodiceans; and that ye also read the epistle from Laodicea". It has been suggested that this letter "from Laodicea" is our "Ephesians", and that the subsequent omission of the name was due to the discredit into which the church fell in consequence of its denunciation in "The Revelation" (III. 14–16). It is, however, unlikely that anyone wishing to omit the reference to the Laodiceans would have done it so clumsily as by leaving a blank; whereas if there was a blank in the original manuscript, faithfulness to the original might well prevent the more scholarly copyists from filling it up.

Purpose

The purpose of the Epistle is not easy to ascertain. Unlike the other Pauline Epistles, except to some extent "Romans", there are no clear indications that it was called forth by any special occasion or by any particular need of those to whom it was addressed. The solution of the problem is to be found in the impact of Greek culture on Christianity. When, on his second missionary journey, Paul crossed the Aegean Sea into Europe he came into intimate contact with Greek culture which had a stimulating effect upon his own intellectual life. Greek philosophers, notably the Epicureans and the Stoics, had solved, to their own satisfaction, the mystery of the universe, the Epicureans by a materialistic philosophy, the Stoics by a pantheistic. Faced with such philosophic speculations Paul must have felt the need of an interpretation of the universe, both theistic and specifically Christian, which would satisfy the intellect and give meaning and purpose to life. Probably after years of meditation, he finally arrived at certain conceptions which he embodied in "Colossians", employing them to refute false doctrines. Shortly afterwards, he wrote "Ephesians", using the same ideas, but developing them apart from any controversial issue. The interpretation is theistic in the fullest sense as it represents God, not only as the Creator, but also as having worked out, even before creation, a course of history for the bringing of men into a right relation with Himself; and it is specifically Christian, as distinct from Jewish, in conceiving Christ as having existed before Creation, and as God's agent as well in redemption, and in declaring that by His redeeming work Gentiles were made equal partakers with the Jews in their relation to God. After writing the Epistle, he sent it as a circular letter by the hand of Tychicus to a group of churches in the province of Asia.

Contents

After the opening salutation, Paul praises God for the blessing which He has bestowed upon him and his readers, for the way in which, even before creation, He had chosen them to be His children, and for the rich gift of wisdom and understanding, enabling them to understand His secret purpose of reuniting all things in Christ (I. 1–10).

The Jews, owing to their favoured position, had been able to put their hope in Christ before the Gentiles, but now the latter have believed the Gospel of salvation, and in consequence of their faith have received the Holy Spirit, according to His promise (I. 11–14).

He thanks God for their faith, and prays that He may give them wisdom and insight that they may know the full blessedness of their position and the greatness of the power with which He assists believers. It was the same power which raised up Christ from the dead and set Him over all things for the Church, which is His body. It was also the same power which raised them, both Jews and Gentiles, when they were spiritually dead, in order that all future ages might recognize the wealth of His grace and goodness (I. 15–II. 7).

It is by faith in Christ that they have been saved, not by works. God has made them what they are through union with

Christ, that they may spend their lives, as He ordained, in doing good (II. 8–10).

He reminds them that though as Gentiles they had once been strangers and aliens from Israel, Christ by His death had broken down the barrier between them, abolishing the Law, so that they now have free access to the Father and are members of the one household of God. They are, as it were, a building that rests on the apostles and prophets as its foundation, with Christ as the corner stone. In Him the whole structure is welded together, and rises into a sacred temple in which God may dwell (II. 11–22).

God has now revealed His secret purpose, hitherto concealed from the ages, that the Gentiles should share equally with the Jews in the divine promises, in order that through the Church the manifold wisdom of God may be made known to the angelic rulers and authorities. Thus all will know of the fulfilment of the divine purpose in Christ Jesus (III. 1–13).

He prays that God may strengthen their inmost life by His Spirit, so that Christ may dwell in their hearts through faith, and that with their own lives based on love, they may come to know the love of Christ, which surpasses all knowledge, and may attain the fulfilment which God intends for them (III. 14–21).

He entreats them to live worthily of the divine call they have received, to live at peace among themselves, and to be zealous in maintaining that unity which the Spirit gives. There is one Church, one Spirit, and one Lord, in whom they all believe and in whose name they have been baptized, and one God who is over all. Each has some special gift from Christ. He has made some men apostles, others prophets, others evangelists, and others pastors and teachers, but they all help in the building up of the Church, till they attain the full measure of development which belongs to the fulness of Christ. Thus they will no longer be like children, easily duped and swayed by every passing wind of doctrine, but will hold steadfast to the truth, but in love. In love the body will grow, each part contributing to the life of the whole, and all united with the Head, which is Christ (IV. 1–16).

They must no longer live like the pagan Gentiles, who are alienated from God and given to sensuality. If they have heard Christ's message and understood its meaning, they must abandon the old corrupt nature and put on the new nature, formed after God's pattern in righteousness and holiness of truth (IV. 17–24).

He presses upon them the importance of self-control, truthfulness, honesty, purity of speech, kindness, gentleness, and forgiveness. As Christians they should imitate Christ, who died for them (IV. 25–V. 2).

He warns them against sexual vice and indecency, and advises them to avoid the company of those who commit these sins, which incur God's anger. They must take care to live wisely, missing no opportunity of doing good. Instead of indulging in wine they should drink deeply of the Spirit, praising the Lord with words and music and rendering thanks to the Father in the name of Jesus Christ at all times and for all things (V. 3–21).

Wives must be subject to their husbands, as the Church is subject to Christ. Husbands must love their wives as Christ loves the Church, His spotless bride. Children must obey their parents as is naturally right and as God commanded. Parents must not irritate their children but train them in the Christian faith. Slaves must obey their masters with good will, as servants of Christ, doing the will of God, while masters must treat their slaves justly, remembering that God is no respecter of persons (V. 22–VI. 9).

Finally, after exhorting them to fight God's battle in His strength and clad in His armour, he asks for their prayers for the Church and for Himself, commends Tychicus to them, and closes with a benediction (VI. 10–24).

Authenticity

External Evidence. The authenticity of the Epistle is well attested by external evidence. There are possibly traces of it to be found in Clement of Rome, but more certainly in Ignatius, Polycarp, and Hermas. It is included in Marcion's Canon under the title of the "Epistle to the Laodiceans". It is mentioned in the Muratorian Fragment and quoted by Irenaeus. From the second century until the nineteenth century it was accepted as the genuine work of Paul.

Internal Evidence. Perhaps the strongest argument in support of the authenticity of the Epistle is the indisputable stamp of genius which is upon it. We know only of one man who was competent to produce such a work, and that man was Paul. If it is not the work of the Apostle, then it must have been written by an unknown person who was his equal in intellectual power and in spiritual insight.

In recent times, however, doubts have been raised against its genuineness by some scholars, who hold that it was written in the second century by a disciple of Paul who was familiar with his master's letters and deeply imbued with his spirit. It is suggested that the use of the phrases, "built upon the foundation of the apostles and prophets" (ii. 20) and "his holy apostles and prophets" (iii. 5), are signs of a later age, when the Apostles had come to be regarded with greater veneration than in Paul's lifetime. The man who, while claiming to be an Apostle, could write of the original Twelve as Paul did in "Galatians" (ii. 1–6), or who could speak of himself as "less than the least of all saints" (iii. 8) would not be likely to represent the Gentiles as a building built upon the apostles and prophets, or to include himself under the term of "holy apostles". But in 1 "Corinthians" xii. 28, he assigns the foremost place in the Church to apostles and prophets. Indeed the collocation of "apostles and prophets" is much more Pauline than was likely at a later age, when the Apostles were given a unique position, and the word "Apostles" is probably used in a wider sense than it would have been later, as applying to all missionaries, since there is no evidence that any Apostle in the restricted sense was responsible for the conversion of the people addressed. Nor is the epithet "holy" in connection with them impossible, since it is employed in its original meaning of "consecrated to the service of God". Used thus, it is not a claim to saintliness but a recognition of dedication.

The vocabulary and style of the Epistle are said to differ too widely from those of Paul's earlier Epistles for it to be the work of the Apostle. It is pointed out that the Epistle contains 38 words which are never used elsewhere in the New Testament and 44 which occur elsewhere but which are never used by Paul. The sentences are long and involved, subordinate clauses being so loosely strung together as to produce frequent ambiguities, and to render the interpretation of the text difficult. Thus in Chapter 1., verses 3–14 and verses 15–23 form two extraordinarily long sentences. But as regards the vocabulary, similar phenomena can be found elsewhere in Paul's Epistles. For example, "Galatians", which is not quite as long as "Ephesians", has 31 peculiar words. The proportion of peculiar words is likely to be largest in Epistles of moderate length; the short Epistles are largely taken up with personal matters, while in the longer the writer is dealing with so many themes that he is likely to repeat what he has said elsewhere. The style, too, has affinities with the Apostle's other writings. Long and involved sentences can be found both in "Romans" and "Colossians": the style of the latter, in fact, forms a connecting link between that of "Romans" and that of "Ephesians", showing that the identity of authorship is quite possible. Moreover, it is an unsound argument that a writer must necessarily have a uniform literary style throughout his career: it may alter considerably in the course of the years, or he may on occasion deliberately adapt it to suit his subject or be carried away by his subject. The difference in style in "Ephesians" can be accounted for on the supposition that the Apostle, who is no longer dealing with controversial matters or with problems of church life, but with mystical universal ideas, adapts his style to suit the sublime nature of his theme.

It is argued that "Ephesians" bears such a close resemblance to "Colossians", both in language and thought, that it must be the work of a later writer, who borrowed his ideas (which he expanded), and frequently his phraseology, from the latter work; that it is, in fact, an expansion of "Colossians" without the personal greetings and local references, produced for the benefit of the Church in general. The resemblances between the two, however, are probably due to the fact that Paul had "Colossians" before him when he wrote "Ephesians" and used some of its ideas and expressions. Again, if there are similarities there are also differences, which tell in favour of the authenticity of "Ephesians". A forger will endeavour to give a correct imitation of his original, whereas a writer, who borrows from his own works, will modify the language and thought, if he thinks it necessary. But above all a forger would surely never have left a blank in the address.

The doctrine of the Epistle is said to be un-Pauline. This is said of the emphasis laid upon the conception of the Catholic Church, uniting all members, including both Jews and Gentiles, in the spiritual fellowship of the body of Christ (II. 11–22). But the same idea is found in 1 "Corinthians" XII. 12–30 and in "Colossians" II. 19. Then it is said that the death of Christ is not so much the means whereby men are reconciled to God, as the means whereby both Jews and Gentiles are reconciled in one Church (II. 13–19). But surely, if his argument leads him to point out the latter result, it is not to minimize the former, especially as the union of Jew and Gentile is brought about only by the reconciliation of both to God. The Second Coming of Christ is not mentioned, but it is implied in Chapter I. 21–22: the point stressed is that the redemptive work of Christ is complete and that He has, and will have eternally, the pre-eminence in all things. What we therefore find in the Epistle is not a difference in doctrine but rather a change of emphasis.

Finally it is urged that the conception of a Catholic Church points to a later age. But Paul always strove for unity in the Church. At Antioch-in-Syria he opposed Peter to his face because he separated himself from the Gentiles. He strove to foster the spirit of fellowship and to develop a sense of unity among all the local Christian communities which he had founded. To this end he raised a relief fund for the poor saints at Jerusalem to which all the Gentile churches were called upon to contribute, and urged upon them their responsibility for the welfare of their Jewish brethren in Palestine (2 Cor. VIII.–IX.). There is no ground at all for assuming that the conception of a Catholic Church arose after Paul's death. It is quite in line both with his thought and action.

Summing up, we may say that the evidence advanced against

the authenticity of the Epistle is considerable but not conclusive, and there is therefore no reason for rejecting the
traditional view of the Pauline authorship.

Historical Value

The view of the Church, that is, the whole body of Christians,
as the body of Christ in a mystical sense, that is to say, in a way
which cannot be seen, because by the gift of the Holy Spirit to
its members they are meant to carry on the work of bringing
the whole world to a knowledge of the truth, and thus continuing
the work which Christ began when He was in a physical body
on earth, has been an immense stimulus. It inspires a sense of
unity by reason of this gift, which is shared by all, and by the
knowledge of a common task, and it is largely responsible for
the feeling which has been expressed in the form that no Church
is a living Church which is not a missionary Church. The Greek
word "working", when Paul constantly speaks of the Holy
Spirit "working" through members of the Church, is the word
from which we derive the noun "energy", and is used in the
exact sense in which it is used by modern physicists. A body is
inert till impelled by a force from without; similarly the human
beings who compose the Church are inert till they are moved
by the Holy Spirit, so the work they do is really done by God.

It is true that the teaching of Paul, and indeed of Christ, on
the subject of the Church, has been corrupted by the identification of the society with its officials, till finally the head of those
officials came to be exalted as God's representative on earth.
No doubt this Epistle is used in support of such views, but it
can hardly be considered to be their source, though when once
they came into existence, it may have helped to maintain them.
It is a natural tendency to identify a society with its leaders,
who are normally its most active members; but the chief cause
of their importance was historical in that organization proved
essential in holding together Christians scattered throughout
the Empire during the centuries of persecution. But, in so far
as officials are over-emphasized, the feeling of responsibility and
the sense of solidarity among the mass of members tend to
decline; the biological unity, which Paul so clearly works out

in his treatment of the relation of the members of the body, is replaced by a mechanical unity such as is seen in totalitarian states. If this Epistle at one time was used in support of the second view, it is now undoubtedly a cause of the revival of the first view, which we are witnessing in the association of missionary effort with a search for unity.

CHAPTER XX

THE EPISTLE TO THE PHILIPPIANS

Philippi

Philippi was a city in eastern Macedonia, situated on the Via Egnatia, the great highway which connected Rome with the East, and about eight miles from its port of Neapolis on the Aegean Sea. Built on an outlying spur of the Pangaean Range, it overlooked a great fertile plain, watered by many springs from which it derived its original name of Krenides ("wells" or "fountains"). In the neighbourhood were gold mines which had been worked in early times by the Thasians. Influenced by its strategic position and by its gold mines, Philip of Macedon, father of Alexander the Great, refounded it and made it one of his frontier strongholds. The gold mines were greatly developed and a large revenue was extracted from them; but their productive capacity must have been taxed to the utmost, for during the Roman occupation little is heard of them. In 168 B.C. Macedonia was subdued by the Romans, who divided the country into four districts, probably to prevent the inhabitants taking concerted action against their conquerors. Philippi was included in the most easterly division of which Amphipolis was the capital. It was in this neighbourhood that Octavian and Antony defeated Brutus and Cassius; and to commemorate the victory Philippi was raised to the rank of a Roman colony, becoming a miniature Rome in its system of officers and legal procedure. Its magistrates, strictly designated duumviri, took the title from Rome, of praetors; their attendants were styled lictors and carried the fasces or rods, while the Philippians called themselves Roman citizens (Acts XVI. 19–40). The official language of the city was Latin. After the battle of Actium in 31 B.C. Octavian refounded the city, settling there some of the defeated veterans of Antony. In "Acts", Philippi is called "A city of Macedonia, the first of the district" (XVI. 12);

this probably means that it considered itself to be the most important city in the district, though strictly speaking, Amphipolis had prior claim to the title. The population consisted of Greeks, Romans, and a small colony of Jews, who had no synagogue, but were accustomed to meet for prayer outside the gate on the banks of the Gangites, a tributary of the Strymon.

The Founding of the Church

In the course of his second missionary journey Paul, accompanied by Silas, Timothy, and Luke, crossed the Aegean Sea from Troas to Neapolis, and thence proceeded to Philippi, where they commenced their work of evangelization by addressing a group of women whom they found at a place of prayer outside the gate on the banks of a river. Their first convert was Lydia, a seller of purple garments from Thyatira, who after being baptized with all her household, invited them to accept the hospitality of her home. Their work was continued without molestation until Paul cured a slave girl possessed by "a spirit of divination", when her owners raised a tumult in which he and Silas were brought before the magistrates, and charged with disturbing the public peace and teaching customs which it was not lawful for Romans to receive or to observe. Without inquiry or trial the two missionaries were scourged and imprisoned. During the night there occurred an earthquake which led to the conversion and baptism of the jailor and all the members of his household. The following morning Paul protested against the injustice committed against them as Roman citizens, and the magistrates, fearing the consequences of their illegal acts, released them and begged them to leave the city. After bidding farewell to the brethren assembled in Lydia's house they departed for Thessalonica (Acts xvi.).

The length of Paul's stay at Philippi is not disclosed, but from the record of his visit preserved in "Acts", especially from the words, "and we were in this city tarrying certain days" (xvi. 12), we judge that it was of short duration; but it was nevertheless long enough to enable him to lay the foundations of what eventually became a strong church.

It would appear that the Apostle kept in touch with his beloved converts, and they with him, by means of messengers and letters, and that he revisited them on two occasions. At the close of his Ephesian ministry we read that he "departed for to go into Macedonia. And when he had gone through those parts, and had given them much exhortation, he came into Greece" (Acts xx. 2). Though it is not definitely stated, we may safely assume that the journey included a visit to Philippi. After a stay of three months in Greece, he set out on his last journey to Jerusalem, passing through Philippi where he kept the Passover before leaving to join his companions at Troas (Acts xx. 3–6).

Purpose

Paul's immediate purpose in writing the Epistle was to thank the Philippians for the gift of money which they had sent him during his imprisonment by the hand of Epaphroditus (II. 25, IV. 14–18). It was apparently their intention that their messenger should not only deliver the money, but also stay some considerable time with the Apostle to assist him in his work and to minister to his needs. Paul calls him "my brother and fellow-worker and fellow-soldier, and your messenger and minister to my need" (II. 25). He performed his duties with such zeal and devotion that his health failed and he became seriously ill; but by the mercy of God his life was spared lest the Apostle might have "sorrow upon sorrow" (II. 27). On his recovery he grew homesick, while the anxiety of his friends at Philippi, who had received tidings of his illness, made him long to see them. Paul sympathized with him and allowed him to return, at the same time seizing the opportunity to send a letter by him, thanking the Philippians for their welcome gift, commending Epaphroditus for his devotion to duty, and exhorting them to receive with him honour (II. 26–30).

The Apostle also wrote the Epistle to check the growing tendency to disunion in the church at Philippi of which he had doubtless been told by Epaphroditus. Though he had the warmest affection for the Philippian brethren, he evidently felt that all was not well with them (I. 9–11). He hinted that he himself was no partisan; he offered prayers and thanksgiving for all; they were all partakers with him of grace; his heart yearned for them all "in the tender mercies of Christ Jesus" (I. 3–8). He tactfully suggested that they were in danger of disunion, when they needed to present a united front to their enemies (I. 27–28); of party spirit and vain glory (II. 3), which were the reverse of the humility shown by Christ in His incarnation, life of obedience, and death (II. 5–11); and of murmurings and disputings which set a bad example to the world (II. 14–16). He mentioned two women, Euodia and Syntyche, who would seem to have been responsible for the dissensions (IV. 2), exhorted them to exercise the spirit of forbearance, to pursue noble ideals, and to follow his example. The divisions were apparently not dangerous, but the Apostle felt that admonition was needed.

It would appear that the Philippians took a pessimistic view of the prospects of Paul's imprisonment and of the future of Christianity. The Apostle therefore wrote to dispel their fears and to deepen their faith in the ultimate success of the Gospel. They had no need to fear lest his imprisonment or even his death might mean the end of Christianity. His imprisonment had actually led to the furtherance of the Gospel, for throughout the whole praetorian guard it had become known that he was in bonds because of his allegiance to Christ. Inspired by his example, "most of the brethren in the Lord" were preaching the Gospel with greater freedom and boldness (I. 12–14). If his life was prolonged, it would mean the further extension of the Gospel and the strengthening of their faith; but if death overtook him, he was confident that Christ would be magnified in his death as in his life. He felt sure that his trial would result in his acquittal and that he would be able to visit Philippi shortly (I. 19–26). He exhorted them not to be over-anxious but to rejoice in the Lord (III. 1).

Finally in his letter Paul took the opportunity to warn the Philippian Christians against the false teaching of the Judaizers and of the Libertines. The Judaizers were dogs, evil-workers and self-mutilators (III. 2), while the Libertines were "enemies of the cross of Christ: whose end is perdition, whose god is the belly, and whose glory is in their shame, who mind earthly things" (III. 18–19).

Contents

After the opening salutation Paul thanks God for their fellowship in maintaining the cause of the Gospel, expresses his confidence that God will complete the good work which He has begun in them, and prays that they may abound in all knowledge and insight, so that they may lead blameless lives and bring forth the fruits of righteousness (I. 1–11).

He assures them that his imprisonment has not hindered but promoted the spread of the Gospel (I. 12–18).

His earnest desire is that by their prayers and by the help of the Spirit of Jesus Christ he may never be ashamed, but that now as ever he may honour Christ by his own fearless courage, whether it be by his life or by his death. He would rather die and be with Christ, but it is needful for them that he should live on. He is confident that he will remain to help them in their spiritual life and to cause them to rejoice over his return to them (I. 19–26).

He urges them to live worthily of Christ and to be steadfast and courageous under persecution. It is their privilege, not only to believe in Christ, but to suffer for His sake, even as he himself suffered at Philippi, and is suffering in prison (I. 27–30).

He pleads with them to make his happiness complete by living in harmony with one another, never acting for private ends or from vanity, but with due consideration for others (II. 1–4).

They should take as their pattern Christ who, though divine by nature, did not set store upon equality with God, but emptied Himself by taking the form, that is, the essential nature, of a servant. Appearing in human form He stooped in His obedience even to die upon the cross. Therefore God raised Him to the highest place and set His name above all others, so that all in heaven and earth should worship Him and confess that Jesus Christ is Lord (II. 5–11).

He exhorts them to work all the more strenuously at their

salvation, so that he may be proud of them at the Last Day because his work has not been in vain (II. 12–18).

He tells them that he hopes to send Timothy to them as soon as he hears the result of his own trial; he is confident that he will be acquitted and that he will soon be able to visit them. He explains the reasons for the return of Epaphroditus, commends his faithfulness and devotion, and asks them to receive him with honour (II. 19–30).

He warns them against Judaizers, who are contemptible curs, wicked workmen, and self-mutilators. Christians are the true "circumcision", who worship by the Spirit of God, take pride in Christ, and rely on no external privileges. He can justly claim pride of race and of religion, and an unblemished moral record, but for the sake of gaining Christ he has parted with them all. He does not claim that he has attained perfection, but he is pressing on, like a runner with his eyes on the goal, to obtain God's prize (III. 1–16).

He urges them to follow his example and warns them against Libertines, who are enemies of the cross and wholly sensual. They are a colony of heaven waiting for the coming of Christ, who will transform the body into the likeness of His own glorified body (III. 17–21).

He pleads with Euodia and Syntyche to be reconciled to each other, and exhorts his readers to rejoice in the Lord, to show forbearance, to take all their troubles to God, joining thanksgiving to their prayers, and to fill their minds with all that is good, beautiful, and true. By so doing God will be with them and His peace will protect their hearts and minds (IV. 1–9).

He gratefully acknowledges their gifts which are a renewed sign of their affection. He realizes that it was lack of opportunity that caused delay. But he is not complaining, for he has learnt the lesson of contentment and can meet wealth and poverty in the sustaining power of Christ. He is amply supplied with what they have sent. God accepts their sacrifice and will of His heavenly wealth supply all their needs (IV. 10–19).

He invokes a blessing upon them, sends salutations from all the brethren, and closes with a farewell benediction (IV. 20–23).

Authenticity

External Evidence. The external evidence for the authenticity of the Epistle is good. Traces of the Epistle are probably to be found in Clement of Rome and Ignatius, but there is no doubt that Polycarp was acquainted with it. It is included in Marcion's Canon as well as in the Old Latin and Peshitta-Syriac Versions. It is mentioned in the Muratorian Fragment, and is quoted directly and assigned to Paul by Irenaeus, Clement of Alexandria, and Tertullian. Until the nineteenth century the genuineness of the Epistle was never questioned.

Internal Evidence. In modern times the German critic Baur and his followers cast doubts upon the genuineness of the Epistle on the grounds: (1) that the reference to bishops and deacons pointed to a post-Pauline stage of ecclesiastical organization, (2) that it showed traces of second-century Gnosticism, (3) that its doctrines differed from those of the earlier Epistles, especially "Galatians", 1 and 2 "Corinthians", and "Romans", and (4) that it was written in the second century to reconcile the Pauline and Petrine parties in the Church. These objections can no longer be maintained and have been abandoned by all but a few extremists. It is now generally agreed that the internal evidence places the genuineness of the Epistle beyond the reach of doubt. The vocabulary and style are typically Pauline, while its doctrines, though doubtless more developed than those of the earlier Epistles, are in harmony with them and do not go beyond what they imply. The vocabulary, style, and doctrine connect the Epistle with the universally accepted group of "Galatians", 1 and 2 "Corinthians", and "Romans". The character revealed in the Epistle is indisputably that of Paul: here we find the Pauline traits of courage, cheerfulness, courtesy, tenderness, independence, affection, and devotion to Christ. It is inconceivable that any forger could have given such a faithful representation of the Apostle's character, or that he could have succeeded in his attempt to palm off a spurious letter on the church at Philippi after Paul's death.

Integrity

It is suggested by some critics that the Epistle is not a unity but a combination of two original documents, which were written by Paul at different times and fused together after his death when the first collection of his letters was made. In support of this view it is maintained that at the beginning of Chapter III. there occurs a sudden change in subject and tone: the Apostle becomes once more the fierce controversialist and denounces the Judaizers and Libertines. The whole passage containing these denunciations is obviously out of place in its context. The word "finally" of Chapter III. 1 seems to point to the conclusion of a letter. Moreover, it is probable that Paul wrote more than one letter to the Philippian Christians, for Polycarp in his letter to them refers to Paul who "wrote to you letters in the which if ye look diligently, ye shall be able to build yourselves up unto the faith given to you". But in refutation of this theory it may be urged that Paul was writing, not a theological treatise with calm deliberation, but an informal letter, probably amid many distractions, and that under such circumstances we should not be surprised to find an abrupt change in subject and in tone. We know, too, from a study of Paul's character that he was quite capable of passing swiftly from one mood to another. The Greek words translated "finally" do not mean "in conclusion", but "for the rest" or "to sum up"; but even if "finally" is retained, it does not necessarily imply the conclusion of an informal letter such as this. As for Polycarp's reference to Paul's letters, of which so much has been made, there is the possibility either that some previous letter or letters did not survive, or that Polycarp was referring to 1 and 2 "Thessalonians", which were written to a neighbouring church and of which copies would naturally be sent to Philippi. There is no manuscript evidence for a break at Chapter III. 1, while those who maintain that the passage is a fragment of another letter are not agreed as to where it ends, whether at III. 16, III. 19, IV. 1, or IV. 3. The evidence for an interpolation is unconvincing, and we therefore accept the view, held by the majority of critics, that the Epistle is a unity.

Historical Value

Doctrine. "Philippians" is historically important because it embodies what are probably Paul's final views on the Person of Christ and on the Second Advent, for it is regarded by many scholars as the last of his extant Epistles.

The Apostle makes clear his belief both in the divine nature and the essential humanity of Christ. Previous to His life on earth He was "in the form of God", that is, He possessed the essential characteristics of deity; but in His pre-incarnate state He did not set store upon equality with God: instead He "emptied himself" of His personality, "taking the form of a servant", and appearing in human form. In obedience to the will of God He humbled Himself to die, reaching the lowest depths of His humiliation in His death on the cross. Wherefore God exalted Him to the highest place, and gave Him the greatest name—that of Lord—in order that He might receive the homage of the whole universe (II. 5–11).

The Epistle shows that Paul retained his belief in the Second Advent till the end of his life, but that he did not look forward to it with the same eager expectation as when he wrote some of his earlier Epistles, notably 1 and 2 "Thessalonians". Death would mean not an insentient "sleep" until the Resurrection, but immediate reunion with Christ (I. 23). It was more important, however, that he should live than that he should enjoy the abiding fellowship of Christ beyond the grave, for longer life would mean greater opportunities for service (I. 25). The Philippians were a colony of heaven waiting for a "Saviour, the Lord Jesus Christ", who would transform the body of humiliation into the likeness of His glorified body (III. 20–21). So they could "rejoice in the Lord alway", showing a forbearing spirit, for "the Lord is at hand" (IV. 4–5). It is evident that towards the close of his life he still looked forward to the time when Christ should appear in triumph to consummate His work, but he did not claim to know the date, nor did he lay stress upon it.

The Condition of the Church at Philippi. The Epistle sheds some light on the history of the Philippian church during the first ten years or so of its history. Greetings are sent "to all the saints in Christ Jesus which are at Philippi, with the bishops and deacons" (I. I), from which we infer that the membership of the church was sufficiently large to require some kind of organization. The Philippian Christians were a generous people and, mindful of the great debt which they owed to Paul, they showed their sympathy and gratitude in a practical fashion. To Thessalonica and to Corinth their messengers followed him with gifts of money (Phil. IV. 16, 2 Cor. XI. 9), and though for several years afterwards they sent him no more financial aid, it was not due to their indifference to his needs, but to lack of opportunity. During his imprisonment their thought for him blossomed forth again and they sent him financial aid by the hand of Epaphroditus, which was gratefully received and acknowledged. They no doubt also contributed to the collection for the relief of the poor Christians at Jerusalem (2 Cor. VIII. 1–2). Paul showed his confidence in them by accepting their gifts, though it was his rule not to accept maintenance from any church, preferring to support himself at his own trade of tent-making.

The Philippians were evidently interested in the work of evangelization, for Paul was grateful, not only for their liberality towards him, but also for their fellowship with him in the furtherance of the Gospel "from the first day until now" (I. 5). At the time when he wrote "Philippians" they were exposed to persecution, for he exhorted them to show no fear of their enemies, but to "stand fast in one spirit, with one soul, striving for the faith of the Gospel", drawing inspiration from the thought that they were suffering in the behalf of Christ (I. 27–30). There is no indication that any section of the church denied his Gospel, or rejected his authority, or sought to undermine his influence by the depreciation of his character. There were dissensions among its members, but they were trivial compared with those which distracted the church at Corinth. Paul denounced the Judaizers and Antinomians, but there is no sign that their teaching had made any considerable impression upon the Philippian Christians. The Apostle would not have commended them in such glowing terms had he learnt that many of them had come to believe that salvation was to be obtained by obedience to the Law or that they were under no obligation to keep the moral law since they were saved by faith. Of all the churches founded by Paul, that of Philippi was the one which gave him the greatest joy and for which he had the deepest affection. Its members were his "brethren beloved and longed for", and his "joy and crown" (**IV.** 1).

PART V

THE PASTORAL EPISTLES

CHAPTER XXI

THE PASTORAL EPISTLES:
2 TIMOTHY, 1 TIMOTHY AND TITUS

Title

The title, "Pastoral Epistles", was given to 1 and 2 "Timothy" and "Titus" in the eighteenth century, because in them Paul is supposed to give two of his assistant missionaries, Timothy and Titus, private instructions in their duties as pastors of the churches of which they had been given temporary charge during his absence. The title, however, is not sufficiently comprehensive, for the Epistles are concerned with other matters as well, but it has been retained largely on the score of its convenience, since it designates a distinct group of Epistles which are closely related in contents, style, and vocabulary, and which are quite different in these respects from the unquestioned letters of Paul.

Authenticity

External Evidence. The external evidence for the authenticity of the Pastorals is good. They were well known to Polycarp and probably to Ignatius. They appear in the Muratorian Fragment and are quoted as the work of Paul by Irenaeus, Clement of Alexandria, and Tertullian. On the other hand, Marcion did not admit them to his Canon, on the ground that they were private correspondence, though this was probably a mere pretext, his real reason for rejecting them being either that he doubted their authenticity or that he disliked their contents. Jerome states that they were rejected by Basilides and "all the heretics", though Tatian made an exception in favour of "Titus". From the time of Irenaeus until the early years of the nineteenth century the genuineness of the Pastorals was never questioned.

Internal Evidence. The genuineness of the Pastorals has been denied on internal grounds more frequently than that of any of the other Epistles attributed to Paul.

Baur's attempt to date these Epistles in the second century may be dismissed at once; it was based on a belief that Gnostic views were unknown in the first century which we know to be incorrect. The view that the form of Church government envisaged in these Epistles represents a stage of development beyond that which is known to have existed in Paul's lifetime cannot be maintained, for it is substantially the same, with no differentiation between the offices of bishop and presbyter.

There are, however, several other serious considerations which make it impossible for many scholars to accept the Pauline authorship of the Pastorals in their entirety, though it is believed that certain fragments of genuine Pauline Epistles have been included. Of these considerations the following may be mentioned:

(1) It is difficult to fix any one of these Epistles at any one date in Paul's career, though particular passages fit in well with events in his life which we know from "Acts" to have occurred at different dates.

It may therefore be well to enumerate these passages which are claimed to be genuine, and to enumerate the circumstances to which they seem to refer.

(a) "Titus" III. 12–15, asking Titus to come to him to Nicopolis, after he had sent Artemas or Tychicus to him, and to help Zenas and Apollos on their way. It is suggested that the occasion for this letter was when Paul had sent Titus from Ephesus to Corinth bearing the letter of rebuke now contained in 2 Cor. x.–xiii. He had expected to meet him at Troas (2 Cor. ii. 12–13), but met him later in Macedonia (2 Cor. vii. 6).

(b) 2 "Timothy" IV. 13–15, 20, 21a, asking Timothy to bring a cloak which he had left at Troas and some documents, informing him of the animosity of Alexander the coppersmith, and telling him that Erastus had stayed on at Corinth and that Trophimus was ill at Miletus. He urges Timothy to come to him before winter. The mention of Alexander the coppersmith dates this letter somewhat after the riot in Ephesus, and therefore probably about the same time as the last.

(c) 2 "Timothy" iv. 16–18a (possibly 18b), recording a successful defence in spite of a general desertion. This is supposed to be written from Caesarea, where he had been taken by Claudius Lysias (Acts xxiii. 33).

(d) 2 "Timothy" iv. 9–12, 22b, asking Timothy to come soon, as he only had Luke with him, since Demas had deserted him and Crescens, Titus, and Tychicus had gone on various missions. He asks him to bring Mark with him. The visit of Tychicus to Ephesus, here mentioned as having taken place, was contemplated in "Ephesians" vi. 21, and Timothy had not yet left him when he wrote "Philippians" (ii. 19), so that the date of this fragment is probably a little after that of the Captivity Epistles.

(e) 2 "Timothy" i. 16–18, iii. 10–11, iv. 1, 2a, 5b, 6–8, 18b, 19, 21b, 22a. This letter seems to be written as a farewell to Timothy, shortly before the Apostle's martyrdom.

If the four passages from 2 "Timothy" be related to the events which we know and which they naturally fit, it becomes obvious that they cannot form part of a single letter written at one date. The references to events in 1 "Timothy" and "Titus" are fewer. In 1 "Timothy" Paul has gone to Macedonia, and left Timothy in Ephesus (1 Tim. i. 3), whither Paul hopes to return (1 Tim. iv. 13); this does not fit the occasion in "Acts" where Paul sent Timothy ahead of him to Macedonia (Acts xix. 22) and himself followed afterwards (Acts xx. 1), and no other occasion is known to us which it would fit. As regards Titus, no visit of Paul to Crete is mentioned in "Acts" or the Epistles.

It should, however, be noted that some of these difficulties disappear if we assume that Paul was released at the end of his two years' imprisonment and was subsequently rearrested and put to death. There is no direct evidence for such a hypothesis, but it is difficult to see how there could be, since the release and rearrest would be later than the close of "Acts" and than all Paul's Epistles if we exclude the Pastorals. But some sort of a case can be made out for it indirectly. Paul was confidently looking forward to an acquittal during his two years' imprisonment in Rome (Philem. 22; Phil. II. 23–24), and his expectations were probably based on a knowledge of the situation. Further, something must have happened at the end of the two years in A.D. 61, and Luke's conclusion of "Acts" would be pointless if it were a condemnation, whereas the persecution of A.D. 64 is the date which, in lack of evidence to the contrary, we should have thought to be most likely for his martyrdom. Clement of Rome asserts that Paul taught the whole world righteousness and reached the farthest bounds of the West, which may mean Spain, but some interpret it as Rome. His journey to Spain is also mentioned in the Muratorian Fragment and also in certain Apocryphal Acts of Peter and Paul, while Eusebius gives it as the current report that the Apostle was released, resumed his missionary activity, and was again arrested and suffered martyrdom in the Neronian persecution. The external evidence is of no great value, since it may be based on inferences from the Pastorals and on Paul's intention to visit Spain as mentioned in "Romans" xv. 28.

(2) The style and vocabulary of the Pastorals are very similar to one another but quite different from those of the unquestioned Pauline Epistles. The style is correct and smooth, but for the most part dull and monotonous; the keen logic, force, warmth, and colour, which we associate with Paul's writings, have disappeared. The difference in the vocabulary is even more remarkable. There are, it is true, many Pauline words and phrases but they are not sufficiently numerous to indicate identity of authorship: they might have been picked up by any keen student of the Apostle's letters. Dr. Harrison shows that in the ten Epistles attributed to Paul, 2,177 words are employed. The vocabulary of the Pastorals, omitting proper names, consists of 848 different words, and of these no less than 306 are found in these three Epistles alone. Not one of them is found in any of the ten Epistles. The vocabulary on the whole stands nearer to that of the Christian writings of the second century than to that of the Pauline Epistles.

Various attempts have been made to account for the altered style and vocabulary but none of them is satisfactory. It has been suggested that a writer's style sometimes changes in the course of time and that Paul is no exception to the rule. This is doubtless true, but such a change could not have taken place in the short period of about three years which separated the composition of the Pastorals from that of "Philippians". It has been urged that the change is due to the fact that the Apostle was dealing with a different subject, which demanded the employment of new technical terms. But the change extends, not only to nouns and verbs, but also to particles and constructions. Moreover, some of Paul's favourite phrases, such as "the God and Father of our Lord Jesus Christ", do not appear at all, while new phrases appear, such as "faithful is the saying", which occurs eleven times in the Pastorals and not once in the unquestioned Pauline Epistles. Further, it has been alleged that Paul employed an amanuensis who expressed the Apostle's ideas in his own way. But we cannot imagine that a man of Paul's intellectual power and force of character would be satisfied with such a method of procedure.

(3) Timothy is addressed in the Pastorals as if he were an immature young man and even a recent convert, whereas he must have been from thirty-five to forty years of age, and had been, not only one of Paul's early converts, but also one of his most trusted friends and companions throughout the greater part of his missionary career. The Apostle calls him "my true child in faith" (1 Tim. I. 2), "my beloved child (2 Tim. I. 2), and "my child" (2 Tim. II. 1), warns him not to allow anyone to despise his youth (1 Tim. IV. 12), and exhorts him to flee youthful lusts and to follow after righteousness, faith, love, and peace (2 Tim. II. 22). Though he knows that Timothy is intimately acquainted with his life as a Christian, he still thinks it necessary to defend his apostolic authority and his character, and to assert that he is speaking the truth, as if he were addressing enemies such as he had to deal with in Galatia and at Corinth.

(4) There is a clear difference of outlook. The ten Pauline Epistles are letters of a missionary to converts while the

Pastorals are concerned with the work of a pastor in a well-established church. We thus miss in the Pastorals the old alternation of "Kerygma" (proclamation) and "Didache" (teaching); Didache is completely dominant. The verb "to believe" and the corresponding noun "faith" are much rarer, as Paul is frequently thinking of the act of accepting Christianity at conversion, while a new word "godliness", expressing the attitude of an old believer towards God, appears eleven times in the Pastorals but never in the ten Pauline Epistles. When "faith" is used in the Pastorals it usually means the body of Christian belief, as in 1 Cor. xvi. 13, Rom. i. 5, Col. i. 23, and 2 Thess. ii. 13, or some particular doctrine, as the Resurrection in Col. ii. 12; it is only once opposed to "the works of the law", as the writer is not arguing against Jews or the original type of Judaizer. The type of error which is combated in the Pastorals is rather that mixture of Judaism, theosophy, and either asceticism on the one hand or Antinomianism on the other which we find in the Captivity Epistles, and it is met by an appeal to primitive Christianity rather than argument on each point. This primitive Christianity is variously called "the faith" (1 Tim. i. 19; 2 Tim. iii. 8; Tit. i. 13; cf. 1 Cor. xvi. 13); "the truth" (1 Tim. iii. 15; 2 Tim. ii. 18; Tit. i. 14; cf. Gal. ii. 5, 14, v. 7; 2 Cor. iv. 2; Eph. iv. 24; 2 Thess. ii. 10); "knowledge of the truth" (1 Tim. ii. 4; 2 Tim. ii. 25; Tit. i. 1); "the teaching of God our Saviour" (Tit. ii. 10); "the commandment" (1 Tim. vi. 14, but this means Christian morals rather than beliefs), "the deposit" (1 Tim. vi. 20; 2 Tim. i. 12); and "healthy teaching" (1 Tim. i. 10; 2 Tim. iv. 3; Tit. i. 9). The denunciation of the semi-Gnostic teachers is stronger than Paul usually uses. Finally, we feel that the Epistles lack the flashes of genius which come out at intervals in all Paul's writings.

The overwhelming character of the linguistic evidence, supported as it is by the other arguments, makes it practically certain that the Epistles as wholes are not by Paul, but by a writer with turns of language which appear through all three works, and an outlook and purpose which are equally common to them.

But there is one point to notice in comparing the "first" and "second" Epistles to Timothy. Both contain a number of passages which purport to be personal statements by Paul or personal appeals to Timothy. In the "second" Epistle there are six, four of which Harrison argues on linguistic grounds to be genuinely Pauline fragments, and we are inclined to add a fifth, namely 2 Tim. i. 3–6, as it contains no words characteristic of the author of the Pastorals and several Pauline words, while the remaining passage, 2 Tim. ii. 17–18, does indeed contain the word "logos" in the sense of "doctrine" or "teaching", which is a favourite with the author of the Pastorals, but is not far from the Pauline usage. On the other hand, there are five such passages in the "first" Epistle, four of which appear to be non-Pauline: (1) 1 Tim. i. 3, with the verb "to teach otherwise" (elsewhere only in 1 Tim. vi. 3), (2) 1 Tim. i. 12–18, containing the favourite phrase of the Pastorals "faithful is the word" and several other non-Pauline words or phrases, (3) 1 Tim. iv. 12–14, which, short as it is, contains four words or phrases suggesting a non-Pauline origin, and (4) 1 Tim. vi. 20–21, which in two verses contains six. The remaining passage is one verse (1 Tim. v. 23), in which Paul urges Timothy to take a little wine for the sake of his digestion. This verse contains no Pauline word and no word used in the Pastorals, but is just composed of ordinary Greek words used in the Hellenistic period; and, as the verse seems to have no point where it is, it may well be a genuine fragment, as, so far as we can see, the writer has no other reason for introducing it. It is reasonably suggested that the author of the Pastorals composed the "second" Epistle first and wrote up a number of genuine Pauline fragments into a continuous letter, of which they form a quarter, the rest being largely reminiscent of Pauline passages: then, pleased with the success of this, he went further and composed the "first" Epistle, in which he stated the views on the present situation which he thought Paul, had he been alive, would have expressed, and invented personal allusions to match the genuine ones included in the "second" Epistle. (The "second" Epistle was placed last by those who made the New Testament Canon because of the passage of farewell to Timothy before his martyrdom.) Such a procedure gives a shock to us who have inherited a far different standard of literary ethics, but it was less strange in an age when it was a literary convention to state the opinions and policy of a public man in the form of made-up speeches. In attributing his letters to Paul he has no wish to misrepresent him; we may almost go so far as to say that Paul would have approved all he says; but a modern writer would have frankly labelled his articles "Paul and the Present Crisis" and stated, with quotations from Paul's genuine letters, what attitude he thought Paul would have taken. Unfortunately no ancient writer ever adopted this method.

Contents

2 Timothy. (Excluding the fragments recognized as Pauline. See pp. 322–3.) Timothy is reminded of his early Christian training, and is exhorted to guard the faith zealously and to hand it on to trusted men, competent to instruct others. He must, like a good soldier, accept his share of suffering, allowing nothing to interfere with the discharge of his duties, and like an athlete obey the rules. Paul himself is in prison for the faith but he can still write, and so by his sufferings others are able to obtain salvation. Those who endure shall reign with Christ (i. 1–15, ii. 1–13).

He must avoid heresies which lead to irreligion. Two persons, named Hymenaeus and Philetus, are saying that "the Resurrection is past already", and are undermining people's faith. If a man keeps clear of false teachers he will be consecrated and equipped for every good work (ii. 14–21).

Timothy must shun the lusts of youth and instruct his opponents with gentleness, in the hope that God will eventually lead them to knowledge of the truth (ii. 22–26).

A time is coming when men will practise manifold vices, becoming lovers of evil and of pleasure instead of lovers of God. All who live godly lives will be persecuted, but he must be faithful to the truths he has learnt from Paul and the inspired Scriptures, which are able to make him "wise unto salvation through faith which is in Christ Jesus", and which are useful for teaching, reproof, correction, and moral discipline. Soon men will refuse to listen to the truth, but whatever happens he must discharge faithfully the duties of his office (III. 1–9, 12–17, IV. 2b–5a).

I Timothy. Timothy is exhorted to oppose certain false teachers, two of whom, Hymenaeus and Alexander, Paul had excommunicated (for false doctrine, cf. Col. II. 8; Eph. II. 1–2, III. 8–11, VI. 12; for the claim to be philosophic cf. I Cor. III. 18–20; and for excommunication cf. I Cor. v. 3–5). These false teachers desire to be teachers of the Law, but they do not understand the subjects on which they dogmatize. The Law is good provided it is used in a lawful way. A law is not enacted for honest people but for the wicked, who are opposed to the wholesome teaching of the Gospel to which Paul, once a blasphemer and persecutor, has been converted (I. 1–20).

Prayer is to be offered for all men, especially for those in authority (cf. Rom. XIII. 1–7; I Pet. II. 13–17). (II. 1–8.)

Women must show their piety by modest dress and by faithful service. They must not teach in public or dictate to men (cf. I Cor. XIV. 34–35). (II. 9–15.)

A bishop must be the husband of one wife, temperate, soberminded, well-behaved, and hospitable, and must possess the ability to teach and to control others. Similarly deacons must be of serious demeanour and of a deep, sincere, religious faith, and must undergo probation before their appointment to office. Women, in the same way, must be serious-minded, temperate, and trustworthy (III. 1–13).

The right management of the Church is important, for it is the pillar and bulwark of the Truth (III. 14–16).

There are false teachers who forbid marriage and insist upon abstinence from certain foods (cf. Col. II. 16–III. 9). Anything that God has created is good, and nothing is to be rejected provided it is eaten with thanksgiving. It is hallowed by the word of God and by prayer. If Timothy impresses these truths on the brethren, he will be a good minister of Christ Jesus (IV. 1–6).

He must practise godliness, not asceticism. Godliness will be attained only as men set their hopes on God, who is the Saviour of all men. He must become an example in life and doctrine of what a Christian minister should be (IV. 7–16).

He must not rebuke members of the church with severity. Aged widows of suitable character must be supported by the church, but in the first instance their children and relatives, if any, must assist them. Young widows would do well to marry, otherwise they are liable to become gossips and busybodies (v. 1–16).

Elders, who are efficient, must be amply rewarded (cf. 1 Cor. ix. 6–11), especially those who have undertaken the "task of preaching and teaching". An elder must not be ordained with undue haste, and no charge must be admitted against him unless it is well attested (v. 17–25).

Slaves must show respect to their masters (cf. Eph. vi. 5–8; Col. iii. 22–25), while those who have Christian masters must not take liberties with them because they are brothers (vi. 1–12).

In conclusion Paul denounces false teachers, issues a warning against the love of money, stresses the responsibility to God in respect of riches, exhorts Timothy to be faithful to his trust, and to keep intact the securities of the faith (vi. 13–21).

Titus. (Excluding the fragment recognized as Pauline. See p. 322.) Paul has left Titus in Crete to organize the Church. An elder (or bishop), as God's steward, must be a man of blameless character, with the ability to give instruction in sound doctrine and to refute objections raised by opponents (i. 1–9).

The many false and insubordinate teachers, particularly those of Jewish origin, must be sharply rebuked, so that they may be sound in the faith instead of studying Jewish fables and the commandments of men (i. 10–18).

Titus must instruct people in what is due to sound doctrine. Aged men must be temperate, grave, sober-minded, and sound in their faith. Aged women must be reverent in demeanour, not slanderers, or slaves to wine; they must play their part in training young married women to be affectionate to their husbands and children, sober-minded, chaste, domesticated, and submissive to their husbands. Slaves must be obedient to their masters and must render honest and faithful service (cf. Col. iii. 18–iv. 6; Eph. vi. 1–8). (ii. 1–10.)

Christian conduct is determined by the fact that the grace

of God is for all men, and is a challenge to renounce ungodliness and worldly desires and to live sober, upright, and pious lives, awaiting the Appearance of Jesus Christ (ii. 11–15).

All Christians must submit to rulers and authorities, and must be ready to undertake any good work. They must be conciliatory, and must display perfect gentleness to all men, remembering their own former sinfulness and their salvation through the grace of God (iii. 1–8).

Foolish controversies with false teachers must be avoided. If, after a second admonition, the factious man proves obdurate, he must be shunned (iii. 9–11).

Purpose

The writer's aims are clear from the preceding summaries. Apart from the wish to maintain the Christian standard of conduct among converts who at times were tempted to revert to their old pagan life, two specific aims are obvious; first, to insist on a high standard for the Christian ministry; and second, to combat certain false doctrines. In both cases a modern parallel will be helpful in trying to appreciate the situation.

In the mission field at the present day a transition is taking place in most of the churches which were founded in the nineteenth century, whereby control is passing out of the hands of the European or American missionaries into those of the local Christians. At this stage the right selection of local ministers is found, now as then, to be all-important, especially in meeting the danger of a revival of old pagan practices in a Christian disguise. The qualities required of a presbyter are dealt with in 1 "Timothy" iii. 2–4, of a deacon in iii. 8–9, of a deaconess in iii. 11, and of widows in v. 9. No presbyter should be appointed without careful inquiry into his character (v. 22), but when once he has been appointed, no charge should be admitted against him unless it is attested by two or three witnesses (v. 19). The appeals to Timothy and Titus to set a good example are intended to emphasize the same points.

The type of false doctrine which the author combats reminds us of the Theosophy, Spiritualism, and Christian Science of the present day. This class of belief appears to appeal to many persons who wish to be considered "intellectuals" but have received little real intellectual training. It has a superficial appearance of being more philosophical than historic Christianity; it has besides the charm of novelty and appeals to curiosity and the love of the abnormal. The motives seem to have been the same, for even the money-making motive (Tit. I. 11) is present in many "mediums" of to-day; but in those days it was Judaism which was used to supply some of the authority required for such beliefs, whereas to-day it is most frequently Buddhism ("Jewish fables", Tit. I. 14; "foolish questionings, and genealogies, and strifes, and fightings about the law", Tit. III. 9; cf. I Tim. IV. 1–4). The ascetic element is found in the forbidding of marriage and in ordering abstinence from certain foods (I Tim. IV. 1–4). The genealogies, which are several times mentioned, are probably part of the beliefs about angels which were in reality an incursion of pagan polytheism into Judaism.

Date of Composition

The date of the Pastorals presents a difficult problem. There is a tendency to place it in the second century. The original reason for so dating the books, that the false teaching which is attacked in them did not arise before that century, has disappeared. It is now formally based on linguistic grounds; the vocabulary of the Pastorals is shown somewhat to resemble the earlier post-New Testament Christian writings. But it will be found that some of the non-Pauline words appear in the Gospels, some in "Hebrews", and some in I "Peter" which, whoever were their authors, are the work of the first generation of Christians, as well as in the Apocalypse and the Johannine writings, and none can be satisfactorily proved not to have arisen till the second century. Because Paul's Epistles are earlier than all, or practically all, the New Testament writings, it would be wrong to assume that the vocabulary of a period can be deduced from any one author; a number of sound classical words appear elsewhere in the canonical writings which do not happen to appear in Paul.

Another factor which has influenced the belief in a second-century origin, is the idea which once prevailed that the Pastorals imply the beginnings of government by single bishops forming an order distinct from presbyters. But the Epistles themselves distinctly present the form of church government as that of presbyters and deacons, assisted by deaconesses and widows. Though prophecy is mentioned in 1 "Timothy" 1. 18 and iv. 14, prophets are not treated as an order of officials; and the organization has passed from the loose form found in the earliest days at Antioch-in-Syria to that set up by Paul in the churches which he founded, which was suggested by that of the Jewish synagogue. It is true that this does not rule out altogether a second-century date, as the writer, in his desire to ascribe a Pauline origin to his work, might have deliberately made Paul speak in terms of his own day and not of the author's.

The question is complicated by our lack of definite knowledge of the date when the transition took place in different localities, of the length of time it took to effect it, and of the intermediate stages. Ignatius, who was martyred early in the second century, assumes the existence of a separate office of bishop as the one and only form of church government with such assurance that it may be assumed that he had never known any other, that is to say in Syria and the province of Asia. But it is only emerging in Rome when the "Epistle of Clement" was written, about the turn of the first and second centuries, though a few years later Ignatius assumes the rule of a bishop in Rome also.

The power of control over presbyters, which the Epistles assume Paul to have conferred on Timothy and Titus, are in fact those of a bishop, though Timothy and Titus are not called bishops and presbyters are still called bishops. But even this fact may be interpreted in either of two ways; it may mean that the writer was in fact acquainted with the existence of bishops but is concealing his knowledge to make the Epistles sound Pauline; or it may mean that the process of change is taking place, but that the thing preceded the name. Indeed, it is likely that among the causes which produced the change was this very need of selecting presbyters with care. Presumably, when there were no longer Apostles living, they were at first chosen by co-optation, and it is clear from these Epistles that the choice was not always satisfactory. It may be noted that two accounts are given of Timothy's ordination; in 1 "Timothy" IV. 14, the writer speaks of the gift "which was given thee by prophecy, with the laying on of the hands of the presbytery", while in 2 "Timothy" 1. 6 he speaks of "the gift of God, which is in thee through the laying on of my hands"; the first suggests the old arrangement, the second the episcopal arrangement.

The only other set of considerations concerning the date arises from the answer to the question, When and where did the author of the Pastorals come into possession of the genuine fragments of the Pauline Epistles, if we admit that they are genuine? It is hardly likely that Timothy and Titus kept such small fragments, whereas it is quite probable that Paul did, for the problem of Paul's letters to the Corinthians is soluble only by assuming that Paul kept drafts of his letters, and the absence of the name of any church to which "Ephesians" was sent points in the same direction. If so, the Pastorals were probably written in Rome, and we cannot allow too long an interval after Paul's death during which his documents remained intact. On the other hand, alleged letters to Timothy and Titus could not have been published during their lifetime. Taking both sets of considerations into account, a date twenty years after Paul's death would appear to be more reasonable than sixty years or than four or five years; it would correspond satisfactorily with the transition period to episcopacy and would not conflict with the linguistic evidence.

Historical Value

In spite of the assignment of letters to Paul which were not really his, the three Epistles have distinct historical value as evidence of the state of Christianity immediately after apostolic times, and have a distinct interest to the modern reader owing to their concern with two problems of the present day, the transfer of control of new churches from missionaries to local leaders, and the growth of syncretistic theosophical religions within the Christian communities.

The unit of organization was the local community, which was predominantly Gentile but which included a number of Jews who were a disturbing element, since many of the false teachers, of whom so much is heard in the Pastorals, were of Jewish origin. Its members were drawn from different classes of society, being apparently similar socially to those belonging to the church at Corinth of whom Paul wrote: "For behold your calling, brethren, how that not many wise after the flesh, not many mighty, not many noble, are called" (1 Cor. 1. 26). That there were both rich and poor among them is apparent from the fact that the former are warned against the temptations of riches and are exhorted to be "ready to distribute" (1 Tim. VI. 9–19). Some were sufficiently prosperous to own slaves. Within the church masters and slaves associated on equal terms, but slaves with Christian masters were prone to show disrespect to them because they were brothers (1 Tim. VI. 1–2). Many members were little more than nominal Christians, being quarrelsome, envious, blasphemous, suspicious, "corrupted in mind" and "bereft of the truth" (1 Tim. I. 4, 19–20, VI. 4–5, 21; 2 Tim. II. 14, 23, III. 6–9; Tit. I. 11–13). Already some had made shipwreck of their faith, and matters were getting worse instead of better (1 Tim. I. 19; 2 Tim. III. 1). Apparently more stress had been laid on mere cleverness than character in the appointment of church officers (cf. 1 Tim. V. 22).

The Pastorals show the perils to which the Church was exposed from heresy. As we have already shown, it was probably similar to that which had appeared in the churches at Colossae and Ephesus, being a combination of Jewish and Gnostic elements. Those who taught it claimed to possess supernatural "knowledge", and were concerned, not with sound doctrine, but with "fables and endless genealogies" (1 Tim. I. 4), and with "Jewish fables, and commandments of men" (Tit. I. 14). This heresy was engendering strife, destroying faith, and eating into the life of the churches like a cancer (2 Tim. II. 17). The author of the Pastorals believed that the remedy for the evil was to be found in a more careful selection of church officers, in the inculcation of sound doctrine, and in stopping the mouths of false teachers (Tit. I. 11).

335

The permanent officials of the local community were elders or bishops (or overseers), deacons, deaconesses, and widows. The terms "elder" and "bishop" were identical: these officers were "elders in rank" (1 Tim. v. 17) and "bishops" in respect of their work and responsibility (1 Tim. III. 1). They had the general oversight of the life of the community, but their chief function seems to have been that of teaching. The office of bishop was one of great dignity and was evidently much coveted (cf. 1 Tim. III. 1). These officers were assisted by a body of deacons who attended to the administrative side of church work. The qualifications for a deacon were similar to those for a bishop except that the latter had to have an aptitude for teaching (1 Tim. III. 2). The diaconate was a stepping-stone to the higher order of bishop. Deaconesses seem also to be mentioned (1 Tim. III. 11), though owing to the Greek word for "women" and for "wives" being the same, the verse has been interpreted as referring to the wives of deacons; but Paul in "Romans" XVI. 1 (probably a fragment of a letter to Ephesus) commends Phoebe who is "a deaconess of the church at Cenchreae". Widows of suitable age and character also seemed to have had certain duties assigned to them. Their names were registered, and it is probable that they were expected to render service to the Church in return for their maintenance from the public funds (1 Tim. v. 3-16).

It appears that little change took place in the order of public worship in the interval between the death of Paul and the close of the century. Reference is made to the reading of the Scriptures, prayer, and exhortation (2 Tim. III. 16; 1 Tim. II. 1-8, IV. 13). The worshipper evidently prayed standing with arms outstretched, implying the expectation of gifts and ritual purity (cf. 1 Tim. II. 8). Women were not allowed to take an active part in public worship. As regards the men, freedom of utterance seems to have been permitted as in the church at Corinth in the days of Paul, when one contributed a song of praise, another a sermon, another a revelation, another a "tongue", and another an interpretation, according to the direction of the Holy Spirit (1 Cor. XIV. 26).

The doctrinal teaching is Pauline. God is "the King eternal, incorruptible, invisible, the only God" (1 Tim. I. 17); He is "the blessed and only Potentate, the King of kings, and Lord of lords; who only hath immortality, dwelling in light unapproachable; whom no man hath seen, nor can see" (1 Tim. VI. 15–16). He gives life to all things (1 Tim. VI. 13), and is the Saviour of all men (1 Tim. IV. 10). He saves men by His grace, not because of their good works (Tit. III. 4–5), but in fulfilment of an eternal purpose (2 Tim. I. 9; Tit. I. 2).

Between God and man there is only one Mediator, the man Christ Jesus (1 Tim. II. 5), who from a pre-incarnate life came into the world to save sinners (1 Tim. I. 15). He abolished death and brought life and incorruption to light (2 Tim. I. 10). He died that He might redeem us from all iniquity and secure for Himself a people zealous for good works (Tit. II. 14). The Holy Spirit is "poured out upon us richly, through Jesus Christ our Saviour" (Tit. III. 6). The time is not far distant when Christ will appear to judge the quick and the dead and to establish His kingdom (2 Tim. IV. 1).

PART VI

THE EPISTLE TO THE HEBREWS

CHAPTER XXII

THE EPISTLE TO THE HEBREWS

Contents

This work is shown to be a letter by its last chapter and by that only. In this chapter the writer expresses a hope that he will shortly visit the recipients; he gives them news about Timothy (XIII. 23), refers to their dead leaders (XIII. 7), and gives exhortations which read as if they are intended for particular people at a particular time. But the letter contains no epistolary opening, giving the name of the writer and sending greetings to the recipients; and the bulk of the work consists of a systematic argument and is such that, if it were not for the last chapter, we should be inclined to call it a theological essay.

The argument aims at showing by citations from the Old Testament, the superiority of Christ to the angels (I., II. 5–9), to Moses (III. 1–6), and to Joshua (IV. 8–10), and to Aaron and the Levitical priests (IV. 14–V. 10, VI. 13–VII. 28), and demonstrating that the sacrifice which He made once for all supersedes the daily and yearly sacrifices of the Jewish law, which were intended only as a shadow and symbol of Christ's one sacrifice (VIII. 1–X. 18). After each of these sections there follows a practical exhortation based on it; and, after the whole of the argument is finished, there follows a longer exhortation, showing that it was through faith that the heroes of the Old Testament became what they were, that they all had to endure suffering (XI.), and that Christians must in both respects imitate them (XII.).

Several views have been put forward to explain the absence of an epistolary beginning. Some writers think that the letter originally contained one, but that the beginning of the manuscript has been lost, as was the end of Mark. Undoubtedly the beginning and ending of the roll, which contained a manuscript, were the parts most liable to such loss. Others think it was written at a time when Christians were in danger from the Roman police, and that the writer wished not to reveal his own identity or that of the recipients should the letter fall into their hands. Our knowledge, however, both of the authorship and of the circumstance in which the letter was written, are not sufficient to warrant any certain conclusion.

Date of Composition

The letter is quoted by Clement of Rome, though not by name. This fixes it as a first-century work, as does the reference to Timothy (XIII. 23). The original leaders are, however, dead, but recently enough to be still remembered (XIII. 7). The whole atmosphere of the Epistle is one of persecution. These facts suggest a date somewhat later than that of Paul's Epistles and probably after Nero's persecution. It therefore becomes necessary to see whether its date can be fixed with reference to the destruction of Jerusalem. At first sight the absence of any reference to the destruction of the Temple in the section in which the author is proving the temporary character of the Jewish rites, would seem to suggest that the Temple was still standing. Against this it is commonly argued that the author's references to the Levitical rites are taken entirely from the Old Testament, and show no familiarity with the worship of the actual Temple in Jerusalem. But, even if he had never been present at the Temple worship, he could not have entirely dissociated it from its Old Testament origin; and the actual disappearance of the Levitical rites would have been so strong a confirmation of his argument that they had been intended to be temporary, that it is hard to believe he would not have used it if, in fact, they had disappeared. Thus a date after the death of Paul and Peter and after the Neronian persecution, but before the destruction of Jerusalem, becomes probable but not certain.

Authorship

The hypothesis of Pauline authorship grew slowly. In the West the Epistle was not included among the canonical books in the Muratorian Canon towards the end of the second century.

In the East it was counted as canonical, but even there it was some time before it was attributed to Paul. It is important to notice that it was known at Rome at a time when it was not recognized there as Pauline or canonical. For, if the collection of Paul's Epistles, as is most probable, was made in Rome, this is clear evidence that it is not a letter of Paul. Possibly at one time the name of the real author was known there. Whether that is so or not, it was soon completely forgotten. Eusebius is quite at a loss on the subject; he discusses several views and has to conclude: "Who wrote this epistle God alone knows." The Pauline theory was eventually adopted, possibly for several reasons. Doubtless there was a strong desire to include so magnificent a piece of writing in the Canon, yet it had come to be agreed that apostolic authorship was necessary for the inclusion of an epistle. Paul was pre-eminently the writer of epistles. Then, too, the emphasis on faith made it look more Pauline than the epistles of other writers; and the reference to Paul's companion, Timothy, may have contributed. But the language and style are quite unlike that of Paul and the main argument is entirely the author's own: Eusebius could see quite well that on linguistic grounds there was nothing to be said for the Pauline hypothesis. At the Reformation these considerations were at once recognized; neither Luther nor Calvin thought it to be by Paul, and Luther put forward a definite suggestion, which is still more favoured than any other, that the author was Apollos. Its non-Pauline character came to be recognized in this country before the Higher Criticism began to be applied generally to the books of the New Testament.

We are thus entirely dependent on internal evidence in discussing the question. From the book itself we can come to a number of conclusions about the author. (a) He is clearly a Jew who is influenced by the Alexandrian tendency to interpret the Old Testament allegorically, a tendency which we associate with the name of Philo. Even omissions in the Old Testament narrative such as that of Melchizedek's parentage and length of days, are credited with allegorical meaning. There is no parallel to this in the writings of Paul or of any other Christian writer. Moreover, we have the use of the word "Logos"

(IV. 12), derived from Philo, which later assumes so important a place in the theology of the Fourth Gospel: in fact, "Hebrews" seems to be a link between the Pauline and Johannine presentation of Our Lord in terms of Stoic philosophy. (*b*) The author is a conscious stylist, in contrast with Paul, whose most impassioned utterances read like inspired impromptus, written with little regard for Greek diction, or with Luke, whose language is literary Greek, perfectly correct but without a touch of rhetoric. (*c*) He was not an original Christian, since he speaks of the message "which having at the first been spoken through the Lord, was confirmed unto us by them that heard" (II. 3). (*d*) Though he is not distinctly Pauline, and though he is clearly a Jew who thinks in terms of the Old Testament, yet he definitely belongs to Gentile Christianity. He and Paul agreed that the Jewish law was intended only as a preparation for the coming of Christ, and that Abraham and the other heroes of Israel had lived and worked through faith. This emphasis on faith is not found in any New Testament writer except Paul and the author of this Epistle.

Most of the persons who have from time to time been suggested as author of the Epistle can be rejected as failing to conform to one or more of these criteria. Had Barnabas been the author no difficulty would have been felt anywhere in accepting the Epistle into the Canon, as it would have been the work of an Apostle. Philip may be rejected because he was an original Christian, and Luke on grounds of diction and style, while the attribution to Priscilla seems quite fanciful. One person only, of those whom we know, satisfies all the conditions, namely, Apollos. He was an Alexandrian, he was noted for his eloquence, he was not an original Christian, and he shared Paul's sphere of labour but did not accompany him. His prominence in the early Church—the Corinthians classed him with Paul and Peter—would secure that his work would be treated with respect though it fell short of apostolic authority. But the argument by exhaustion is in this case no proof, as we do not know all the workers in the early Church; and the Epistle may be the work of some person totally unknown to us.

Recipients

The title "To the Hebrews" is not original. If it is meant to apply to the general body of Palestinian Jews, it is certainly incorrect. Yet most writers seem to consider that the Epistle was addressed to some group of Jewish Christians. But the reference in XIII. 9 to food laws, as among the things which diverted them from the true belief, rather points to Gentiles who were being attracted by the teaching of Judaizers. It would be to such readers that the argument for the temporary character of the Jewish law would be most appropriate. Even Paul indignantly denied making any attempt to prevent Jewish Christians from keeping the Law; and it is most unlikely that any Christian writer would have gone beyond him.

As regards locality, we are dependent on XIII. 24, "They of Italy salute you". The Authorized Version translates this as if it meant "those in Italy", that is, as if it was written from Italy to persons outside. But a more natural translation is "The people who come from Italy", in which case it would appear to be written among a body of Christians, some of whom had lived in Italy, to a group still living there. Many writers think that it was written to some house group in Rome, and that the past leaders of XIII. 7 include Paul and Peter, and that among the present leaders of XIII. 17 may have been Clement, who quotes from the Epistle.

A theory has recently been put forward that it was written to the Colossians or to some neighbouring church, on the ground that the kind of erroneous teaching to which they are being subjected is similar to that against which Paul warns the Colossians. This theory assumes that Paul had a copy of "Hebrews" by him when he wrote his own Epistle, and that it was due to this circumstance that it was preserved. It would further explain how it was known at Rome not to be by Paul but was nevertheless associated with him. In view of the difficulty in coming to any certain conclusion on the authorship and date of the Epistle, it would be unwise to reject this hypothesis outright, but it is difficult to reconcile it with the mention of dead leaders and of Timothy's imprisonment, or with the atmosphere of persecution which pervades the Epistle.

Historical Value

We live in an age dominated by physical science. Science has no place for oratory; and for the first time in history, we have come to suspect it as something intended to misguide our reason. Science reasons and does not declaim. In our politics we call for statesmen who can convince us, not for orators who can carry us away. In the political sphere we are probably right; the modern broadcast is a safer guide than the declamation of a public meeting or even the eloquence of a Chatham or a Gladstone. But conviction is one thing, incentive to action is another. In 1939 conviction, not oratory, was needed. In 1940 conviction was already there; hope, resolution, self-sacrifice, and readiness to face even death were needed. Oratory came to its own again in Churchill's speeches. The situation when this Epistle was written was similar. Paul, as he constantly affirms, had converted men, not by the charm of oratory, but by the plain substance of his message. But more than mental assent was needed to meet the lions in the amphitheatre or the fires in Nero's gardens. We begin to realize the strength with which early Christianity met and overcame persecution when we peruse the eloquence, born of firm conviction, with which a Christian leader, ready himself to face the worst, appeals to his brethren to do the same. Throughout the ages the Epistle has been a source of inspiration in times of persecution. But even for the ordinary Christian in a quiet time a tepid assent is not enough. Christianity is a religion to be practised, not merely believed. Faith, hope, and charity, are feelings, not mathematical conclusions. There is still room for the great preacher. The feeblest sermons may hope for assent; only a few sermons stir us to action. These come from men with blazing zeal, intense desire, and an ardent love of God and men. Oratory really helps to convey such emotions. Hardly any passages in the new Testament maintain this high level of appeal so long as the latter half of this Epistle, and there are few who fail to be inspired by it.

The greatness of the Epistle is then due to the personality of its author. It has little to do with his actual argument. His argument, indeed, is in some ways out of date, and in his own day was perhaps peculiar to himself. Early Christianity urged its claims on two bases. The one embraced the Resurrection, the personality of Jesus, His teaching, and His powers of healing. This ground we accept. The second was founded on quotations from the Old Testament. To this our attitude is different. We accept the general trend of Old Testament teaching, but argument based on isolated texts, which were used by all early Christian writers, are not in accord with modern ideas; and they were never carried quite to such an extreme as in this Epistle.

Nevertheless, though we cannot accept all his arguments, we all accept his conclusion—the complete separation of Christianity from the older Judaism. His view of the temporary character of Judaism was a forward move; it gave a theoretic foundation to what was in fact the practice of Gentile Christianity in not requiring of Gentile Christians obedience to the Law. It marks the permanent attitude of the Christian Church. Gentiles were not to be regarded as mere associates, allowed, as it were, in the outer court of what was primarily a Jewish society; on the contrary, the Jews were rather the forerunners of what was meant to be a world-wide religion.

The Epistle helps us to understand the diversity of gifts in the early Christian community, and we owe a deep debt of gratitude to those who secured its admission to the Canon, even though their recognition of its value led them, by attributing it to the greatest of the Apostolic writers, to conceal for a time the existence of another great personality in the early Church. It is the one great literary product of the persecutions, and it enriches our knowledge of that terrible period. We understand more fully how the blood of the martyrs became the seed of the church.

PART VII

THE CATHOLIC EPISTLES

CHAPTER XXIII

THE CATHOLIC EPISTLES:
THE EPISTLE OF JAMES

The Catholic Epistles

Seven writings were classed together by the early Church under the title of "Catholic Epistles". They were "James", "Jude", 1 & 2 "Peter", and 1, 2, & 3 "John". The origin of the title is uncertain, but the most probable explanation is that the Epistles constituting the group were addressed to the Church in general rather than to particular communities. The title, however, is misleading, since some of them are not "Catholic" in the accepted sense of the word; 3 "John", for example, is a private letter written to a person named Gaius, who was a member of a particular Church. Again the title suggests a group of Epistles possessing certain common characteristics, but each Epistle has its own purpose and character. The title, however, may be retained more as a matter of convenience, as denoting the non-Pauline Epistles, than as the expression of a truth.

THE EPISTLE OF JAMES

Authorship

External Evidence. The ultimate acceptance of this Epistle into the Canon of the New Testament was based on the identification of the author with James, "the Lord's brother", head of the church in Jerusalem, an identification which, it must be noted, is not made in the Epistle itself. Apostolic authorship, it must be remembered, was considered necessary for the inclusion of Epistles, though not of Gospels.

The Epistle was little known to the early Church. It is possibly known to Clement of Rome (*c.* A.D. 96), certainly to Hermas a little later; after that it is first mentioned by Origen in the third century, who refers to it as the work of James the Lord's brother and quotes it as Scripture, though he is hesitant on the subject and speaks of the "Epistle which goes under the name of James". Eusebius, our great authority, classes it among the disputed books, as does Jerome. In the West it was finally admitted to the Canon by the third Council of Carthage (A.D. 397); in the East it first appears in the Syriac version (early fifth century). After that it was accepted till the Reformation when Luther attacked it as "an epistle of straw" on account of its supposed antagonism to Paul's doctrine of justification by faith.

Internal Evidence. This yields a totally different result. The author states that he is a "teacher" (III. 1). "Do not many of you become teachers, my brothers, knowing that we [i.e. we teachers] shall undergo a severer scrutiny." The whole of the contents bears out this claim: the Epistle is unmixed "teaching" (didache), addressed to persons already Christians, and it is thrown into the form of an "epistle" only because there was no other recognized form of contemporary Greek literature into which it could be put; but it is addressed to all Christians, "the twelve tribes which are of the Dispersion" (I. 1)—Christians claiming to be the true Israel on the analogy of 1 "Peter" (I. 1).

Almost the whole of the work is based on parallels from the Old Testament, the Wisdom books of the Apocrypha, the Gospels, the Pauline Epistles, and 1 "Peter", and it is written in the form of the Wisdom books, that is to say, of commands, given in the imperative mood on various points of conduct in a somewhat disjointed manner. A difficulty arises from the author's habit of giving the substance, not the exact words, of the author to whom he is indebted, though he often preserves striking words or phrases, so that when the teaching is similar to that of the Gospels or other Epistles, we cannot always be sure whether he has them before him, or whether both he and they are drawing on a common stock of Christian teaching in general use. Where the analogy is very close and contains some striking word or phrase, it is safe to assume that he is making direct use of the other work; but in many cases we have to remain doubtful.

The position will become plainer if we run through the Epistle, giving analogies to each passage in turn, with some hints regarding their closeness.

I. 1. "To the twelve tribes".	1 Pet. I. 1.
2, 3. Trials a blessing.	1 Pet. I. 6–7 (close); Rom. v. 3, 4 (close); Mt. v. 10 (M); Lk. vi. 22 (Q).
4, 8. Ask wisdom without doubting.	Mt. xi. 24; Rom. iv. 20; Lk. xi. 9 (Q).
9–12. Poor should rejoice; trials; "garland of life".	Ecclus. xxxi. 8–10 and Wisd. v. 16 (close; see below); "garland of life", 1 Pet. v. 4.
13–18. Temptations not from God but from our own appetites; all good things from God.	Rom. vii. 7–25, viii. 1–6 (see below); idea of our being first fruits. Rom. viii. 19–29.
19–20. Against anger.	Often in Prov.; Col. iii. 8; Eph. iv. 26–31; Mt. v. 22.
21. Associates foulness and malice, welcoming the word which is able to save.	1 Pet. ii. 1, same association and same leading up to salvation.
22–24. Doers of the word, not hearers only.	Rom. ii. 13; cf. Lk. vi. 46.
25. The perfect law of liberty.	'Perfect', Mt. v. 48 (M), lightness of yoke, Mt. xi. 30 (M).
26. Curbing his tongue.	Counsels against ill-natured talk innumerable in Paul.
27. To care for widows and orphans.	Mt. xxv. 36–40 (M).
II. 1–9. Deference to wealth; God has chosen the poor; "Love thy neighbour as thyself".	Lk. vi. 20 (Q) "Heirs of the Kingdom"; 1 Cor. i. 27, chosen "the weak things of the world"; Mk. xvi. 31, Gal. v. 14 "Love neighbour as self".
10–11. Breaking one commandment is breaking all.	Gal. v. 3.
12–13. Judgment to those who do not pity.	Mt. v. 7, vii. 1; Lk. vi. 36, but see below.
14–26. Uselessness of faith without works.	A reply to Rom iv. 13–25; instances Mt. xxv. 35, 36 (M).

III.	1. Teachers to be judged by stricter standard.	Lk. XII. 47–48.
	2–10. The tongue untameable.	No exact parallel.
	11–12. Can fig tree produce grapes? etc.	Lk. VI. 44 (Q).
	13–18. True wisdom inconsistent with jealousy and selfishness, need of peacefulness.	True wisdom, 1 Cor. II. 13; Peacemakers, Mt. v. 9 (M).
IV.	1–2. Fightings among them result from craving for pleasure.	Rom. VII. 21.
	4–5. Friendliness with World hostility to God.	Rom. VIII. 6. cf. Mt. VI. 24 (Q).
	6. God resists proud but bestows favour on humble.	Prov. IV. 34.
	7–10. Humbling oneself before God.	1 Pet. v. 6 (close); Lk. XIV. 11 (Q).
	11–12. Disparagement and judgment of others.	Rom. II. 1; Lk. VI. 37 (Q).
	13–16. Planning without God.	Lk. XII. 17–20 (L).
	17. If you know but do not do, it is sin.	Lk. XII. 47 (L).
V.	1–3. Decay of wealth, including reference to moth and rust.	Moth and rust, Mt. VI. 19 (M, Q, similar); Lk. VI. 24 (Q).
	4–6. Defrauding of pay is murder.	Ecclus. XXXIV. 22 (clear source).
	7–9. Patience till coming of the Lord.	"Now is salvation nearer to us than when we first believed" (Rom. XIII. 11).
	10–11. Patience of prophets and Job.	Job 1.
	12. Against oaths.	Mt. v. 36–37 (M), identity of phrase.
	13. Prayer in sorrow, melody in joy.	Col. III. 16, Eph. v. 19.
	14–15. Healing by prayer with anointing.	Mk. VI. 13. (Association of cure with forgiveness, Mk. II. 5–12.)
	16–18. Power of prayer, e.g. Elijah.	1 Kings XVIII. 42–46.
	19–20. Recalling a sinner "covers a multitude of sins".	Prov. X. 12, quoted 1 Pet. IV. 8.

Where we find similar passages in James and the Old Testament (including the Apocrypha), we know that James has the Old Testament book before him (in the Greek Septuagint version): we can therefore see with certainty how he uses his originals. Let us take as an example, namely, James I. 9–12. It is based on two passages from the Apocrypha. One is "Ecclesiasticus" xxxi. 8–10, "Blessed is the rich that is to be found without blemish, and hath not gone after gold. Who is he? and we will call him blessed: for wonderful things has he done among his people. Who hath been tried thereby, and found perfect? then let him glory". The other is "Wisdom" v. 16, "Therefore shall they receive a glorious kingdom, and a beautiful crown [really, "garland"] from the Lord's hand". In "James" we have the essential words "blessed", "tried", "glory", "crown", which show how much he is affected by the language of the Wisdom literature, but the actual substance is greatly changed, from praise of a rich man who has done good with his wealth, to a warning of the futility of riches and a praise of poverty; in other words, James uses the language of the Wisdom literature to teach, not a Jewish but a Christian ethic consonant with "Luke" vi. 20. "Blessed are ye poor: for yours is the kingdom of God", and vi. 24, "But woe unto you that are rich! for ye have received your consolation".

We can now turn to his use of Christian literature. The degree of closeness which warrants belief that James is consciously following Paul is to some extent a matter of individual opinion; but it may be safely asserted that competent judges think the evidence to be sufficient as regards "Romans", I "Corinthians", and "Galatians", while as regards "Colossians" and "Ephesians" it is a matter of uncertainty. A clear case where James is referring to "Romans" is one where he differs from what he supposes Paul to be asserting (II. 14–36), namely, Paul's doctrine of justification by faith contained in "Romans" IV. 13–25. James argues the matter out from Paul's own instance, Abraham, and even quotes the text already used by Paul, that his faith "was imputed to him for righteousness"; he goes with Paul as far as he can; but by inserting Abraham's readiness to sacrifice Isaac he turns the argument into one that faith must be shown by works. (The sacrifice of Isaac is also mentioned as an instance of faith in "Hebrews" XI. 17–19, but this is not enough to prove that James was acquainted with "Hebrews".) A case which is not so clear is to be found in "James" I. 13–18, where he argues that no temptation comes from God, from whom only good things come. This may well be a comment on "Romans" VII. 7–13, where Paul argues that the law produces bad desires and that in "finding occasion, through the commandment beguiled me"; for, since Paul and James would both agree that the Law came from God, James may well argue that Paul's doctrine implies that God tempts to sin. This suspicion is increased when we find that almost immediately afterwards James, in speaking of Christians as "the firstfruits of his created things", seems to have in mind a passage in the next chapter of "Romans" (VIII. 19–23), in which the whole body of created things is represented as ultimately to be redeemed through the redemption of "our-selves also which have the first-fruits of the Spirit".

Anyone reading the references to I "Peter" in the list of passages given above will be convinced of a close similarity, the phraseology being more similar than in references to Paul's Epistles.

The case as regards the Gospels is more difficult. Not only is much of Our Lord's direct teaching given in almost identical language in "Matthew" and "Luke", but there is reason to believe that there was a considerable overlap between Matthew's two sources, Q which he shares with "Luke", and M which he alone uses. So, though no doubt may exist that James is drawing on Synoptic material in any particular case, we are doubtful whether it is our existing Gospels, or their immediate sources, or something even older than those sources. Before we can proceed further, we shall have to consider the date of "James".

Date

This cannot be earlier than "Romans" and, if it be judged that the resemblances of "Colossians" and "Ephesians" are more than accidents, is probably after Paul's death. On the other hand, "Romans" would have hardly occupied the author's mind so much were it not comparatively recent. In the second century Paul's Epistles were already treated as Scripture (2 Peter III. 15, 16), whereas James, though following them in the main, is prepared to differ on occasions. The complete absence of any trace of either the thought or the language of the Fourth Gospel, or of the Epistles of John, or of the Apocalypse, requires a date earlier than the general spread of these works. Moreover, the atmosphere is not one of acute persecution, recent or expected; indeed Christianity seems to be receiving a welcome from the well-to-do. This suggests the possibility that Streeter was right in the conjecture that the ring which the rich men wear is the ring which marked the equestrian (or knightly) rank, and that the date is the earlier period of Domitian's principate, when even the heir-apparent was favourable to Christianity. This date suits both the literary allusions and the contemporary atmosphere. It remains to see how it bears on the use of Synoptic material.

Rome is more probable than any other quarter as the place of origin. It is based on Hellenistic rather than Palestinian Judaism. The first certain use of it is by Hermas, writing in Rome. The writer makes use not only of correct, but of effective, stylish Greek. The date would surely have to be put considerably earlier to escape all influence of John the Elder if it were written in the province of Asia.

What was then the position of the Christian world at the probable date as regards the Gospels? "Mark" had been written in the seventh decade of the century and was known everywhere. "Luke" and "Matthew" were written after the Fall of Jerusalem; "Luke" was known in Rome before A.D. 90 and had reached Asia before the Fourth Gospel was written. "Matthew" was "the Gospel" in Syria but Streeter argues that it was not accepted in Rome till A.D. 119. James contains parallels with all three. Critics have generally been most struck by resemblances with "Matthew"; but this may merely be because "Matthew", using both Q and M, has more direct teaching of Our Lord than "Luke": for passages similar to James appear not only in Q but in M and L, and even in "Mark", whose Gospel contains so little direct teaching, as distinct from parables and arguments with the Jews on doctrine.

Exactly the same question arises regarding the use of Gospel material by Clement of Rome, and, by a coincidence the passage of Clement which Streeter uses to support his theory regarding that writer, contains passages which are also paralelled by James. The passage (1 Clem. xiii. 1) runs: "Specially remembering the words of the Lord Jesus which he spoke teaching mercy and long suffering: for thus he said, 'Pity that you may be pitied; forgive that you may be forgiven; as you do so it shall be done to you; as you give so it shall be given to you; as you judge so you shall be judged; as you do kindly, so shall kindness be done to you; with what measure you measure shall it be measured to you'". Streeter points out that Clement uses a formula of quotation, but that it is not a direct quotation either from "Luke" (vi. 36–38) or from "Matthew" (v. 7, vi. 14, vii. 1, 12). James' version runs, "For judgement is pitiless to those who do not show pity" (Jas. ii. 13). The association of pity and judgment is common to Clement's version and "Luke", whereas in "Matthew" they appear in separate passages; but the point is this: if we possessed "Matthew" only we should think James was quoting two separate passages in "Matthew". If we possessed "Matthew" and "Luke" but not "Clement", we should be inclined to think he was quoting "Luke"; but the addition of "Clement" makes it possible that he was quoting some third version. It is highly probable that Q was the fullest of several versions and was therefore adopted by Luke and the compiler of "Matthew"; and that in turn Matthew, by incorporating M also became so much the fuller that in time his Gospel came to be considered as the great compendium of Our Lord's direct teaching. But all we can say of James is that he was acquainted with some version or versions.

Not much evidence can be got from passages which are not direct teaching, but taken from incidents or parables. The all-embracing character of the text, "Thou shalt love thy neighbour as thyself" (Jas. ii. 8, Mk. xii. 31) may possibly not be taken from "Mark" but from "Galatians" v. 14, and the need of faith in prayer (Jas. I. 6, Mk. XI. 24) may have found its way into some compendium of direct teaching; so that direct dependence on "Mark" cannot be proved, though there is no difficulty as regards date. There is one passage on planning to get wealth when we have no idea what God may have in store for us (Jas. IV. 13) which very strongly suggests a parable in "Luke" (XII. 17–20), peculiar to his Gospel; by itself it can only suggest a probability, not a certainty; once more, "Luke" was known in Rome early enough to raise no difficulties. But, as regards "Matthew" we can find no passage which is not of the character of direct teaching in the imperative, though the passage on swearing (Jas. V. 12) is very close to teaching recorded in "Matthew" only; but there is no reason why we should assume that it should not appear in some other digest of teaching, when once we know that such existed.

The Author

The attribution to James the Lord's brother, which was made at a date long after the Epistle was written, was not unnatural. It was the easiest way of explaining the respect in which it was held in certain churches: and its criticism of Paul's doctrine of justification by faith appeared to come naturally from the leader of the party in the Church which was most opposed to Paul. But there is nothing Judaistic in the Epistle, and it clearly reflects Hellenistic, not Palestinian, Judaism; and the author claims no higher rank than that of teacher. James was an exceedingly common name, being merely the Greek form of Jacob, and it is unnecessary to assume that the name was a later addition added to make the ascription to the Lord's brother acceptable. Of James the author, whom we may call "James the teacher" little can be inferred from his Epistle. The notion that his character can be inferred from the number of imperatives he uses, can be dismissed when once it is realized that this is the traditional form of didactic literature from the days of "Proverbs", "Ecclesiasticus" and "Wisdom" onwards. The idea that he speaks with authority is the exact opposite of the truth; he says nothing for which he cannot find warrant in previous recognized authorities. He writes good Greek; his advice is sound, and we feel that, if he is an example of early Christian ethical teaching, that teaching was a healthy continuation of that of the first generation.

Contents

The Epistle may be divided roughly into the following sections:

(1) Trial and Temptation (I. 1–8, 12–18).
(2) Rich and Poor (I. 9–11, II. 1–4, 5–13, IV. 13–16, V. 1–6).
(3) Faith and Works (I. 22–25, II. 14–26, IV. 17).
(4) Control of Speech (I. 19–21, 26–27, III. 1–12, IV. 11–12, V. 12).
(5) Patience and Prayer (V. 7–11, 13–20).
(6) The Evils of Strife (IV. 1–10).
(7) The True Wisdom of Life (III. 13–18).

(1) *Trial and Temptation.* The author exhorts his readers to rejoice amid trial, for trial bravely borne in reliance upon divine wisdom, results in moral perfection. Divine wisdom is given to those who ask for it in faith (I. 1–8). Temptation comes, not from God but from man's own evil desires which produce sin and death. All that men are given is good, and all their endowments are faultless and come from the Father (I. 12–18).

(2) *Rich and Poor.* The poor brother should rejoice when he is promoted, while the rich brother should rejoice in being brought low. The position of the rich man is insecure, for in the midst of his occupations he fades away (I. 9–11).

Christians should not show respect of persons. If they assign a man adorned with a gold ring and fine clothing a good place in their synagogue, and a shabbily dressed man an obscure seat or mere standing room, they are making distinctions and showing partiality (II. 1–4).

God has chosen the poor to be heirs of His kingdom. It is the rich who oppress the poor, drag them into the law courts, and even revile the name of Christ to whom they belong. It is a good thing to fulfil the royal law of love to one's neighbour; to transgress that command in any respect is to transgress the whole law (II. 5–13).

The trader in pursuit of wealth presumes on his own powers and forgets God. Life is transient, and the plans of men are futile until they submit to the will of God (IV. 13–16).

The author denounces the rich for their exploitation of the poor. The Lord of Hosts has heard the cry of their workmen whom they have robbed of their dues, and He will repay. They have lived self-indulgent lives and have condemned and murdered the righteous man who has offered no resistance (V. 1–6).

(3) *Faith and Works.* Men must not only hear God's word but also obey it, otherwise they delude themselves. He who obeys the Christian rule of life (the law of liberty) will find blessing in the act of obedience (I. 22–25).

Faith is of no avail apart from works. It is futile to wish the poor well if no provision is made for their bodily needs. A faith that does not express itself in deeds is dead in itself. Faith and works are inseparable. Both Abraham and Rahab were accounted righteous before God on account of their works. If a man knows what is right and does not do it, he commits a sin (II. 14–26, IV. 17).

(4) *Control of Speech.* The Christian must be slow to speak and slow to be angry, for human anger does not promote divine righteousness. If he cannot curb his tongue his religion is worthless. Religion is not shown by an unbridled tongue but by charity and purity of life (I. 19–21, 26–27).

No one should become a teacher unless he can control his tongue. It is a world of wickedness among the members of the body, in that it sets fire to the circle of existence and is itself fired by the flames of hell. All living things have been tamed but no man can tame the tongue. The same tongue blesses God and curses man, but this ought not to be (III. 1–12).

Christians should not speak evil of one another. To speak evil of others is opposed to the law of the divine judge (IV. 11–12).

Christians should renounce all oaths; they should be so truthful and straightforward that their bare word will suffice (V. 12).

(5) *Patience and Prayer.* They should exercise patience while

they wait for the speedy return of the Lord. The prophets, especially Job, provide examples of suffering patience (v. 7-11).

Those who are suffering should pray, and those who are thriving should sing praise to God. He who is sick should summon the elders of the church and let them pray over him. The earnest prayers of a righteous man have a powerful effect, as may be seen in the case of Elijah who prayed first for drought and then for rain, and his prayers were answered (v. 13-20).

(6) *The Evils of Strife.* Conflicts and feuds are born of men's passions, which are at war within the body. Men wrangle and fight because they are envious and jealous and cannot acquire what they want. They pray with the wicked intention of wasting what they acquire on sinful pleasures. Friendship with the world means enmity to God. They should repent and humble themselves before God, and He will exalt them (IV. 1-10).

(7) *The True Wisdom of Life.* The wise and well-instructed man will show by his good conduct that he is guided by the humble modesty of wisdom. If men are bitterly jealous and quarrelsome, they should not boast of it and so be false to the truth. Such wisdom is not of heavenly origin but is earthly, unspiritual, and devilish. Jealousy and strife mean disorder and every evil deed. But the heavenly wisdom is first of all pure, then peaceable, gentle, conciliatory, full of mercy and wholesome fruit, and free from insincerity (III. 13-18).

Faith and Works.

It is often maintained that there is a fundamental difference between Paul and James on the question of "Faith and Works". According to Paul, man is saved by faith in Christ whereas James affirms that he is saved by works, while each takes the example of Abraham to prove his own doctrine. There is, however, no real contradiction between the two, for each places a different interpretation on the term "faith". To Paul "faith" involves an attitude of dependence, trust, and love towards God as revealed in Christ, and results in a new kind of life which produces the fruits of the Spirit. To James "faith" means simply intellectual assent to a doctrine, which is devoid of any driving power; such a faith could be held by devils, but no one reading "Romans" or "Galatians" can imagine that devils could believe in the Pauline sense of the word. Paul guards against the idea that mere intellectual assent is sufficient (Rom. ii. 6–20), and is never tired of exhorting his fellow Christians to be "stedfast, unmoveable, always abounding in the work of the Lord" (1 Cor. xv. 58). The only "works" which he disparages are "works of the law" (Rom. iii. 20, 28), by which he means the observance of the Jewish ceremonial law. When James speaks of "works", he too, like Paul, has in mind the deeds which are consistent with the Christian life, but when he demands obedience to the royal law of liberty (ii. 8), he is thinking, not of Jewish ceremonial law, but of the Gospel regarded as a new law. There is also a difference in their use of the term "to justify". Both use it in the sense of "to account righteous" but they apply it differently. What matters to Paul is the initial act of justification by which a man, estranged by sin, is accounted righteous before God through faith in Christ. But according to James, a man is accounted righteous before God, when by the performance of good works, inspired by faith, he proves the reality of his Christian character. In short Paul means that a man is brought into a right relation to God, not by obedience to the law, but by faith in Christ, whereas James means that he is brought into a right relation to God by obedience to a new law (the royal law of liberty), and that it is futile for him to profess faith in Christ unless his life is consistent with the Christian ideal. With Paul "works" are the result of an inner compulsion, consequent upon the new life in Christ, but with James they are the result of a discipline from without, namely, obedience to the new law of liberty. James perhaps never really understood Paul's profound conception of justification by faith.

Historical Value

The Epistle reveals something of the state of Christian society for which it was written. It is often represented as revealing a generation which had lost the ardour of the first generation and become commonplace. On the other hand, there is very little reference to sins of the flesh, such as we find in "Romans" and "Corinthians", or to the crimes of the backwoodsman, which are not entirely absent from Christian literature. The faults are those of a "respectable" society, which seems to include some well-to-do members; and the section on deference to wealth—an unusual topic in the New Testament —appears to be a response to a real situation. Hence we are less surprised at another passage in which defrauding the labourer of his hire is attached. This concern with a community much like that of many Christian congregations to-day gives the Epistle a value still, and it must always occupy a prominent position in the life of the Church. Man in his essential nature does not change, and the sins which James condemns appear in every age. The dangers inherent in the possession of wealth, and undue respect paid to rank and position, the sins of speech and of harsh and hasty judgment of others, the attempt to compromise with the world—all these things are prevalent in the world to-day in other but not less dangerous forms than those which the author of the Epistle attacked. The Epistle in many respects is singularly modern, and the wise counsels it contains are as relevant to-day as when they were first written.

CHAPTER XXIV

THE FIRST EPISTLE OF PETER

Authorship

External Evidence. The Epistle is quoted by James, and passages in Clement of Rome (end of first century) and Polycarp (early second century) seem to be echoes of it. According to Eusebius is was known to Papias, who "used testimonies from the First Epistle of John and likewise from that of Peter". There is no reference to it in the Muratorian Fragment, but its omission may be an accident, as the only surviving copy of the document in question is mutilated. But it is not till later that it is quoted as the work of Peter by Irenaeus, Clement of Alexandria, Tertullian, and Origen, and that it is placed by Eusebius among the generally accepted Epistles. It seems to have been more popular in the East than in the West. "The actual traces of the early use of 1 'Peter' in the Latin churches are very scanty. There is not the least evidence to show that its authority was ever disputed, but, on the other hand, it does not seem to have been read much."[1]

Internal Evidence. Several objections have been raised to the traditional view of authorship on internal grounds. The objection that Peter would have given us more facts about the life of Jesus carries no weight; early Christian preachers were concerned with the great moments only—His Death, Resurrection, and Exaltation. More serious is the objection that the references to persecution (iv. 16) imply a time when the profession of Christianity was in itself a crime punishable by death, and that this was not earlier than the reign of Trajan (A.D. 98–117). But it is a mere matter of chance that we possess Trajan's edict to Pliny (A.D. 112), and it is highly probable that Christianity had been an illegal religion since the time of Nero, but that the enforcement of the law on a large scale

[1] Westcott, *Canon of the New Testament*, 1896, p. 263.

was often allowed to elapse, as in later times. An objection might be brought on the ground of the use of the word "Babylon" of Rome; this will be considered later.

But there are two serious objections. One is that Peter's use of Greek could not have reached the standard of this Epistle; for, though its Greek cannot be compared with that of "Hebrews" or "James", it is far above that of Mark, who is stated to have acted as Peter's "interpreter". The other is the dependence, not only on the thought, but on the verbal expressions of Paul in "Romans" and "Ephesians" (cf. i. 14 and Rom. xii. 2; i. 21 and Rom. iv. 24; i. 22 and Rom. xii. 9–10; ii. 5 and Rom. xii. 1; ii. 6–8 and Rom. ix. 32–33; ii. 13–14 and Rom. xiii. 1–4; ii. 24 and Rom. vi. 18; iii. 8–12 and Rom. xii. 14–19; iii. 22 and Rom. viii. 34; iv. 1 and Rom. vi. 7; iv. 10–11 and Rom. xii. 3–8; v. 1 and Rom. viii. 18; i. 3 and Eph. i. 3; i. 10–11 and Eph. iii. 5–6; i. 13 and Eph. vi. 14; ii. 4–7 and Eph. ii. 20–22; iii. 1 and Eph. v. 22; ii. 18 and Eph. vi. 5; iii. 22 and Eph. i. 20–21). Now any writer may use the content of another's work, and occasionally a very striking word or phrase; but the constant use of another's phraseology implies that a writer is steeped in his model to an extent which we cannot believe Peter was steeped in the writings of Paul.

To both these objections the Epistle itself provides a very possible answer. The letter proper, having closed with a doxology, a note is appended stating that it was written by the hand of Silvanus (who is the Silas of Acts). This does not necessarily mean more than that Silvanus was the amanuensis, but it does not exclude his taking a much larger share in its composition. In fact the Epistle is just what we should expect Silvanus to write. He was at one time Paul's right-hand man (Acts xv. 40) and is mentioned as joint author of the two letters to the Thessalonians (1 Thess. i. 1 and 2 Thess. i. 1), and would be saturated in Paul's phraseology. It is easy to picture a situation which would lead to the dispatch of a letter with the authority of Peter but actually composed by a secretary. Paul had presumably already been martyred: he had "had the care of all the churches" and used what we may call a headquarters staff to help him. This staff had not been entirely broken up; but it would not have the moral authority of Paul. The only man who could come near such authority was Peter. For a short period, till he, too, was captured and put to death, he could well lead Paul's staff. He could see where Paul would have written a letter of encouragement, but had not the literary power to do it himself. The natural person to do it was Timothy, but Timothy was probably in prison (Heb. xiii. 23). Silvanus was evidently still free. We might fill up this conjectural picture by supposing that, after Peter's death, the leadership fell to Apollos and that "Hebrews" continued the work of encouragement, and that with the production of Mark's Gospel the work of the first generation, associated with Paul, came to an end.

It is thus possible to combine the traditional Petrine attribution of the Epistle with what we know of the situation towards the end of Nero's persecution, which is unhappily far less than we should like to know. But we must not omit mentioning Streeter's brilliant guesswork. According to his theory, it really consists of two documents: (1) a baptismal address by a bishop (i. 3–iv. 11) and (2) a letter of encouragement written in a time of persecution. The address (i. 1–2) and salutation (v. 12–14) are interpolations added at a later date, perhaps in the reign of Trajan (c. 112). These two interpolations secured the admission to the New Testament Canon of an Epistle, which otherwise might not have been preserved. He also suggests that the author was Aristion, who was Bishop of Smyrna at the time of the persecution mentioned in "The Revelation". It must be noticed that this theory consists of two parts, that which divides the Epistle into two parts—this depends on an analysis of the contents, and needs nothing else—and the conjectural work which follows an acceptance of the first part of the theory. The evidence for the division is strong, as we shall see; but it is not inconsistent with the attribution to Silvanus or the genuineness of Peter's beginning and ending. Silvanus might well conduct a baptism; we know that Paul rarely baptized himself, and he might agree with Peter that this baptismal sermon contained enough encouragement under persecution to make it the basis of the required pamphlet, and might expand it at the end to make it still more suitable.

The division of the Epistle was first suggested by the presence of two doxologies marking an end (IV. 11 and v. 11). Next, a consideration of I. 3–IV. 11 shows that it begins by thanking God for giving us a new birth (I. 3) and works up to the meaning of baptism (III. 21) as an end of sin (IV. 1) and the start of a new life (IV. 2–5), parallel to the death and resurrection of Christ. The theme of this part may be summed up as, "Now is the Crisis of History; how are we to react to it?" Those to whom the Epistle is addressed are entering on an indestructible life through Christ's resurrection, which should in spite of temporary hardships give them a sense of triumphal joy. It is the great period pre-arranged by God, foreseen (though dimly understood) by all the prophets and which even angels desired to understand; it brings a new birth direct from God, which results in a holy life; they become stones in a holy edifice, of which Christ Himself is the chief corner-stone. The author then addresses various classes on their specific duties as members of this holy society. The crisis may call for suffering, but they are showing the sufferings of Christ, of whose resurrection to an eternal life with God baptism is a counterpart; they must lead a new life on earth, and the end is approaching, when they will obtain the consummation of the new life.

There is a completeness in this sermon, which meets the needs of new converts, to whom the breach with the heathen past and the starting on a new course could well be called a death and a new birth, in a way which admission into the Christian community by baptism nowadays possesses only in missionary lands. But, when it is incorporated into a letter of encouragement to Christians of longer standing who were being persecuted, the emphasis on different parts is somewhat altered, and it is the references to hardships which the new readers would feel to be most appropriate to themselves, though they do not seem to have been composed with an eye to such serious persecution as is envisaged in the second part of the Epistle. In an analysis of the Epistle as a whole we must therefore think of it as it would appeal to these readers.

Contents

The author sends greetings to the elect of the Dispersion in Pontus, Galatia, Cappadocia, Asia, and Bithynia (I. 1–2).

Persecution must not prevent a triumphant feeling of joy, for they are living in an age appointed by God and foretold by all the prophets. They must fix their hopes calmly and un-falteringly on their salvation and be holy in their lives even as God Himself is holy, remembering that the price of their salvation was nothing less than the life-blood of Christ (I. 3–21).

Knowing that their new life comes of God, they must have brotherly love and eschew all unbrotherly faults; for they are all stones in the holy building of which Christ Himself is the corner-stone and have been made God's chosen people. They must, by the sanctity of their lives, make their accusers glorify God for all their good works (I. 22–II. 12).

He then passes on to particular duties; of subjects to the Emperor and his officials; of slaves, of wives, of husbands, and of all brethren to one another (II. 13–III. 12).

They must not fear threats but consecrate Christ as Lord in their hearts. They must be ready to give a reason for the hope which they cherish, and have a clean conscience, so that their slanderers may be put to shame (III. 13–16).

It is better to suffer for doing right than for doing wrong, for then we share the sufferings of Christ, who died for the sins of others and who saves us, as Noah was saved in the ark, by baptism through His Resurrection and Exaltation (III. 17–22).

The conviction that they who have suffered are quit of sin, should nerve them to pass the remainder of their lives governed, not by earthly passions, but by the will of God (IV. 1–6).

The end is at hand, and therefore they must be steady, tem-perate, and prayerful, exercising brotherly love and hospitality, and ministering to others according to the gift of God imparted to each, in order that in all things Christ may be glorified (IV. 7–11).

He repeats his counsel to rejoice in Christ's sufferings; they must not suffer as evil-doers, but must not be ashamed of suffering as a Christian (IV. 12–16).

He warns them that the time has come for judgment to begin

at the house of God, and exhorts those suffering in accordance with the will of God to entrust their souls to a faithful Creator (IV. 17–19).

The Elders must discharge their duties faithfully; the younger men must submit to the Elders, while all must be humble, sober, alert, and steadfast in the face of persecution, knowing that the same trials beset their brethren everywhere (v. 1–11).

After a brief reference to Silvanus and a final exhortation to steadfastness, the letter closes with greetings from the church in Babylon and from Mark, and with a benediction (v. 12–14).

Destination

The Epistle is addressed to "the elect who are sojourners of the Dispersion in Pontus, Galatia, Cappadocia, Asia, and Bithynia". The reference to the "Dispersion" suggests Jewish Christians, but most probably the work is used to describe all the Christians of the five districts mentioned who form part of the true people of God scattered abroad in an alien world. Since there were colonies of Jews in these districts, it is probable that the local churches included some members of Jewish origin, but the contents of the Epistle show that its readers were largely Gentiles. Before their conversion they moulded themselves according to the passions which ruled them in the days of their ignorance (I. 14). God had called them "out of darkness into his marvellous light" (II. 9); in time past they were no people, but now they are the people of God (II. 10). In their former state they had "wrought the desire of the Gentiles" and had walked in "lasciviousness, lusts, wine-bibbings, revellings, carousings, and abominable idolatries" (IV. 3). The implied contrast between the past and present in the matter of obedience to husbands suggests that they had recently become descendants of Sarah when they became Christians (III. 5–6).

On the South Galatian theory, the churches addressed were confined to the districts in the northern half of Asia Minor which had not been founded by Paul. It would appear that the author had not visited the districts to which he wrote (I. 12); but there had been ample time since Paul's missions to the south of the peninsula for the evangelization of the north by other Christian missionaries.

Place and Date of Composition

At the close of the Epistle Peter sends greetings to his readers from "she that is in Babylon" (v. 13). It is now generally agreed that "she" means the local church with which the author was associated at the time of writing. There is nothing to connect Peter with either the great Babylon on the Euphrates, or a little Babylon in Egypt, whereas tradition has always connected him with Rome, and Rome was the most likely place for Paul's old companions, Silas and Mark, to be together. One point of difficulty arises: the use of the name "Babylon" for Rome is best known to us from "The Revelation" and is often thought to have been first used there. It seems to us that this difficulty can be met by the following consideration. In "The Revelation" XVII. reference is made to seven emperors, five past, one present, and one for a short time in the future (vv. 10, 11): in other words, this chapter was certainly (and the whole book probably) written in the reign of the sixth emperor, Vespasian, and in it the term "Babylon" is introduced. Many critics regard this chapter as derived in part from a Jewish apocalypse: if so, the use of "Babylon" for Rome may well be of Jewish origin, and have been invented by the Jewish terrorists who had been working up anti-Roman feeling since the rule of Felix. The Jews had been terribly alarmed by the projects of Caligula and this feeling culminated in the rising of A.D. 66. Christians did not share these feelings till the persecution of Nero, and certainly the writer of this Epistle did not (1 Pet. II. 13, 14); but they would be well acquainted with the Jewish attitude, and the writer may well have used the term "Babylon" as a disguise, since it would be understood by his readers but not by the Roman police if the letter should fall into their hands.

Purpose

Even if we suppose that a large part of the Epistle was originally a baptismal address, yet the purpose of including it

371

in a letter and adding new material, if it was actually sent by the authority of Peter to the Christians of Northern Asia Minor, was to comfort them in persecution. The author reminds them that their afflictions are only temporary and that they have the great hope of salvation at the revelation of Jesus Christ (I. 3–6). Suffering is the common lot of Christians throughout the world (IV. 12, V. 9). It is in accordance with the divine will (I. 2), its purpose being to test the genuineness of faith (IV. 12), and should be ground for rejoicing (I. 6). Suffering strengthens and purifies the soul (I. 7), and is a way of entering into fellowship with Christ (IV. 13). He who suffers for Christ's sake has done with sin (IV. 1), and he who is denounced for bearing the name of Christ is blessed, for the Spirit of God rests upon him (IV. 14).

The original purpose of the sermon, if such it be, is to rouse the newly baptized Christians to an appreciation of the place which the Gospel has in God's plan for the world and the importance of their living in a manner worthy of it.

Doctrine

Though the author does not discuss theology, he nevertheless employs certain theological ideas concerning God, Christ, the Church, and the Second Advent, as a basis for his teaching.

God. God is a faithful Creator (IV. 19), and mighty in power (V. 6). He is the Holy One who demands holiness from His children (I. 15–16), and gives them through Jesus Christ the assurance of an incorruptible inheritance (I. 3). He is also a loving Father, to whom those who suffer in accordance with the divine will may entrust their souls (IV. 19), and upon whom they may cast all their anxieties knowing that He cares for them (V. 7). He is no respecter of persons and judges every man according to his works (I. 17). He is the God and Father of our Lord Jesus Christ (I. 3).

Christ. Christ is the eternal Son of God (I. 3), predestined to be the Redeemer of mankind before the foundation of the world (I. 20). During His life on earth He suffered, "the righteous for the unrighteous, that he might bring us to God" (III. 18). After His Resurrection He visited the realms of the dead and preached the Gospel "unto the spirits in prison" (III. 19). This was suggested by the "Book of Enoch", one of the Jewish apocalyptic books written not long before. Having died in the flesh He was made alive in the Spirit, exalted to the right hand of God, and made supreme over angels, authorities, and powers (III. 22). He is the Shepherd and Bishop of the souls of men (II. 25), the supreme object of love and faith (I. 8, 9, II. 7), the sinless example (II. 21–22, IV. 1, 13), the means of access to God (II. 5, IV. 11, V. 10), and the corner-stone of the spiritual temple (II. 4).

The Church. The Church is composed of believers in Christ who is its Head (II. 4), and constitutes the true Israel of God (II. 5, 9–11). It is a brotherhood which embraces the whole world (V. 9) and which has not only privileges, but also responsibilities and duties.

The Second Advent. Christ is returning in the near future (IV. 7) when believers will obtain the outcome of their faith in the salvation of their souls (I. 9), and will become partakers of the glory that shall be revealed (V. 1). At His Coming there will be a final judgment when God will judge impartially (I. 17), and righteously (II. 23), both the living and the dead (IV. 5). In view of the approaching end of the present world order, men should spend in reverent fear the time of their stay on earth (I. 17).

Historical Value

The Epistle was written in the first century to meet a specific situation in Asia Minor, but it has a universal significance, for suffering is the common lot of man, and many have tried to find a satisfactory answer to the question, "Why should men suffer?" The author of the "Book of Job" believes that God allows His children to suffer to test their loyalty. In his delineation of the Suffering Servant, the author of "Second Isaiah" (LIII.) expresses the conviction that suffering finds its glorification in service to others. The author of 1 "Peter" teaches that suffering is ordained by God to test the genuineness of faith, and is a means of purifying and ennobling the soul (I. 7). It brings a man into closer fellowship with Christ, and enables him to attain to that higher life which Christ imparts (II. 1–11). The Epistle, therefore, will always appeal to Christians, since it offers a satisfactory solution to the age-old problem of human suffering and helps them to justify the ways of God to man. Moreover, the exhortation of steadfast faith and hope, to patience and fortitude, and to consistent Christian conduct in all human relationships in time of persecution, will always bring comfort, strength, and inspiration to Christians, who are called upon to live out their lives in the midst of a hostile environment.

CHAPTER XXV

THE EPISTLES OF JOHN

Canonicity

1 John. The Epistle is known and valued by Christian writers before the middle of the second century, for it is cited by Polycarp, and, according to Eusebius, employed by Papias. Towards the close of the same century it is closely associated with the Fourth Gospel in the Muratorian Fragment, while Irenaeus uses it freely, and refers to it as the work of "John, the disciple of the Lord", evidently meaning the Apostle John. It is also quoted as the Apostle's work by Clement of Alexandria, Tertullian, and Origen. The only persons who refused to acknowledge its genuineness were the Alogi because they rejected the doctrine of the Logos, and Marcion, who accepted no books of the New Testament except Paul's Epistles and Luke's Gospel. Thus, by the close of the second century the Epistle had won a secure place in the Canon of the New Testament and was generally attributed to the Apostle John.

2 and 3 John. There are no traces of these two Epistles in the writings of the Church Fathers during the first half of the second century. The first reference to 2 "John" appears towards the close of the same century in the Muratorian Fragment which, after mentioning 1 "John" in connection with the Fourth Gospel, refers to two Epistles of John as received in the Catholic Church. That probably means 2 and 3 "John", though it is possible that 1 and 2 "John" are meant. Irenaeus quotes a passage from 2 "John" as if it came from 1 "John". Clement of Alexandria, by a reference to 1 "John" as "the greater Epistle", shows that he was acquainted with one at least of the shorter Epistles. There is no mention of 3 "John" till the first half of the second century, and its genuineness, together with that of 2 "John", was doubted down to the fourth or, in some places, to the fifth century. Origen states that they were not accepted by all as genuine, while Eusebius describes them as disputed by some, and alludes to the possibility that they may be the work of the Elder John. The two Epistles were finally accepted as canonical at the end of the fourth century by the Council of Laodicea, and the Third Council of Carthage.

Form and Character

1 "John" is grouped among the so-called "Catholic Epistles", but it is something of a misnomer to describe it as an epistle, since it contains no greetings at the beginning and end, and there is no clue to the identity of the author or to the destination to which it is to be sent. It is not so much a letter as a tract or sermon, addressed to a group of churches, well known to the author. This is shown by the fact that the heresies condemned are evidently confined to a particular locality, not to the whole of Christendom, and by the fact that there is a certain warmth of personal feeling between the author and his readers, whom he addresses as "my little children" (II. 12).

2 "John" is in the form of a private letter, written by a person who styles himself "the elder" (I. 1), addressed to "the elect lady and her children, whom I love in truth" (I. 1), and containing the usual introduction and conclusion. The address may possibly refer to a lady and her family, but it is highly probable that it is a figurative expression for a local church. The transition from the second person singular to the second person plural at the sixth verse (cf. vv. 6, 8, 10, 12) suggests a Christian community rather than an individual. The use of personification in describing a church has the support of 1 "Peter" v. 13, where we have the words, "She that is in Babylon, elect together with you, saluteth you". Moreover, the language in which the author expresses his affection, and the contents are more appropriate to a local congregation than to a lady and her family.

3 "John" is a genuine private letter written by the Elder to Gaius (I. 1), who was evidently a friend and convert of the author (v. 4), and a member of the same Christian community to which 2 "John" had been addressed.

376

Authorship

The authorship of the three Epistles is closely connected with that of the Fourth Gospel.

Relation between 1 "John" and Fourth Gospel. There is a close similarity between 1 "John" and the Fourth Gospel in thought, style, and language, which is obvious even to a superficial reader. There is hardly a thought in the Epistle which does not find its parallel in the Gospel. In both we find similar ideas concerning the Incarnation (cf. Jn. i. 14 and 1 Jn. iv. 2), union with God (cf. Jn. xv. 1 and 1 Jn. ii. 24), the love of the brethren (cf. Jn. xv. 12 and 1 Jn. iii. 23), eternal life (cf. Jn. iii. 15 and 1 Jn. ii. 25, iii. 15, v. 11, 13, 20), and Christian believers as children of God (cf. Jn. xi. 52 and 1 Jn. iii. 10, v. 2). As regards style the two writings have certain common characteristics, such as the employment of disconnected sentences, the combination of positive and negative statements, and the use of contrast, such as light and darkness, life and death, love and hate, children of God and children of the devil. In the matter of language the list of words and phrases common to both is very striking: in the Epistle no less than in the Gospel we find frequent allusions to "life", "light", and "love", and the recurrence of certain phrases, such as "to be of the truth", "of the devil", "of the world", "the only begotten Son", "knowing God", "walking in the light", and "overcoming the world".

The close similarity between the Epistle and the Fourth Gospel does not prove identity of authorship but it does point in that direction. Unfortunately the problem is further complicated by the presence of certain differences between the two documents in thought and language. The Old Testament is never cited in the Epistle and there are only two explicit allusions to the former in it (1 Jn. ii. 7–11, iii. 12). The Gospel, on the other hand, contains numerous quotations and implicit allusions to the Septuagint. Greater stress is laid in the Epistle than in the Gospel on the fact of sin, and on Christ as the propitiation for sin (cf. 1 Jn. ii. 2, iv. 10, and Jn. i. 29). In the Epistle the term "paraclete" is applied to Christ himself (1 Jn. ii. 1) not to the Spirit as in the Fourth Gospel (Jn. xiv. 16). Whereas in the Epistle the return of Christ is understood in a literal sense (1 Jn. II. 28), the Gospel either gives it a spiritual interpretation or seems hesitant on the point. In the matter of language the Epistle employs the preposition "apo" instead of "para" with words of receiving and asking, omitting entirely the "oun" of the Gospel. The former, too, never uses "men . . . de" the favourite Greek antithesis while the latter does. The vocabulary of the Epistle is smaller than that of the Gospel, as might be expected; but the Epistle has nearly forty words which do not occur in the Gospel, while over thirty words characteristic of the Gospel are absent from the Epistle.

It is suggested by some critics that the two documents are the work of two different writers who belonged to the same school of thought. But it is unlikely that two contemporary writers living in the same place would produce books which had so much in common. Moreover, the differences are not fundamental and are insufficient to outweigh the striking resemblances. On the supposition of identity of authorship, they may be accounted for by some interval of time between the two writings and by a difference in their theme and aim. We conclude, therefore, that the Epistle is probably the work of John the Elder, who is to be distinguished from the Evangelist. (See Chapter IX.)

The Relation of 2 and 3 "John" to 1 "John" and to the Fourth Gospel

A study of the phraseology and point of view of 2 and 3 "John" proves that these two Epistles were written by the same person who wrote 1 "John" and the Fourth Gospel. It therefore follows that they, too, must be the work of John the Elder. It is significant that in both of them the author styles himself "the elder" (2 Jn. I. 1; 3 Jn. I. 1).

Place of Composition

The place of composition of the three Epistles is unknown, but we may hazard a good guess. We have already shown that the first evidence of 1 "John" is to be found in the writings of Polycarp and Papias, Bishops of Hierapolis and Smyrna respectively—cities situated in the province of Asia. On the hypothesis that 2 and 3 "John" are by the same author, we may assume that these, too, emanated from the same place. Irenaeus tells us that the Fourth Gospel was written by "John, the disciple of the Lord" (whom he probably confused with John the Elder) at Ephesus. We also know that the school of thought which produced the Fourth Gospel, the Epistles of John, and the Apocalypse, had its centre at Ephesus. From the facts aforementioned, it is reasonable to assume that 1, 2, and 3 "John" belong to the province of Asia, presumably to Ephesus. This view receives further confirmation from the use of the title "Elder" to designate, not a member of a board of elders, but one of a group of teachers or "disciples of the Apostles"—a use which was apparently confined to the same province.

Date of Composition

The question of the date of the Epistles involves the question whether they were written before or after the Fourth Gospel, and this in its turn is dependent on our choice between the theory that they are the work of different authors and the more usual assumption that they are the work of the same author.

The important linguistic differences are not the use of a certain number of different nouns, verbs, and adjectives, since these necessarily vary with the subject-matter, but of prepositions and conjunctions which are used whatever the matter discussed may be. Scholars have pointed out that a different preposition is used to express "from" after verbs of receiving, etc., in the Gospel and in the Epistles, that the Gospel frequently uses the particles "men" and "de" which express anthithesis in all normal Greek while the Epistles do not, and that the Epistles hardly ever connect sentences by "therefore" where normal Greek would do so, but by "and". At first sight such differences suggest a difference in authorship. But another explanation is forthcoming. If they are both written by John the Elder, then they are the work of a bilingual person whose original language was Aramaic, but one who had spent much of his life in a region where he must have spoken Greek almost exclusively. In these circumstances he would naturally acquire a more idiomatic Greek as time went on; but a reasonable interval must be allowed. Now in all three cases it is the Gospel which has the natural Greek idiom, so it would appear that the Epistles were written some time before the Gospel. On the other hand, if the Epistles were written by a different person, he must have been one who was full of the ideas of the Gospel, and the Epistles must come later.

Have we any other evidence as regards priority in the works themselves? There are two indications which, though not conclusive, suggest a priority of the Epistles. In 1 "John" ii. 1 the Greek word "paraclete" is used of the Son in His relation between Man and the Father; in the Gospel it is used of the Holy Spirit as a medium between the Father and Man, and it becomes almost a technical term. The word was not originally technical and could well be used as it is in the Epistle before the Gospel had been written; but it is hard to believe that, after the Gospel had made it into an expression for the Holy Spirit as the means whereby the Father influences Man, anyone should use it of the Son as the means whereby Man influences the Father. The second indication is given by a difference of attitude on the Second Coming; in 1 "John" the author accepts the traditional view of Paul and the Synoptists, but in the Gospel he is beginning to hesitate and to think that Pentecost may have been the Second Coming foretold by Christ Himself. A novel view like this is likely to be the result of longer thought.

On the other side, the existence of the Docetic heresy, which affirmed that the Passion was a mere appearance or even that Christ's whole life was such, is often brought forward as evidence of a late date. But this specific form of heresy is not clearly marked as it is in the Epistles of Ignatius (c. A.D. 115); it seems to be mixed up with other Gnostic and Antinomian heresies, all of which were arising at the time when Paul wrote his Epistle to the Colossians; and Luke's insistence on the Apostles touching the risen Lord (xxiv. 39) and His eating (xxiv. 42, 43), would appear to be indications of a knowledge of Docetic views.

Tradition made John live till the reign of Trajan (A.D. 98–117), and it is quite possible that this is a true recollection of John the Elder, though it could hardly be true of John the

Apostle; but in 1 "John" 1. 1 the author claims to be an eye-witness, and had he been sixteen years of age at the time of the Crucifixion (if in A.D. 30) he would be 84 in A.D. 98 and 102 in A.D. 117, so he could not have lived far into Trajan's reign. A date of *c.* A.D. 100 for the Gospel and *c.* A.D. 80 for the Epistles is not impossible. If, however, the Epistles were written by someone other than the author of the Gospel, and later, then the latest date for the Epistles has to be fixed by relation to the Epistles of Ignatius. In the time of Ignatius episcopacy was firmly established in the province of Asia under that name and Ignatius is quite unaware that any other system had ever been known, whereas in the Johannine third Epistle, though Diotrephes may be exercising an episcopal function in excommunicating the writer's adherents, the writer never uses the term "bishop" of him, and episcopacy is at most only rudimentary. This points to a difference of at least twenty years, especially as Ignatius, who mentions Paul's connection with Ephesus, never refers to John. A date of *c.* A.D. 95–100 for the Epistles would therefore push the Gospel earlier—to *c.* A.D. 90–95 at least—but there is nothing impossible in this as the only limiting earliest date to the Gospel is that it must be later than Luke. It may be noted that the Judaizing movement within the Church is not mentioned in these Epistles; but, as the only possible reference to such tendencies in "The Revelation" concerns Philadelphia (Rev. III. 9), this helps us little as regards date.

Purpose and Contents of 1 "John"

Purpose. The author's purpose in writing the Epistle was to warn his readers against certain false teachers, who were Docetists in doctrine and Antinomians in practice, and to build them up in the Christian faith. These false teachers refused to recognize the reality of the Incarnation (II. 22), since, in their opinion, a righteous God could have no communion with sinful man. They maintained that Christ only appeared to take a human body (cf. IV. 2). The "aeon" (that is, the celestial being, Christ) descended upon Jesus at His baptism and left Him before His crucifixion. Salvation depended upon knowledge

381

(gnosis) of divine mysteries. This doctrine tended to produce Antinomianism, for the initiated, who claimed to possess this supernatural knowledge, believed that they were under no obligation to obey the moral law, and that they could not sin. They therefore denied the need of forgiveness (i. 8-10), and felt no need of fellowship and brotherly love (ii. 9-11, iv. 20-21). Antinomianism was the direct result of Paul's doctrine of justification by faith, from which some drew the conclusion that since salvation was conditioned by faith in Christ alone, they were exempt from the moral law.

The author exhorts them to cleave to the Gospel, and in opposition to the "false knowledge" of the heretics, sets before them the "true knowledge" which is eternal life (cf. v. 18-20). Against their false doctrines he proclaims the love of God, the reality of the Incarnation, the great fact of sin, the work of Christ in the redemption of mankind, the possibility of union with God through Christ, and the necessity of brotherly love.

Contents

The Epistle is difficult to analyse, but it may be divided roughly into the following sections:

(1) Introduction. Eternal life made manifest in Jesus (i. 1-4).
(2) Fellowship with God who is Light (i. 5-ii. 28).
(3) Fellowship with God who is Righteousness (ii. 29-iv. 6).
(4) Fellowship with God who is Love (iv. 7-v. 12).
(5) The assurance of eternal life through the Son (v. 13-21).

(1) The author's theme is the manifestation of eternal life in the Incarnation, which the Apostles, by their association with Jesus, were qualified to declare, and his aim is to bring the faithful into fellowship with the Father and the Son (i. 1-4).
(2) God is light. Fellowship with God must therefore show itself in moral goodness. Those who have fellowship with God have fellowship with one another, and are cleansed from their sins through the atoning death of Christ (i. 5-7). The denial of the existence of sin is a denial of the truth.

Sinners have an Advocate with the Father in Jesus Christ, who is the propitiation for the sins of the whole world (I. 8–II. 2).

Knowledge of God reveals itself in obedience to His commandments. Union with God involves conformity to His character as revealed in Christ (II. 3–6).

Those who profess to be in the light and disobey the law of brotherly love are still in darkness. Christians, however, must not love the "world", which is doomed to destruction. Those who love God and obey his will continue for ever (II. 7–17).

The appearance of many Antichrists is a sign of the approaching end of the world. He who denies the Father and the Son is Antichrist. But those who remain loyal to the Gospel will be able to face the final Judgment with confidence (II. 18–28).

(3) God is righteous, and all who lead righteous lives are His children and will purify themselves, as He is pure (II. 29–III. 3).

There is a marked contrast between righteousness and sin. Christ came to abolish sin; the child of God, by virtue of the divine life within him cannot sin (III. 4–10).

Christ bids us love one another. Hatred is murder and no murderer has eternal life in him. Love for man is a sign that we already have eternal life (III. 11–15).

We know what love is from Christ's action in laying down His life for us. It is our duty to imitate His sacrifice: we must love not only in word, but in deed and truth. If our conscience is clear on this matter, we may address God in confidence and our prayers will be answered (III. 16–24).

All spiritual phenomena cannot be regarded as the work of the Spirit. The test by which the Spirit may be recognized lies in the confession of Christ as the Son of God. The children of God can discriminate between true and false teaching (IV. 1–6).

(4) Love is of divine origin and those who love are children of God. God is love. His love is manifested in the coming of Christ to be the propitiation for our sins (IV. 7–10).

To love one another is to live in union with God. Love is complete when it does not fear the Judgment, because we are living as He lives. There is no fear in love (IV. 11–18).

Everyone who believes that Jesus is the Christ is a child of

God, for he who believes that Jesus is the Son of God conquers the world. This faith rests on the threefold witness of His baptism, His death, and the Spirit. The witness is that God has given us eternal life in His Son (IV. 19–V. 12).

(5) The Christian's assurance of eternal life means that God answers prayer, especially prayer for a fellow Christian who has committed a venial and not a mortal sin (V. 13–17).

Christians can be certain that the children of God are preserved from sin, that the world is in the power of the devil, and that through the Incarnate Son they know God and live in union with Him. This is the real God and eternal life. All meaner conceptions of God must be rejected (V. 18–21).

Purpose and Contents of 2 "John"

Purpose. The purpose of the Epistle was to warn the members of the church, to which the author was writing, against certain false teachers who were planning to visit them. The heresies, which these false teachers were propagating, were similar to those in 1 "John", involving Docetism and Antinomianism.

Contents. The Elder sends greetings to "the elect lady and her children" (a Christian community), and expresses his pleasure in the knowledge that some members are living the true life (vv. 1–4).

He beseeches them to obey the law of love, given in the beginning by Christ (vv. 5–7).

He warns them against certain "deceivers", who deny that "Jesus Christ cometh in the flesh", exhorts them to remain true to the orthodox doctrine of Christ, and enjoins them not to extend hospitality to anyone who teaches a different doctrine (vv. 8–11).

After expressing his hope of visiting them, the Elder closes with greetings from members of his own church (vv. 12–13).

Purpose and Content of 3 "John"

Purpose. The author's purpose in writing the Epistle was to commend Gaius for the hospitality which he had shown towards certain travelling missionaries who had recently visited his church, and to exhort him to receive such visitors and to set them on their journey in a manner worthy of his fellowship with God (v. 6). At the same time he urged him not to imitate the example of a fellow church member, Diotrephes, an ambitious leader who defied his authority, "prating against us with wicked words" (v. 10), and who not only refused to receive travelling missionaries, but drove out of the Church those who did.

Contents. The Elder sends greetings to Gaius, praying that he may enjoy prosperity and health commensurate with his spiritual well-being, and expressing his delight at the witness borne to his fidelity to the truth by certain brethren (vv. 1–4).

Gaius has given proof of his fidelity by offering hospitality to these brethren. They have set out again on a missionary journey in the cause of Christ, making no provision for their journey, and refusing to accept help from the pagan Gentiles. Gaius is asked to forward them on their way, in a manner worthy of a true Christian (vv. 5–8).

The Elder has written to the church, but Diotrephes, an ambitious leader, repudiates him, refuses to welcome the brethren, and excommunicates the party favourable to them. Gaius should not imitate his example (vv. 7–11).

After commending Demetrius (perhaps the bearer of the letter) the Elder expresses his hope of visiting Gaius, and closes with greetings from friends in his own church (vv. 12–14).

Historical Value

The Epistles of John are important as showing the way in which the doctrine and organization of the Church were developing at the time they were written. Many Christians, deeply influenced by Hellenistic philosophy and religion, were propagating doctrines which struck at the very heart of the Gospel. Had they been generally accepted, it would have meant the separation of the historical Jesus from the exalted Christ, of religion from morality and of faith from works, while Christianity would have degenerated into a mere speculative philosophy, practically devoid of any religious or ethical content, and lacking any dynamic power. The writer of the Epistles took up the challenge, denouncing the heretical teachers, who denied the reality of the Incarnation, as liars (1 Jn. II. 22) and proclaiming the validity of the Gospel as taught by Jesus (1 Jn. II. 7; 2 Jn. 4–6, 9). His Epistles, by their emphasis on the love of God and on the Incarnation, proved a powerful weapon in the struggle of the Church against heresy—a struggle which eventually resulted in the victory of the orthodox faith.

In the sphere of organization we see the Church at a stage in her history when she is in process of transition from the primitive apostolic ministry, in which the local churches of a district, each with its own board of elders, are under the general supervision of an Apostle (or a disciple of an Apostle, as in 2 and 3 John) to the episcopal system in which each local church is under a monarchical bishop, who is independent of any central authority. There is no definite evidence that Diotrephes (3 Jn. 9–11) is a monarchical bishop, as Harnack and other critics suggest, but there is no doubt that he is the leader of a party in the church which resents outside interference. He speaks disrespectfully of the Elder, refuses to receive his itinerant missionaries, and drives out those who offer them hospitality (3 Jn. 10). On this point Professor Dodd says, "Whether the church to which Diotrephes belonged already possessed a fully episcopal constitution, we cannot say. The churches of this region are represented in the 'Acts of the Apostles' and the Pastoral Epistles as governed by a board of presbyters who might also be called bishops (Acts xx. 17, 28; Tit. I. 5–9). In the Ignatian Epistles (about A.D. 115) they are governed by bishops, assisted by a board of presbyters. At what stage this church stood at this moment, we do not know. All we can say is that Diotrephes acted in the capacity of a bishop, as understood from the second century onwards. But what was his actual position? There seems to be three possibilities: either (1) he was the acknowledged bishop of the church, pursuing a policy hostile to the Presbyter; or (2) he was one of the board of presbyters who by force of character, or by successful demogogy, overrode his colleagues; or (3) he was a layman, who had usurped quasi-episcopal functions. The Presbyter regards him as nothing but an ambitious demagogue. From this point of view at least, Diotrephes was no bishop. In any case, however, he must have secured the support of a majority of the congregation; also we should have been told, not that he excommunicated people from the church, but that he separated from the church with his followers (like the false teachers of 1 John)."[1]

The Epistles, too, have a permanent significance, for to every age they proclaim the message of the love of God manifested in Jesus, which to him who believes is eternal life.

[1] Dodd, *The Johannine Epistles*, 1945, pp. 162–3.

CHAPTER XXVI

THE EPISTLE OF JUDE

Canonicity

The Epistle was little known in the West until the beginning of the third century. It is included in the Muratorian Fragment and is quoted by Clement of Alexandria, Tertullian, and Origen, but not by Irenaeus. Its use by earlier patristic writers is a matter of dispute, but there are possibly traces of it in Polycarp and the "Didache". Eusebius places it among the disputed books, while in the time of Jerome many rejected it. It was finally admitted to the Canon by the Council of Carthage in A.D. 397. The silence of the early patristic writers regarding the Epistle may be accounted for by its brevity and comparative unimportance, while its references to Jewish apocalyptic literature would explain its rejection in some quarters in the third and fourth centuries.

Authorship and Date of Composition

The author of the Epistle and its date of composition are uncertain. The author describes himself as Judas "a servant of Jesus Christ, and brother of James"; and this would seem to imply that the James to whom he was related was a person of some importance in the Church. It was natural, therefore, that the early interpreters should identify him either with the brother of the Lord, mentioned in "Mark" vi. 3 or with the Apostle, called "Judas of James", mentioned in "Luke" vi. 16 and "Acts" i. 13. The view that the author was one of the original Twelve can be dismissed at once on the ground that: (1) he makes no claim to be an Apostle; indeed, he distinguishes himself from the Apostles; and (2) the natural meaning of the phrase "Judas of James" is not "brother of James" but "son of James". Of Judas, the brother of the Lord we know nothing except in connection with a story (told by Hegesippus and quoted by Eusebius) of his grandsons, who were brought before the Emperor Domitian (A.D. 81–96) as descendants of David and possible claimants to the throne. At the time of the interview which, it would appear, took place early in the principate of Domitian, Judas was dead. On the hypothesis that Judas was the author of the Epistle, it was probably written before A.D. 85; and since there are reminiscences in it of Paul's Epistles, it could hardly have been written until after the Apostle's death in A.D. 64. Accepting this hypothesis, we should have to fix the date of its composition within the period A.D. 64–85.

There are indications in the Epistle, however, which suggest that the author was not the brother of the Lord. If he were the author, it is difficult to understand why he should have styled himself "a servant" of Jesus Christ and not a "brother". The explanation that he was silent from motives of reverence or that he thought it a greater honour to be considered a "servant" of Christ rather than a "brother", carries little weight. The author's exhortation to his readers, "to contend earnestly for the faith which was once for all delivered unto the saints" (v. 3), suggests that at the time of writing Christianity was already old and well-established, and that he did not regard himself as belonging to the first generation of Christians. The Apostolic Age lay in the past, for he urged his readers to recall how the Apostles had foretold the coming of mockers who should walk "after their own ungodly lusts" (v. 18). The Gnostic tendencies, vaguely described in the Epistle, bear a close resemblance to those found in "The Pastoral Epistles", and the writings of Ignatius, which belong to the close of the first century or the beginning of the second. On the internal evidence, therefore, it is reasonable to assume that Jude the Lord's brother was not the author of the Epistle. At the same time it is not necessary to suppose that the Epistle was a pseudonymous work. The two names, Jude and James, were quite common in those days, and it is highly probable that the Epistle was written by an unknown person, named Jude, who had a brother, James. In fact, it is all the more likely on the assumption that James, the brother of the Lord, and head of the church of Jerusalem, was not the author of the Epistle which bears his name. Rejecting the traditional view of the authorship of the Epistle, we conclude that it was probably written towards the close of the first century or in the early years of the second. A suggestion has been put out that the words "brother of James" were a marginal note which got incorporated in the text, and another that it originally read "Judas of James" that is, "son of James", to which "brother" was added, and the phrase was then put after the words "servant of Jesus Christ". Streeter believes that he had even identified this "Judas of James" as the third bishop of Jerusalem according to one list.[1] At least the date would be suitable.

Destination and Purpose

Destination. The Epistle is addressed "to them that are called, beloved in God the Father, and kept for Jesus Christ". Since there is no mention of a particular church or locality, it was probably addressed to the Church at large.

Purpose. The author's main purpose in writing the Epistle was to denounce certain false teachers who had crept into the Church and to warn its members against them. It would appear that these false teachers claimed to be in possession of a secret knowledge (v. 16), denied the Lordship of Christ (v. 4), defied Authority (v. 8), railed at angelic beings (v. 8), and propagated the Antinomian doctrine that the truly spiritual man was free from the moral law (v. 4). It was their immoral practices especially which roused the author's indignation; for he recognized that if allowed to continue unchecked, they would undermine the foundations of the Christian faith. In his anxiety for the moral and spiritual welfare of the Church, he gave up the idea of writing on "our common salvation" to launch an attack upon those who were turning the grace of God into lasciviousness (v. 4). Unlike Paul, however, he made no attempt to contravert the pernicious doctrines of these false teachers, but contented himself with scathing denunciation and warnings of their impending destruction. In his view safety lay in strict adherence to the Christian faith, as taught by the Apostles (v. 3), and in the reclamation of the false teachers themselves.

[1] Streeter, *The Primitive Church*, 1929, pp. 178–80.

Contents

The author greets his readers, praying that mercy, peace, and love, may be abundantly granted to them (vv. 1–2).

He urges them to defend the Christian faith against the ungodly persons, who are making the grace of God a plea for their immorality and are denying Christ (vv. 3–4).

Their doom has been long predicted, and is as certain as that which overtook the Israelites in the wilderness, the fallen angels, and the cities of Sodom and Gomorrah (vv. 5–7).

Despite the warnings of history these dreamers continue in their wickedness, defying Authority, and railing at the Angelic Orders. Their conduct is different from that of the Archangel Michael, who, when he was contending with the devil for the body of Moses, did not pronounce judgment against his adversary but committed his cause to God. They scoff at anything they do not understand, stain the Christian love-feasts by their presence, and care for none but themselves (vv. 8–13).

Enoch prophesied of the divine judgment which would overtake them, and the Apostles foretold that such persons would rise in the last days (vv. 14–19).

The author exhorts his readers to steadfastness and prayer and to efforts for the salvation of the backsliders, and concludes with an ascription of praise to God, who alone can keep them from falling (vv. 20–25).

Historical Value

This short Epistle is important for the light it sheds on the state of Christianity towards the close of the New Testament period, revealing that at that time heresy was becoming a menace and a challenge to the Church. The author's use of the "Book of Enoch" and "The Assumption of Moses" as inspired Scripture (vv. 6, 9, 14, 15) also shows that Jewish apocalyptic literature was popular among Christians about the close of the first century. As an inspired utterance the Epistle cannot be compared with any of Paul's Epistles or with "Hebrews", and has little abiding spiritual significance. But if it had no historical or inspirational value, its preservation in the Bible would be worth while, for it contains what is perhaps the noblest

Doxology in Christian literature. "Now unto him that is able to guard you from stumbling, and to set you before the presence of his glory without blemish in exceeding joy, to the only God our Saviour, through Jesus Christ our Lord, be glory, majesty, dominion and power, before all time, and now, and for evermore. Amen."

CHAPTER XXVII

THE SECOND EPISTLE OF PETER

Authorship and Date

External Evidence. There are possible traces of the Epistle in the latter half of the second century, but the first undeniable reference to it comes at the beginning of the third century, from Origen, who doubts whether it is a genuine work of Peter. Eusebius says, "As for that which is said to be the Second Epistle we have not received a tradition that it is canonical, but nevertheless, as it has appeared useful to many, it is studied with the rest of the Scriptures"; he himself does not accept it. It was finally admitted to the Canon at the Council of Carthage in A.D. 397, "partly on its religious and ethical merits, partly, we may surmise, because it seemed fitting that Peter, as well as Paul and John, should be represented by a plurality of Epistles".[1]

Internal Evidence. Its artificial and somewhat obscure style, with its conscious striving after effect, renders it unlikely to be a work of Peter, but as this might be due to a secretary, other grounds for rejection must be considered.

1. The standpoint is that of a period later than the Apostolic Age. Paul's Epistles are treated as "Scripture" (III. 15–16), a term applied in the Apostolic Age only to the Old Testament. The words, "For, from the day that the fathers fell asleep, all things continue as they were from the beginning of the creation" (III. 4), would seem to imply that the original Apostles and Evangelists were dead when the Epistle was written.

2. Almost all the "Epistle of Jude" is incorporated in Chapter II. 2–17. It is unlikely that the author should make up a whole letter by taking a section out of 2 "Peter"; whereas the author of 2 "Peter" might easily take the short "Epistle of Jude" and make it a third of his own work. Further, 2 "Peter" II. 11–12

---

[1] Streeter, *The Primitive Church*, 1929, p. 391.

is obscure till we turn to "Jude" 8–9, and find that it refers to a story in "The Assumption of Moses", an apocryphal Jewish book.

3. The passages in which the writer, claiming to be Peter, refers to two Gospel incidents in which Peter figures, imply by their wording that the readers were familiar with those incidents, and, as neither is likely to have been part of the "Kerygma" preached orally to the Gentiles, this means familiarity with the Gospels. In the reference to the Transfiguration we have "the holy mount" (1. 18); and the prophecy of the manner of Peter's death (Jn. xxi. 18–19), mentioned in 2 "Peter" 1. 14, would require some explanation to readers who were not familiar with the Fourth Gospel. The second of these two instances pushes the date at which 2 "Peter" was written beyond the end of the first century, when the Fourth Gospel was written, to some date in the second century when it was generally known.

We therefore conclude that the Epistle is the work of a pseudonymous author, who wrote under Peter's name in order to claim apostolic authority for his views.

Destination

It is intended for Gentile readers (1. 1, "those who have been allotted a faith of equal privilege with ours"), and, according to Chapter iii. 1, the same readers as those of 1 "Peter"; but in reality it is a treatise of a general character with no local reference which can be detected.

Purpose

The analysis of the contents will show that it had two main purposes: (1) to counteract Antinomian teaching—most of this part of the Epistle is taken from "Jude"; and (2) to strengthen the faith of Christians in the second Advent and make them live accordingly.

Contents

The author sends greetings to his readers who have been admitted to the full privileges of the Christian faith (1. 1–3).

God has bestowed upon them exceeding great and precious promises in order that they may become sharers in the divine nature. They must exhibit a noble character, cultivating knowledge, self-control, endurance, godliness, and love (I. 4–11).

As regards the power and the Coming of the Lord, the author himself had been an eyewitness of the Transfiguration, and had heard the divine voice confirming prophecy to which they must pay heed, remembering that no prophecy is a matter of private interpretation, but is given to men by the Holy Spirit (I. 12–21).

False teachers will appear who will deny the Lord and cause apostasy in the Church, but they will bring destruction upon themselves. The punishment of the wicked angels, the destruction of the ancient world by water, and of Sodom and Gomorrah by fire, are a pledge and proof of the final Judgment. Audacious and self-willed, the false teachers do not fear to speak evil of the angelic Orders. They have no shame, rolling in luxury in broad daylight, revelling as they feast with Christians, and using sensual pleasures to delude people who are just escaping from those who live in error. They promise freedom but they are themselves the slaves of corruption (II.).

It had been foretold that a sign of the last days would be the rejection by some persons of the belief in the Coming of the Lord (III. 1–7).

Judgment may be delayed, but it is only a sign of the long-suffering of God, who does not desire that anyone should perish but that all should repent. Time is not reckoned by God as it is by man (III. 8–9).

In spite of all denial the "day of the Lord" will come unexpectedly, when the present universe will be destroyed, to be followed by a new world in which righteousness dwells. That day may be hastened by holy living: it behoves them, therefore, in view of the approaching end, to consider what manner of lives they ought to live (III. 10–14).

Paul held similar views on the Coming of the Lord and on the final Judgment (III. 15–16).

Finally, the author warns his readers against the errors of

the false teachers, exhorts them to remain steadfast in the faith and to grow in the grace and knowledge of Jesus Christ, and closes with a brief doxology (III. 17–18).

Historical Value

This is chiefly concerned with the evidence it throws on the two subjects of Antinomian teaching and the Second Coming; but, as we do not know where it was written, nor when (within limits from A.D. 110 to 150), this is not considerable.

Antinomian teaching in Asia Minor appears first in "Colossians" and "Ephesians". It figures in the letters to the seven churches in "The Revelation", probably in the principate of Vespasian; and there seems to be an undercurrent of anxiety on the subject in the Johannine Epistles at the end of the first century. The Pastoral Epistles, too, seem to have Asia primarily in mind. As there is no evidence to whom "Jude" is primarily addressed, we have little indication how far other areas were affected.

With regard to belief in the Second Coming, many books in the New Testament give us evidence. Roughly, the expectation of the immediacy of that event increased in times of persecution and diminished in more peaceful times; but it varied with the mental constitution of authors. In Paul's Epistles it diminishes from 1 and 2 "Thessalonians" onwards. Pre-Neronian Apocalyptic is represented by "Mark" XIII., but it is clear that there was already a feeling of surprise at the delay when Mark arose, since he finds it necessary to give an explanation that the delay is to enable the Gospel to be preached to the Gentiles (XIII. 10). Mark's Gospel represents the attitude at the time of the Neronian persecution. The siege and fall of Jerusalem probably increased the expectation (Matthew's Gospel lays more stress on the Second Coming than any). Then came a diminution; but Domitian's persecution probably increased it. The Fourth Gospel is Anti-apocalyptic and almost identified the Second Coming with the gift of the Holy Spirit. In 2 "Peter" we find a doctrine which marks a landmark on the way to the permanent attitude on the subject in the Christian world, namely, that, as with God a thousand years are as one day, the event may be a long way off; but he believes that a conviction of its possibility at any moment is essential to right living. The permanent attitude, which was soon to take its place, is that the event is certain but probably in the far distant future. Another feature in his attitude to the Second Coming is his adoption of the Stoic idea that the world would be destroyed by fire, which appears nowhere in the Gospels or in "The Revelation", but has become an integral part of subsequent Christian belief. It is noteworthy as an attempt to harmonize religion and science, as then understood; and it is curious that, on this particular subject, little disturbance to traditional belief has been caused in modern times, because science is emphatic that life on the earth is not permanent but is uncertain whether it will end by being frozen out or suddenly extinguished by a conflagration due to a collision. It is certain that a recognition of the impermanence of life as we know it is a powerful factor in the belief in something permanent outside the material universe, though we have discarded the fantastic imagery of the Apocalypses.

PART VIII

THE REVELATION

CHAPTER XXVIII

THE REVELATION

Introduction

Of all the books included in the New Testament, "The Revelation" has been always considered to be the most difficult to understand. Even now, after scholars have ceased to accept it as having any reference to our own day or even as containing a detailed programme of future events, and have devoted their attention to finding its meaning for the author's contemporaries and how he came to hold the beliefs which he expresses in it, though comprehension is now far easier and agreement in broad outline is more assured, yet it is possible to see that all difficulties have not been removed from the differences among commentators on many points, from the attempts to simplify by re-arranging many of the later sections in a different order, and from the numerous allegations of inconsistency between statements made in different visions.

Conditions under which Written

Before considering this book two preliminary studies are necessary, namely, those of the generally accepted eschatological views of the early Church, and of the position of prophets in it.

(1) *Eschatological Views.* The early Christians had inherited certain ideas from the Jews, but had had to make one radical alteration in them because Jesus, whom they accepted as Messiah, was not in the least like the Messiah expected by the Jews, and His Death and Resurrection were at first astonishing to them, though they soon found passages in the Old Testament prophets which appeared to refer to them. But they left the rest of the Jewish ideas unaltered, except that they interpreted Israel as meaning themselves, not Israel "according to the flesh". The Jewish views of the time, so far as they included a period of bitter persecution of "Israel", the coming (that is, in Christian thought, the Second Coming) of the Messiah, the

26

Resurrection, Judgment, and permanent allotment of bliss in heaven to the righteous, and punishment in Gehenna to the ungodly, were taken over by all, together usually with the idea of a personal Antichrist leading the persecution, which was accepted by the Synoptists, and, at one time at least, by Paul, but with more doubt by the author of the Fourth Gospel. The early Christians believed that Jesus Himself had taught these views, though this is very doubtful. He certainly taught that His earthly ministry had been predicted, that He was establishing the Kingdom of Heaven on earth and that it would be consummated in heaven, that His followers would be persecuted, and that in the world to come the good would inherit bliss and the wicked punishment. But Q represents in its purest form the teaching of Our Lord, and the Q account, preserved in "Luke" xvii. 20–37, seems to set aside the spectacular elements in Jewish Apocalyptic by its emphatic opening that "The kingdom of God cometh not with observation". Undoubtedly He foretold the destruction of the Temple—this was part of the evidence on which He was convicted—and the substitution of a temple not made with hands, and probably, therefore, of the Jewish state and Jerusalem, to make way for the new dispensation; but the Kingdom itself would not come apocalyptically. But, to understand "The Revelation", it is not what Our Lord really taught but what contemporary Christians thought He had taught that matters: and they thought that He must have taught what they believed they found in the Old Testament prophets. Many went further and accepted the later apocalyptic books which were not included in the Old Testament; thus the "Book of Enoch" is accepted in 1 "Peter", "Jude", and 2 "Peter".

(2) *Prophets in the Early Church.* The Jews believed that prophecy ceased with Malachi, and new apocalyptic books gained acceptance only by pretending to be written by older persons, such as Enoch, Solomon, and Ezra. But Christians believed that prophecy had been renewed in the Christian Church, or rather with John the Baptist. They form what may almost be called a regular church order but for the fact that the holder of some other office might also be a prophet, as was

Paul, as we see in the account of the church at Antioch (Acts xiii. 1). In 1 "Corinthians" xii. 28, prophets are placed next after apostles. They remained important till the end of the century, as is shown in the directions in 1 "John" iv. 1-3, to test the spirits; and existed in the second century, since it is provided in the Didache that a prophet, if present, shall substitute an extempore Eucharistic thanksgiving for the liturgical form used by presbyters.

Relation to Preceding Writers

In the light of these conditions we have to consider the relation of the writer to the Old Testament prophets and previous apocalyptic works, as on this turns the whole conception of the character of the book.

Modern readers, whose acquaintance with the prophets is in most cases limited to a few well-known passages, will fail to realize on a first reading of "The Revelation" that from Chapter iv. onwards every scene and often most of the language are derived from Old Testament sources. Yet it claims to be a series of visions experienced by the writer himself. Thus it is possible to maintain either of two views or some compromise between them. The first view is that the visions are merely stage machinery used by apocalyptic writers, and that the book is really a systematic gathering together of older prophecies, in which the author wholeheartedly believed, into a scheme of events which he imagined, as a result of his studies and not of visions at all, would take place within the lifetime of many of his readers. The argument in favour of this view is based on the systematic arrangement of the book into three series of seven woes, each followed by a compensating picture of the blessedness of the saints.

A preliminary view of heaven (iv., v.).
The woes of the seven seals (vi.).
The bliss of the redeemed (vii.).
The woes of the seven trumpets (viii.–xiii.).
Another account of the bliss of the redeemed (xiv., xv. 1-4).
The woes of the seven bowls and the final collapse (xv. 5-xx.).
The final blessedness (xxi., xxii.).

Further arguments for the view are the difficulty of visualizing some of the things said to have been seen in visions, the obvious pains taken to harmonize in one scheme apparently conflicting accounts given in the prophets, and the subordination of everything to the central purpose of encouraging and exhorting the faithful under an impending persecution.

The second and opposite view never goes so far as to hold that the book is nothing but a recital of visions exactly as they were experienced. But it holds that the visions were real, though they were worked up into a telling literary form later. Exponents of this view can hardly in the nature of things prove their case, but they can remove objections and show that it accords with the use of "prophecy" in the early Church. Paul had visions of heaven (2 Cor. xii. 1–4), and Ignatius believed he had received instructions from the Spirit. Hermas is obviously genuine, though his visions are humdrum and dull. So the writer was not extraordinary in seeing visions. Further, we know much more about the psychology of dreams than was known fifty years ago. We know that the dreamer's beliefs can be turned into visual and symbolic form, that what has been gained from reading can be reproduced, and that a considerable sequence of happenings can be experienced in a dream. In fact the dream represents, often in a more connected form, what was in the dreamer's mind already. A man whose knowledge of Old Testament prophecy and of Apocalyptic was as great as the writer's and whose interest was as intense would, if he saw visions, see the kind of visions recorded in "The Revelation". Before coming to any conclusion between these opposing views we must examine the contents of the book in more detail.

The First Three Chapters

The first three chapters differ from the rest of the book and may be disposed of quickly.

After a preliminary vision of the glorified Christ (i.) they consist of letters to the "seven churches" of the province of Asia, that is, the western part of Asia Minor, containing praise and rebuke. (1) Ephesus is praised for past zeal but warned of a decline (II. 1–7); (2) Smyrna is praised for its opposition to certain pseudo-Jews and encouraged to face a coming persecution (II. 8–11); (3) Pergamum, the "seat of Satan", has bravely endured persecution but tolerates the Nicolaitans (II. 12–17); (4) Thyatira is commended generally, except for the immoral teaching of a certain prophetess (II. 18–29); (5) the zeal of Sardis is almost extinguished (III. 1–6); (6) Philadelphia is commended and encouraged in persecution (III. 7–13), and (7) Laodicea is rebuked as "neither hot nor cold" (III. 14–22).

The only point of difficulty is the meaning of the "angels" of these churches, to whom these letters are addressed. One view maintains that the guardian angels of the churches—nations in Jewish belief are under the guardianship of such angels—are so identified with the churches that the merits and faults of the churches are credited to their angels. Others think it impossible that angels—guardian angels are good angels—would ever be represented even in allegory as suffering from human imperfection, and see in the angels the heads of the churches who would later have been called bishops. As a matter of dating there is nothing impossible in this, for Episcopacy was probably first established in the province of Asia and seems to have been in existence at the close of the century, ten to twenty years later.

Abstract of the Rest of the Book

Readers are advised to look up the Old Testament references if they wish to appreciate the extent of the borrowing; it would take up too much space to print them here. As a rule references are given only when the substance is taken from the Old Testament; use of biblical phrases is enormous, for instance in the various hymns.

Introductory. A vision of God being worshipped in heaven (IV., V.). This is a combination of the visions by which Ezekiel and Isaiah were called to the prophetic office (Ezek. I., Is. VI.), and fulfils the same role towards John; but it also uses "Zechariah" (IV. 1–3). The throne and the four living creatures are from the passage in Ezekiel, the six wings and "Holy, holy, holy" from Isaiah, and the seven lamps from Zechariah. The

four-and-twenty elders are not from the Old Testament, but
are supposed to be the Babylonian star-gods, and possibly come
from a lost Jewish apocalypse.

In God's hand is a book which none could open till the Lamb
appeared to break the seals; He is received with a hymn of
praise. The book is from "Ezekiel" (II. 9–10); the Lamb is the
ordinary symbol for Jesus Christ; the title "lion of the tribe of
Judah" is from "Genesis" XLIX. 9–10 and "the root of David"
from "Isaiah" XI. 1, 10; the seven eyes come from "Zechariah"
IV. 10. The seven horns are not from the Old Testament, but
are parallel to the ten horns of the Beast, Christ's antagonist.

(1) The breaking of the Seven Seals (VI.). In "Daniel" XII.
9, the prophet is told that his words will be sealed up till the
time of the end (doubtless this was inserted to explain to the
Maccabaean readers why a book purporting to be written by
Daniel had been unheard of till then). The writer of "The
Revelation" naturally assumes that it is meant, not that the
book was unknown but that its meaning was unknown, and he
generalizes this to cover all ancient prophecy about the last
things. His task is to be to receive the meaning. Hence the
unsealing. But the first of the series of seven revelations is,
compared with its two successors, short and conventional. The
first four seals reveal four different coloured horses, representing war, civil disturbance, famine, and pestilence, the fifth the
souls of the martyrs under the altar (that is, under God's protection), the sixth the general cataclysm which precedes the
end, while the seventh, which should give us the end itself, is
deferred. The four horses are from "Zechariah" VI. 1–8; the
bow is to symbolize the Parthians; the rationing of good by
weight comes from "Ezekiel" IV. 8–10; four plagues come in
"Ezekiel" XIV. 13–21. The question "How long?" which is the
point of the sight of the martyrs is from "Zechariah" I. 12.
The sixth seal combines "Joel" II. 21 (sun and moon), "Isaiah"
XXXIV. 4 (heavens rolled together as a scroll and the host falling
as figs), "Isaiah" II. 19–21 (hiding in clefts) and "Hosea" X. 8
(calling on mountains to fall on them).

The alternation from the plagues of the wicked to the happiness of the faithful occupies Chapter VII., which recounts the

sealing of the 144,000 and their bliss in heaven. The sealing comes from "Ezekiel" IX. 14. The hymn is largely made up of Old Testament phraseology.

(2) The seventh seal is then broken, but, instead of the end we have a fresh series of seven terrors, each proclaimed by the blowing of a trumpet (VIII.–XIII.). The first six are given in somewhat greater detail than the woes of the seals; then we get great detail when the seventh trumpet sounds. The first plague, a shower of hail and fire, the second, a fiery mountain mass, the third, a star called wormwood, and the fourth, an eclipse, destroy one-third of the land, sea, springs, and light; the fifth, blast looses locusts with the stings of scorpions, and the sixth, 200,000,000 horsemen from beyond the Euphrates (VIII., IX.).

The hail, the turning of the water into blood, and the locusts are of course suggested by the plagues of Egypt, with additional terrors added to them. Wormwood is from "Jeremiah" IX. 15, and effects on sun and moon are from the passage of "Joel" already mentioned. The locusts are amplified from "Joel" I. 6–7 and II. 4–5. Prophecies of Assyrian and Babylonian invasions are numerous; but the idea that Rome would succumb to a Parthian invasion is a favourite one with the author.

Before the seventh trumpet, as previously before the breaking of the seventh seal, there is a pause: the prophet hears seven thunders, but is forbidden to write what they say. He then has to eat a scroll, sweet to the taste but bitter in digestion (X.). The sealing of the prophecies is from "Daniel" XII. 4, 9, the oath from XII. 5, and "no delay" corresponds to Daniel's three times and a half, a conventional expression for a very short period; but no satisfactory reason has been given for the appearance of the passage here. The swallowing of the roll is from "Ezekiel" II. 8–10.

From this point onwards there is somewhat of a change in the character of the prophecies; instead of being terrors which by themselves need not be associated with the end, they become a consecutive series of events leading up to the destruction of the evil powers, the victory of righteousness, and the Judgment. The prophet is told to measure the temple but not the outer court which is given to the Gentiles (XI. 1–2). There is a very detailed measurement of the temple in "Ezekiel" XL.–XLII. and a short mention in "Zechariah" II. 1, 2; the idea here is protection. The forty-two months (time, times and half a time, or 3½ years) are from "Daniel" VI. 25 and XII. 7. Next we see two witnesses, who are killed but return to life and are taken to heaven (XI. 3–13). The two witnesses come from "Zechariah" IV. (described as olive trees in vv. 3, 11, which are interpreted as two anointed ones in v. 14; there is only one lamp in "Zechariah"). In "Zechariah" they presumably represent Zerubbabel as king and Jeshua the high priest; but the author of "The Revelation" interprets them as Elijah and Moses, as they have power to prevent rain and to turn water into blood, and many Jews believed that not only would Elijah appear before the day of the Lord (Mal. IV. 5), but also Moses. There is no Old Testament suggestion of their death and resurrection; but Herod's suspicion that John the Baptist had risen from the dead shows how consistent it was with Jewish belief and it may have appeared in some unknown apocalypse. Their ascension into heaven after their death, of course, was suggested by the original ascension of Elijah in 2 "Kings" II. 12 and of Moses in the apocryphal "Assumption of Moses". The statement that their bodies lay in Jerusalem ("the great city, which spiritually is called Sodom and Egypt [cf. Isaiah I. 8–10] where also their Lord was crucified"), not in "Babylon" will be considered later.

The seventh trumpet at last sounds (XI. 15–19) and there appears a woman in heaven who bears a child, against whom the Dragon fights; but he is cast down from heaven by Michael and his angels, whereupon he wages war against the rest of her offspring on earth (XII.) and is helped by two wild beasts. The first, with ten horns and seven heads, one of which is wounded but cured, is allowed forty-two months to persecute the saints: he is aided by the second; he is identified by a cipher, 666 (XIII.).

The scene in heaven is believed to be based on a pagan myth of Isis the mother, Horus the child, and Typhon the dragon, or in its Greek form of Leto the mother, Apollo the child, and Python the dragon, which expressed no more than the change of seasons as the sun passes through the signs of the zodiac; but it has certainly changed in "The Revelation', where the dragon is clearly the devil and the child is Christ. The woman is obviously the counterpart on the good side of the scarlet woman on the bad; and, as the scarlet woman is a community, so must this woman be; it is therefore reasonable to regard her as the faithful remnant of Israel (who continued in the Christian community), from whom came Christ according to the flesh. The dragon, like the beast, has ten horns; he may be identified, too, with leviathan (Is. xxvii. 1). His sweeping down of stars comes from "Daniel" viii. 10 and the iron flail from Psalms; the 1260 days we have met before: the only suggestions of seeking safety in the desert are the flight of Moses (Exod. ii. 15) and the escape of the Israelites from Egypt. The source of the casting out of the dragon is unknown; the drying up of the waters with which he tried to drown the woman is probably suggested by the safe crossing of the Red Sea, interpreted in the light of "Isaiah" xlii. 15, xliii. 2, and l. 2.

The plot now gets well under way with the Beast rising from the sea and persecuting the saints, and another beast, subsequently called the False Prophet, arising from the land and performing miracles, the two insisting on all men taking the mark of the beast and the cipher 666 (xiii.).

The key passage to all this is "Daniel" vii. In "Daniel" there are four beasts—a lion, a bear, a leopard, and a monster with ten horns (vv. 4–8); features of these four are combined in "The Revelation" (xiii. 2) into one. In "Daniel" there is a little horn, who prevails till he is identified with the Beast; in "The Revelation" there is one head, which is wounded and recovers and is identified with the Beast. The persecution of the saints is from verses 7 and 21 in "Daniel" vii.; "Daniel" viii. begins with a ram with two horns who may have suggested the second beast. The idea of the powers of evil being able to work lying miracles was a part of early Christian Apocalyptic (cf. Mk. xiii. 22) and can be traced back to "Deuteronomy" xiii. 1–5. The mark of the Beast and the cipher are the author's own application to his own days. The acceptance of the mark is a figurative way of expressing the sacrifice to the Emperor

409

which was demanded of Christians. The cipher is obtained from the fact that in Hebrew, Greek, and Latin alike, letters were used to express numbers; by adding the numerical value of the letters in a man's name a cipher could be obtained. There can be little doubt that Nero is intended. Rome and Nero become identified, and Nero is Antichrist. This is the really new feature in the author's Apocalyptic; there is no suggestion of identifying Antichrist with the Roman Empire in Mark's Apocalypse or in 2 "Thessalonians".

Before the last series of seven plagues (the bowls), we have an interlude of the worship of the Lamb by the 144,000 martyrs (xiv. 1–5), the promise of the coming fall of Babylon (xiv. 6–11), showing that death is worth while (xiv. 12–13), the reaping of the grapes and the winepress of the wrath of God (xiv. 14–20), and the song of Moses and the Lamb (xv. 1–4).

The One "like unto a son of man" sitting on the cloud is from "Daniel" vii. 13, 14, the author's favourite chapter, the reaping and winepress from "Joel" iii. 13, and the blood as high as a horse's bridle from "Enoch". The song of Moses is contained in "Deuteronomy" xxxii., of which phrases appear: it is not the same as the song of Miriam over the Egyptians.

(3) The third series of seven plagues really carries us to the end. It consists of the pouring out of the seven bowls (xv. 5–xx.).

The first five differ little from the preceding series (xvi. 1–11). The temple filled with smoke is from "Isaiah" vi. 4; the blains, the turning of the water into blood, and the darkness are from the plagues of Egypt. But in the sixth the Parthian host is let loose and mustered at Armageddon (xvi. 12–16), and in the seventh "All is over", the great city is shattered by an earthquake and there is a mighty hailstorm. The waters are dried up like the Red Sea; the frogs are one of the plagues of Egypt; the armies come from "Ezekiel" xxxviii. and "Jeremiah" l. 9; the localization at Megiddo is from "Zechariah" xxii. 11. The disappearance of mountains is from "Isaiah" liv. 10 and the battle is suggested by "Ezekiel" xxxix. The hail is another plague of Egypt.

A further description and explanation of the harlot are given in XVII. 1–10. The seven hills identify her with Rome. The eighth head, which was and is not, refers to the common belief that Nero would reappear, as he was the fifth emperor. The description of a city which forsakes God for idols as a harlot is used of Nineveh in "Nahum" III. 4, of Tyre in "Isaiah" XXIII. 15, and of Jerusalem both by Isaiah and Ezekiel. The phrase "drunk with the wine" is from "Jeremiah" LI. 7, and "upon many waters" from LI. 13. This section is the key to the writer's specific ideas: it is very important to notice that it is Antichrist here who destroys Babylon (LI. 16).

A whole chapter is now devoted to the triumph in heaven and laments on earth over the fall of Babylon (XVIII.). The angels' triumph in the first three verses takes its "Babylon is fallen" from "Isaiah" XXI. 9 and the loathsome birds from "Isaiah" XXXIV. 11–17. The next voice (vv. 4–8) takes its "Come out of her" from "Jeremiah" L. 8 and LI. 6, 45. The cry to treat her as she has treated others is from "Jeremiah" I. 29, and her sense of security from "Isaiah" XLVII. 8. The lament for her by kings, merchants, and seafarers, is based on Ezekiel's dirge for Tyre (XXVII.). In what follows the millstone is from "Jeremiah" LI. 63–66, the cessation of minstrels, milling, and marrying from "Jeremiah" VII. 34, XVI. 9, XXV. 10. The marriage-feast of the Lamb (XIX. 1–10) contains only phrases from the Old Testament.

The great moment is at last reached. Heaven is opened wide and Christ appears, but in a different guise from what we should have expected. He does not come as judge or to inaugurate the general resurrection, which is postponed till after the millennium, but as a conquering king (XIX. 11–16); "Isaiah" LXIII. 1–6 is its true Old Testament counterpart. Then Armageddon is described again; the feast of the birds of prey is from "Ezekiel" XXXIX. 17–20 and the fate of the Beast from "Daniel" VII. 11.

We now come to a strange pronouncement. The dragon is not yet destroyed for ever but bound for a thousand years; there is only a partial resurrection of the martyrs who reign during this millennium; then he is released and there is a second gathering of the hosts, now called Gog and Magog, and a second battle before the final consignment of the dragon to the lake of fire (xx. 1–10). The explanation would seem to be that the prophets often foretold a reign of the saints on earth (e.g. Isaiah xi.) while in "Daniel" vii. 21 their dominion is everlasting; the author therefore provides both. Again "Daniel" xii. 2 speaks of a partial resurrection, whereas most Jews at the time "The Revelation" was written and all Christians believed in a general resurrection: once more the author provides both. Gog is from "Ezekiel" xxxix. 1–21.

Then follows the general Judgment (xx. 11–15). Apparently not Christ, as in the Gospels, but God the Father is judge, as in "Daniel" vii. 9–10, where the books are mentioned.

The counterpart of the final conquest of the wicked is naturally the final and eternal bliss of the faithful—the new heaven and new earth, or the New Jerusalem descending from heaven (xxi., xxii. 1–5). Isaiah and Ezekiel both speak of God's tabernacle being with men, and Isaiah frequently of the drying of tears. The thirsty drinking of the water of life is from "Isaiah" xliv. 3 and lv. 1. A picture of a revived triumphant Jerusalem is given at the end of "Zechariah" (xiv. 16–21); the same prophet describes a measurement of the city (ii.). But the chief description, a very long one, of a revived Jerusalem and temple, with elaborate measurements, is in "Ezekiel" xl.–xliii., following the overthrow of Gog. The precious stones come ultimately from "Exodus" xxviii. 17–20 (Philo and Josephus connect them with the twelve signs of the zodiac); their use in the building of Jerusalem is from "Isaiah" liv. 12; they also appear in "Ezekiel" xxvii. 13. The kings who bring treasures and the ever open gates are from "Isaiah" lx. 1–11 (cf. Hag. ii. 7–9). The river and the tree of life come from the garden of Eden in "Genesis" by way of "Ezekiel" xlvii. 12.

Chapter xxii. 6–15 is an epilogue and 16–21 a declaration of authenticity.

Treatment of Sources

It is obvious that the author's knowledge of prophetic literature is exhaustive. The most detailed prophecies used are from "Daniel" and "Zechariah"; "Ezekiel" contributes a large amount; "Isaiah" has more references perhaps than any, but they are of a more general character; "Jeremiah" and "Joel" appear not infrequently. Several others appear at least once. Of the historical books, the parts of "Exodus" dealing with the plagues of Egypt are to the fore.

Three fundamental principles control his treatment.

(1) The main outline follows strictly the general Christian apocalyptic pattern revealed in Mark's apocalyptic chapter and in 1 and 2 "Thessalonians". First we have wars, famines, pestilences, and earthquakes, which are only the "beginning of troubles" (v.–x.). Next come the great persecution, with the appearance of Antichrist and of lying wonders (xi.–xiii.), and finally the disturbances in heaven, the Second Coming, and the Judgment (xiv.–xxii.).

(2) He illustrates and amplifies this outline from the Old Testament and, to some extent, from later Jewish apocalypses. He absolutely accepts the Old Testament predictions, as we see in his going so far as to assume two resurrections and two final battles, with the millennium in between, in order to harmonize different prophecies.

(3) He has his own system of interpretation, by which Babylon means Rome and the Beast is revived Nero, and the invading armies for the final battle are the Parthians. In all Paul's Epistles, in 1 "Peter", and in the Gospels, Rome as a civil power should be obeyed, and there is no connection whatever between Rome and Antichrist. But the author of "The Revelation" is at pains to make his position unmistakably clear.

The question arises whether he introduces any features from Old Testament prophecies not required under (1) and (3). The answer would seem to be that he occasionally does so. For instance, he retains the ten horns of Daniel's beast as ten future kings (xvii. 12, 13), though he cannot identify them in his scheme. He seems to be so convinced of the truth of his sources that he believes some things will happen on the strength of those sources even though he cannot understand them. The two witnesses are probably another case (xi. 3–12). It is useless therefore to look for forced interpretations of every detail.

We are now in a position to return to the question whether

the visions are merely stage machinery or whether the prophet really saw visions. In "Daniel" they are mere stage machinery; Chapter XI. in "Daniel" is a detailed description of minor wars between Ptolemaic Egypt and Seleucid Assyria. "Daniel" is consequently for the most part exceedingly dull. When the author of "The Revelation" is merely arranging his sources, he can become as dull as Daniel, for instance, in the account of the war which follows the millennium (xx. 7–10). But for the most part he is intensely vivid. No one denies his imaginative power. Which is more likely, not in the twentieth-century poet but in a first-century prophet, that he used his imaginative power to invent visions or that his imaginative power caused him to see visions? Paul saw the seventh heaven in a vision; even matter-of-fact Peter saw a vision (Acts x. 9–16). When once the psychological principle is admitted that a man will see in a vision what his mind is already filled with, but that his ideas become visualized and turned into symbols, we can see how the prophet's mind worked. First he studied the old prophets; then he believed in them and thought over them—so much for the intellect—then in a vision he clad the work of the intellect with the work of the imagination. Then he sat down and worked up his imaginations into literature. This view explains, too, why substantially the same elements are repeated in the first four visions of each series of seven with different images. He is reproducing visions he saw at different times. True, they attain greater detail, and the repetition has an effect on the mind of the reader; but the material had to be there before he could use it to produce an effect.

Date of Composition

For this we must refer to Chapter XVII. 10, where the seven heads of the beast are interpreted as seven emperors, five past, one present, and one future. The existing, or sixth, emperor was Vespasian, the five past emperors being Augustus, Tiberius, Caligula, Claudius, and Nero: the generals who held the office for a few weeks only, Galba, Otho, and Vitellius, are not counted; even if they are, and it were written in the reign of Galba, as a single year covers the three, it would not affect the date much.

But there is a general reluctance to accept a date in the reign of Vespasian, as we know of no great persecution in that reign; so commentators have escaped by regarding this section as part of a Jewish apocalypse, because it was in that reign that the siege and fall of Jerusalem occurred. This apocalypse, they hold, was included in "The Revelation" without the necessary alterations. Such a theory is not in accord with the author's treatment of his known sources, and has one fatal objection. The author believes that the eighth emperor will be one of the five, and later chapters make it clear that that one will be Nero, and that he will destroy Rome. This seems to rule out a date in Domitian's reign completely; Christians living in the days of Domitian's persecution might well identify him as a revived Nero, but no one from his accession onwards could have regarded him as a Nero who had won the Empire at the head of the Parthians and destroyed Rome before he turned on the Christians. The role of Nero redivivus is so integral to the plot of "The Revelation" that no theory about sources can explain it away.

But is there evidence that an acute persecution was taking place while the book was being written? The author expects it; but Antipas is the only martyr mentioned in the letters to the churches, and the author himself was only imprisoned. The persecution under Nero was enough to account for his passion; that it is which he believes will be repeated. And his belief is based on previous prophecy, not on inference from the existing policy of the Empire.

It must be acknowledged that there is one cause of surprise, whenever the book was written, that there is no reference to the fate of Jerusalem which took place in A.D. 70, the second year of Vespasian. It plays a prominent part in Synoptic apocalypse: and "Luke" and "Matthew" must be nearly contemporary with the Apocalypse. Jerusalem is ignored. There is one apparent exception—Chapter XI. 8—where it is said that the bodies of the two witnesses are exposed in the great city, spiritually called Sodom and Egypt, "where also their Lord was crucified". Were it not for these last words we should certainly have identified the "great city" with "Babylon";

and it is hard to see how they could lie in a destroyed city. We suspect these words to be a gloss which has crept into the text; they are not integral to the plot but on the other hand are an interruption; they are just the sort of comment which a reader might write who fully accepted the book but was puzzled by it. For Rome had not fallen; Jerusalem had; therefore, in spite of all the author had done to identify the great city with Rome, he must have meant Jerusalem, if he was a true prophet. The ignoring of an event, which nearly 1900 years later we recognize as an epoch in religious history, can only make us feel that, great as was the author's imagination and intense as were his feelings, this outlook was as narrow as it was concentrated. He has his scheme and is concerned with nothing else. If he were alive to-day we should call him a fanatic and a crank.

Authorship and Purpose

The author describes himself simply as John (Rev. 1. 1) and later as "your brother and partaker with you in the tribulation and kingdom and patience which are in Jesus" (Rev. 1. 9): the only other facts which his book supplies are his connection with "Asia" and his prophetic status. It was inevitable that he should later be identified with John the Evangelist, who was in turn identified with John the son of Zebedee, the Apostle. The identification with the Evangelist first appears in Justin Martyr.

Language makes it well-nigh impossible. The Evangelist uses a Semitic idiom but writes quite correct Greek. The author of "The Revelation" writes Greek which is absolutely ungrammatical. Mark's Greek is not idiomatic Greek; but that of this book might well be called "pidgin Greek". These linguistic difficulties combined with dislike of the subject-matter in making recognition of the book a matter of controversy for two centuries; and its use by various heretics added to the dislike felt for it by many orthodox Christians. Early in the third century a Western writer, named Gaius of Rome, went so far as to attribute its authorship to the arch-heretic Cerinthus, and in the East the opposition was stronger. A writer, named Dionysius of Alexandria, who did not go so far as to reject it altogether, regards it as the work of "a holy and inspired person", but, on linguistic grounds, not the Apostle. On the whole it was accepted in the West, but it was not till A.D. 450 that the opposition was overcome in the East.

It is to be noted that, unlike all Jewish apocalypses, it is not attributed to any great figure of the past, and the writer is clearly writing to churches to whom he is known. There is no reason, therefore, for not accepting the fact that he bore the common name of John, but we cannot identify him with any John known to us.

His purpose is obviously to strengthen his readers in the persecution which he apprehends. The book may well be almost contemporary with 1 "Peter", and the apprehension be caused by the same happenings. But what a contrast! Both writers use the brevity of troubles and the greatness of reward, and there the likeness ends. 1 "Peter" counsels endurance, hope, and charity; "The Revelation" consoles by the thought of terrible retribution to their persecutors. The difference is between the saint and the fanatic.

Historical Importance

The book is so unlike anything else in the New Testament, that the very reasons which make us wish it had not been included give it a kind of historical importance, as revealing ideas which in some quarters and at certain times became prominent in the early Church and left a permanent mark behind them.

Patience under persecution and prayer for persecutors are the teaching of Christ and the Apostles. But some even of the Apostles, before they were taught otherwise, wished to call down fire from heaven on their opponents. We have to remember that the first Christians had all been Jews and retained Jewish beliefs after they had become Christians. Some elements of Apocalyptic were universally accepted and by their inclusion in "Mark" XIII. became part of the orthodox belief, such as the symbolism (as it originally was) of the clouds of heaven, the last trump, the destruction of sun and moon and fall of the stars, and Antichrist. Only in Q do we find apparently no apocalyptic, in fact a caution against it (Lk. XVII. 20-24). Paul in 1 and 2 "Thessalonians" seems to go as far as Mark. But many went still further and later apocalyptic writings were popular among them, such as "Enoch" and the "Assumption of Moses", as we have seen in the chapters on 1 "Peter" and "Jude". It is true that it produced a reaction; the evangelist John is inclined to explain away Apocalyptic (1 Jn. IV. 3). But, when these Jewish apocalypses were lost, "The Revelation", by its inclusion in the Canon, remained and secured a puzzled acceptance, though it was not understood.

Though it is the only example of Christian prophecy which has been included in the Canon, it is not typical. The "Shepherd" of Hermas, for instance, is commonplace, harmless, and often trivial, and Ignatius says merely what he probably would have said if he had not been a prophet. In fact we may assume that there were as many kinds of prophecy as there were kinds of mind in the early Church.

It is not easy to assess the influence of "The Revelation". It appealed to fanatics; it is therefore hard to say whether it helped to make men fanatics or was merely seized on by them because they were fanatics already. We cannot say whether it contributed largely to the bitterness which persecution produced; for the persecutions would tend to produce bitterness without it. Nor can we tell whether the terrible pictures of the Judgment which we see in mediaeval stained glass windows would have formed so prominent a part in the religion of the Middle Ages but for its existence. But it is fairly certain that it tended to promote fanaticism at the Reformation, when the denunciations of pagan Rome were transferred by Protestants to the Papacy. In the last hundred years it has ceased to exercise direct influence on any but eccentric individuals who have no knowledge of modern theological scholarship; but there is probably still a residuum in popular Christianity which has been handed down from the days when "The Revelation" was better known, though its origin is forgotten.

But, once accepted into the Canon, the book has kept its place largely through the consolation which certain passages have always given and to the influence which its imagery has had on art and literature. Passages like VII. 9–17 and XXI. 10–XXII. 5 have always had a profound effect on the human heart.

Ruskin could not read the last verse of Chapter VII. without being deeply moved. Estlin Carpenter in his book *The Johannine Writings*, says: "The variety and vividness of the pictures have suggested manifold themes for literature and art. Its mysterious visions supplied Dante, himself a traveller along the path of many prior souls, with the symbols of moral and spiritual realities as he ascends from Hell to Paradise. The splendid embodiments of mediaeval piety, such as the majestic figure of the 'Christus Regnans' looking down the long vista of the Cathedral at Pisa, the exquisite radiance of the 'Adoration of the Lamb' by Van Eyck at Ghent (about 1420), the tremendous force of the 'Last Judgment' of Michael Angelo in the Sistine Chapel at Rome, the sublime gathering of the saints and martyrs, the prophets and the heroes in the 'Paradiso' of Tintoret in the Doge's Palace at Venice—down to the pathetic form of the 'Light of the World' by Holman Hunt—these and innumerable other scenes wrought into stone in our cathedrals and churches or into allegory like 'Pilgrim's Progress', or into popular hymns like 'Jerusalem the Golden', testify to the abiding power of the appeal made by the Apocalypse to the imagination of the Church."

PART IX

APPENDICES

BIOGRAPHICAL NOTES

Augustine (A.D. 354–430)

Augustine was born at Tagaste in Numidia in A.D. 354 of a heathen father (Patricius) and a Christian mother (Monica). He was educated first at Madaura and afterwards at Carthage. At nineteen years of age he began to study the Scriptures, but they seemed to him "unworthy to be compared with the dignity of Cicero". Next he came under the influence of Manichaean teachers and was for nine years an adherent of their sect, living partly at Tagaste and partly at Carthage in study and teaching. Growing dissatisfied with the principles of Manichaeism he broke with it, and was for a time a sceptic. In A.D. 383 he removed to Rome, and in the following year was appointed a teacher of rhetoric at Milan. Under the powerful influence of the preaching of Ambrose and of Paul's Epistles he was converted and baptized. In A.D. 387 he returned to Tagaste and four years later, much against his will, was made Presbyter in Hippo Regius. Later, in A.D. 397, he became Bishop of Hippo Regius, remaining in that office till his death in A.D. 430. He exercised his influence both within and outside the Church by means of lectures, sermons, and numerous writings of great length. His best known works are *The City of God* and *Confessions*.

Basil (A.D. 330–379)

Basil was born of a prominent Cappadocian family and was educated at Constantinople and Athens. About A.D. 357 he yielded to the ascetic tendencies of the age, practically adopted the monastic life, and became the great propagator of monasticism in Asia Minor, drawing up the Rule which has remained the Code of Greek and Slavic monasticism till the present day. In A.D. 370 he was appointed Bishop of Cappadocian Caesarea, a position which gave him ecclesiastical authority over a large part of eastern Asia Minor. He produced numerous sermons and theological treatises, and is honoured as a "Doctor of the Church".

Basilides

Basilides was a celebrated Gnostic teacher who taught in Alexandria in the principate of Hadrian (A.D. 117–138).

Clement of Rome

Of Clement little is known. He appears in the Roman tradition as the second or third Bishop of Rome. He is well known as the author of 1 "Clement", an epistle written about A.D. 96 and addressed to the Corinthian church to put an end to the discord which prevailed in that community. It is written anonymously in the name of the Roman church.

Clement of Alexandria (c. A.D. 150–215)

Clement was born about A.D. 150 at Athens. His writings show an intimate knowledge of the ceremonies of pagan religions, and there are indications that he had been initiated into some of the "Mysteries". The facts of his conversion are not known. He became a presbyter in the church at Alexandria and succeeded Pantaenus as head of the catechetical school in that place. Origen was his most distinguished pupil. Clement was a theologian who united the tradition of Greek philosophy with Christianity, considering the latter more as the perfect philosophy than as a religion. He drew on many schools of philosophy for his doctrines, in particular those of the Stoics and Neo-Platonists. Among his writings are *A Hortatory Address to the Greeks*, *Miscellanies*, and *Adumbrations*.

Cyprian (A.D. 200–258)

Cyprian was born about A.D. 200 at Carthage and spent all his life in his native city. A wealthy pagan scholar, he was converted to the Christian faith about A.D. 246 and two or three years later was appointed Bishop of Carthage, in which office he showed conspicuous administrative ability and much kindliness of spirit. His writings show strongly the influence of Tertullian whom he called "Master", and whose works he studied. In A.D. 258 he was martyred during the persecution of the Emperor Valerian. He left a collection of letters and other writings, which are valuable as sources of Church history.

Eusebius (c. A.D. 265–350)

Eusebius was born probably in Palestine. In early youth he became acquainted with Pamphilus, Bishop of Caesarea, and founder of a theological school there. After the death of his friend he withdrew to Tyre and later to Egypt, where he seems to have been imprisoned. But he was soon released and became Bishop of Caesarea, holding the office till his death. He is best known as the author of the *Ecclesiastical History* (*c.* A.D. 325) which is an invaluable source of information for our knowledge of the early Church.

Hermas

Hermas was educated by a slave dealer and sold to a lady. Like many other freedmen he married and became a prosperous tradesman. The Muratorian Fragment says (probably incorrectly) that his brother was Pius, Bishop of Rome. He wrote *The Shepherd*, a collection of visions, precepts, and parables (*c.* A.D. 100).

Irenaeus (*c.* A.D. 142–200)

Irenaeus was born probably at Smyrna in Asia Minor, for he tells us that in his childhood he heard the preaching of Polycarp, Bishop of Smyrna. From Asia Minor he removed to Lyons and eventually became its bishop. His name is chiefly associated with his activities against the Gnostics, and with his attempt to prevent a rupture between the Eastern and Western churches on the question of the day on which Easter should be kept. His chief work is *Against Heresies*.

Jerome (*c.* A.D. 340–420)

Jerome was born about A.D. 340 in Dalmatia of Christian parents, and was educated at Rome where he studied philosophy. During a serious illness at Antioch in A.D. 373 he had a vision in which he saw Christ who reproached him for his devotion to the classics. He now turned to the Scriptures, studying Hebrew and leading the hermit life. In A.D. 379 he was ordained a presbyter and journeyed to Constantinople where he studied under Gregory Nazianzus. In A.D. 382 he removed to Rome where he devoted himself to writing, preaching, and teaching Hebrew. Two years later he retired to Antioch and afterwards travelled through Palestine to Egypt, returning to Bethlehem in A.D. 386 to preside over one of the four monasteries built by Paula, a wealthy Roman lady. Here he remained till his death in A.D. 420.

He was undoubtedly the greatest scholar of his age: he knew Hebrew as well as Greek, a rare accomplishment in those days. During the period *c.* A.D. 382–400 he completed the revision of the Old Latin version of the New Testament, and translated the Old Testament into Latin, making the Hebrew text rather than the Septuagint the basis of his translation. This Latin version is known as the Vulgate and is still in use in the Roman Catholic Church.

Justin Martyr (c. A.D. 100–165)

Justin Martyr was born about A.D. 100 at Flavia Neapolis, the modern Nablus in Palestine. His wide reading and deep study of philosophy resulted in his becoming in turn a Stoic, a Pythagorean, and a Platonist. After his conversion to Christianity he became a wandering religious teacher of a type common in that age. He was martyred about A.D. 165. His writings include the *First Apology*, the *Second Apology*, and the *Dialogue with Trypho the Jew*.

Marcion

Marcion was born of wealthy parents at Sinope, a port on the northern coast of Asia Minor. About A.D. 139 he visited Rome and joined the local church. He was a heretic, denying the reality of the Incarnation and rejecting the Old Testament and its God. Failing to gain acceptance for his heretical views, he withdrew from the church and formed a separate community of his own. For its use he compiled a Canon, consisting of a mutilated version of Luke's Gospel and a collection of ten Pauline Epistles (omitting "Hebrews" and the three Pastorals). His church spread extensively, but from the fourth century it began to die out, more rapidly in the West than the East, where it survived till the seventh century when it finally disappeared. Of Marcion's later history nothing is known.

Montanus

Montanus belonged to Phrygia in Asia Minor. According to a tradition recorded by Jerome, he had been a priest of Cybele. About A.D. 156 he proclaimed himself to be a prophet and the mouthpiece of the Holy Spirit. He also declared that the end of the world was at hand, and in expectation of that event practised extreme asceticism and insisted that his followers should do likewise. The movement spread from East to West and caused a serious division in the Church by which it was eventually condemned. It gradually died out in the fourth century.

Origen (c. A.D. 185–253)

Origen was the son of Leonidas, an Alexandrian Christian. After receiving both a classical and a Christian education, he was appointed at the early age of eighteen to succeed Clement as head of the famous catechetical school of Alexandria at which his lectures drew many followers. In A.D. 215 jealousy on the part of Demetrius,

Bishop of Alexandria, caused him to return to Caesarea in Palestine, but he was subsequently recalled only to leave the city finally in A.D. 231. At Caesarea he not only preached, but also established a school which flourished rapidly. He was martyred at Tyre in A.D. 253. Origen was one of the most learned and famous scholars of the age. Among his literary works may be mentioned his commentaries and the *Hexapla*, an edition in which the Old Testament is set out in the original Hebrew with the different Greek versions in parallel columns.

Papias

Papias, according to Irenaeus, was a companion of Polycarp. He became Bishop of Hierapolis and wrote *Expositions of the Oracles of the Lord.*

Pliny the Younger (c. A.D. 61–114)

Pliny, frequently called the Younger, was the nephew of Pliny the Elder who lost his life in the eruption of Vesuvius (A.D. 79) which overwhelmed Pompeii and Herculaneum. He became well known as an author and orator. He had also a distinguished public career, holding the positions of Senator, Tribune, Consul, and Governor. For two years he was Governor of Bithynia, a province of Asia Minor. Among his friends were the Roman historian Tacitus and the Emperor Trajan. Many of his letters have survived, of which the best known are that describing the destruction of Pompeii and Herculaneum and that to Trajan on the Christians.

Polycarp (c. A.D. 65–155)

Little is known of Polycarp's early career. According to Irenaeus he was taught in early life by the Apostles and lived in familiar intercourse with many who had seen Christ. He was Bishop of Smyrna for nearly fifty years in which capacity he welcomed Ignatius as the latter passed through Smyrna on his way to Rome to be martyred. Later, Ignatius wrote to him, charging him to write to all the churches between Smyrna and Antioch, requesting them to send either delegates or letters to the church at Antioch to congratulate its members on the cessation of persecution and to establish them in the faith. This illustrates the commanding position which Polycarp held in the churches of Asia Minor. The Philippian Christians wrote, asking him to forward their letters to Antioch: in his reply he promised to carry out their request and enclosed a number of letters of Ignatius which he had in his possession. When over eighty years of age he visited Anicetus, Bishop of Rome, and soon afterwards suffered martyrdom. Throughout his career he was a staunch defender of the faith, not only against paganism, but also against heresy within the Church.

Tatian

Tatian was a Christian apologist, missionary, and heretic of the second century. He was born in Mesopotamia, educated in Greek learning, and initiated into the "Mysteries". Removing to Rome he became a disciple of Justin Martyr, but after the death of the latter he developed Gnostic ideas. He went on a missionary journey to the East and worked in Cilicia and Pisidia, using Antioch-in-Syria as his headquarters. His chief importance lies in the fact that he compiled a Harmony of the Four Gospels, known as the *Diatessaron* (*c.* A.D. 170).

Tertullian (*c.* A.D. 150–225)

Tertullian was born in Carthage of well-to-do parents and was given the education usual to a youth of good family. After studying Law he practised at Rome, but the greater part of his life was spent in his native city. In middle life he was converted to Christianity and was for a time a presbyter in the church at Carthage. Finally, however, he became a Montanist and remained a member of that sect till his death at an advanced age. He was the first prominent theologian to use Latin instead of Greek as the medium for the expression of his thoughts. He was a prolific writer, his best-known works being the *Apologeticus*, the *De Anima*, and *Adversus Marcionem*.

WORKS OF THE POST-APOSTOLIC AGE

1. *Epistles.* 1 Clement; the Seven Epistles of Ignatius, namely those to the Ephesians, Magnesians, Trallians, Romans, Philadelphians, and Smyrnaeans, and that to Polycarp; the Epistle of Polycarp to the Philippians; the Epistle of Barnabas.

2. *Gospels.* The Gospel according to the Hebrews; the Gospel of the Egyptians; the Gospel of the Ebionites; the Gospel of Peter; the Protevangelium of James; the Gospel of Thomas; the Gospel of Philip; the Gospel of Bartholomew; the Gospel of Nicodemus; the Gospel of Gamaliel.

3. *Acts.* The Acts of Paul; the Acts of Peter; the Acts of John; the Acts of Andrew; the Acts of Thomas.

4. *Apocalypses.* The Apocalypse of Peter; the Shepherd of Hermas; the Apocalypse of Paul; the Apocalypse of Thomas; the Apocalypse of Stephen.

5. *Manuals of Instruction.* The Didache or the Teaching of the Twelve Apostles; the so-called Second Epistle of Clement; the Preaching of Peter.

THE DIDACHE

The Didache is an early Christian document (*c.* A.D. 100), discovered in Constantinople in 1875 and published in 1883. It falls into two well-defined parts, namely, (1) a book of precepts, and (2) a manual of church ordinances.

PART I

The Two Ways. This part is a modified version of an earlier document entitled "The Two Ways", which may have been a Jewish manual adapted for Christian usage. The two "Ways" are the Way of Life and the Way of Death. The Way of Life is to walk in love, and especially to obey the commandments of the Second Table. Among other matters the author includes a number of passages from the Sermon on the Mount, in which the language of Matthew's Gospel is blended with that of Luke's. Of the Way of Life he writes: "Thou shalt never forsake the commandments of the Lord; but shall keep those things which thou hast received, neither adding to them nor taking away from them. In church thou shalt confess thy transgressions, and shalt not betake thyself to prayer with an evil conscience. This is the way of life."

The Way of Death is the exact opposite of the foregoing. The author gives a mere catalogue of vices and vicious types of men, praying that his "children" may be delivered "from all these things", and warning them lest they be led astray. "For if thou art able to bear the whole yoke of the Lord, thou shalt be perfect; but if thou art not able, do that which thou art able."

PART II

This part deals with questions of baptism, fasting and prayer, the Eucharist, the treatment of apostles and prophets, travellers, and bishops and deacons, the whole closing with a solemn exhortation to watchfulness in view of the Second Coming.

Baptism. Baptism is to be "in the name of the Father and of the Son, and of the Holy Spirit". Directions are given as to the manner of baptism and the preparations for it.

Fasting and Prayer. Fasting is to take place on the fourth and on the sixth day of the week. Prayer is to be as the Lord commanded in His Gospel: then follows the Lord's Prayer almost exactly as in Matthew's Gospel, with a brief doxology: "For thine is the power, and the glory for ever and ever." This prayer is to be said three times a day.

The Eucharist. The Eucharist is to be on the Lord's Day. It must be preceded by public confession and mutual forgiveness. Three Eucharistic thanksgiving prayers are given, which are to be said over the cup and the bread, and after the meal. In accordance with "Luke" XXIII. 17–19, the cup is first partaken of and then the bread. The prophets are not to be confined to any particular form, but can offer thanksgiving as much as they desire. No one is to partake of the bread and the wine unless he has been baptized "into the name of the Lord".

Apostles. An Apostle is to be received as the Lord, but he must stay only a day or two, and on his departure must take no money, but only bread for the journey. If he stays three days or asks for money, he is a false prophet.

Prophets. A Prophet who chooses to settle in a church is to receive some of the first-fruits which would otherwise go to the poor, "for they are your chief priests".

Travellers. Any person who comes "in the name of the Lord" is to be received, but he must not stay more than two or three days. No one is to live among them in idleness. If a person will not work for his food, "he is trafficking upon Christ".

Bishops and Deacons. Those appointed to be bishops or deacons must be worthy of the Lord—"men who are meek and not lovers of money, and true and approved; for unto you they also perform the service of the prophets and teachers".

Final Exhortation. The book closes with an exhortation to watchfulness, for Christians are living in the last days before the coming of the world-deceiver (Antichrist) which will precede the Coming of the Lord.

THE MURATORIAN FRAGMENT

Origin

The Muratorian Fragment, published in 1740 by the Italian scholar Muratori, appears to have been composed in Rome, perhaps by Hippolytus, about A.D. 170. It is unfortunately only a fragment of what seems to have been a longer treatise, but it is important since it contains the writer's judgment on the Canon of the New Testament.

Contents

Gospels of Matthew and Mark. The Fragment begins with the words, ". . . at which, however, he was present, and so set them down". From the context it would appear that these words refer to Mark. That the writer had also spoken of Matthew may be taken for granted.

Gospel of Luke. "Luke" is spoken of as the Third Gospel. "The third book of the Gospel [according to Luke[, Luke, that physician whom after the ascension of Christ Paul had taken with him as companion of his journey, composed in his own name on the basis of report. However, he did not himself see the Lord in the flesh, and, therefore, as he could 'trace the course of events' he set them down. So also he began his story with the birth of John."

The Gospel of John. Next we are told how John came to write the Fourth Gospel. "The Fourth Gospel is that of John, one of his disciples. When his fellow disciples and bishops intreated him, he said, 'Fast ye now with me for the space of three days, and let us recount to each other whatever may be revealed to each of us'. On the same night it was revealed to Andrew, one of the Apostles, that John should narrate all things in his own name as they called them to mind. And hence, although different points are taught us in the separate books of the Gospels, there is no difference as regards the faith of the believers, since by the one sovereign Spirit all of them give all the details concerning the Lord's Nativity, His Passion, His Resurrection, His conversation with His disciples, and His twofold advent—the first in the humiliation of rejection, which is now past, and the second in the glory of royal power, which is yet

432

in the future. What wonder is it then that John brings forward each detail with so much emphasis even in his Epistles, saying of himself (or of his own accord), 'What we have seen with our eyes and heard with our ears and our hands have touched, this we have written'. For thus he professes himself to have been not only a spectator but also a hearer, (and not only a hearer) but also a writer of all the wonderful things of the Lord in order".

"Acts". "Acts" is accepted and Luke the physician is named as its author. "But the Acts of all the Apostles were written in one volume. Luke compiled for 'most excellent Theophilus' what things were done in detail in his presence, as he plainly shows by omitting both the death of Peter and also the departure of Paul from the city, when he departed for Spain".

Paul's Epistles. Paul, following the example of his predecessor John, wrote only to seven churches, and in the following order: "first to the Corinthians, second to the Ephesians, third to the Philippians, fourth to the Colossians, fifth to the Galatians, sixth to the Thessalonians, seventh to the Romans, for though two letters each were written to the Corinthians and the Thessalonians by way of reproof, yet that there is but one Church scattered throughout the whole world is made plain, for John also in the Apocalypse, though he writes to seven churches, yet speaks to them all".

"Philemon" and the three Pastoral Epistles are regarded as private letters. "But he wrote one letter to Philemon, and one to Titus, and two to Timothy from affection and love. Yet they have been sanctified by the ordinances of ecclesiastical discipline in the honour of the Catholic Church."

The author regards as spurious the Epistles to the Laodiceans and to the Alexandrians, which had been attributed to Paul by some people. "There are many others which cannot be received in the Catholic Church, for gall cannot be mixed with honey."

Other Writings. The "Epistle of Jude", two Epistles of John, the "Book of Wisdom", and the Apocalypses of John and Peter are accepted, though the author acknowledges that the last of these is rejected by some. The "Shepherd" of Hermas is commended but excluded from the Canon on the ground of its date. "But Hermas wrote the Shepherd quite recently in our own times, in the city of Rome, while his brother Pius was seated on the episcopal throne in Rome."

Omissions. "James", 1 and 2 "Peter", and "Hebrews" are not

28   433

included, but since there are certain lacunae in the manuscript, we cannot attach any importance to their omission, except in the case of "Hebrews".

Heretical Writings. The author repudiates the works of certain heretics, including Valentinus and Basilides.

NOTE.—The account of the writing of the Gospel of John at a time when all the Apostles were alive and together is quite impossible, and shows that the Muratorian Fragment must be used with great caution.

THE PRINCIPAL MANUSCRIPTS AND VERSIONS OF THE GREEK NEW TESTAMENT[1]

Our knowledge of the Text of the Greek New Testament is derived from three sources: (1) Greek Manuscripts, (2) the Versions, and (3) the Fathers.

(1) PRINCIPAL GREEK MANUSCRIPTS

The vellum Greek manuscripts are divided into (a) Uncials, which date from the fourth century onwards, and (b) Minuscules (or Cursives), which are not earlier than the ninth century.

(a) Uncials

B. *Codex Vaticanus.* 4th cent. In the Vatican Library at Rome. Originally contained the whole of the Bible but parts of both Testaments are now lost. New Testament lacks "Hebrews" IX. 14 to the end, the Pastoral Epistles, "Philemon", and the Apocalypse.

א (*Aleph*) *Codex Sinaiticus.* 4th cent. In British Museum. Contains the whole of the Bible with the addition of the "Epistle of Barnabas" and a mutilated fragment of the "Shepherd" of Hermas.

A. *Codex Alexandrinus.* 5th cent. Presented to Charles I by the Patriarch of Constantinople. In the British Museum. Contains Old and New Testaments, but the latter has lost Mt. I–xxv. 6; Jn. VI. 50–VIII. 52; 2 Cor. IV. 13–XII. 7. Contains also portions of 1 and 2 "Clement". Originally included the "Psalms of Solomon", now lost.

C. *Codex Ephraemi.* 5th cent. In the National Library in Paris. A palimpsest, several works of Ephraem the Syrian having been copied over the original text in the twelfth century. Now includes portions of the Old Testament and fragments of every book of the New Testament except 2 "Thessalonians" and 2 "John".

D. *Codex Bezae.* 5th cent. In Cambridge University Library. Contains (with omissions) the Gospels and "Acts". Originally included the Catholic Epistles but these have been lost except

---

[1] See McNeile, *Introduction to the New Testament,* 1927, pp. 368–99, and Kenyon, *The Story of the Bible,* 1936, pp. 145–50.

3 Jn. 11–16. A Graeco-Latin manuscript with Greek and Latin on opposite pages.

W. Codex Washingtonensis. Late 4th or 5th cent. In Freer Museum in Washington. Contains Gospels.

D2. Codex Claromontanus. 6th cent. In the National Library in Paris. Contains Paul's Epistles (with omissions). A Graeco-Latin manuscript.

E2. Codex Laudianus. 7th cent. In Bodleian Library at Oxford. Presented by Laud in 1636. A Graeco-Latin manuscript of "Acts" with Latin and Greek (in that order) on opposite pages.

L. Codex Regius. 8th cent. Contains the Gospels (with omissions).

Codex Koridethianus. 9th cent? Discovered at Koridethi in the west of Caucasia. In museum at Tiflis. Contains the four Gospels (with omissions).

B2. Gregory 946. *Codex Vaticanus.* 8th cent. In the Vatican. Contains the Apocalypse and some writings of Basil, Gregory of Nyssa, and other Fathers.

P45. Chester Beatty Papyrus I. Early 3rd cent. Contains portions of Gospels and "Acts".

P46. Chester Beatty Papyrus II. Early 3rd cent. Contains Paul's Epistles (with omissions).

P47. Chester Beatty Papyrus III. Late 3rd cent. Contains the Apocalypse (with omissions).

(b) *Minuscules (or Cursives)*

Family 1. The group of minuscules numbered 1, 48, 131, 209.

Family 13. The group of minuscules numbered 13, 69, 124, 346, with which 211, 543, 713, 788, 826, 828, have affinities.

Minuscule 33. 9th cent. In National Library in Paris. Contains Gospels, "Acts", and Epistles.

Minuscule 81. A.D. 1044. In British Museum. Contains "Acts".

(2) PRINCIPAL VERSIONS

Latin

(a) *Old Latin.* 2nd cent. Two main classes known as (1) African, represented chiefly by Codex Bobiensis (*k*), at Turin, Codex Palatinus (*e*) in Vienna, the Speculum (*m*), perhaps of Spanish origin, and quotations in Cyprian and Priscillian; (2) European, represented chiefly by the manuscripts Codex Vercellensis (*a*), Codex Veronensis, and many others.

(b) *Vulgate.* Made by Jerome, A.D. 382–400.

Syriac

(a) *Old Syriac.* 2nd cent. Represented only by two imperfect manuscripts of the Gospels, namely the Sinaitic (4th or 5th cent.) and the Curetonian (5th cent.).

(b) *Peshitta.* Made about A.D. 411 by Rabbula, Bishop of Edessa. The accepted version of the Syrian Church. Contains New Testament (with omissions).

Coptic

(a) *Sahidic.* 2nd–3rd cent. Contains fragments of all the books of the New Testament, except "Titus" and "Philemon".

(b) *Bohairic.* 3rd–4th cent. Contains the whole of the New Testament. The accepted version of the Coptic Church.

(3) QUOTATIONS FROM FATHERS

Many quotations are found in the works of patristic writers, including Justin Martyr (*c.* A.D. 100–165), Irenaeus (*c.* A.D. 142–200), Clement of Alexandria (*c.* A.D. 150–215), Tertullian (*c.* A.D. 150–225), Origen (*c.* A.D. 185–253), Cyprian (A.D. 200–258), Eusebius (*c.* A.D. 265–350), Chrysostom (*c.* A.D. 347–407), Jerome (*c.* A.D. 340–420), and Augustine (A.D. 354–430).

NOTE.—Symbols. Capital letters denote Uncials, numerals, Minuscules (or Cursives), and small italic letters the manuscripts of the Old Latin Versions.

437

WRITING MATERIALS

None of the "originals" or "autographs" of the New Testament books has survived, but it is practically certain that they were papyrus rolls. Papyrus was used as a writing material many centuries before the Christian era. A papyrus sheet was made of strips of pith taken from the papyrus reed which once flourished on the banks of the Nile in Egypt. Strips of pith were laid vertically side by side to the required width, thus forming a layer across which another layer was laid at right angles. These were then soaked in water from the Nile, treated with some glutinous matter, pressed together, dried in the sun, and polished with an ivory roller or a smooth shell. The sheet was then ready for use.

The ordinary size of a papyrus sheet was from five to five and a half inches in width and from nine to eleven inches in height. Frequently sheets were pasted together side by side to form a roll, the length of which varied, but it rarely exceeded thirty-five feet. A single sheet would suffice for a short letter like "Philemon", but "Matthew", "Luke", and "Acts", the longest books in the New Testament, would each have required a roll of from thirty to thirty-five feet.

The side of the papyrus sheet on which the strips ran horizontally was known technically as the "recto" and provided a smooth surface for the pen. The writing was usually done on this side, but sometimes it was carried over to the back ("verso"). The matter was arranged in columns from two and a half to three and a half inches in width, with narrow intervals, usually about half an inch, between them, and wider margins at the top and bottom. The words were generally joined together, though occasionally they might be separated by dots. There was no punctuation apart from an occasional insertion of a dot above the line to divide words, or a slight space to mark an important break in the sense. The paragraphs so formed were also divided from one another by a short horizontal line below the line in which the pause occurred.[1] The pen was a reed cut to the required shape, and the ink was made from soot, gum, and water.

[1] *Christianity in the Light of Modern Knowledge*, 1929, p. 278.

In the second century A.D. vellum, made chiefly from the skins of sheep, goats, and calves, began to enter into competition with papyrus and gradually superseded it as the principal material for books. It was more durable, provided a better surface for writing, and in codex form could contain a much greater quantity of matter than the papyrus roll. From the fourth century vellum continued to be used as a writing material until the invention of paper and printing at the close of the Middle Ages.[1]

[1] Kenyon, *The Story of the Bible*, 1936, pp. 24–25.

APPENDIX G

THE FAMILY OF HEROD THE GREAT

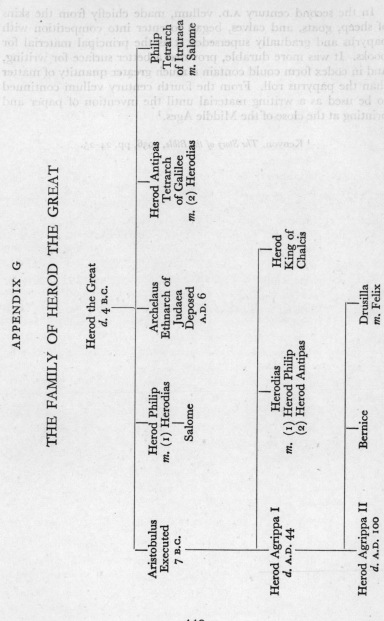

ROMAN EMPERORS 27 B.C.–A.D. 138

		B.C.
Augustus		27
		A.D.
Tiberius		14
Caligula		37
Claudius		41
Nero		54
Galba	June 68–Jan.	69
Otho	Jan.–April	69
Vitellius	April–Dec.	69
Vespasian		69
Titus		79
Domitian		81
Nerva		96
Trajan		98
Hadrian	117–138	

APPENDIX I

BIBLIOGRAPHY

HISTORIES

GREECE

Bury, J. B., *A History of Greece.*
Livingstone, R. W. (Ed.), *The Legacy of Greece.*
Murray, G., *Five Stages of Greek Religion.*
Zimmern, A. E., *The Greek Commonwealth.*

ROME

Bailey, C. (Ed.), *The Legacy of Rome.*
Fowler, W. Warde, *The Religious Experiences of the Roman People.*
Heitland, W. E., *The Roman Republic.*
Jones, H. Stuart, *The Roman Empire.*

ISRAEL

Deane, A., *The World Christ Knew.*
Oesterley, W. O. E., and Robinson, T. H., *History of Israel.*
Schürer, Emil, *The Jewish People in the Time of Christ.*
Smith, Sir G. A., *The Historical Geography of the Holy Land.*

ENCYCLOPAEDIAS

Hastings, J., *Dictionary of the Bible.*
     Dictionary of Christ and the Gospels.
     Dictionary of the Apostolic Church.
Encyclopaedia Biblica.
Encyclopaedia Britannica (relevant articles in).

GENERAL COMMENTARIES

Gore, C., *A New Commentary on Holy Scripture.*
Manson, T. W., *A Companion to the Bible.*
Peake, A. S., *Commentary on the Bible.*

SPECIAL COMMENTARIES

The Century Bible Commentaries.
The Clarendon Bible Commentaries.

442

APPENDIX I

The International Critical Commentaries.
The Moffatt New Testament Commentaries.
The Westminster Commentaries.

INTRODUCTIONS TO THE NEW TESTAMENT

Bacon, B. W., *The Making of the New Testament.*
McNeile, A. H., *An Introduction to the Study of the New Testament.*
Moffatt, J., *An Introduction to the Literature of the New Testament.*
Peake, A. S., *A Critical Introduction to the New Testament.*

CANON AND TEXT OF THE NEW TESTAMENT

Gregory, C. R., *Canon and Text of the New Testament.*
Harnack, A., *The Origin of the New Testament.*
Kenyon, Sir F. G., *The Story of the Bible.*
Souter, A., *The Text and Canon of the New Testament.*

SEPARATE GOSPELS

MATTHEW

Allen, W. C., *St. Matthew.*
Bacon, B. W., *Studies in Matthew.*
Green, F. W., *The Gospel according to St. Matthew.*
Kilpatrick, G. D., *The Origins of the Gospel according to St. Matthew.*

MARK

Bacon, B. W., *The Beginnings of the Gospel Story.*
Blunt, A. F. W., *St. Mark.*
Rawlinson, A. E. J., *St. Mark.*

LUKE

Cadbury, H. J., *The Making of Luke—Acts.*
    The Style and Literary Method of Luke.
Creed, J. M., *The Gospel according to St. Luke.*
Easton, B. S., *The Gospel according to St. Luke.*

JOHN

Bernard, J. H., *St. John.*
Burney, C. F., *The Aramaic Origin of the Fourth Gospel.*
Carpenter, J. E., *The Johannine Writings.*
Drummond, J., *The Character and Authorship of the Fourth Gospel.*
Gardner-Smith, P., *St. John and the Synoptic Gospels.*
Hoskyns, E., *The Fourth Gospel.*

443

Howard, W. F., *Christianity according to John.*
      The Fourth Gospel in Recent Criticism and Interpretation.
Macgregor, G. H. C., *The Gospel of John.*
Scott, E. F., *The Fourth Gospel.*
Strachan, R. H., *The Fourth Gospel: its Significance and Environment.*
      The Fourth Evangelist, Dramatist or Historian.

GENERAL WORKS ON THE FOUR GOSPELS

Burney, C. F., *The Poetry of Our Lord.*
Burkitt, F. C., *Jesus Christ: an Historical Outline.*
      The Gospel History and its Transmission.
Crum, J. M. C., *The Original Jerusalem Gospel.*
Dibelius, M., *From Tradition to Gospel.*
      Gospel Criticism and Christology.
Dodd, C. H., *History and the Gospel.*
      The Parables of the Kingdom.
Easton, B. S., *The Gospel before the Gospel.*
Glover, T. R., *The Jesus of History.*
Gore, C., *Jesus of Nazareth.*
Grant, F. C., *Form Criticism. A Translation of the Study of the Synoptic Gospels* by R. Bultmann, *and of Primitive Christianity in the Light of Gospel Research* by Karl Kundsin.
Harnack, A., *The Sayings of Jesus.*
      The Date of the Synoptic Gospels and Acts.
Headlam, A. C., *The Fourth Gopsel as History.*
Hoskyns, E., and Davey, F. N., *The Riddle of the New Testament.*
Lightfoot, R. H., *History and Interpretation of the Gospels.*
Manson, T. W., *The Teaching of Jesus Christ.*
Montefiore, C. G., *The Synoptic Gospels.*
Redlich, E. B., *Form Criticism.*
Ropes, J. H., *The Synoptic Gospels.*
Sanday, W. (Ed.), *Oxford Studies in the Synoptic Problem.*
Scott, E. F., *The Validity of the Gospel Record.*
Stanton, V. W., *The Gospels as Historical Documents.*
Streeter, B. W., *The Four Gospels.*
Taylor, V., *The Foundation of the Gospel Tradition.*
Torrey, C. C., *Our Translated Gospels.*

ACTS

Clarke, A. C., *The Acts.*
Henshaw, T., *The Foundation of the Christian Church.*
Jackson and Lake, *The Beginnings of Christianity.* Vols. 1–5.

PAUL AND HIS TEACHING

Dean, J. T., *St. Paul and Corinth.*
Deissman, A., *Paul.*
Dodd, C. H., *The Mind of Paul.*
Duncan, G. S., *St. Paul's Ephesian Ministry.*
Glover, T. R., *Paul of Tarsus.*
Inge, W. R., *Essay on Paul* in *"Outspoken Essays"* (First Series).
Kennedy, H. A. A., *St. Paul and the Mystery Religions.*
       The Theology of the Epistles.
Lake, K., *The Earlier Epistles of Paul.*
McNeile, A. H., *St. Paul, His Life, Letters, and Christian Doctrine.*
Nock, A. D., *St. Paul.*
Ramsay, W. M., *St. Paul, the Traveller, and Roman Citizen.*
Scott, C. A., *Christianity according to Paul.*
Stewart, J. S., *A Man in Christ.*

PAUL'S EPISTLES

Burton, E. D., *Galatians.*
Dodd, C. H., *Romans.*
Frame, J. S., *1 and 2 Thessalonians.*
Moffatt, J., *1 Corinthians.*
Plummer, A., *2 Corinthians.*
Scott, E. F., *Colossians, Philemon, Ephesians.*
Michael, J. H., *Philippians.*

THE PASTORAL EPISTLES

Easton, B. S., *The Pastoral Epistles.*
Falconer, Sir R., *The Pastoral Epistles.*
Harrison, P. N., *The Problem of the Pastoral Epistles.*
Lock, W., *The Pastorals.*

HEBREWS

Moffatt, J., *Hebrews.*
Robinson, T. H., *Hebrews.*
Westcott, B. F., *Hebrews.*

THE CATHOLIC EPISTLES

Barker, C. J., *The Johannine Epistles.*
Brooke, A. E., *The Johannine Epistles.*
Dodd, C. H., *The Johannine Epistles.*

445

Moffatt, J., *James, Peter, and Judas*.
Ropes, J. H., *James*.
Selwyn, E. G., *1 Peter*.

REVELATION
Charles, R. H., *Revelation*.
Scott, E. F., *The Book of Revelation*.
Swete, H. B., *The Apocalypse of John*.

INDEX

447

449

GEORGE ALLEN & UNWIN LTD
LONDON: 40 MUSEUM STREET, W.C.1
CAPE TOWN: 58–60 LONG STREET
SYDNEY, N.S.W.: 55 YORK STREET
TORONTO: 91 WELLINGTON STREET WEST
CALCUTTA: 17 CENTRAL AVE., P.O. DHARAMTALA
BOMBAY: 15 GRAHAM ROAD, BALLARD ESTATE
WELLINGTON, N.Z.: 8 KINGS CRESCENT, LOWER HUTT

ENCYCLOPAEDIA OF RELIGION AND RELIGIONS

by Royston Pike DEMY 8VO 30S NET

Here in one volume may be found information—clearly written, unbiassed, accurate, and up to date—on the Founders and other great personalities, the theological tenets and philosophical ideas, the rites and ceremonies and practices, the scriptures, the creeds and confessions of faith, the Churches or other divisions and organizations of all the religions that have played a vital part in the life of the human race. The articles have been submitted for approval to recognized authorities and are written by one who has devoted many years to the subject and is a trained encyclopaedist.

REFORMED DOGMATICS

by Henrich Heppe DEMY 8VO 50S NET

This volume provides a summary of the doctrines held by leading Reformed theologians from Calvin onwards. Each "place" of doctrine grows out of a condensed statement into a chain of citations from the great Reformed theologians, and is fully documented in Scripture.

It is thus a compendium from a great school of theology with a vast literature which the student cannot hope to assimilate in its entirety. The student of dogma can follow the 300 years from Geneva to Westminster, a body of doctrine exhibiting variety with orthodoxy, elastic enough to be comprehensive, charitable enough to tolerate lesser "difficulties", yet thoroughly grounded in Holy Scripture.

LIGHT IN DARKNESS

A BOOK OF DAILY READINGS

compiled by Helen Olney F'SCAP 8VO 7s 6d NET

Readings for each day of the year are arranged under headings which embrace almost every human need and in which the reader can find just what is required to inspire and comfort. Mrs. Olney has striven to make these extracts from prose, poem and prayer blend into a comprehensive whole and to make it a unique book in which only the beautiful and true in thought is depicted and the hackneyed and too well known avoided.

As a young woman the authoress first experienced the influence of the Divine and witnessed two instantaneous healings of very sick people. From that day, throughout a most varied and adventurous life, she has always felt the guidance and influence of the unseen. She has compiled this book of daily readings in an effort to provide a source of help and encouragement to which one could turn in trouble and distress.

GEORGE ALLEN AND UNWIN LTD